SHAKESPEARE STUDIES

SHAKESPEARE STUDIES

Volume XXXV

EDITOR
SUSAN ZIMMERMAN

Queens College

The City University of New York

ASSOCIATE EDITOR
GARRETT SULLIVAN
Pennsylvania State University

ASSISTANT TO THE EDITOR
LINDA NEIBERG
The Graduate Center, CUNY

Madison • Teaneck

Fairleigh Dickinson University Press

Associated University Presses
2010 Eastpark Boulevard
Cranbury, NJ 08512

The paper used in this publication meets the requirements of the American National Standard for Permanence of Paper for Printed Library Materials Z39.48-1984.

International Standard Book Number: 978-0-8386-4123-1 (vol. xxxv)
International Standard Serial Number: 0-0582-9399

All editorial correspondence concerning *Shakespeare Studies* should be addressed to the Editorial Office, *Shakespeare Studies,* English Dept., Queens College, CUNY, Flushing, NY 11367. Orders and subscriptions should be directed to Associated University Presses, 2010 Eastpark Boulevard, Cranbury, New Jersey 08512.

Shakespeare Studies disclaims responsibility for statements,
either of fact or opinion, made by contributors.

PRINTED IN THE UNITED STATES OF AMERICA

Contents

6 Contents

Review Articles

Reviews

Foreword

W<small>E ARE PARTICULARLY</small> pleased to feature two members of our editorial board in volume 35. Ewan Fernie's essay on the oeuvre of Jonathan Dollimore ("Dollimore's Challenge") was prompted by publication of the third edition of *Radical Tragedy:* Fernie takes this occasion to assess Dollimore's singular and invigorating intellect, and the continuing challenges of his critical practice. We are also featuring a forum organized by Jean E. Howard that addresses an issue with which Howard's own work has been deeply engaged: "English Cosmopolitanism and the Early Modern Moment." Introduced by Howard and including commentary by Alison Games, Barbara Sebek, Jonathan Gil Harris, Crystal Bartolovich, Alan B. Farmer, and Pamela Allen Brown, the forum offers fresh perspectives on a complex topic that requires the consolidation of interdisciplinary perspectives.

Volume 35 is also notable for four contributions that concentrate on Shakespeare—two articles that analyze the transformation of cultural discourses in the plays and two review articles that deal with the development of the so-called Shakespeare industry. In his essay on *Antony and Cleopatra,* Alan Stewart argues that the theatricality of Shakespeare's tragedy challenges the epistolary grounds of Roman historiography; in an essay on *Hamlet,* Paul D. Stegner considers the play's ambiguous representations of interiority in terms of the irreconcilable tensions between Catholic and Protestant confessional practices. The review articles focus on modern practices. Bruce R. Smith, curious about the "Shakespeare Book Biz," collectively considers no fewer than nine critical works with broad popular appeal in an attempt to identify what an "appeal to a general readership" might mean; and Alexander C. Y. Huang examines the "performative afterlife" of Shakespeare's plays in terms of the localities—both geocultural and critical—in which the plays have been appropriated globally.

Finally, the wide-ranging reviews in this volume explore, as is customary, the cultural history of early modern England and the place of Shakespeare's productions within it. They include such topics as gender and literacy, the concept of the monstrous in religious discourse, the significance of rogues and of the working poor in early modern society, early modern sexuality, theatrical collaborations and theatrical companies, manuscript culture, the book trade, and (complementing the forum) cultural interactions between England and Italy.

Susan Zimmerman, Editor

Contributors

CRYSTAL BARTOLOVICH is Associate Professor of English at Syracuse University. Her current project takes up varieties of utopian Commons in early modern England.

PAMELA ALLEN BROWN is Associate Professor of English at the University of Connecticut, Stamford. She is at work on a book about foreign women performers and the plays of Shakespeare and his contemporaries.

MARK THORNTON BURNETT is Professor of Renaissance Studies at Queen's University, Belfast. He is the author of *Masters and Servants in English Renaissance Drama and Culture: Authority and Obedience* (1997), *Constructing "Monsters" in Shakespearean Drama and Early Modern Culture* (2002), and *Filming Shakespeare in the Global Marketplace* (2007), and is also the editor or co-editor of numerous other works.

WILLIAM C. CARROLL is Professor of English at Boston University. He is the author of *Fat King, Lean Beggar: Representations of Poverty in the Age of Shakespeare.*

BART VAN ES is a Fellow and University Lecturer at St. Catherine's College, Oxford. He has recently edited *A Critical Companion to Spenser Studies* and is now writing a book on Shakespeare and the early modern acting company.

ALAN B. FARMER is an Assistant Professor of English at The Ohio State University. He is co-editor of *Localizing Caroline Drama: Politics and Economics of the Early Modern English Stage, 1625–1642* (2006), and is currently completing a monograph on playbooks and newsbooks in Caroline England.

EWAN FERNIE is Senior Lecturer in Shakespeare and Renaissance Literature at Royal Holloway, University of London. He edits the

"Shakespeare Now!" series of "minigraphs" with Simon Palfrey, with whom he is also writing a book that begins the day after *Macbeth.*

CHARLES R. FORKER, Professor of English Emeritus at Indiana University, Bloomington, has recently published a monograph-length article in volume 19 of *Medieval and Renaissance Drama in England* (FDUP, 2006) attributing *A Speedy Post,* a seventeenth-century manual of model letters, to John Webster. He is currently working (with Joseph Candido and Deborah Curren-Aquino) on the Variorum edition of *King John.*

ALISON GAMES is the Dorothy M. Brown Distinguished Professor of History at Georgetown University. She is finishing a book on English expansion around the world in the sixteenth and seventeenth centuries.

DARRYLL GRANTLEY teaches in the School of Drama, Film and Visual Arts at the University of Kent and publishes mainly in medieval and early modern drama. His publications include *Wit's Pilgrimage: Drama and the Social Impact of Education in Early Modern England* (2000) and *English Dramatic Interludes: A Reference Guide* (2004). He is the co-editor of *Christopher Marlowe and English Renaissance Culture* (with Peter Roberts, 1996) and *The Body in Late Medieval and Early Modern Culture* (with Nina Taunton, 2000). He is completing a book about early modern English drama.

STEPHEN GUY-BRAY is Associate Professor of English at the University of British Columbia. He has just published his second book—*Loving in Verse: Poetic Influence as Erotic* (2006).

ALEXANDRA HALASZ is an Associate Professor of English at Dartmouth College. She works on the early modern English book trade.

JONATHAN GIL HARRIS is Professor of English at George Washington University. He is currently completing a book on the relations between materiality and temporality in the time of Shakespeare.

DAVID HILLMAN is Lecturer and Director of Graduate Studies in the Faculty of English at the University of Cambridge and Fellow of King's College, Cambridge. He is the author of the recently published *Shakespeare's Entrails: Belief, Scepticism and the Interior of the Body.*

JEAN E. HOWARD is George Delacorte Professor in the Humanities at Columbia University. Her new book, *Theater of a City: The Places of London Comedy 1598–1642,* was published in 2007.

ALEXANDER C. Y. HUANG is Assistant Professor of Comparative Literature at the Pennsylvania State University (University Park). He has published on Shakespearean performance in *The Shakespearean International Yearbook, Shakespeare Bulletin,* and *Shakespeare Yearbook.* He is currently completing a book on visuality and Shakespearean appropriation.

IAN FREDERICK MOULTON is Associate Professor of English in the Division of Humanities and Arts, Arizona State University. He is author of *Before Pornography* (2000), and editor and translator of Antonio Vignali's *La Cazzaria* (2003).

MARCY L. NORTH is Associate Professor of English at the Pennsylvania State University and the author of *The Anonymous Renaissance: Cultures of Discretion in Tudor-Stuart England.*

WILLIAM A. ORAM is Helen Means Professor of English at Smith College. He is the Coordinating Editor of *The Yale Edition of the Shorter Poems of Edmund Spenser* (1988) and the author of *Edmund Spenser* (1997).

RICHARD PREISS is Assistant Professor of English at the University of Utah. He is currently completing a book on the relationship between stage clowns and dramatic authorship in early modern England.

DIANE PURKISS is Fellow and Tutor in English at Keble College, Oxford. Her most recent book is *The English Civil War: A People's History* and she has also published *Literature, Gender and Politics during the English Civil War* (2005). She is now working on a book on food and history.

KIERNAN RYAN is Professor of English Language and Literature at Royal Holloway, University of London, and a Fellow of New Hall, University of Cambridge. He is currently completing a study of Shakespearean comedy.

BARBARA SEBEK is Associate Professor of English at Colorado State University. Her essays on merchants and factors are forthcoming in Jyotsna Singh, ed., *A Companion to the Global Renaissance,* and Brinda Charry and Gitanjali Shahani, eds., *Early Modern Emissaries in Literature.*

BRUCE R. SMITH is College Distinguished Professor of English and Professor of Theatre at the University of Southern California. In addition to *Homosexual Desire in Shakespeare's England, The Acoustic World of Early Modern England,* and *Shakespeare and Masculinity,* he has published *Roasting the Swan of Avon: Shakespeare's Redoubtable Enemies and Dubious Friends,* the catalog of a special exhibition at the Folger Shakespeare Library. He is completing a book on the color green.

PAUL D. STEGNER is Assistant Professor of English at California Polytechnic, San Luis Obispo. He is currently completing a book on ritual confession, memory, and desire in early modern English literature.

ALAN STEWART is Professor of English and Comparative Literature at Columbia University. He is currently completing a book on the letters in Shakespeare's plays.

VALERIE WAYNE is Professor of English at the University of Hawai'i at Mānoa. She is currently at work on an edition of *Cymbeline* for the Arden Shakespeare, third series.

HEATHER WOLFE is Curator of Manuscripts at the Folger Shakespeare Library. She recently edited *The Literary Career and Legacy of Elizabeth Cary, 1613–1680,* and is currently researching filing practices in early modern England.

SHAKESPEARE
STUDIES

FORUM

English Cosmopolitanism and the Early Modern Moment

Introduction

JEAN E. HOWARD

IN 1571 QUEEN ELIZABETH came to the corner of Cornhill and Thread-needle streets to attend the opening of Sir Thomas Gresham's grand new building, a bourse to which she gave the name the Royal Exchange. The edifice was extremely imposing. Modeled on the Antwerp bourse with which Gresham had become familiar during his time in the Low Countries, the Exchange was one of the first London buildings to show strong Continental influences. Designed by a Flemish mason, Hendryck van Paesschen, and partly erected by foreign workmen brought over—along with wainscoting, slate, and other building materials—from the Continent, Gresham's new building signified London's arrival as a cosmopolitan center of international trade. It put London on the map as a city, like Constantinople, Venice, Marseilles, or Antwerp, that staked a claim to leadership in long-distance trade and new forms of commercial transactions. In the large interior of the Exchange was a courtyard where merchants from France, the Netherlands, Italy, and Spain assembled to conduct business. These merchants all had designated places in the courtyard so that they could easily be found by those seeking to make deals, to negotiate a bill of exchange, or to inquire about news from their quarter of the world. The queen's attendance at the official opening ceremony of the Exchange indicated the building's importance. It seemed, above all, to signal London's status as a player in an international arena, a place where the people and the goods of many nations commingled.

The existence of this building in London in 1571, however, is something of a puzzle. There were not many even vaguely like it in the city; its erection, treated with great fanfare by the queen, nonetheless caused protests by the London bricklayers who felt that foreign workmen were taking jobs away from them; and the seeming cosmopolitan nature of the place was belied by the parochial pride both city and queen took in having an *English* bourse to signal their own uniqueness and accomplishments (however much both building and trading practices were modeled on foreign prototypes). These paradoxes raise questions about the extent to which early modern England really was cosmopolitan in its practices and attitudes, or, by contrast, how much it maintained an indifference or hostility to things and people perceived as foreign or alien. Of what, in short, was Gresham's bourse a sign or symptom—a confident worldliness or an anxious insularity? One of the first plays about this place, William Haughton's *Englishmen for My Money,* has it both ways. It makes vicious fun of foreigners who can't speak English properly even as its main plot ends in the marriage of three English suitors to the three daughters of a wealthy Portingale, a Jewish merchant and usurer who is the most powerful figure on the floor of the London bourse. This ending might be taken to signal the happy incorporation of foreign wealth and alien blood into the English polity. In this case a cosmopolitan gesture fortifies an insurgent nationalism.

This forum takes up in a number of ways the question of early modern English cosmopolitanism. Did it exist? If so, what forms did it take? What were its effects? Scholars such as Laura Yungblut have suggested that early modern England was a xenophobic place in which antialien sentiment ran strong even though considerable numbers of Continental merchants plied their trade in London and even though waves of French Huguenots and Flemish artisans, many fleeing religious persecution, had settled throughout England in the sixteenth century. Antialien riots and restrictions on strangers' rights to engage in trade are evidence of persistent dis-ease with this foreign presence. These views are countered, however, by a number of critics working, in particular, on England's economic development throughout the sixteenth and seventeenth centuries. Participation in long-distance trade not only led foreign merchants to congregate at the Royal Exchange, but it forced English merchants and their factors to travel to Spain, to Aleppo, and to the Moluccas, forced them to live among strangers in these polyglot entrepôts, and led them to bring back to England the products of their trading encounters. Whether one focuses on the homely products, like sugar and currants, that increasingly made their way to the houses of the English middling sort or on the luxury goods that Linda Peck has shown were purchased by the very rich, English bodies were everywhere affected by foreign goods in the form of foodstuffs, fabrics, and fashions. Whatever their conscious attitudes toward foreigners, in their domestic lives English men and women to some extent lived their engagement with aliens through their habits of consumption.

These simple observations suggest, of course, that there was not a monolithic "England" or even a monolithic "London" whose views about aliens and alien matter can be discerned, nor would a focus solely on consciously held beliefs necessarily illuminate practices that in some instances might belie those beliefs. Moreover, in the very concept of *cosmopolitanism* lies a tangle of contradictory implications. Drawn from a Greek root, the word *cosmopolite* was employed in a text reprinted by Richard Hakluyt in *Principal Navigations* to refer to a citizen of "one mysticall citie universall." Cosmographers and even armchair travelers might be cosmopolites if their worldly interests led them to explore in maps and books the customs of alien peoples and the contours of a globe that stretched far beyond the English Channel. The positive promise of cosmopolitanism, then and now, is that it eschews the parochial and the sectarian, embraces difference, and opens to a tolerant universalism. And yet, *cosmopolitan* has not always been a term of praise. It can also imply rootlessness and overripe sophistication, questionable qualities that can be opposed to what is sturdily native and seemingly transparent. Moreover, even in its most utopian conceptions, cosmopolitanism often remains committed to boundaries and borders; it often implicitly sets limits to its own inclusiveness. There is frequently someone, and usually more than one someone, who does not belong in the "mysticall citie universall" but whose religion, habits, or language place them outside the pale of inclusion, sometimes outside the definition of the human.

In the thought pieces that follow, a lively group of early modern scholars stakes out different positions on the cosmopolitan strands in early modern culture. They engage the term's positive connotations with varying degrees of skepticism and resistance, some, such as Alison Games and Barbara Sebek, exploring the extent to which traffic and trade actually encouraged an acceptance of difference on the part of those who went to live, for example, among the native inhabitants of Japan. These factors and merchants were to an unusual extent forced to experience themselves as "others" situated within the gaze of a community that did not necessarily recognize or accept their customs, language, diet, and dress. Other members of the forum, such as Jonathan Gil Harris, focus more on the prob-

lematics of the term *cosmopolitan* and on the ways in which an interest in aliens can also involve a relegation of them to a past that
in no way intersects with the present temporality of the English
subject. Harris tellingly explores how this is so in John Stow's engagement with "Old Jewry" and with the Jewish inhabitants of the
city he memorialized.

Nearly every participant in the forum in some way and to some
extent wants to resist the simple binary between the cosmopolitan
and the xenophobic, instead seeing them as everywhere inter-
implicated and coexistent. But for Crystal Bartolovich, despite the
contradictions and the exclusions everywhere adhering in cosmopolitan projects and imaginings, there is nonetheless value in continuing to stress the utopian dimensions of these undertakings.
Focusing on women's translations of foreign texts, Bartolovich sees
the practice of translation as, in Margaret Tyler's resonant phrase,
"giving entertainment to a stranger, before this time unacquainted
with our country guise." The utopian possibilities of translation as
hospitality, refiguring the gendered labor of women, must be given
their due, she argues, even in texts that in some ways and to some
extent remain entangled in forms of class privilege or Eurocentric
bias.

In many of these essays, travel is a key term. Englishmen were
certainly in motion in the period, their travels a primary means by
which they encountered foreign ways. They not only went abroad;
they also wrote about their going. Merchants, factors, and clergy
attached to the great trading companies sent home letters and diaries and reports; gentlemen like Thomas Coryate traveled across the
face of Europe and recorded their adventures as they went, often
with an eye to the money to be made from their writings; religious
refugees made their way to Rome or to Douai, sites from which is-
sued a steady stream of recusant literature, texts meant to travel
back to England and fortify a beleaguered Catholic community. As
the last example makes clear, neither the people nor the texts in
motion necessarily shared a cosmopolitan goal. Sectarianism remained a defining feature of the period, a point tellingly addressed
in Alan Farmer's exploration of the trade in two different kinds of
books printed abroad and imported into England. On the one hand
were Latin books of Christian and humanist scholarship, brought
in, he argues, to be consumed by a relatively elite group of readers
who were nonetheless committed to a transnational community of
learning. On the other hand, there was also a large market in sectar-

ian books. Written in English, but printed abroad, they were meant to fuel partisan controversy and accentuate divisions within the Christian fold. Within the book trade itself, then, one can discern two quite different uses of "foreign matter."

But books and people were not the only things that traveled. So did products and cultural forms. In a lively essay, Pam Brown explores how jests traveled across national boundaries, as did traditions of clowning and foolery, often enacted by performers such as Will Kemp or nameless "Italian women" who performed in Norwich in 1574. While jest and foolery never ceased to trade in xenophobia and sexism, Brown nonetheless points to the many ways in which traditions of popular clowning opened to hybridity, intermingling, and impurity, in short, to practices that resisted the closure of a purely national imaginary. Her essay lingers on the contradictions that everywhere mark the contact zones where boundaries are breached and native and foreign intermingle.

I close by asking the obvious question, but one we too seldom ask of our scholarship: why should one care about early modern cosmopolitanism? It is important, I would argue, because the world continues to press the question of difference upon us—in the trivial form of ads that promise an easy assimilation of strangers in the form of marketplace consumption (we are all brothers and sisters when we wear Prada) and in the nontrivial form of the mass migration of peoples from poverty and sectarian strife. It may be easy to see the limits of tolerance (read "compassionate conservatism") when a government imagines erecting a physical wall between itself and its southern neighbor, but the ruses of exclusion are often more subtle. To dream of being a citizen of the world, rather than of a national or parochial polity, is a noble dream. The never-realized utopian longing embodied in the phrase "citizen of the world" marks an aspiration not to be slighted. Yet in the mirror of the past we can glimpse some of the contradictions that have historically attended its instantiation and that require practices of vigilance lest we, too, merely assimilate difference without allowing ourselves to be changed by it, or acknowledge others while simultaneously relegating them to a different temporality. These are the dangers that haunt the cosmopolitan project, glimpsed in William Haughton's contradictory fiction about Gresham's Royal Exchange, but remaining with us even today.

England's Global Transition and the Cosmopolitans Who Made It Possible

Alison Games

THE SINGLE MOST DRAMATIC shift in English history in the early modern period lay in the kingdom's altered status in a transformed world beyond its shores. For all the upheavals and transitions at home, from the consolidation of the national state to the tumult of civil war, from the turmoil of successive religious reformations to the population explosion and ensuing economic strains of the late sixteenth and early seventeenth centuries, it was England's new position as an emerging world power that defined England's early modern moment. Cosmopolitanism—and especially cosmopolitans—were central to this transition.

Perched on the western fringes of Europe, the most remote sovereign kingdom in a trading world centered around the Mediterranean, England was a nation characterized above all by its weakness in the middle of the sixteenth century. Annual fleets carrying silver and other treasures from the Americas enabled Spain to achieve unprecedented power in Europe and the Mediterranean while the English and other rivals watched in frustration. England's geographic position, however, turned out to be crucial. After Columbus's voyage in 1492 and especially after Spain's spectacular conquests on the American mainland in the early sixteenth century, a European trading world once oriented toward the Mediterranean shifted toward the Atlantic. Through no initiative of its own, these larger geopolitical shifts transformed England from a kingdom on the European margins to one well positioned to take advantage of new opportunities to the west. But it took considerable enterprise and ingenuity for the English to turn this accidental geographic advantage into a real opportunity, and in the period between 1560 and 1700 they did so. In this remarkable period the

English dislodged the Spanish from some of their holdings in the Americas, challenged Spanish dominion over the American continents, established new long-distance trade routes to the eastern Mediterranean and the East Indies, and emerged in the seventeenth century as a kingdom on the rise. Cosmopolitanism and cosmopolitans facilitated this shift. Men and women voyaged overseas in numbers sufficient to secure colonial holdings, and they traveled around the globe on commercial ventures that pushed English trade routes into America, eastern Europe, the Mediterranean, and India. And in their travels they demonstrated their interest in and sympathy for foreign mores, worked with and for foreigners, sometimes immersed themselves in foreign worlds, and gradually dislodged themselves from unthinking attachments to a single nation.

These cosmopolitans were most evident in the world of commerce. Tangibly centered around the circulation of goods, commerce first required the circulation of people who traveled abroad, inserted themselves in foreign communities, and brought back their treasures. Everywhere, the appearance of cultural understanding was crucial to successful trade. The advice merchants offered to each other invoked themes of humility and restraint: there was no place for xenophobia in this world. Merchants needed to acquire cultural understanding in order to facilitate trade, and they required strategies to enable themselves to perch in foreign ports. We might now consider much of this behavior to be private and personal—what men wore, how they dressed and ate, with whom and how they socialized—but for these enterprising traders, personal attributes facilitated commercial relations. In this era when many English merchants were the first of their nation to open new markets, to assess new commodities, to persuade foreign merchants that they wanted to buy English goods, to cement trade relations with strangers, and to blunder their way through unfamiliar diplomatic rituals, men had to rely on their social acuity to establish trade. Merchants were ambassadors, not simply traders.

Successful merchants had to be willing to acknowledge their cultural ignorance and to be guided by European competitors and by their foreign hosts in diplomatic and commercial conventions. One false step might imperil an entire venture; thus merchants had to be prepared to place their pride secondary to other interests and they had to learn quickly whom to trust. If they did not master the history and meaning behind religious practices, they soon ascertained what the culturally appropriate ways were to demonstrate respect for indigenous traditions. If they did not value the erudition of indigenous priests, they knew to mask their disdain. They played the roles of gracious host and guest constantly. In pursuit of these goals, they required a social competence—measured in their enthusiasm for new pursuits—which must have made the best of these traders charming companions. Richard Cocks, who led the English trade factory in Japan, worked strenuously to read the preferences of his Japanese friends, visitors, potential patrons, and customers, and organized entertainment at a moment's notice. He threw together banquets and waited all night if he thought guests might appear. Cocks even organized a pickup chamber ensemble composed of a ship's carpenter and a sailor to divert Japanese music lovers.[1]

Merchants needed, moreover, to be quick studies. They required a keen awareness of commercial preferences: what people wanted, what they wore, what they ate. They compiled lists of commodities they hoped to sell and sought to understand local tastes. In one such list Captain John Saris detailed the fabrics and minerals he thought would sell profitably in Japan, but also recommended "Pictures paynted, som lascivious, others of stories of warrs by sea and land, the larger the better."[2] Thomas Roe likewise wrote quite sternly to the East India Company of the type of wares that were marketable in India, and particularly urged that goods "must be made by Indian patternes."[3] Responding to cultural cues, merchants learned trading preferences slowly, through trial and error.

English merchants acquired this information on cultural predilections, which translated into commercial acumen, in matters ranging from diet to art to clothing, by befriending local merchants, meeting their families, observing fashions and tastes, and by visiting people in their homes. Conventions of buying and selling introduced people to foreign tastes in deeply intimate ways. The English house at Japan was simultaneously a residence, a storehouse, and a showroom. The head of the factory entertained visiting merchants and brought out his wares for display, a system that enabled traders to scrutinize each other's reactions to the goods offered. Once newcomers learned the body language of strangers, they could read a gesture or an expression as easily as they could an overt comment on wares.

Often real understanding and empathy followed this cultural facility. Some English immersed themselves in foreign lands, embracing local customs, rituals, and people. So Richard Cocks did in Japan, where he befriended a Chinese merchant, intruded in the Japanese judicial system, rented a garden plot where he tenderly cultivated the plants friends procured for him in their travels—including fruit trees given by a Buddhist priest—attended concerts and plays, secured sexual companionship with multiple Japanese women, and by the end of his time in Hirado dated his diary entries with Japanese months. Merchants conformed to local customs, and in their desire to acquire cultural bilingualism, they obtained the best tutors they could: local women. Sexual alliances were at the heart of commercial success, or so Richard Wickham suggested when he praised another trader's woman as his "language tutor."[4] East India Company merchants and mariners seem to have strewn the children of such unions around the Indian and Pacific oceans, leaving, in some cases, other men to provide for their care. One such child was not abandoned by his father. Instead, William Eaton arranged for his son, William, to follow him to England from Japan. The son attended Trinity College, Cambridge, and was made a denizen of England in 1639 (denization gave foreigners certain legal rights as English subjects, and it is interesting in this case that having an English father did not automatically give William Eaton Jr. the rights of other English subjects). The boy's mother and sister stayed behind in Japan.

Some traders deplored the sexual latitude of East India Company trading posts, while some ambassadors rebuked traders for their tendency toward cultural immersion. At the heart of such apprehension lay English ideas about the mutability of identity: travel might alter an individual at his core. Indeed, one English mariner, in service to the Dutch, was so shaken in his perception of who he was after a stint in foreign service that, "staring as yf he had byn agast," he confessed to Richard Cocks that "he was dowbtfull whether he might tell me he was an English man or no."[5] The diverse ways in which merchants integrated themselves as outsiders and foreigners into unfamiliar communities reveal that there was no single English style of interaction with foreign people. The English, by necessity, followed the cultural cues they were able to perceive. In some posts, English merchants lived gently and discretely, both a part of and apart from the dominant host culture. So they did in Lisbon, where as Protestants they lurked on the margins of a Catholic world. Elsewhere, the English sought to immerse themselves in the varied opportunities of foreign ports. The ability of the English to accommodate these different expectations reflects the improvisation and adaptability, the forced or voluntary cosmopolitanism, central to trade relations.

Although it is easy to appreciate the willingness of traders to absorb the novelties of the world around them, they were not the only travelers to do so. Perhaps the most unexpected expression of cosmopolitan sentiments came from English clerics, men hired to provide the most visible symbol of English culture (expressed through the national church) abroad. English ministers, bulwarks of English Protestant faith in their chaplaincies overseas, were often lured to their foreign posts *because* of their cosmopolitan inclinations. The cleric Thomas Smith, who was in Istanbul in the 1660s, described this trait as "an inbred curiosity."[6] Edward Pocock, already a linguist, was appointed to the Aleppo chaplaincy in 1629. He was a reluctant voyager who complained about his residence among "the barbarous people of this country."[7] Yet his sojourn in Aleppo enabled him to continue the language studies he loved. He studied Hebrew, until he concluded that he could not learn the language fruitfully there; worked on Syriac; and especially studied Arabic, hiring a doctor or sheik to teach him and attended by a servant with whom he conversed in Arabic. He collected books and manuscripts for Archbishop Laud, befriending local religious figures in the process. His language studies enabled him to revise his scriptural translations, and, for all his gripes, he traveled overseas again.

Another minister, John Covel, shared this intellectual posture. He visited mosques and synagogues. He went to services of Greeks ("a hundred times," he reported later), Armenians, Georgians, and Russians. Not only did he visit services, but he also spoke with religious leaders, read their books, and copied their manuscripts. He interrogated strangers. He marveled at the array of "superstitions" he encountered among Turks, Greeks, Jews, and Armenians. When the Ragusean ambassador came to visit, Covel befriended him, too, and when he learned from him of a Jewish woman who was believed to be a witch, he insisted that he meet her as well.[8] There was no limit to his enthusiasms.

Covel's travels and his interrogation of the priests and laity he met led him, as such encounters did most travelers, to some remarkable conclusions for a preacher. He believed that in "outward practice and profession" all religions were the same, with saints and learned leaders whom people followed. "They all have strange fancyes and human conceits of ye stations in eternity. they all have factions and furiously persecute, censure, damn one ye other . . .

they all stricktly persist in their own way."[9] His ecumenism is the clerical version of the merchant's cosmopolitanism, and it got Covel in trouble.

After his stint in Istanbul, John Covel went to Rome to serve the English community there. In Rome, Covel heard rumors being spread by Jesuits that he had converted to Catholicism. The inveterate sightseer deployed his interests in Catholic sights to defend himself. At the site of a miracle in Naples, for example, he was banned entry because he refused to say he was Catholic. Thus how could he have converted? The evidence against him, he speculated, was his attendance at several functions of the pope and cardinals in Rome, events that were also attended by other English gentlemen. The accusations made him irate and indignant. They suggested that a man should not read and view the religious practices of others, lest he invite such criticism. Covel insisted that he was no more Catholic than he was Greek or Jewish or Muslim or Armenian. In his defense Covel articulated a cosmopolitan posture: he could not be any one thing without being equally another. And yet he knew with certainty that he was Protestant—so he signed his letter quite clearly, as "a true son of ye protestant church."[10]

If it is easy to see the centrality (and occasional perils) of cultural accommodation and understanding, and the cosmopolitanism and ecumenism that often resulted from these behaviors and interests in trading posts far from England, it is more difficult to discern this intellectual posture at home. Cosmopolitanism facilitated survival and success overseas, and thus emerged in part as a series of learned behaviors, but was less urgent—and thus less visible—in England. Yet this cosmopolitan world seeped into England. The docks where vessels landed their goods and passengers were vibrant places. English mariners died in high numbers on long ocean voyages, the victims of scurvy, infectious diseases, and fevers, and English merchant ships always sailed home with sailors acquired along the way. When John Saris left Japan in 1613, his East India Company ship carried a crew of fifteen Japanese, forty-six English, and five men simply described as "Swarts," likely a reference to sailors hired in India.[11] And the mariners themselves brought back pets, including monkeys and parrots, whose cries added to the babel of voices heard at the port.[12] But above all, these vessels carried foreign goods that were coveted by English consumers—textiles such as luxury silks and colorful calicos, spices, both necessities (salt and pepper for food preservation) and luxuries (like nutmeg and mace), and dyegoods for the vital English textile industries. The visual, tactile, and olfactory presence of new commodities generated a festival for all the senses and brought distant lands into the domestic setting of English households well beyond the metropolis.

Ships also carried goods collected by travelers, including live animals to entertain royal patrons. The manuscripts and books travelers gathered filled English libraries, and the antiquities they dismantled, purchased, or plundered overseas adorned private collections of men such as the Earl of Arundel. Travelers returned not just with reeking and tattered clothes, but with their memories of their journeys, often laboriously recorded on paper sealed in watertight pouches for safekeeping. Some labored to make public their experiences, and the most popular books went through multiple editions. As these works circulated, they made the foreign world so familiar that already by 1663, one Scottish father told his son not to bother to write down everything he saw on his travels. "Som days," he remarked, there would be nothing important to record, and much of what the son had to write would already be available in print.[13]

To assert the centrality of cosmopolitanism in England's transition from a weak kingdom to an emerging power is not to deny the reality and pervasiveness and importance of its opposite: xenophobia. Not all English who traveled abroad embraced the unfamiliarity of new surroundings, and many English overseas enterprises were predicated around the displacement of indigenous people and foreign rivals, not a cultural embrace. The son of the trader William Eaton, like Thomas Rolfe, the son of the planter John Rolfe and Pocahontas, represented one possible English response to a world beyond its shores, but these offspring (who lived simultaneously in England) were also part of a world of vicious loathing of foreigners, both within Europe and far from home. Cosmopolitanism in this context was not a coherent system of behavior or a cohesive worldview. Rather, it emerged organically and by necessity from a willingness (for some, a predisposition) to learn how to respond to new circumstances. And this willingness, with each individual who sailed from England, embedded England in a transformed global world.

Notes

1. October 1613, *The Voyage of Captain John Saris to Japan, 1613,* ed. Ernest M. Satow (London: Hakluyt Society, 1900), 160.

2. Letter from Saris to the East India Company, October 17, 1614, *Voyage of Captain John Saris,* appendix A, 204.

3. William Foster, ed., *The Embassy of Sir Thomas Roe to the Court of the Great Mogul, 1615–1619* (London: Hakluyt Society, 1899), 486–87.

4. Wickham at Edo to Nealson at Hirado, May 25, 1614, in Anthony Farrington, ed., *The English Factory in Japan, 1613–1623,* 2 vols. (London: British Library 1991), 1:164.

5. Edward Maunde Thompson, ed., *Diary of Richard Cocks,* 2 vols. (London: Hakluyt Society, 1883), June 1617, 1:269.

6. Thomas Smith, *An Account of the Greek Church* (London, 1680), A2r.

7. Quoted in Zachary Twells, *The Lives of Dr. Edward Pococke . . .* (London, 1816), 15.

8. Covel to George Davis (consul at Naples), July 5, 1678, Rome, Add. 22910, fol. 164v, British Library; Add. 22912, fol. 227r, fol. 188v, British Library.

9. August 10, 1675, Add. 22912, fol. 237v, BL.

10. Covel to George Davis (consul at Naples), July 5, 1678, Rome, Add. 22910, fols. 164r–165r, BL.

11. *The Voyage of Captain John Saris to Japan,* 183.

12. Thompson, ed., *The Diary of Richard Cocks,* 1:291.

13. "Instructions for my sone going abroad," January 30, 1663 (1663/4?), MS 3234, n. 118, Yule Collection, National Library of Scotland.

Morose's Turban

Barbara Sebek

Given the explosion of critical interest in the "global" as a paradigm in literary and cultural studies—not to mention the recent resurgence of anti-immigrant hysteria in the United States—the question of English cosmopolitanism and xenophobia is timely and important, approachable from many possible angles. It might seem circuitous, then, to use Jonson's *Epicene,* a play set squarely in London, as a point of entry into the discussion. Over half of the play takes place within the house of that most insular of characters, Morose, who feverishly tries to isolate his domestic domain from the noise and bustle of outside life. Despite his resistance to penetration from the wider world, however, Morose invokes that world admiringly in his first appearance onstage during a farcical "interaction" with his bowing and gesticulating servant Mute:

> Your Italian and Spaniard are wise in these [gestures]! And it is a frugal and comely gravity. . . . The Turk in this divine discipline is admirable, exceeding all the potentates of the earth; still waited on by mutes, and all his commands so executed; yea, even in the war, as I have heard, and in his marches, most of his charges and directions given by signs and with silence. An exquisite art! And I am heartily ashamed and angry oftentimes that the Princes of Christendom should suffer a barbarian to transcend 'em in so high a point of felicity. I will practise it hereafter.
>
> $(2.1.19-35)^1$

Even before Morose compares his household's disciplined regimen of enforced silence to foreign modes of communication and rule, Truewit describes his elaborate headwear as a "huge turban of nightcaps on his head buckled over his ears," a getup that Clerimont explains to be "his custom when he walks abroad" (1.1.139–41). Associated with the Turk when he is "abroad" in the streets of

London, and imagining his rule at "home" in relation to the practices of Italians, Spaniards, and Turks (at least insofar as he "[has] heard" of these practices), Morose must be read in the context of English engagements with and perceptions of the non-English.[2]

The topic of this forum encourages us to do more than note the *fact* of the presence of the foreign in this London-based satire.[3] We need to nuance how we understand the possible range of contemporary responses to this presence, both in this particular instance and in the culture in general. Does Morose's admiration and emulation of Spaniards and Turks, emblemized in Truewit's "turbanization" of the homely nightcaps, simply or automatically serve to ridicule him? How does it relate to Dauphine's "urbanization" of the nightcaps later in the play? "Oh, hold me up a little!" Dauphine laughs as he describes Morose sequestering himself in the roof beams: "I shall go away i'the jest else. He has got on his whole nest of nightcaps and locked himself up i'the top o'the house, as high as ever he can climb from the noise. I peeped in at a cranny and saw him sitting over a crossbeam o'the roof, like him o'the saddler's horse in Fleet Street, upright" (4.1.20–25). Among class- or status-conscious spectators in the Whitefriars Theater, might not Morose's transformation into a shop sign (perhaps just a few doors down from the theater on Fleet Street) get a bigger, or more mocking, laugh than the turbanized Morose earlier in the play? Rather than primarily registering insular hostility to a predilection for imitating the customs of foreigners, the nightcapped Morose resonates here with class-based cultural anxiety about an increasingly prominent commercial culture in London. It is after all not Morose's *openness* to external influences but his tyrannical *refusal* to be penetrated by the outside that fuels much of the satire of him. Further, in the final scene, his public declaration of his incapacity as penetrat*or* finally seals his humiliation: "I am no man, ladies. . . . Utterly unabled in nature, by reason of frigidity, to perform the duties or any the least office of a husband" (5.4.41–44). Emasculation overrides Turkification in Jonson's skewering of Morose. In short, we must remember how multiple axes of difference—religion, nationality, gender, class, occupation, even neighborhood[4]—impinge on the range of responses Jonson's satire might elicit. I don't think that an overarching sense of "English xenophobia" nor "English cosmopolitanism" adequately captures these intricate discursive operations. Given that "Englishness" in our period was an unevenly developing construct, itself shot through with differences, a totalizing sense of xenophobia will not do, since it implicitly posits a coherent, stable English identity. Informed by the insights of post-structuralism and historicism, we cannot address the question of English cosmopolitanism without attending to particular discourse communities and to the conventions governing the forms of textual output associated with them.

Moreover, Morose's first speech captures a deep ambivalence toward the foreign that pervaded early modern culture: the simultaneous denigration and admiration of national and religious "others," particularly those actively embarking on imperial projects. Rather than merely foolish or misguided, Morose's admiration of the "barbarian" illustrates a larger set of cultural responses: a complex dynamic of fascination and fear, celebration and denunciation, at work in a process of negative self-definition vis-à-vis "others" who were often positively construed. If it seems I am belaboring the early moment in the play, or rehashing familiar critical axioms, consider the Norton's gloss of "Turk" in 2.1.28: "The Sultan of Turkey was considered a cruel despot by most Western Europeans." Despite the weak qualifier—not *all,* but *most*—the explanatory gloss perpetuates the notion that this static stereotype held sway, not just in England, but "Western Europe" generally. Recent critics have amply demonstrated how English perceptions of and experiences with the Ottoman world or the "East" were shiftier and far more variable than this static stereotype of the "cruel despot" allows.[5] The whole field of postcolonial studies has engaged in historicizing or dismantling the "Orientalist" paradigm in which the "Turk-as-cruel-despot" stereotype is enmeshed. Any editorial gloss can impose interpretive blinders, of course, so it behooves teachers to encourage students to work with and against whatever textual apparatus they are given. To assume this kind of automatic xenophobia potentially serves (to use language that has a quaint, old-fashioned whiff) to reinscribe what we aim to critique. At the very least, the assumption closes down interpretive and critical questions, blinds us to shades of meaning in textual evidence, and disables awareness of important differences and specificities (of region, class, occupation, and so on).

Moving beyond this general pronouncement on the importance of specificity, I want to target a particular occupational group/discourse community to reveal how openness to alterity is most salient when we foreground those directly involved in long-distance trade, both abroad and in England. As Ottoman historian Daniel

Goffman points out, it is in the sphere of commerce that shared purposes across national and religious lines often emerge. Without effacing hostilities between Ottomans and other Europeans, Goffman argues that the two civilizations "converge in some areas" and that "such intersections of character and purpose . . . are most visible, perhaps, in the economic sphere, in which trade within the Mediterranean basin served to bind the two worlds."[6] Serving as factor for the Turkey and Levant companies in various Mediterranean locales from 1582–1602, John Sanderson illustrates how English traders in the region and the company governors back in London were just as preoccupied with conflicts and negotiations *among* the English and other western European traders as they were with the Turks. Sanderson's correspondence and other documents open a window onto how attention to specific trade conditions can destabilize English/non-English binaries.[7]

Trade not with the Ottomans but with the Far East becomes a focal point in a text that Jonson wrote in the same year that *Epicene* was first performed. Commissioned by William Cecil to celebrate the opening of the New Exchange in the West End, the *Entertainment at Britain's Burse* presents the Master of a "china house" who offers an openly (perhaps facetiously, perhaps strategically) adulatory view of the "other" as he hawks his wares: "O your Chinese! The onely wise nation under the Sun: They had the knowledge of all manner of Arts and letters, many thousand's yeares, before any of these parts could speake" (135–36).[8] The relative backwardness or belatedness of "these parts" vis-à-vis the Chinese is signaled in muteness, the very condition that Morose tries to impose on those around him as he emulates the "frugal and comely gravity" of the Italians and Spaniards and the "exquisite art" of the Turkish sultan. The shop Master's claim of English or European belatedness echoes and refracts Morose's "shame" that the sultan "transcend[s]" the "Princes of Christendom." While we cannot take the Master's exaggerated praise of the Chinese at face value, as Baker argues (174–75), the Master's revaluation of European development in comparison to a foreign power becomes thinkable in the commercial venue. Encouraging consumption of foreign wares provides incentive to engage, even celebrate, alterity, including England's own alterity.

A final example. In the very years when antagonisms between England and Spain were at their height, Bristol-based merchant John Browne wrote and published a manual of practical and moral advice, *The Marchants Avizo* (1589), addressed to the "sons and servants" of merchants venturing "to Spain or Portingale or other countries" (title page). The text is remarkable for many reasons, but I want to call attention to what it does not say. First published in the year after Spain's unsuccessful naval invasion, the *Avizo*— Spanish for warning—is pointedly devoid of chauvinistic zeal. Browne's muteness on this score attests to how out of sync merchants' concerns could be with nationalist rhetoric. Not only does Browne fail to evince animus against the Spanish, but, as McGrath notes, he even enjoins factors to defer with courtesy and lowliness to the Spaniards with whom they deal (19).[9] Here, national and religious conflicts are subordinated to promoting the harmonious conduct of profitable traffic. Calling attention to his locality in the sign-off to the dedicatory epistle that appeared in the first edition— "from my house in Bristow 26 Oct."—Browne might serve as a test case for the idea that London is a unique locus of openness to foreign influences and intercultural exchange.[10]

I am self-conscious about sounding as if I am glorifying the power of commerce to foster cross-cultural harmony or openness to foreigners and foreign influences. Benefiting from inequities of wealth and differential access to education and networks of influence, it was merchant and aristocratic elites who most immediately profited from foreign trade and who could most comfortably afford to purchase luxury imports.[11] Just as transglobal trade depends on exploited labor, cosmopolitan communities are often a consequence of persecution, poverty, and dislocation. Nonetheless, those English citizens actively engaged in trade with the non-English, especially, though not only, those who lived and worked abroad, had to temper and filter xenophobic sentiments as they experienced and represented *themselves* as others.

Notes

1. All quotations from the play are from *English Renaissance Drama: A Norton Anthology* (New York: W. W. Norton, 2002).

2. Especially, though not only, the Ottoman world. The servant's name alone, Mute, conjures the sultan's seraglio. M. Miles, working from the perspective of the history of disability, points to the "communications achievements of the Ottoman court," achievements obscured by current historians' and critics' unwitting participation in later travelers' Orientalist stereotypes. "Signing in the Seraglio: Mutes, Dwarfs and Jestures at the Ottoman Court 1500–1700," *Disability and Society* 15:1 (2000): 115–34. Compare this to Barbara Fuchs's formulation that critics of early modern English culture, working within an isolated national framework, "unwit-

tingly replicate the effects of Elizabethan propaganda" about Spain (84). "Imperium Studies: Theorizing Early Modern Expansion," in *Postcolonial Moves: Medieval through Modern,* ed. Patricia Clare Ingham and Michelle R. Warren (New York: Palgrave, 2003), 71–90.

3. Others have noted the presence of the exotic and foreign in Jonson's city comedies. Crystal Bartolovich reads *Bartholomew Fair* as saturated with the new world in "'Baseless Fabric': London as a 'World City'," in *"The Tempest" and Its Travels,* ed. Peter Hulme and William H. Sherman (Philadelphia: University of Pennsylvania Press, 2000), 13–26. Also see Vitkus, *Turning Turk: English Theater and the Multicultural Mediterranean, 1570–1630* (New York: Palgrave, 2003), 28.

4. Deborah Harkness shows how natural science practitioners in certain neighborhoods in Elizabethan London were "particularly international in composition and outlook," engaged in collaborative and competitive working relationships that cut across differences of nation, culture, gender, and educational level. "'Strange' Ideas and 'English' Knowledge: Natural Science Exchange in Elizabethan London," in *Merchants and Marvels: Commerce, Science, and Art in Early Modern Europe,* ed. Pamela H. Smith and Paula Findlen (New York: Routledge, 2002), 137–60.

5. Linda McJannet, *The Sultan Speaks: Dialogue in English Plays and Histories about the Ottoman Turks* (New York: Palgrave, 2006); Emily Bartels, *Spectacles of Strangeness: Imperialism, Alienation, and Marlowe* (Philadelphia: University of Pennsylvania Press, 1993); Daniel Vitkus, *Turning Turk;* Jonathan Burton, *Traffic and Turning: Islam and English Drama, 1579–1624* (Newark: University of Delaware Press, 2005). As Fuchs remarks regarding English perceptions of Spain, critics tend to sidestep "the messy dynamics of simultaneous admiration for and vilification of Spanish influences that characterize so many English texts of this period" (85).

6. Daniel Goffman, *The Ottoman Empire and Early Modern Europe* (Cambridge: Cambridge University Press, 2002), 8.

7. William Foster, ed., *The Travels of John Sanderson in the Levant, 1584–1602* (London: Hakluyt Society, 1931).

8. Reference to the play is from Knowles. Butler suggests that the absence of the *Entertainment* from Jonson's 1616 *Works* signals Jonson's attempt to distance himself from the city and the kinds of commerce associated with it (17–18). Butler and Orgel read the *Entertainment* as a celebratory vision of foreign trade, a reading that Baker problematizes. Knowles, "Jonson's *Entertainment at Britain's Burse,*" in *Re-Presenting Ben Jonson: Text, History, Performance* (New York: St. Martin's 1999), 114–51; Martin Butler, "Jonson's London and Its Theatres," and Stephen Orgel, "Jonson and the Arts," in *The Cambridge Companion to Ben Jonson* (Cambridge University Press, 2000); David J. Baker, "The Allegory of a China Shop: Jonson's *Entertainment at Britain's Burse,*" *ELH* 72 (2005): 159–80.

9. *The Marchants Avizo* (London, 1589); Patrick McGrath, introduction to *The Marchants Avizo* (Boston: Baker Library, 1957).

10. Perhaps Browne suggests that we entertain the idea of *port town* exceptionalism. McGrath explains that Bristol was especially well positioned to benefit from the Iberian trade, so the impact of the crisis of 1586–87 was particularly severe (xii–xiii). In addition to his location at a remove from the imminent naval threat in 1588, Browne's wariness about his book facing censorship abroad, indi-

cated in the dedicatory epistle, might account for his effacement of anti-Spanish sentiment.

11. For a quick overview of debates about the expansion of a consumer economy and the role of luxury in it, see Levy Peck, 10–13. Throughout her study, Levy Peck provides ample evidence of the English eagerly borrowing manners, values, and goods from abroad. *Consuming Splendor: Society and Culture in Seventeenth-Century England* (Cambridge University Press, 2005).

The Time of Shakespeare's Jewry

Jonathan Gil Harris

Like its twenty-first-century counterpart, early modern London has recently become a good deal more cosmopolitan. Literary critics and cultural historians increasingly regard it as not just an English but also a British and even international city. Ruled by a Scottish king, it teems with émigré Irish costermongers, Dutch textile workers, and Portuguese merchants. Nor is it any longer monolithically Christian. We have learned from Inquisition records about London Jews celebrating Passover in 1605; we are aware, too, of London's African visitors, such as the presumably Muslim Moroccan ambassador whose portrait is often reproduced in editions of *Othello*. New economic criticism supplements this multicultural picture by reminding us of how London's rapidly growing involvement in global commerce flooded its markets with exotic commodities from Asia and the Americas, creating new cosmopolitan consumers of the kind parodied by Dekker and Middleton in *The Roaring Girl*. The picture is supported also by the widespread popularity of the joke that the Englishman's clothes comprise the fashions of the world. As Portia says of her English suitor in *The Merchant of Venice:* "How oddly he is suited! I think he bought his doublet in Italy, his round hose in France, his bonnet in Germany and his behavior everywhere"(1.2.68–70).[1]

This is not to say that we now read these signs of London's globalization as evidence of inclusiveness or tolerance. Scholars of early modern London recognize that globalization and xenophobia are often partners, as the city's growing immigrant populations knew all too well from the riots against foreign artisans, the Dutch Church libel, the edicts to expel "blackamoors," or the slanders against Dr. Lopez. But even as we complicate early modern London's cosmopolitanism by insisting on its complicities with practices of exclusion, we can all too easily reproduce an interpretive

tendency endemic to modern multiculturalism: that is, understanding the relations between London's different cultures
(whether linguistic, religious, or ethnic) in simply secular and spatial terms, as the favored American images of the mosaic and the
rainbow or, less rosily, the ghetto and the gated community all suggest.

The tendency toward secularization is underscored by the *Oxford English Dictionary (OED)*. It defines the "cosmopolite," an
early cognate of "cosmopolitan," as "a citizen of the world," listing
as the first recorded instance Richard Hakluyt's 1598 reference to
"cosmopolites" in his tale of King Edgar's travels.[2] So long as we
think of the cosmopolitan in purely secular terms, we are likely to
accept the *OED*'s implicit assurance that the word originated in a
genre devoted to mapping transnational movement within a newly
global conception of geographical space. But the *OED* doesn't note
how Hakluyt's "cosmopolites" derives less from experiences of
global travel than from fantasies of universal religion. King Edgar's
travel narrative first appears in John Dee's 1577 treatise on the arts
of navigation, in which he defined the *"Cosmopolites"* as "A Citizen, and Member, of the whole and only one Mysticall City Vniuersall: And so, consequently, to meditate of the Cosmopoliticall
Gouernment therof, vnder the King Almighty."[3] Dee's conception
of the cosmopolitan "City Vniuersall" has roots that can be traced
back to the New Testament. One of its scriptural antecedents is St.
Paul's first letter to Corinthians, which powerfully yokes together
supposedly different peoples in a universal church: "For as the
body is one, and hath many members, and all the members of that
one body, being many, are one body: so also is Christ. For by one
Spirit are we all baptized into one body, whether we be Jews or
Gentiles, whether we be bond or free" (1 Corinthians 12:13). Thus
St. Paul, like Dee, imagines religious cosmopolitanism with a spatial metaphor—albeit in his case not a world city, but a mystical
body.

By focusing exclusively on the spatial dimensions of the "Vniuersall" city or body, however, we lose sight of how cosmopolitan
discourse often employs not just space but also time as a way of
organizing the relations between different cultures. After all, St.
Paul's universal cosmopolitan body was predicated on a temporal
movement, one that shifted God's favor from a prior oriental Judaism to a future occidental church, typologically superseding physical circumcision with spiritual baptism (and Jewish Saul with

Christian Paul).[4] I want to reflect briefly here on how Shakespeare's Jewry is similarly marked by temporal distance from the present—and in ways that parallel certain contemporary American discourses of world cultures. By Shakespeare's Jewry, I do not mean just his representations of Venetian Jewry in *The Merchant of Venice.* I refer also to a London neighborhood that he doubtless knew well: the Old Jewry, north of Cheapside. Both Shakespeare's Jewish-Venetian play and the London neighborhood are implicated in a cosmopolitan discourse that organizes the relations between cultures not just spatially but also temporally.

This tendency is perhaps most familiar to us from Hegel's *Philosophy of History,* in which Europe embodies the present, while Asia is eternally stuck in the past. Just as the sun rises in the east but moves west, so has world Spirit—Hegel's agent of progress—dawned in Asia only to move to Greece and Rome prior to its present location in Germany and its possible future in America.[5] But lest we think of Hegel's conception of *History* as simply an apotheosis of Enlightenment occidental-centrism, we might also reflect on the following:

> Almightie Lord, who from thy glorious throne
> Seest and rulest all things ev'n as one:
>
> . . . .
> But above all, thy Church and Spouse doth prove
> Not the decrees of power, but bands of love.
> Early didst thou arise to plant this vine,
> Which might the more indeare it to be thine.
> Spices come from the East; so did thy Spouse
>
> . . . .
> The course was westward, that the sunne might light
> As well our understanding as our sight.

(193)[6]

This extract is from George Herbert's "Church Militant," published in *The Temple* in 1633. For Herbert as for Hegel, the globe is not just a space, but a temporal movement "westward," from sunrise to sunset, from primitive to contemporary, from Asia to Europe. Herbert's model of time can seem modern, not least in his Hegel-like prediction that the future will belong to America: "Religion stands tip-toe in our land, / Readie to passe to the *American* strand" (199). But it is also antique, inasmuch as it resurrects St. Paul's temporal distancing of the Jews. For Herbert, religion's purposeful movement from East to West emblematizes his typological understanding of history—that is, his relentless insistence on the supersession of the Old Testament by the New, Moses by Jesus, and Jew by Christian.[7]

As countless critics have noted, *The Merchant of Venice* is likewise suffused with the traces—whether serious or ironic—of typology. Most notoriously, Portia trumps old Jewish law with supposed Christian mercy. But the courtroom scene is simply one instance of the play's preoccupation with the typological relations between Jew and Christian. The "streaked and pied" lambs of Shylock's parable about the Old Testament Jacob (1.3.71) are eclipsed by Antonio's Christlike lamb or "tainted wether of the flock" (4.1.113). Similarly, "Old" Gobbo is a type of blind Isaac from the Old Testament, while his son Launcelot—who performs a twin spatial and temporal movement from "old" Jewish to "new" Christian master (2.4.18)—is a type of the New Testament prodigal son. Venice is presented as the exemplary cosmopolitan city, in which "trade and profit . . . / Consisteth of all nations" (3.2.30–31). But the space this compact reserves for Jewishness is not only physically circumscribed within the ghetto; it is also temporally distanced from the present, even as it continues to supply the multicultural city with rich typological and economic resources. Lorenzo, enriched by Portia's alienation of Shylock's estate, tells her that "you drop manna in the way / Of starved people" (5.1.292–93); old Jewish matter ("manna") survives anachronistically in the Venetian present, but only as a figure with which to feed the Christian future. The play thus makes explicit the workings of what we might call typological cosmopolitanism.

Many readings of *The Merchant of Venice* have drawn parallels between early modern London and Shakespeare's Venice as cosmopolitan cities situated within new global networks of commerce and migration. But the cities' shared typological cosmopolitanism is arguably what most connects Venice's Old Jew (who refers to himself as "Old Shylock" [2.5.2]) to London's Old Jewry. As its name suggests, the Old Jewry implies not just a location, but also a temporality. The street in London EC2 that now bears the name was for two centuries the location of the city's Jewish community. Although the area had already begun to be called Old Jewry prior to the expulsion of England's Jews in 1290, by Shakespeare's time the "Old" of Old Jewry worked to ossify its noun and make the phrase designate a singular Jewish place, people, and time, all of which were defined by their irrevocable pastness. Even three hundred years after the Expulsion, Londoners had a keen sense of the past occupants of the present Old Jewry and the historical rupture that had made it "Old": Gabriel Harvey, criticizing the possible readmission of Jews to England, wrote that "I am beholding to the old Jewry, but have no great fancy to a new."[8]

The temporal distancing of both Jews and Old Jewry is particularly apparent in John Stow's *Survey of London,* which displays an unlikely fascination with England's Jewish past. In his first edition of 1598, Stow discusses numerous episodes from Anglo-Jewish history; but he had developed a full-blown obsession by the time of his revised 1603 edition, to which he added four new pages on Jewish history from the Conquest to the Expulsion. In these pages, Stow makes London's Old Jewry a synecdoche for an entire religion and people apprehended under the mark of belatedness: the Jews who dwelt there appear in his narrative as always already vanished, such as one "Benomy Mittun" (or "Bonevia Mitun") who had been the owner of a house deeded by Henry III to Semane the crossbowman, or one "Moses of Canterbury" whose house had been escheated to a Christian.[9]

Stow doubtless knew that there were Jews living in his London. But the time of the Jews is, in his *Survey,* pluperfect passive—they are not has-beens, but *had*-beens, always already absent because irrevocably past. Yet their material relics have a curious presence. We might call this tendency Stow's Neutron Bomb historiography: the people are vaporized, but the buildings remain. Stow repeatedly identifies old Jewish structures that have assumed new identities: the synagogue at Threadneedle Street in the Broad Street Ward that has become St. Anthony's Hospital (1:280); a Jewish stone house at the northeast side of Ironmonger's Lane that is now the King's "Wardrobe"(1:291); a synagogue in Old Jewry that became first the Lord Mayor's house and then the Windmill Tavern (1:278); and a Jew's house, forfeited to Henry III, that was transformed into a Domus Conversorium for Jewish converts to Christianity (2:42–43). In Stow's reading, Old Jewry yields convertible matter that—like Lorenzo's manna—sustains the Christian present.

The *Survey*'s most telling instance of typological cosmopolitanism appears in Stow's description of Ludgate, one of the city's seven ancient gates. Describing the repair of Ludgate's crumbling wall—a civic project undertaken in 1586—Stow relates a remarkable discovery. As workmen toiled to restore a structure that commemorated King Lud, the supposed pagan founder of the city, they found instead the remains of another, unexpected religious past: a stone "ingrauen in Hebrewe Caracters."

Stow recorded the inscription; but he was no polyglot, and his Hebrew is mangled (see below). He makes sense of the Hebrew

builded.

Iewes houses spoiled.

ken down to be newe builded, there was found couched within the wall thereof, a stone taken from one of the Iewes houses, wherein was ingrauen in Hebrewe Caracters these wordes following, הרם מצב חר משת בן הרב ר יצחק. Hæc est statio Rabbi Mofes, filij infignis Rabbi Ifaac: which is to fay, this is the Station, or Ward of Rabby Mofes, the fonne of the honozable Rabby Ifaac, and had béene fired vppon the front of one of the Iewes houses

characters via a Latin gloss: *"Haec est statio Rabbi Mosis filii insignis Rabbi Isaac;* which is to say, this is the Station, or Ward of *Rabby Moses,* the sonne of the honorable *Rabby Isaac"* (1:38). The original Hebrew, however, if we can deduce it correctly from Stow's garbled characters, is probably "matzevat rabbi Moshe ben harav rabbi Yitzhak." The word "matzevat" interests me here. It corresponds to what Stow renders in Latin as "statio" (station or ward); but it means, more accurately, "monument" or "gravestone." In all likelihood, what Stow saw in 1586 was the remainder not of a house, but of Rabbi Moshe ben Yitzhak's gravestone. If so, the historical event that Stow misreads as a looting of a private Jewish house entails a transparently supersessionary logic. Desecrated yet converted, temporally distanced yet saved, the sacred matter of Old Jewry—or rather, of the city's Jewish cemetery—was anachronistically sutured into the cosmopolitan fabric of London's New Jerusalem.

This brief sketch of early modern London's typological cosmopolitanism has repercussions for us now. When Herbert imagined religion passing from Europe to America's "strand," he was fantasizing not the Puritan exodus, but Edenic Native Americans with a commendable disregard for gold. Yet there is a way in which Herbert's prophecy of religion's temporal and geographical movement to America has come true. Just as the supposedly tolerant decision in 1656 to readmit Jews to England was driven in part by an apocalyptic version of typology—that retrograde Jews might be converted to Christianity to usher in the Second Coming and the end of days—so does a certain strain of fundamentalist Christianity in the

United States embrace Jews as the backward agents of salvation, as Jerry B. Jenkins and Tim LaHaye's best-selling *Left Behind* series makes clear. The series, a projected fourteen-part novelization of the events of the book of Revelation, imagines the conversion of 144,000 Israeli Jews who evangelize for Christ during the Tribulation and the global war against the terror of the Antichrist. These events take place in a fallen world "left behind" by true Christian believers who have experienced the Rapture—that is, ascended body and soul to heaven. Inasmuch as Jews are barred entry to heaven by their outmoded convenant, they exemplify what must be "left behind"; Judaism is the "old" superseded past within the cosmopolitan present that nonetheless secures the movement of history toward redemption.

We may want to dismiss the *Left Behind* series as the snake oil of Christian extremists. Yet its popularity makes it hard to ignore. *Desecration,* the ninth volume of the *Left Behind* series, was the best-selling hardcover novel in the United States in 2001; the next in the series, *The Remnant* (2002), was just as successful. Indeed, one wonders if its many readers include the architects of recent American foreign policy. For Jenkins and LaHaye, the Israeli Jew is the Old believer who must be converted to the New covenant, which means Israel must be violently protected by the Christian faithful from all threats posed to it and hence to human salvation. Baghdad, by contrast, is Satan's headquarters and irredeemably evil, and the United Nations is a godless organization against which believing Americans must crusade. That these details resonate eerily with the current Bush administration's rhetoric tells us something about not just the persistence but also the current power of typological cosmopolitanism.

The administration's "war on terror" has rhetorically presumed a cosmopolitan, democratic community of nations temporally divided from backward religious and political cultures, whether a "medieval" Islam in need of (Protestant?) "reformation," or an "Old" Europe superseded by "New" converts to America's democratizing mission. The political costs of temporally distancing cultures—of putting them "in the waiting room of history"—have been famously laid bare by Dipesh Chakrabarty.[10] But by tracing this supposedly secular tendency back only to nineteenth-century European historicisms, Chakrabarty's analysis ignores its religious coordinates, whether now, in early modern England, or in the ancient Christian church. As much as secular liberals may regard the

Bush administration's foreign policy as the antithesis of cosmopolitanism, its temporalization of geographical space is closer to the religious fantasy of the "cosmopolites" that we find in early modern writing. No, neither Jenkins and LaHaye's nor the neoconservatives' typological cosmopolitanisms are the same as Stow's or Shakespeare's. But we ignore at our peril the troublesome histories of the cosmopolitan if we understand it only in spatial and secular terms. We need to rethink, then, what we mean by a cosmopolitan early modern London. In a literal as well as figurative way, it is about time.

Notes

1. All references to *The Merchant of Venice* are from *The Norton Shakespeare,* ed. Stephen Greenblatt, Walter Cohen, Jean E. Howard, and Katherine Eisaman Maus (New York: Norton, 1997), and are cited in the text.

2. *OED,* "Cosmopolite," 1; Richard Hakluyt, *Principal Navigations, Voyages, Traffiques and Discoveries of the English Nation* (London, 1598), 1:35.

3. John Dee, *General and Rare Memorials Pertayning to the Perfect Arte of Nauigation* (London, 1577), 54.

4. Here I depart from, even as I am influenced by, Alain Badiou's extraordinarily compelling argument that Paul offers an alternative to notions of identity grounded in cultural affiliation. Badiou sees Paul as indifferent to temporal as well as cultural difference, and suggests that Christianity's distancing of Judaism is instead the legacy of St. John, who argued for the supersession of Jewish law by Greek logos. See Badiou, *Saint Paul: The Foundation of Universalism,* trans. Ray Brassier (Palo Alto, CA: Stanford University Press, 2003), esp. 43.

5. Georg W. F. Hegel, *The Philosophy of History,* trans. J. Sibree (Amherst, NY: Prometheus Books, 1991), 1–110.

6. References are to George Herbert, "The Church Militant," in *The English Poems of George Herbert,* ed. C. A. Patrides (London: Dent, 1974).

7. For a brilliant study of Christian typology and its persistence in modern "secular" thought, see Kathleen Biddick, *The Typological Imaginary: History, Technology, Circumcision* (Philadelphia: University of Pennsylvania Press, 2003).

8. Gabriel Harvey, *Pierce's Supererogation or A New Praise of the Old Ass* (London, 1593), 51–52.

9. John Stow, *A Survey of London, by John Stow: Reprinted from the Text of 1603,* ed. Charles Lethbridge Kingsford (Oxford: Clarendon Press, 1908), 1:279, 280. All further references are cited in the text.

10. Dipesh Chakrabarty, *Provincializing Europe: Postcolonial Thought and Historical Difference* (Princeton: Princeton University Press, 2000), 8.

Utopian Cosmopolitanism

CRYSTAL BARTOLOVICH

Borrowed from the ancient Greek, the early modern English "cosmopolitan" or "cosmopolite" designated a "citizen" of the "one mysticall citie universall," as one of the extracts collected in Richard Hakluyt's *Principal Navigations* uses it to describe the "perfect Cosmographer." "Hard word" books in the seventeenth century explained to the perplexed that it meant "citizen of the world." We know that some English men so designated themselves at the time, and even rendered London "Cosmopoli," but it seems pertinent to ask, given the word's association with citizenry, what it might have meant for women.[1] That is, if substantial cultural impediments (legally it was, in theory, possible) prevented English women from becoming citizens of London for the most part—indeed, barred them from being recognized as independent political subjects of any kind, except in exceptional circumstances—to what extent could they imagine themselves "citizens" of the *world?*[2] I will suggest they could in a very specific sense: *utopianly.* The cosmopolitanism that I will be examining here, in other words, was fulfilled "nowhere," but it can be traced as an incipient desire in women's writing, though more in hints, textual disruption, and contradictions than in positive description.[3] In its most radical form, of course, men's cosmopolitanism was necessarily utopian, as well, as we shall see; however, as a desire, *utopian cosmopolitanism* was arguably more potent—and imaginable—for women because their social roles were more circumscribed than those of their male counterparts in each class, and this structural subordination made it more likely for them to long for participation in a universal community that exceeded local constraints without simply collapsing them into a preexisting male normativity, as the default understandings of cosmopolitanism in early modern England demanded. Thus, while the utopian cosmopolitanism I have in mind did—and

does—not exist, I will suggest that aspiration to it served as a hitherto unexplored incentive for women to produce translations, one
of the most prominent forms of early women's writing.

Typically this highly active site of female production is explained in negative terms: public display by women being considered unseemly, women migrated to a site of publication deemed
more socially acceptable because, as John Florio put it, it was "delivered at the second hand."[4] I do not dispute this position entirely,
but think it is incomplete; women's translations often indicate, at
the very least, that a virtue was made of necessity. They were a
means by which women could aspire to a more expansive world—a
cosmopolitan conversation—*as women,* even if they did so only
partially conscious of disrupting the status quo. Margaret Tyler, for
example, who audaciously translated a Spanish romance into English in 1578, does seem to dismiss her own role as secondary ("the
invention, disposition, trimming, & what els in this story, is wholly
an other mans, my part none therein but the translation"), but she
goes on to describe translation in an unmistakably transculturally
engaged, or cosmopolitan, way—as "giving entertainment to a
stranger, before this time unacquainted with our country guise"—
and to defend a woman's fitness for such a task.[5]

Affirming this cosmopolitan dimension, Walter Benjamin insisted that in good translation all languages reveal their "kinship"
and an aspiration toward convergence in a lost unifying universal
language, pointing the way toward the relation between translation
and a utopian cosmopolitanism. In Benjamin's theorization, all languages are equivalent, though not identical: Tagalog or Farsi are as
significant as French or English as far as unfolding the mysteries of
"true" language are concerned, each being a unique fragment of its
"broken vessel" in his evocative image. Only by way of moving
through *all* languages in their specificity can the lost "true" pre-
Babelic language be recovered to usher in a redeemed world; from
this perspective, language itself might be understood as a utopian
cosmopolitan formation. For Benjamin, humans can participate in
this utopian cosmopolitanism of language most immediately via
good translation—and this is its significance. It indicates the for-
eignness permeating one's own language and each language's aspiration toward connection with all others: a cosmopolitan agenda
inhabiting every tongue whether its speakers recognize it consciously or not.[6]

One might have to go back all the way to the Renaissance to find a moment that saw translation in as august a light as Benjamin did. Translation was an important, visible and much-debated practice in early modern England because of its centrality to the school curriculum and because of self-consciousness about the status of the English language in relation to others.[7] John Florio thus stoutly defends translation in terms that are resolutely cosmopolitan in an at least potentially utopian form by declaring it the medium through which collective human knowledge is dispersed and preserved—or, in Benjamin's terms, has an *afterlife* (Florio puts it: "had its offspring"). His famous preface to his translation of Montaigne emphasizes that the Greeks are the source of knowledge for Europeans "and the Greekes drew their baptizing water from the conduit-pipes of the Egiptians, and they from the well-springs of the Hebrews or Chaldees." He goes on to assert that nothing can be written without translation, at least indirectly, since all knowledge depends on the font of prior wisdom, which is necessarily transcultural—and therefore polylinguistic—in its origins: "What doe the best then but gleane after others harvest? Borrow their colours, inherite their possessions? What doe they but translate?"[8] His rousing defense of translation can be read, then, as a celebratory and expansive view of human interchange via translation as a cosmopolitan medium—indeed, an English "cosmopolitan" (from "Greek" roots) is an example of this very process—which does not mean, of course, that any actual practice of translation has realized this condition in a liberatory form. Nevertheless, the strenuous debates about the effects of translation in which Florio's preface participates indicate how important—and potentially disruptive—a medium it was considered to be.

Indeed, Florio opens up the possibility of free exchange via translation not only transnationally, but also locally, by encouraging nonelite users to participate in universal human knowledge; against those who would criticize translation for making learning "common," opening up the possibility that children and "olde wives" or "coblers" might encroach presumptuously, he insists that "Learning cannot be too common," so long as it is used well.[9] Still, he is not divested of all gender elitism. He dedicates the Montaigne translation to the uncommon Countess of Bedford, who had set him the task, naming her ostentatiously as a patron of the community of learning whose circle he seeks to expand. At the same time, however, he wonders, contradictorily, whether he need apologize for engaging in the production of a translation, a genre of texts that were "reputed femalls," and he unfolds at length a metaphor of masculine birth that curiously inverts the gender roles, designating translations female for being "delivered at the second hand," while he describes his former writing as in "birth . . . masculine (as are all mens conceits that are their own)." Though he elaborately praises his female patrons (he includes the countess's mother in the dedication) as the genre demands, declares the translation their servant, and even describes himself at one point as enjoined to wear "the coller you [the Countess] have put about my neck with your inscription, *noli me cadere, nam sum Diana,*" femaleness is nonetheless associated in the dedication with translation as secondary.[10] And yet translation itself is so aggrandized in the ensuing epistle to the reader, as we have seen, that its supposed secondariness inverts: the "reputed femalls" turn out only a few pages later to be primary, an indispensable cosmopolitan medium, irreducible to the collective human accumulation of knowledge. What is going on with this contradictoriness? In Florio's discussion of translation no man's "conceits" are entirely his "own," while in the dedication he is eager to declare his earlier "conceits" a possession, "though but by their collecting." Inhabiting the transition to private property, he suggests that writing is common *and* "own[ed]" through the dramatically different content of the dedication and the epistle to the reader. Women translators were often contradictory in a different but related way, expressing a desire to engage in a universal conversation *and* remain female, while reproducing class elitism, Eurocentrism and xenophobia intact.

It seems important to recall at this point that then (as now) "cosmopolitan" is a site of struggle between those who use it to designate a group of elites who travel, know languages, or at least have a passionate curiosity about the world's peoples and places (the example from Hakluyt cited above), and its underlying concept of a universal human community. Furthermore, as egalitarian as the latter formulation may sound in comparison to the first, it, too, has tended to be an elitist formulation, predicated on recreating the world in the image of a privileged group, typically male, Christian, and European, and sometimes even more narrowly defined. For this reason, as Timothy Brennan has argued, the concept would come to be viewed with suspicion by anticolonial insurgents, who saw it as a Eurocentric attempt to refuse or limit the unsettling difference that they might bring to a redefined understanding of the human and civilized.[11] Brennan's point is important; we must con-

stantly be vigilant against falling into the trap of an insidiously subordinating cosmopolitanism. Nevertheless, other theorists have
struggled to recuperate the term in hopes of producing a nonelitist
form because at the current juncture of "globalization," the stakes
of such a project seem high. Ulrich Beck, for example, has argued
that "cosmopolitan ideas have not yet had the opportunity to ex-
haust their utopian potential." He insists on reclaiming the term,
but replacing the conformity logic of the older cosmopolitanism
with a "both, and" logic of "cosmopolitanization": a "dialectical
process in which the universal and the particular, the similar and
the dissimilar, the global and the local are to be conceived not as
cultural polarities, but as interconnected and reciprocally interpen-
etrating principles."[12] It may be difficult to imagine how such a
process would work in practice, but in a properly utopian project,
this is to be expected.[13]

At first glance, Margaret Roper's 1526 translation of Erasmus's
Precatio Dominica—Devout Treatise on the Pater Noster—seems
distant from such a utopian project since it reproduces the Christian, Eurocentric, and elitist cosmopolitanism of its Latin precursor.
Erasmus conceives of the Christian community as a (motherless)
family, with a fatherly God extending his care over beloved sons,
and this "family" is understood as, properly, a universal one.
"When thy sonne was here in erth," Roper's Englished version
reads, "he nothing more fervently desired than that thy most holy
name shulde appere and shyne not onely in Judea but also thorowe
all the worlde." It laments the refusal of the "gentyls" and "the
jewes" to heed this call to fellowship in Christ, and sees the contin-
uation of earthly divisions as a symptom of the fall: "for as yet that
tyrannous fende hath a do with many and divers nacions: there is
nat yet one herde and one herde master."[14] The cosmopolitanism
of the treatise—its vision of a universal "herde" of humanity in
Christ—comes at the cost of subordination to a Christian, European, male norm.

However, in relation to the last term, at least, we can detect in
Roper's translation an alternate dynamic, and her subtle contesta-
tion of the gender norm calls the text's whole subordinating structure into question and offers the possibility of a unity-in-difference.
The potential attractiveness to a woman—well-educated, but constrained by the gender expectations of her moment—of a cosmopolitanism conceived in *family* terms, is perhaps self-evident. It
reinscribes the narrowed female sphere into a universal one, which

greatly expands its reach, and extends it to a public significance. That Margaret Roper chooses to translate the work of perhaps the most well-known and sought-out humanist scholar in Europe—and vicariously to circulate in circles to which her access is severely constrained by insinuating herself into "his" text—can easily be seen to exceed the modesty that others are always carefully claiming for her. Her father insists that he knows that he and her husband would be audience enough for her, indicating his own assessment of the limits of female aspiration, if not Margaret's own.[15] And, most immediate to the text, Richard Hyrde's preface seeks to contain and domesticate a piece of writing impertinently extending itself to a readership well beyond Roper's immediate family. Addressed to one of the female pupils in More's household school, Margaret's cousin, Frances Staverton, Hyrde's preface pulls the text back toward its most local situation: the very house in which it was produced. He urges young Frances to be learned like her (unnamed) cousin, and virtuous like both her cousin and her mother. Admitting that "many" men look askance at learned women, he undertakes to defend female acquisition of Latin and Greek by attributing male doubt to ignorance and envy. He defends women's virtue as well, claiming that it is men who are usually more culpable, since they are not only less steadfast and inclined to shame, but have more opportunity for vice, because they "lyveth more forthe abrode amonge company dayly," whereas women "abyde moost at home occupied with some good or necessary busynesse."[16] He points out, too, that Roper's marriage is happier because of her learning. The preface, in short, praises Roper and female learning, but underscores her ties to home and family, refusing even to give her accomplishment a public proper name.

In contrast to the enclosure, subordination, or obliteration of the female evident in the Erasmian text and Hyrde's preface, however, a woman's *act* of translation insists on the participation of women in a cosmopolitan project—and, in many cases, insists on acting specifically as a women. Most significantly along these lines, Roper regularly translates as "children" Erasmus's references to the members of God's family as "sons" (filiorum). Crucially, her term includes both male and female at once, without subordinating or denying either.[17] Neither the role of honorary male nor secondary female will do: the shift in terms insists on equality of women and men, without obliteration of the female term to privilege the male—a utopian cosmopolitan desire in the context of a text imagining a universal human family. In any case, a female translator, as much as a male, participates in a transcultural conversation, a collective human project of interchange and accumulation of learning, as Florio described it. Context, Benjamin has taught us, is crucial: to wrench a text into a new situation is to alter its potentialities, what it can mean. When a woman "writes" the Erasmian commentary in English, it is translated in the strong Renaissance sense of the term: displaced, transformed.[18] That on the title page the unnamed Roper is described as a "yong woman" is, then, a certain gender triumph, although it comes at the sacrifice of her individual identity. Whatever the printer's intention in identifying the translator's gender but not her name, this gesture asserts a utopian cosmopolitanism via gender, the participation of a woman as a woman in a transcultural conversation—Margaret Tyler's entertainment of strangers—and refuses obliteration, rocking the normative project of the Erasmian text, which recognizes the cosmopolitan subject only as male, Christian, and European. Once one normative term is called into question, so, too, may others, a move toward a utopian cosmopolitanism to which Roper's text aspires, however vestigially.

Aphra Behn's translation of Bernard de Fontenelle's *A Discovery of New Worlds* over a century later reminds us that this battle for female participation in a cosmopolitan community was by no means quickly won. Structured as a conversation between a Marquesa and a male guest at her chateau, the dialogue considers the possible inhabitation of the moon and other astronomical bodies. As the possibility of "creatures" existing on other worlds emerges, the earth is consolidated as a single—cosmopolitan—unit in relation to its planetary rivals. The male speaker imagines himself "hanging in the Air" watching the rotation of the Earth as humanity flows past, "some white, some black, some tawny, others of an Olive-colour . . . all the variety that is to be seen upon the face of the Earth." He further fleshes out this vision with traveler-tale vignettes: "then will appear the Canibals, eating some prisoners of war alive . . ." and so on.[19] The interlocuters make it clear, however, that people are not only different, but unequal: in "the new discovered World of America . . . the inhabitants there . . . [are] hardly Men, but rather a kind of Brutes in humane shape, and that not perfect neither." Yet even this hierarchy of difference seems to have limits, because Fontenelle's male character also describes the excitement of the possibility of confronting "creatures" off Earth since travel on Earth, for all the variety, can become dull, "crawling as it were with difficulty from one point of this Globe to another, and still to see nothing but Men and Women over and over again." Indeed, he concludes, though "Europeans and Africans seem to have been made after different models," it is nonetheless the case that "We, the Inhabitants of the Earth are but one little Family of the Universe" in contrast with the vast differences of otherworldly creatures that were likely. Still, this does not keep the conversation from straying into unflattering assumptions about some members of the earthly "family": in comparison to the inhabitants of Venus, "our Morrs of Granada are . . . as the Inhabitants of Lapland, or Greenland, for Coldness and Stupidity."[20] At once imagining a unified world—and a hierarchical one—this text continues the cosmopolitan fantasy of Erasmus's, but also its Eurocentric assumptions, albeit in a secular form.

Behn's translator's preface, however, raises questions of a woman's place in such a world; she underscores that she was attracted to Fontenelle's text because a woman is introduced as one of the speakers. Though annoyed with the author's implication that he resorted to this device to indicate that anyone should be able to understand his argument, she identifies with the Marquesa as a woman participating in an important intellectual inquiry. That Behn herself aspires to participation in a cosmopolitan conversation is evident in her decision to translate, and in the text she selects. Her fascinating preface explicitly inserts her voice into a number of weighty, transnational learned debates, ranging from the challenges of translation to—most daringly—the reconciliation of the Bible with the new science. Whereas Fontenelle keeps the lady in his text isolated in her estate to receive the tutelage of a more learned male guest, Behn's preface unabashedly takes on several of the most contentious issues of the time and implies that women should be part of them *as* women, as her pointed identification with Fontenelle's Marquesa makes evident. She also, cosmopolitanly, espouses a theory of languages that emphasizes their kindred, intermingled qualities, which, she observes, facilitate translation, but, at the same time, she sees absolute differences in "humours" among nations as impediments, picking up on the inequality theme that also haunts Fontenelle's book. Hence she attempts to bring English speakers into conversation with French authors and ideas, but cannot do so without commenting that "every Body knows there is more affinity between the English and Italian People, than the English and the French," and lamenting that the English "chop and change our Language, as we do our cloths, at the pleasure of every French tailor."[21] This does not stop her from translating a French text, however, nor with responding to a French cleric in defense of Copernicus. As contradictory as an ideology of inequality of nations might be with her attempt to assert female equality to observe it, we can still see that a feminist cosmopolitanism animates her project to affirm a woman's participation in such debates, and that, at least as an aspiration, she thrusts women into a cosmopolitan publicness at considerable remove from the domestic isolation of Fontenelle's Marquesa.

I have examined texts by female translators widely separated in time, then, not to underscore their differences, which are ample, but rather to indicate a persistence: both participate in a utopian cosmopolitanism in the form of a fantasy of universal belonging without gender obliteration. To be sure, marked by the limits of their moment and the source texts, these translations also carry with them baggage of xenophobia, religious narcissism, and other elitist assumptions. Nevertheless, Roper and Behn incipiently engage a utopian cosmopolitanism in their dreams of being women in and of the world: a step forward in the long revolution, even if they left us many battles to wage.

Notes

1. Richard Hakluyt, *The Principal Navigations* (London, 1599), 1:6; Thomas Blount's *Glossographia* (1656) and Elisha Coles's *An English Dictionary* (1660) include it as an entry, though *OED* claims it was "common" usage; several books in the period give their place of imprint as "Cosmopoli" instead of London, including a 1611 book by Thomas Preston, *Apologia Cardinalis Bellarmini pro jure principum.*

2. See Steve Rappaport, *Worlds Within Worlds* (Cambridge: Cambridge University Press, 1989): "There may have been no legal impediment preventing a woman from obtaining the freedom, but in reality very few women became citizens" (36).

3. By "utopian" I mean the aspiration to a just and satisfying social order that cannot be fully theorized (conceptualized) under the existing conditions, nor concretely realized, so it inhabits texts negatively, emerging primarily in contradictions and lacunae rather than positive description (even when such description is offered). See Fredric Jameson, *Archaeologies of the Future* (London: Verso, 2005); Christopher Kendrick, *Utopia, Carnival and Commonwealth in England* (Toronto: University of Toronto Press, 2004); Louis Marin, *Utopics,* trans. Robert A. Vollrath (Amherst, NY: Humanity Books, 1984).

4. In *Desiring Women Writing* (Stanford, CA: Stanford UP, 1997), Jonathan Goldberg gives an overview of this critical tendency and provides a counternarrative, 75–131.

5. Margaret Tyler, "M.T. to the Reader," in *The Mirrour of Princely Deedes* (London, 1578), A3v. Anthropomorphizing translated texts as strangers is commonplace in the period, but Tyler's figure of hospitality ("giving entertainment")—coming together on respectful, equal terms—is notable (other translators describe themselves as dressing their texts in English fashion, teaching them to speak English, etc.). Similarly, she defends a woman's equal access to print culture: "it is all one for a woman to pen as story, as for a man to addresse his story to a woman," A4v.

6. Walter Benjamin, "The Task of the Translator," in *Selected Writings,* vol. 1, trans. Harry Zohn, ed. Marcus Bullock and Michael W. Jenning (Cambridge, MA: Harvard University Press, 1996).

7. On the importance of translation in early modern England, see, for example, R. F. Jones, *The Triumph of the English Language* (Stanford University Press, 1953); F. O. Matthiesen, *Translation: An Elizabethan Art* (Cambridge, MA: Harvard University Press, 1931); Tejaswini Niranjana, *Siting Translation* (Berkeley: University of California Press, 1992); Patricia Parker, *Shakespeare from the Margins* (Chicago: University of Chicago Press, 1996).

8. John Florio, "To the Curteous Reader," in *Essayes* (London, 1603), A5r.

9. Ibid.

10. John Florio, "To . . . Lucie Countesse of Bedford," in *Essayes* (London, 1603), A2–A3.

11. Timothy Brennan, *At Home in the World: Cosmopolitanism Now* (Cambridge, MA: Harvard UP, 1997).

12. Ulrich Beck, *Cosmopolitan Vision,* trans. Ciaran Cronan (Cambridge: Polity, 2006), 44, 73.

13. Fredric Jameson, for example, observes that utopia is necessarily *negative* because realization of social justice and happiness is a historical project, not a textual one, so attempts to forecast transformed existence will necessarily be contaminated by the bad world prevision seeks to replace. See *Archaeologies of the Future* (London: Verso, 2005).

14. Desiderius Erasmus, *A Devout Treatise Upon the Pater Noster,* trans. Margaret Roper (London, 1526), Civ, D3r.

15. See Elizabeth McCutcheon, "The Learned Woman in Tudor England," in *Women Writers of the Reniassance and Reformation,* ed. Katherina M. Wilson (Athens: University of Georgia Press, 1987), 460.

16. Richard Hyrde, "Unto the Moost Studyous and virtuous yonge mayde," in *Devout Treatise upon the Pater Noster,* trans. Margaret Roper (London, 1526), A3v.

17. The opening line of Erasmus's text, for example, is "Audi, Pater in coelis habitans, vota *filiorum* tuorum," which Roper renders, "Here O father in hevyn the petyciones of thy *children*." Goldberg also calls attention to this shift, but to make a point concerning Roper's relation to her earthly father, which has been so important to interpretations of her translation. (Erasmus's text is collected in *Opera Omnia,* vol. 5 [Hildescheim: Georg Olms Verlagsbuchhandlung, 1962]). She also refers to petitioners to God as "brothers," indicating a limit to how far she can take her gender challenge, however.

18. On the extended Renaissance senses of translation, see Parker *Shakespeare from the Margins.*

19. Bernard de Fontenelle, *A Discovery of New Worlds,* trans. Aphra Behn (London, 1688), 34–35.

20. Ibid., 61, 81, 94, 99.

21. Aphra Behn, "Translator's Preface," in *A Discovery of New Worlds* (London, 1688), A5r, A6r.

Cosmopolitanism and Foreign Books in Early Modern England

Alan B. Farmer

WHEN DISCUSSING COSMOPOLITANISM in early modern England, scholars have tended to stress its development within royal court culture and the trade in luxury goods. R. Malcolm Smuts, for example, has noted the "fascination for European culture" in the court of Charles I, while Linda Levy Peck has examined how "the well-off increasingly identified themselves as cosmopolitan through the appropriation of continental luxuries."[1] In her study of the effects of this fascination with Continental culture, Anna Bryson has shrewdly analyzed how the manners and social behavior of English men and women were influenced by courtesy literature and translations of foreign conduct books.[2] In this essay, I want to look at English cosmopolitanism in connection with a more diffuse, less courtly, and less luxurious set of commodities: books in Latin of Christian and humanist scholarship, and books in English of Puritan and Catholic polemic, both of which were printed abroad and imported into England. These two types of foreign books helped foster intellectual exchange but also stimulated religious discord, contradictory effects, I argue, that contributed to an emerging split in the meaning and politics of early modern cosmopolitanism.

As the English book trade grew in the sixteenth and seventeenth centuries, its printers and booksellers maintained close ties to Continental authors, papermakers, printers, booksellers, and merchants. English stationers relied in particular on their Continental counterparts to supply them with one specific type of book, Latin texts of Christian and humanist scholarship. These books were part of what was known as the Latin trade, and they were books that English stationers tended to avoid publishing themselves. Printers on the Continent were able to produce them more cheaply and

58

more accurately than English printers could, and after the books were printed the Continent had a larger potential readership for them than England did.[3] This does not mean, however, that these publications were unprofitable for English *booksellers;* in 1616, members of the Stationers' Company established the Latin Stock in an attempt to monopolize the market for these books. Though the stock company lasted little more than a decade and was largely unsuccessful, its very existence testifies to the financial gains that could be realized from importing Latin books from abroad and selling them in English bookshops.[4]

The prevalence of books in the Latin trade can be difficult to determine since most of its titles are not included in Pollard and Redgrave's *Short-Title Catalogue (STC).*[5] But various lists of the holdings of sixteenth- and seventeenth-century libraries, especially those of early modern intellectuals, academics, and university students, suggest how plentiful these books could be. Over 90 percent of the 194 printed books listed in the library of Bishop Richard Cox following his death in 1581 were Continental publications, almost all in Latin.[6] Books that survive from the libraries of John Donne and Ben Jonson show a similar tilt toward Continental publications (80 percent).[7] Of course, not all readers shared this taste for Continental or Latin publications; in 1625, only about 40 to 50 percent of the books in Roger Townshend's library were Continental publications, while of the 241 books in the wide-ranging library of Frances Egerton, the Countess of Bridgewater, none was in Latin or Greek, though eighteen were in French.[8]

The division in the English book trade between foreign and domestic books was often blamed on English printers, whom authors lambasted for "carelessness," "lack of skill," and being "absolutely ignorant of the liberal arts." Edward Grant, for example, asked in exasperation, "Where amongst us is that noble printer, Robert Estienne?" not to mention his sons Henri and Charles Estienne and other learned Continental printers like Aldus Manutius, Sebastian Gryphius, Jean Crespin, Christopher Plantin, and Johann Heruagius.[9] The reputation of English printed books for poor quality even led some printers, most famously John Wolfe, to print surreptitiously books in foreign vernacular languages (with false imprints listing fictitious Continental origins) as a way to avoid the stigma of an English imprint.[10]

The author Richard Vernam attributed the poor quality of English books not simply to the "ignorance" of printers but also to their

excessive desire for "profit and greed." "Humane learning flour-
ishes on all sides" in Germany, Vernam pointedly observed,
whereas England has "only a few printers and those are either quite
ignorant of their art or else care more about profit and greed than
advancement of letters."[11] Richard Montagu would voice substantially the same complaint almost fifty years later, impugning "the
stupidity and stinginess of printers," which led them to favor
cheap "garbage" over "serious" works:

> On top of the hundreds of difficulties with which we are afflicted we
> have unfortunately had to put [up] with the stupidity and stinginess of
> printers. For they are accustomed to work for profit, they are only fol-
> lowing a mercenary trade. And so they load whole waggons and carts
> with hackneyed twopenny-halfpenny garbage. They have no taste for
> serious things. Latin writings are not read, and as for Greek, they ex-
> claim against them as if they were heretical.[12]

English printers and publishers were choosing to invest in books
that would reliably turn a profit, in Montagu's analysis, with the
unfortunate result that "whole waggons and carts" of cheap English books were being printed and almost no "serious" Latin ones.

   If economic motives caused English printers and booksellers to
import many of the books in the Latin trade, domestic political
measures helped create the other primary market for foreign books
in early modern England: radical Protestant and Catholic works.
According to the calculations of Maureen Bell and John Barnard,
about seven percent of *STC* entries from 1475 to 1640 are for books
that were printed abroad, the vast majority of which originated in
the Netherlands or France.[13] Unlike the books in the Latin trade,
which were intended to facilitate intellectual exchange across Europe, these books were meant to further religious sectarianism. Ecclesiastical licensers for the press would never have allowed these
texts to be printed in England, so strident Puritan and Catholic authors, printers, and booksellers were forced to print them abroad.

   Once in Europe, Puritan authors often turned to printers in Dutch
cities like Amsterdam and Leiden, while Catholics availed themselves of the Jesuit English College presses in Douai and St. Omer,
France. As the author of *A True, Modest, and Just Defense* explained in 1618, "it is not safe" for nonconformist Puritans "to suffer the Printers to know that wee haue any such Coppy to bee
printed," and, as a result, they must hire, at "great charge and haz-
ard," "the printing of [our books] in some other Land." After their

books were printed, religious extremists then faced the problem of distribution, for "open sale in every Booke-sellers shop" was not possible; if their books were "taken by the Bishops," then the publications would be "burnt, or otherwise utterly suppressed."[14] Both radical Protestants and Catholics, as a result, had to distribute their books through secret networks of merchants, congregations, and booksellers.[15]

These two types of foreign books—learned works circulating through the Latin trade and sectarian works distributed through clandestine Puritan and Catholic networks—give us some idea of what "foreign books" signified in early modern England. But this split in the market, I want to suggest, also points to an important aspect of English cosmopolitanism. When writers discussed what we would now call cosmopolitanism, they tended to do so in one of two ways. On the one hand, they used the term "cosmopolite" to denote "a citizen of the world," a person who sought greater knowledge through studying and traveling to foreign countries. It was this type of person who would have been expected to purchase the scholarly works of the Latin trade. On the other hand, writers used "cosmopolite" to describe a base sinner who delights in worldly pleasures like fighting, feasting, cheating, and whoring, a sense that forward Protestant authors sometimes used to disparage their religious adversaries. This division in the semantic meaning of "cosmopolite" registers a key tension in early modern English culture surrounding the influence of Continental writers, books, and religious beliefs.

The *Oxford English Dictionary* lists the earliest usage of "cosmopolite" in 1598, but John Dee used the term two decades earlier in his *General and Rare Memorials Pertayning to the Perfect Arte of Nauigation* (1577).[16] In this work, Dee includes a "Little Discourse" criticizing the "Publik Behauiour," "Ciuile Conuersation," and "Industry" of the "the People of this *ALBION*" (sig. G3v). In order to rectify these deficiencies in social behavior as well as increase "the Common-Wealths Prosperity," Dee recommends studying "the State of Earthly Kingdoms, Generally, the whole World ouer" so that a person might "fynde hym self, *Cosmopolites:* A Citizen, and Member, of the whole and only one Mysticall City Vniuersall." Dee here draws on the Stoic political philosophy that held a person should strive to be a citizen of the world (*kosmopolitis*), an idea emphasized in his book by printing the word *"Cosmpolites"* in a marginal note. Studying other cultures, Dee suggests, is necessary not only to improve the behavior of the English people but also to promote the nation's political and economic health. Doing so, he argues, will allow "this Brytish Monarchy" to surpass "any particular Monarchy, els, that euer was on Earth, since Mans Creation."[17]

Dee was not alone in propounding the Stoic notion of *kosmopolitis*. The English translation of Justus Lipsius's *A Direction for Trauailers* (1592) offers examples of biblical, classical, and contemporary travelers who believed "it a great staine and dishonour to the libertie which nature hath geuen them . . . to bee restrained within the narrowe precincts of a little countrie, as poore prisoners kept in a close place." Instead, these travelers viewed themselves as *"Cosmopolites,* that is Cytizens of the whole world." "For as with the wise *Sacrates,* they counted euerie place their country," allowing them to "profite, and inrich themselues with experience, and true wisedome."[18] As Francis Meres would later remark, "a contented Cosmopolite, though banished from his owne country, may liue as well in an other."[19] It was ultimately this sense of the word that the lexicographer Thomas Blount drew on in his *Glossographia, or A Dictionary Interpreting all such Hard Words* (1656), the first English dictionary to include an entry for "cosmopolite," which he defined as "a Citizen of the World; or Cosmopolitan."[20]

In opposition to the Stoic theory of the cosmopolite, the Protestant poet John Vicars offered a more caustic characterization of "proud *Cosmopolites"* in 1618, describing them as "carnall Worldlings" consumed with material desires:

> Goe then, you godlesse *Heliogabolites,*
> You carnall *Worldlings,* proud *Cosmopolites,*
> Goe please your selues in swearing, feasting, fighting,
> And not what's *iust,* but what's your *Lust* delight in.

These lustful delights included possessions like "wealthie Mannours," "stately tenements," "*Ward-roabes* stuft with proud Apparell," and "Coffers full of treasure," in addition to sinful practices like filling one's mouth "with oathes" and one's "*thoughts* with *strife* and quarrell." Cosmopolites, according to Vicars, were not dedicated to God but bewitched by "*Mammon, Sin-bane, Soules-decay.*"[21]

In a similar manner, Thomas Adams separated "they that liue by the Gospell" from "the Cosmopolite," preaching in 1614 that "the vanitie of carnall ioyes, the varietie of vanities, are as bitter to vs [i.e., true Christians], as pleasant to the Cosmopolite or world-ling."[22] In another sermon Adams returned to the idea of the cos-mopolite, claiming that "semi-atheisticall Cosmopolites . . . bring as many sinnes with them euery day to Church, as they haue beene all their liues in committing. Their hands are not washed from as-persions of lust and bloud: their eyes are full of whoredome, their lips of slander, their affections of couetousnes, their wits of cheat-ing, their soules of impiety."[23] For Adams, as for Vicars, cosmopo-lites were sinners ensnared by covetousness and the carnal joys of the world rather than committed to the heavenly delights of God.

The difference between viewing "cosmopolites" as citizens of the world or seeing them as sinful worldlings not only parallels the division in early modern England between foreign books of schol-arly humanism and religious sectarianism, but I think points to a certain reciprocal influence. The Latin trade was an important site for the spread of Stoic cosmopolitanism in early modern England, whereas radical Continental publications helped establish the no-tion of a gulf separating true believers from vain, carnal sinners. But this apparent contradiction might perhaps be better regarded as opposite sides of the same coin. Many of the controversial religious books imported into England were marked by an insistence on the absolute categories of orthodox and heretical, but at the same time they also tended to advocate moving the English Church either closer to or further away from the Catholic Church of Rome or one of the Protestant churches of Europe.[24] In contrast to the intellec-tual commitments of scholarly works, these radical foreign books might thus be seen as arguing for a type of cosmopolitanism that privileged the religious over the intellectual, the circulation of ideas among a narrow segment of the Christian world rather than among all the members of the educated world. From this point of view, then, it might be more accurate to talk of two different kinds of cosmopolitanism in foreign books—one intellectual, the other religious, both open to Continental influences, just not the same ones.

Notes

1. R. Malcolm Smuts, *Court Culture and the Origins of a Royalist Tradition in Early Stuart England* (Philadelphia: University of Pennsylvania Press, 1987), 187;

Linda Levy Peck, *Consuming Splendor: Society and Culture in Seventeenth-Century England* (Cambridge: Cambridge University Press, 2005), 18.

2. Anna Bryson, *From Courtesy to Civility: Changing Codes of Conduct in Early Modern England* (Oxford: Clarendon, 1998).

3. Julian Roberts, "The Latin Trade," in *The History of the Book in Britain, Vol. 4, 1557–1695,* ed. John Barnard and D. F. McKenzie, with the assistance of Maureen Bell (Cambridge: Cambridge University Press, 2002), 141–73; for the contents of a typical shipment, see esp. 157.

4. Roberts, "The Latin Trade," 161–62; R. J. Roberts, "The Latin Stock (1616–1627) and Its Library Contacts," in *Libraries and the Book Trade,* ed. Robin Myers, Michael Harris, and Giles Mandelbrote (New Castle, DE: Oak Knoll Press, 2000), 15–28.

5. A. W. Pollard and G. R. Redgrave, eds., *A Short-Title Catalogue of Books Printed in England, Scotland, and Ireland and of English Books Printed Abroad, 1475–1640,* 2nd ed., rev. W. A. Jackson, F. S. Ferguson, and Katharine F. Pantzer, 3 vols. (London: Bibliographical Society, 1976–91).

6. E. S. Leedham-Green, "Bishop Richard Cox," in *Private Libraries in Renaissance England: A Collection and Catalogue of Tudor and Early Stuart Book-Lists,* ed. R. J. Fehrenbach and E. S. Leedham-Green, 5 vols. (Binghamton, NY: Medieval and Renaissance Texts and Studies, 1992), 1:3–39.

7. Mark Bland, "The London Book-Trade in 1600," in *A Companion to Shakespeare,* ed. David Scott Kastan (Oxford: Blackwell, 1999), 450.

8. R. J. Fehrenbach, "Sir Roger Townshend's Books," in Fehrenbach and Green, eds., *Private Libraries,* 1:79–135; Heidi Brayman Hackel, *Reading Material in Early Modern England: Print, Gender, and Literacy* (Cambridge: Cambridge University Press, 2005), 250–51.

9. Edward Grant, "Candido lectori," in Roger Ascham, *Familiarium Epistolarum Libri III* (London, 1576), sigs. A15r–v; trans. and quoted in J. W. Binns, *Intellectual Culture in Elizabethan and Jacobean England: The Latin Writings of the Age* (Leeds: Francis Cairns, 1990), 400–401.

10. Denis B. Woodfield, *Surreptitious Printing in England 1550–1640* (New York: Bibliographical Society of America, 1973), esp. 9–10, 20–21.

11. Richard Vernam, "Methodo Geographica," in Nicholas Carr, *De Scriptorum Britannicorum* (London, 1576), sig. B8v; trans. and quoted in Binns, *Intellectual,* 402–3.

12. Richard Montagu, *Analecta Ecclesiasticarum Exercitationum* (London, 1622), sig. a5v; trans. and quoted in Binns, *Intellectual,* 403. For a similar take on the greed of printers penned by a Puritan author, see George Wither's *The Schollers Purgatory* (London, 1624), in which he excoriates the "meere Stationer" who "exercizeth his Mystery without any respect either to the glory of God, or the publike aduantage," making him "the aptest Instrument to sowe schismes, heresies, scandalls, and seditions through the world" (sig. H4r). See also Zachary Lesser's insightful discussion of claims like Montagu's and Wither's in relation to the economics of early modern publishing in *Renaissance Drama and the Politics of Publication: Readings in the English Book Trade* (Cambridge: Cambridge University Press 2004), esp. ch. 1.

13. Maureen Bell and John Barnard, "Provisional Count of *STC* Titles 1475–1640," *Publishing History* 31 (1992): 48–64. They list 88 percent of foreign *STC* books as being printed in France or the Netherlands (including Belgium).

14. "To the Christian Reader," in *A True, Modest, and Just Defense* ([Leiden], 1618), sigs. A3r–v.

15. Keith L. Sprunger, *Trumpets from the Tower: English Puritan Printing in the Netherlands 1600–1640* (New York: Brill, 1994), ch. 6.

16. *Oxford English Dictionary,* 2nd ed, s.v. "cosmopolite," *n.* and *a.*; John Dee, *General and Rare Memorials pertayning to the Perfect Arte of Nauigation* (London, 1577).

17. For a perceptive discussion of Dee's thought on this issue, see William H. Sherman, *John Dee: The Politics of Reading and Writing in the English Renaissance* (Amherst: University of Massachusetts Press, 1995), 143–45.

18. Justus Lipsius, *A Direction for Trauailers,* trans. John Stradling (London, 1592), sigs. A3r–v.

19. Francis Meres, *Wits Common Wealth: The Second Part* (London, 1634), 519.

20. Thomas Blount, *Glossographia, or A Dictionary Interpreting all such Hard Words* (London, 1656), sig. L4r.

21. John Vicars, *A Prospective Glasse to Looke Into Heaven, or The Celestiall Canaan Described* (London, 1618), sig. E3r.

22. Thomas Adams, "The Shot, or The wofull price which the wicked pay for the Feast of Vanitie," in *The Diuells Banket* (London, 1614), sig. Y3v.

23. Thomas Adams, "Gods House, or The Place of Prayses," in *The Happines of the Church* (London, 1619), 218–19.

24. Anthony Milton, *Catholic and Reformed: The Roman and Protestant Churches in English Protestant Thought, 1600–1640* (Cambridge: Cambridge University Press, 1995).

"I care not, let naturals love nations": Cosmopolitan Clowning

Pamela Allen Brown

"**I** AM HUMAN: nothing human is alien to me." So says the busy-body Chremes in Terence's comedy *The Self-Tormentor,* answering a neighbor who tells him to mind his own damn business.[1] His off-the-cuff retort is often quoted solemnly today, having shed its lowly origins as a laugh line to re-emerge as "something like the golden rule of cosmopolitanism," in the words of Kwame Anthony Appiah. Chremes succinctly and unwittingly expresses "a tenable cosmopolitanism [that] tempers a respect for difference with a respect for actual human beings—and with a sentiment best captured in the credo, once comic, now commonplace"—*Homo sum: humani nil a me alienum puto.*[2]

The way jest can congeal into earnest over time may help explain the tenor of some oddly cosmopolitan moments in early modern foolery. In Davenport's *The City Night Cap,* an Italian insists that his wife follow the English fashion and allow his guest to kiss her in greeting. Warned that his eccentricity will be taken ill by his countrymen, he explodes: "I care not, let naturals love nations. My humour's my humour."[3] His experiment ends badly, but his pun on "naturals" lingers in the mind for the way it aligns narrow obedience to gender codes and "native"/national feeling with a natural fool's imbecility. This point of view is not particularly tolerant, but qualifies as satire that a cosmopolitan could enjoy.

Similar animus against blind obedience to local custom punctuates the satiric squib *Haec Vir.* The womanish man criticizes the outlandish, un-English dress of the mannish woman, Hic Mulier. She responds with a rant against the tyranny of habit, concluding "*Custome* is an idiot."[4] Again, custom is equated with dribbling folly, slavish subjection and tiny mental horizons. Applauding her own flexibility of temper and arguing for the liberty to shop, think, debate, and walk the streets unmolested, Hic Mulier celebrates a city of "mingle-mangle" encompassing both new and old, familiar and foreign, inviting the free woman to strap on her dagger and stride boldly through town. Her joy is mobility, her keyword is freedom, and her London is cosmopolitan.

In both cases the counterconventional position is articulated by a jesting figure: a comic character whose open-mindedness leads to his being cuckolded, and a ramping virago of cheap print. The important thing to recognize is how often cosmopolitan ideas appear in the guise of Folly, sporting its tattered livery. As Susan O'Malley has discovered, some of Hic Mulier's arguments are lifted from an essay by Montaigne,[5] and it is oddly fitting that his words should reappear in the mouth of a witty fool wrangling on the streets of London. Behind these instances of cosmopolitan clowning lie two linked figures, the specialist in stage clowning and the artificial court fool. Both were greedy collectors and transmitters of usable theatrical knowledge, serving as go-betweens in culture, picking up tricks of the trade wherever they could and putting them into circulation. While some fools were naturals indeed and stuck close to one patron and nation all their lives, others were mobile and curious, voyaging afar in fact or in fancy, and offering a conduit to ideas, places, and people few of the English would ever encounter on their own. Bearing "mad packets of mad letters," peripatetic jest-fools and stage clowns enter the scene breathlessly, offering "new news" from fabulous places like "Roame," "Eutopia," and "Purgatory." The clown's skills were eminently exportable because of his wide gestural and verbal repertoire, his ability to shape macaroni out of many tongues and make it comprehensibly funny. From the ludicrous nonlanguage in *All's Well That Ends Well,* invented to perplex the pretentiously polyglot Parolles, to Dario Fo's commedia-inspired *grammelot* four centuries later (a mix of real words, nonsense, and onomotopoeia that gets the point across),[6] the skilled comic performer sells a cosmopolitan openness and linguistic adaptability masquerading as confusion.

High and low participated in these comic personations. The Renaissance humanist discourse on Folly was elaborately learned, and thoroughly impure and transnational. Playing to a footloose, politically powerful international elite, Erasmus and More pretended to be a pair of wise fools batting quips in Latin in *Utopia* and *Praise of Folly*. Both works continually echo classical cosmo-politanism derived from Seneca, the Stoics, Plato, and St. Paul. Eras-mus's Folly extends a benevolent welcome to everyone from every nation and, like Hic Mulier, she despises the pettiness of custom:

> I don't leave a single mortal without a share in my bounty, though the gifts of the other mortals are unevenly bestowed. . . . I don't expect pray-ers, and I don't lose my temper and demand expiation for some detail of ceremony that has been overlooked. [. . .] I hold the view that I'm worshipped with truest devotion when all men everywhere take me to their hearts, express me in their habits, and reflect me in their way of life—as in fact they do. . . . The entire world is my temple, and a very fine one too.[7]

By recognizing and affirming the bonds that unite all humanity Folly adheres to the Senecan ideal described by Nicholas de Cusa: "[E]ach of us dwells in two communities—the local community of our birth, and the community of human argument and aspiration that is, in Seneca's words, 'truly great and truly common, in which we look to neither this corner nor to that, but measure the boundary of our nation by the sun.'"[8]

This saintly homily might have raised a laugh in early modern London, whose citizens (many of them recent immigrants from the countryside) were prone to displays of xenophobic rudeness and outbursts of violence.[9] In spite of attacks on strangers and diatribes against foreign fashion, glamorous strangers were imported (or fab-ricated) for the humble as well as the mighty. All and sundry grazed on the common marketplace of cheap print and public spectacles, a mélange of the near and far. At the annual fair, "Rare Works and Rarer Beasts do meet; we see / In the same street *Africk* and *Ger-many*," wrote one observer of the Oxford fair.[10] At the market cross one might see the traveling duo of Banks and his famous horse, newly returned from Italy (reports of their deaths by fire for sorcery in Rome having proved premature), or thrill to the harangues of tur-banned quacksalvers who might be anything from barbers, players, and peddlers to true exotics, "runagate Jews, the cut-throats and robbers of Christians," according to one hysterical citizen.[11] At the social summit was the rarefied courtly world of liveried fools, dwarves, and jesters whose monikers, whether grand or simple, figured them as denizens of a mimic *mappamundo* beyond family and nation: "Jane Fool," "Monarcho," "Madame Thomasine de Paris," "Dego," "Patch," "Ippolyta the Tartarian."[12]

Courtly clowning and street theater mingled as influences on the public stage and its star player-clowns, whose roles mixed the utterly familiar with the new-fangled and absurdly strange. Untold numbers of foreign japes, plots, roles, speeches, texts, and ideas circulated through these interrelated arenas, imported like burrs by courtiers, travelers, and players returning from abroad, then taken up by those in the business of selling spectacle and driving away the time. The influx of the foreign and its intermingling with the native created a polymorphic dynamic on the stage and street. Sometimes the thin transparency of an Italian mask allowed the native-born jester to delight an audience under the cloak of the strange, and English yahoos wander through plays with nonce names like Assinico and Brothello and Dildo, as if ribald onomastics alone will work the magic of the famed *comici* who were their teachers and rivals. Such identifications were not always bawdily satiric: the clown-playwright Robert Armin proudly styled himself "Clunnico del Curtanio Snuffe," paid homage to the mountebank Scoto in a jest-dialogue, and praised and translated a jest book by Straparola, writing modestly, "I but light a Taper at his Torch . . . for your Italians are in this (as in all) neate."[13]

Louise George Clubb coined the useful term "theatergram" to describe the manifold "recombinatory units" of Renaissance theater—texts, *lazzi*, playing skills, roles, and plots—that flowed back and forth across borders, and found their most famous purveyors in the players of the commedia dell'arte. Shakespeare, Armin, and their colleagues were intimately familiar with the trends on the Continent and the wares of the Italian *comici,* "the sellers of theater," who offered matter and skills of every sort, including "the scenarios, the lazzi and the masks . . . and their dexterity with theatergrams of each kind."[14] From this commerce flowed Armin's mock-Italian regalia, Touchstone's lecturing on dueling *alla* Saviolo, and Trinculo's "lazzo of the four legs" with Caliban. These comic enactments demonstrate what Keir Elam calls "intercorporeality," the process of imitation and translation, which fashioned chameleonic "English bodies in Italian habits."[15]

In the rapidly expanding city, this traffic in new habits fostered a rough familiarity, a process that Appiah sees as vital to becoming-cosmopolitan; the sense of the stranger's strangeness is muted through "imaginative engagement with the experience and the ideas of others across boundaries of identity." Harping on difference or even reaching consensus is not a goal of such conversation:

"it's enough that it helps people get used to each other."[16] Theater
seems inimical to fostering an attitude of live and let live, but that
discounts the crucial role of genre and expectation in successful
comic action. Some forms of comic spectacle traded on shock and
novelty, but many more were based on traditions evolved over
years of intercourse, contamination, and mimicry. Punch, a totem
of Englishness, began life in Naples as Pulchinella and emigrated
via traveling entertainers to London, where he slowly Britified,
though his hunchback and rasping voice are relics of the Neapoli-
tan ninny. At the highest social levels, acculturation was a by-product
of the long-standing royal practice of importing talented foreign artists, musicians, players, and acrobats to court, often at great expense. During the sixteenth century these players show up more
and more often in the payment records of towns and great houses,
and occasionally excite xenophobic outbursts, such as that of the
Norwich citizen who contemns the "shameless and unnaturall
tomblinges of the Italion Woemen" who performed there in 1574.[17]
But these performances brought a vocabulary of actions and gestures, costumes and patter that became so common that by 1600 the
disguise of an Italian player-acrobat was often used as a false identity for spies operating in London. Theatrical practice made the foreign somewhat familiar over time, and the wearing-out of newness
was both inevitable and necessary to the evolution of a more cosmopolitan London.

Will Kemp was a past hand at combining the foreign and familiar, and devised a singularly cosmopolitan sort of clowning. The
first mention of him appears in a letter in 1580; next he is hired as
a special player at the lavish alternative court of Robert Dudley,
Earl of Leicester, in the Netherlands; he acts as a jester-cum-
diplomatic messenger for Leicester, then performs on his own in
Denmark and Germany before heading to London, eventually joining the Lord Chamberlain's Men.[18] He leaves for unknown reasons
in 1599/1600 and performs his famous jig to Norwich, inventing
a new kind of entrepreneurial clowning by "dancing carnival into
market" and producing a pamphlet in which he is no simple jester
but "a witty, urbane and ironic commentator."[19] Next he heads for
Rome, where he meets Sir Anthony Shirley, the self-proclaimed
ambassador to Persia. In Day, Rowley, and Wilkins' *The Travels of
the Three English Brothers,* Shirley asks Kemp to collaborate in an
extempore bout with "Harlequin and his wife"—a face-off Kemp
wins by playing dumb about the Italian practice of using actresses

to play women's parts. Kemp is game and ready to take up the challenge—nothing human is alien to him—but his ad-libs upset the rehearsal of the supposedly improvisatory comici. Though "hard of study," he beats the Italians at getting laughs without a script.[20]

In blending his urbane mobility with a common-man persona, Kemp managed to offer a commodity that was "friendly, familiar, foreign and near," in the words of Canada's come-on to U.S. tourists. As he put it in *Nine Daies Wonder,* he is "Cavaliero Kemp, head-master of morris dances, high-headborough of hays."[21] *The Return to Parnassus,* staged in 1601, features a student audition run by Kemp and Burbage. Penniless Cambridge students welcome Kemp in terms that combine curious wonder with arch familiarity:

> *Philomusus.* . . . What Master Kemp, how doth the Emperor of Germany?
> *Studioso.* God save you, Master Kemp. Welcome Master Kemp from dancing the morris over the Alps.
> *Kemp.* Well, you merry knaves, you may come to the honour of it one day. Is't not better to make a fool of the world as I have done, than to be fooled of the world, as you scholars are? But be merry, my lads you have happened upon the most excellent vocation in the world. For money, they come north and south to bring it to our playhouse.[22]

Kemp's expansive boast about customers from "north and south" can be imagined to extend well beyond the provinces around London, indeed beyond England's island borders, to the transnational worlds of playing that the students were so eager to hear about. This was the market that lured the players and comedians who crisscrossed Europe in search of audiences with ready money. Some saw Kemp's farflung fame as a source of national pride: here at last was a performer who ranked with the dazzling pantheon of performers abroad. Thomas Nashe dedicated *An Almond for a Parrot* to Kemp and pretended to have met the great "Francatrip Harlicken" himself in Italy, where he had the pleasure of hearing the Italian beg to kiss the hand of the man who knew the supreme "Chiarlatano Kempino."[23] As with "Monarcho" and "Clunnico del Curtanio Snuffe," the mock-Italian marks the clown-body to which it is attached as a praiseworthy cultural hybrid, a commodity whose worth cannot be named in correct Italian *or* in correct English, for the court of judgment lies somewhere in between, beyond nations.

Salman Rushdie, a theorist-practitioner of postmodern clowning, applauds the farcical-historical mixmastery of his own novels, particularly *The Satanic Verses,* which celebrates "hybridity, impurity, intermingling, the transformation that comes of new and unexpected combinations of human beings, cultures, ideas, politics, movies, songs. It rejoices in mongrelization and fears the absolutism of the Pure. Melange, hotchpotch, a bit of this and a bit of that is how newness enters the world."[24] One could (by replacing "movies" with "plays, jokes and jigs") take this as a fair sketch of how the strange and new entered early modern England. Willy-nilly, through thousands of voyages both real and imaginary, a more expansive world was diced, repackaged, and sold piecemeal, in artful catachresis, macaronic jibes, publicity stunts, and zany antics. Though the clowns' words were often xenophobic, their bodies and names bore the news from nowhere and everywhere, from "Cokayne" to "Tartaria." Worn and soiled with foreign travel or marathon jigs, Kemp's and Coryate's shoes became homely relics of bizarre mobility, mongrel mementoes for all to gape at. In outlandish liveries a special kind of comic cosmopolitanism was performed for an audience of stay-at-homes—new ideas presented first as foolery, emerging only much later as part of a new geopolitical ethics, "in which we look to neither this corner nor to that," as Seneca said, "but measure the boundary of our nation by the sun."

Notes

1. Terence, *Phormio & Other Plays.* Trans. Betty Radice (Baltimore: Penguin, 1967), 86.

2. Kwame Anthony Appiah, *Cosmopolitanism: Ethics in a World of Strangers* (New York: Norton, 2006), 113.

3. Quoted in A. J. Hoenselaars, "Italy Staged in English Renaissance Drama," in *Shakespeare's Italy: Functions of Italian Locations in Renaissance Drama,* ed. Michele Marrapodi et al., (Manchester: Manchester University Press, 1997), 40.

4. Susan O'Malley,*"Custome Is an Idiot": Jacobean Pamphlet Literature on Women* (Urbana: University of Illinois Press, 2003), 291.

5. Ibid., 255.

6. For a discussion of *grammelot* in performance, see Dario Fo, *The Tricks of the Trade,* trans. Joe Farrell (London: Methuen, 1987), 56–59.

7. Erasmus, *Praise of Folly,* trans. Betty Radice (Harmondsworth, UK: Penguin, 1971), 139–40.

8. Quoted in M. C. Nussbaum, "Kant and Stoic Cosmopolitanism," *Journal of Political Philosophy* 5.1 (1997): 6. In his *Idiota de sapientia et de mente,* translated in 1650 by John Everard as *The Idiot in Four Books,* de Cusa presented the unedu-

cated, apolitical man of faith as Pauline counterweight to the oversophisticated man of affairs.

9. See Lien Bich Luu, " 'Taking the Bread Out of our Mouths': Xenophobia in Early Modern London," *Immigrants and Minorities* 19.2 (2000): 1–22.

10. William Cartwright, *Plays and Poems,* ed. G. Blakemore Evans (Madison: University of Wisconsin Press, 1951), 455.

11. Bella Mirabella, "Quacking Delilahs: Female Mountebanks in Early Modern England and Italy," in *Women Players in England, 1500–1660: Beyond the All-Male Stage,* ed. Pamela Allen Brown and Peter Parolin (Aldershot: Ashgate, 2005), 100.

12. See indexes in John Southworth's *Fools and Jesters at the English Court* (Stroud: Sutton, 2003) and Enid Welsford's *The Fool: His Social and Literary History* (London: Faber & Faber, 1935).

13. Robert Armin, *The Italian Taylor and His Boy* (London, 1609; repr., London, 1810), 3.

14. Louise George Clubb, *Italian Drama in Shakespeare's Time* (New Haven: Yale University Press, 1989), 280.

15. Keir Elam, " 'The continent of what part a gentleman would see': English Bodies in European Habits," in *Shakespeare and Intertextuality: The Transition of Cultures Between Italy and England in the Early Modern Period,* ed. Michele Marrapodi (Rome: Bulzoni, 2000), 39.

16. Appiah, *Cosmopolitanism,* 85.

17. Kathleen Marguerite Lea, *Italian Popular Comedy: A Study in the Commedia dell'arte, 1560–1620,* 2 vols. (Oxford: Clarendon, 1934), 1:354.

18. David Wiles, *Shakespeare's Clown: Actor and Text in the Elizabethan Playhouse* (Cambridge: Cambridge University Press, 1987), 31–37.

19. Max W. Thomas, "Kemps Nine Daies Wonder: Dancing Carnival into Market," *PMLA* 107.3 (May 1992): 520.

20. David Mann, *The Elizabethan Player: Contemporary Stage Representation* (New York: Routledge, 1991), 70–72.

21. Wiles, *Shakespeare's Clown,* 111.

22. Mann, *Elizabethan Player,* 144.

23. Southworth, *Fools and Jesters,* 164.

24. Quoted in Appiah, *Cosmopolitanism,* 112.

ARTICLES

Lives and Letters in
Antony and Cleopatra

ALAN STEWART

W HEN OCTAVIUS CAESAR receives the news of Antony's suicide, at the end of act 5, scene 1 of *Antony and Cleopatra,* he invites his Council of War to

> Go with me to my Tent, where you shall see
> How hardly I was drawne into this Warre,
> How calme and gentle I proceeded still
> In all my Writings. Go with me, and see
> What I can shew in this.
>
> (5.1.73–77)[1]

Octavius is anxious to furnish textual evidence that will support his account of his "calme and gentle" actions toward Antony and his reluctant entry into war against him. He is not alone in valuing how he will be viewed by posterity. Antony applauds the "Noblenesse in Record" (4.14.100) that suicide brings, and Cleopatra famously frets lest Rome's "quicke Comedians / Extemporally will stage vs," and, while still alive, she will be forced to witness "Some squeaking *Cleopatra* Boy my greatnesse / I'th' posture of a Whore" (5.2.215–16, 219–20). W. B. Worthen notes that "*Antony and Cleopatra* is, of course, centrally concerned with how events are written into narrative, transformed into history, literature, and myth";[2] C. C. Barfoot has suggested that "the chief protagonists in *Antony and Cleopatra* are above all committed to fulfilling the destiny of their names," acutely aware "of how the future will regard them when they are entirely in the past";[3] indeed, as Garrett Sullivan sums up, *Antony and Cleopatra* is "a play dominated by the retrospective characterization of people and events."[4]

In an important essay, Linda Charnes has demonstrated how, de-

spite their shared concern for posterity, the characters' approaches
to posthumous reputation—and their success in achieving it—vary
widely. While noting that "all the 'actors' in this play are obsessed
with playing to reviewers near and far," she argues that "they are
not equally in control of the effects of their performances" since
Rome is "the play's 'original' center of the narrative imperative, of
the incitement to discourse that drives imperialist historiography."
In her reading the play "represents the ultimate triumph of Octavius, who will later sculpt himself into the Augustus of Virgil,
Horace, and Ovid," writers who had a profound influence on Renaissance readers such as Shakespeare. Not only did he have "a
monumental machinery of language at his disposal," but "[a]s Augustus Caesar, Octavius was to become chief executive of a massive
discursive empire, the productions of which would be referred to
again and again, from Dante to Pope, as models of literary, moral,
and historical 'authority.' "[5]

The historical Octavius certainly provided for posterity, not only
through his patronage of great writers, but also by leaving to the
safekeeping of the Vestal Virgins "a catalogue of his achievements
which he wished to be inscribed on bronze tablets and set up in
front of his mausoleum"; in the sixteenth century, a copy of this
text was found inscribed in the temple of Rome and Augustus in
Ancyra in Galatia (modern Ankara), and fragments of the text were
later found in Apollonia and Antioch in Pisidia, testifying to the
emperor's success in disseminating his version of his life.[6] This emphasis on documentary culture chimes with the portrait of Octavius given in one of Shakespeare's sources, Sir Thomas North's
Englishing of "The Life of Octavius Cæsar Augustus" by the French
Calvinist Simon Goulart (included in the 1603 edition of Plutarch's
Lives). Goulart depicts Octavius as "learned in the liberall sciences,
very eloquent, and desirous to learne," a bookworm for whom reading is a favorite and enthralling pursuit. Delighting in the great authors, he would plunder their works for "sentences teaching good
maners," and "hauing written them out word by word, he gaue out
a copy of them to his familiars: and sent them about to the gouer-
nours of prouinces, and to the magistrates of ROME and of other
cities." He was, Goulart reveals, "not curious to set himselfe out, as
litle caring to be shauen, as to weare long haire: and in stead of a
looking-glasse, reading in his booke, or writing, euen whilest the
Barber was trimming of him." Even "in the middest of all his infinite affaires" while at war, "he did reade, he wrote, and made

orations amongst his familiars." This was no *sprezzatura* performance, but a painstakingly careful and prepared campaign. Although
he "had speech at commaundement, to propound or aunswer to
any thing in the field," Octavius "neuer spake vnto the Senate nor
people, nor to his souldiers, but he had first written and premedi-
tated that he would say vnto them." In order not to "deceiue his
memory, or lose time in superfluous speech," the emperor "determined euer to write all that he would say" (Goulart claims he was
"the first inuenter" of this habit). No matter to whom he was talking—even his wife—"he would put that downe in his writing tables, because he would speake neither more nor lesse."[7]

For Shakespeare's Octavius similarly, the image he will present
to posterity lies in "all my Writings." Charnes's account assumes a
triumphalist narrative not only of Octavius's imperialism, but of
the Renaissance humanist claims for the continuing dominance of
Roman textual achievements. But, as I shall argue, the play's attitude to such a narrative is by no means secure:[8] while Charnes's
argument may be a valid claim for the lasting success of Octavius's
version of historiography into the Renaissance, it fails to address
the complexities of the characters' multifarious bids for posterity
in *Antony and Cleopatra.* To return to the specific incident of inviting his officers into his tent to view his writings: this moment,
surely a crucial point in Octavius's propaganda campaign,[9] is taken
directly from Plutarch's life of Antony:

> *Cæsar* [i.e., Octavius] hearing these newes [of Antony's death], straight
> withdrewe himselfe into a secret place of his tent, and there burst out
> with teares, lamenting his hard and miserable fortune, that had bene his
> friend and brother in law, his equall in the Empire, and companion
> with him in sundry great exploits and battels. Then he called for all his
> friends, and shewed them the letters *Antonius* had written to him, and
> his answers also sent him againe, during their quarrell and strife: and
> how fiercely and proudly the other answered him, to all iust and rea-
> sonable matters he wrote vnto him.[10]

But the play's adaptation of this passage seriously weakens the
force of Octavius's appeal to his writings. Plutarch tells how Octavius produces "the letters *Antonius* had written to him," as well
as "his answers also sent him againe," and depicts an ongoing, responsible epistolary exchange, as Antonius "fiercely and proudly
. . . answered . . . all iust and reasonable matters [Octavius] wrote
vnto him." In the play, however, we are promised only "all my

Writings,'' only one side of a supposed correspondence. Moreover, on hearing the news, Shakespeare's Octavius does not retire to his tent to weep, but instead launches into his eulogy for Antony, only to interrupt himself:

> Heare me good Friends,
> But I will tell you at some meeter Season,
> The businesse of this man lookes out of him,
> Wee'l heare him what he sayes.
>
> (5.1.48–51)

The interruption, "this man," turns out to be an *"Aegyptian,"* his "businesse," a message from Cleopatra. Octavius sends the man back with assurances that he will not be "vngentle" to his prisoner (5.1.60), but is struck with the idea that Cleopatra might kill herself and sends Proculeius, Gallus, and Dolabella to prevent it;[11] only then does he issue his invitation to view his "Writings." The effect of this interruption is twofold: first, it hints at the likelihood of Cleopatra's suicide in the following scene; and second, it en-sures—as Octavius dispatches his men on various missions—that the writings are presented to a sadly depleted Council, probably only numbering two, Agrippa and Maecenas. It betrays the fact that Octavius' letters are going to mean little to posterity compared with the iconic act of Cleopatra's suicide.

   As I shall argue, this incident is just one of a series of moments when Octavius's textual bid for history is pitted against a nontex-tual bid by Cleopatra. Far from leading to Octavius's posthumous dominance, *Antony and Cleopatra* consistently challenges the grounds on which Roman historiography is to be built—Octavius's "Writings," his letters—and, in so doing, offers a different, and de-terminedly theatrical, challenge to the sway of Roman epistolary historiography.

   It is, of course, a commonplace to read *Antony and Cleopatra* as a confrontation between two civilizations, west and east, Rome and Egypt, Caesar and Cleopatra.[12] In the words of John F. Danby, Shakespeare is writing "the vast containing opposites of Rome and Egypt, the World and the Flesh,"[13] or as Maurice Charney puts it, "Rome and Egypt represent crucial moral choices, and they func-tion as symbolic locales in a manner not unlike Henry James's Eu-rope and America."[14] The play's imagery pits Rome against Egypt relentlessly: cold versus hot, rigour versus luxury, scarcity versus bounty, masculine versus feminine, political versus domestic, rational versus irrational, Attic versus Asiatic, *virtus* versus *voluptas*.[15] Rome takes a passive role in this battle of binaries, often suggested as the negative of Egypt, rather than being fully portrayed in its own right: Rome is not, simply because Egypt is, a place of pleasure, sensuality, sex, appetite, shifting moods, sudden violence, infinite—and destabilizing—variety. In these readings, Antony is torn between the two: though Roman-born, he is easily swayed by Egyptian pleasures—Danby memorably summarizes his choice as between "soldiering for a cynical Rome or whoring on furlough in reckless Egypt."[16] Recent criticism has successfully complicated this binary model, while still preserving its basic terms: we now see the Rome in Egypt and the Egypt in Rome, their complementarity, the specularity of the two cultures, the complex ways in which we are led to see one through the eyes of the other.[17] But an examination of the modes of communication used by the two cultures—letters, messages, messengers, the kinds of communication that by their very nature have to work *across* those cultures—provides us with a way of understanding not only the differences between Egypt and Rome, but also their points of contact, practical and ideological.[18] *Antony and Cleopatra* is a play overrun with messages and messengers,[19] and necessarily so. With its action spread across two continents, disparate events have to be reported, verbally or by letter, in order to provoke a response; its characters spend much of the play recounting, hearing of, and commenting on what has happened elsewhere. While scholars have commented on this abundance and the effect of reportage they produce,[20] the play's various letters—the letters that Octavius evokes to prove his historiographic case—have yet to be scrutinized in any detail.

Rome's power is built on its use of letters, its geographically vast empire controlled by an epistolary network.[21] Messages from Rome arrive in letter form. In Alexandria, Antony receives letters containing the details of Fulvia's death in Sicyon (1.2.123–28); he is petitioned by "the Letters too / Of many our contriuing Friends in Rome" (1.2.188–90). Silius asks Ventidius if "thou wilt write to *Anthony*" (3.1.30). Rather than mere verbal agreements, Rome insists on written, sealed contracts: we see Pompey asking that "our composi[ti]on may be written / And seal'd betweene vs" (2.6.58–59), and Enobarbus reports of Pompey's collaborators that "The other three are Sealing" (3.2.3). This Roman empire is epitomized by Octavius Caesar, significantly first encountered by the audience in the act of "*reading a Letter*" from Alexandria (1.4.0, SD), an entrance motif that is repeated later (4.1.0, SD). He sees letters as documentary evidence, orally paraphrasing to Lepidus "the newes . . . From Alexandria" (1.4.3–4) but then offering the letter containing the news in support of what he says: "You / Shall finde there a man, who is th' abstracts of all faults, / That all men follow" (1.4.8–10).[22] He uses letters to control: in planning the sea battle, he commands Taurus with written instructions: "Do not exceede / The Prescript of this Scroule" (3.8.4–5). He has respect for petitions submitted in letter form: in temporarily holding back an assault against Antony, he tells his sister Octavia that it was "your Letters did with-holde our breaking forth" (3.6.81). And, as befits a man with such investment in letters, he shows himself to be hyperefficient in matters epistolary. When he recites to Agrippa Antony's charges against him, Agrippa urges "Sir, this should be answer'd," but Octavius is a step ahead: "'Tis done already, and the Messenger gone" (3.6.31–32). He sees letters as evidence: when he turns on Lepidus, after their joint victory against Pompey, he "accuses him of Letters he had formerly wrote to *Pompey*" (3.5.9).[23] Material gains from war can be "Put . . . i'th'roll of Conquest" (5.2.180); even physical injuries take on a textual form, as he reassures his prisoner Cleopatra that "The Record of what iniuries you did vs, / Though written in our flesh, we shall remember / As things but done by chance" (5.2.117–19).

Against Rome's literate culture, Egypt is presented as predominantly oral—a choice that seems to be the playwright's, rather than an effect of dominant opinion. Indeed, discourses about Egypt circulating in the early modern period, recently surveyed by John Michael Archer, point to the respect paid to Egypt as an early, if not originary, civilization in the development of writing.[24] Philemon Holland, writing in 1603, provides a typical summation: "The wisdome and learning of the Aegyptians hath bene much recommended unto us by ancient writers, and not without good cause: considering that *Aegypt* hath bene the source and fountaine from whence have flowed into the world arts and liberall sciences, as a man may gather by the testimony of the first Poets and philosophers that ever were."[25]

Shakespeare's Cleopatra, however, is seen to prefer spoken messages to letters. For the queen, news arrives in bodily form, moving violently from the throat to the ear: "Ramme thou thy fruitefull tidings in mine eares" (2.5.24); "Powre out the packe of matter to mine eare" (2.5.54). She refuses to *hear* that Antony is dead: "If thou say so Villaine, thou kil'st thy Mistris" (2.5.26–27), "The Gold I giue thee, will I melt and powr / Downe thy ill vttering throate" (2.5.34–35). The messenger pleads to be *heard:* "Good Madam heare me . . . Wilt please you heare me?" (2.5.35, 41). By contrast to the Roman emphasis on written and sealed contracts, for Cleopatra (as Antony acknowledges) a "Kingly Seale, / And plighter of high hearts" is not made of wax and affixed to a letter, but "My play-fellow, your hand" (3.13.130–31).

Cleopatra's understanding of news in bodily terms renders her incapable of distinguishing the message from its physical vessel, the messenger. When news arrives of Antony's marriage to Octavia, she lectures the messenger:

> Though it be honest, it is neuer good
> To bring bad newes: giue to a gratious Message
> An host of tongues, but let ill tydings tell
> Themselues, when they be felt.
>
> (2.5.85–88)

Her analysis is borne out by her behavior, as the messenger bears the brunt of her anger at the message he bears. Even before he makes the announcement, Cleopatra has said that his reward will depend on the news he brings:

> I haue a mind to strike thee ere thou speak'st:
> Yet if thou say *Anthony* liues, 'tis well,
> Or friends with *Caesar,* or not Captiue to him,
> Ile set thee in a shower of Gold, and haile
> Rich Pearles vpon thee.
>
> (2.5.42–46)

Ultimately, of course, she "*Strikes him downe*" (2.5.61, SD) calling down "The most infectious Pestilence vpon thee" (2.5.61); she "*Strikes him*" (2.5.62, SD) again, and "*hales him vp and downe*" (2.5.64, SD), claiming she'll "spurne thine eyes / Like balls before me: Ile vnhaire thy head, / Thou shalt be whipt with Wyer, and stew'd in brine, / Smarting in lingring pickle" (2.5.63–66). Finally she "*Draw*[s] *a knife*" (2.5.73, SD) and the messenger flees. "Gratious Madam," he claims, "I that do bring the newes, made not the match. / . . . What meane you Madam, I haue made no fault"

(2.5.66–67, 74). But for Cleopatra, there is no distinction: he is not merely the carrier of written news, but the embodiment of the news itself.

Although this binary of literate, letter-bound Rome versus oral, physical Egypt is attractive, strictly dichotomous models of message-bearing are, perforce, impossible to sustain, since the carrying of messages is by its nature transactive, moving not only within a single culture, but *across* the play's two cultures. So Cleopatra is shown as literate: when Antony leaves her, she proves her love by twice calling for her writing implements: "Inke and paper *Charmian*. . . . Get me Inke and Paper, / he shall haue euery day a seuerall greeting, or Ile vnpeople Egypt" (1.5.68, 79–81). Once separated geographically, Egypt seems to engage in "Roman" letter writing. But, despite her intentions, there is nothing in the text to suggest that Cleopatra ever does write a letter. She certainly sends an army of messengers to her beloved, asking Alexas "Met'st thou my Posts?" "I Madam," he answers, "twenty seuerall Messengers. / Why do you send so thicke?" (1.5.64–6).[26] The queen replies portentously "Who's borne that day, when I forget to send to *Anthonie*, shall dye a Begger" (1.5.66–68). Later, having beaten Antony's messenger, Cleopatra again appears to resort to letter writing. Plying the hapless messenger with gold, she informs him that

> I will employ thee backe againe: I finde thee
> Most fit for businesse. Go, make thee ready,
> Our Letters are prepar'd.
>
> (3.3.35–37)

But it turns out that in fact the letters are not prepared—or at least that Cleopatra is not finished with them. Within ten lines, she announces that she has "one thing more to aske him yet good *Charmian:* but 'tis no matter, thou shalt bring him to me where I will write; all may be well enough" (3.3.44–46). Even in her final moments, when she produces for Caesar "the breefe: of Money, Plate, & Iewels / I am possest of," assuring him "'tis exactly valewed, / Not petty things admitted" (5.2.137–39), it turns out to be incomplete, and even her treasurer will not endorse it. These incidents show Cleopatra equipped with the understanding and skills to enter into the Roman epistolary world, but temperamentally unsuited to it, refusing to respect its rules.

Antony, as one might expect, is depicted as torn between these two cultures. In Plutarch's account, Antony, in common with every other major political player of his day, is involved in extensive epistolary correspondence, and his affair with Cleopatra is kept afloat during lengthy periods of separation through letters, some-times to his detriment: Antony is specifically charged "That di-uerse times sitting in his tribunall and chaire of state, giuing audience to all Kings and Princes: he had receiued loue letters from *Cleopatra,* written in tables of Onyx or Christall, & that he had red them, sitting in his Imperiall seat."[27] It's a great image, but one that Shakespeare chooses not to use: his Antony does not read love let-ters. In other early modern accounts, by contrast, Antony makes good use of letters. Samuel Brandon's dramatization of his relation-ship with Octavia hinges on the fact that Antony halts Octavia's journey to him at Athens by sending her letters; Brandon even com-posed a fictional pair of letters between husband and wife on this emotionally fraught occasion, while Samuel Daniel similarly con-fected "A Letter sent from Octauia to her husband Marcus Anto-nius into Egypt."[28]

In the play, however, when in Cleopatra's company, Antony is seen to opt out of, if not refuse completely, his native Roman letter-writing culture. Octavius complains to Antony that "I wrote to you, when rioting in Alexandria you / Did pocket vp my Letters: and with taunts / Did gibe my Misiue out of audience" (2.2.76–79). Al-though Antony weakly objects that Octavius's messenger had vio-lated protocol by entering without being properly admitted,[29] Octavius's anger is warranted: Antony publicly humiliated his messenger (and therefore Octavius himself), and was seen to "pocket vp" the letters instead of affording them his attention. An-tony's decline from Roman etiquette is measured by his perform-ance in diplomatic relations with Caesar. He decides to send "our Schoolemaster" (3.11.72) as an ambassador, a choice that Dolabella correctly interprets as "An argument that he is pluckt, when hither / He sends so poore a Pinnion of his Wing, / Which had su-perfluous Kings for Messengers, / Not many Moones gone by" (3.12.3–6) The schoolmaster-ambassador himself expresses amaze-ment and shame at his appointment: "Such as I am, I come from *Anthony:* / I was of late as petty to his ends, / As is the Morne-dew on the Mertle leafe / To his grand Sea" (3.12.7–10). As an ambassa-dor, he is shockingly incompetent, presenting a verbal petition and then immediately, in the same sentence, assuming it will not be granted: Antony "Requires to liue in Egypt, which not granted / He

Lessons his Requests" (3.12.12–13). It is only when the schoolmas-
ter has returned with Caesar's denials that Antony returns to writing letters, as he challenges Caesar (for the second time) to single
combat:

> I dare him therefore
> To lay his gay Comparisons a-part,
> And answer me declin'd, Sword against Sword,
> Our selues alone: Ile write it:
>
> (3.13.25–28)

Presumably this is the letter that Caesar is shown reading at the beginning of act 4 ("*Enter Cæsar, Agrippa, & Mecenas with his Army,
Cæsar reading a Letter*" [4.1.0, SD]), as he complains

> He calles me Boy, and chides as he had power
> To beate me out of Egypt. My Messenger
> He hath whipt with Rods, dares me to personal Combat.
> *Cæsar* to *Anthony.*
>
> (4.1.1–4)

Antony has by this point fallen away from epistolary protocols,
allowing his prejudice against Octavius's youth to find its way into
a letter (which Octavius characteristically sees as evidence), as well
as physically abusing his letter-bearer.

But this anti-Roman attitude is by no means consistent. Although
enthralled by Cleopatra, Antony necessarily remains part of the
Roman epistolary world. As we have seen, he receives news of his
wife Fulvia's death by letter, and petitions from his friends in Rome
to return home. After his defeat at sea, Antony dismisses his attendants, but uses letters to recommend them to posts elsewhere:

> Friends be gone, you shall
> Haue Letters from me to some Friends, that will
> Sweepe your way for you.
>
> (3.11.15–17)

It is revealed in passing that Antony is in correspondence with Octavius: when challenged that he was complicit with attacks against
Octavius by his brother and wife, Antony points out that "Of this,
my Letters / Before did satisfie you" (2.2.56–57).

Rome and Egypt, then, can be seen to have different attitudes to the bearing of messages, Rome fixating on written epistolary documentation, Egypt preferring the personally conveyed oral message, although both civilizations are capable—perhaps through necessity—of drawing on the other's techniques. In terms of the posterity of historiography, Rome might seem to have the upper hand here, its messages preservable in written form while Egypt's are by their nature transient. But this notion is not allowed to pass unchallenged. In the figure of Antony—the Roman in Egypt, ostensibly rejecting but often complicit in the culture of Roman letters—we are presented with an uncertain resistance to Roman historiography, focused on his claim to be a Roman, at the moment of his death.

*   *   *

In Antony's final words he paints a self-portrait of how he should be remembered:

> The miserable change now at my end,
> Lament nor sorrow at: but please your thoughts
> In feeding them with those my former Fortunes
> Wherein I liued. The greatest Prince o'th' world,
> The Noblest: and do now not basely dye,
> Not Cowardly put off my Helmet to
> My Countreyman. A Roman, by a Roman
> Valiantly vanquish'd. Now my Spirit is going,
> I can no more.
>
> (4.15.53–61)

According to Antony, he did not submit to a fellow "Countreyman," but was "Valiantly vanquished," in the only way a Roman should be, by an equal, a Roman. The "Countreyman" must be Octavius Caesar, whose control he has escaped, since the two Romans are both Antony, vanquisher and vanquished—he has already claimed that "Not *Cæsars* Valour hath o'rethrowne *Anthony,* / But *Anthonie*'s hath Triumpht on it selfe," and Cleopatra has confirmed approvingly that "none but *Anthony* should conquer *Anthony*" (4.15.15–18). Self-killing is, of course, understood by the Renaissance as the classic Roman gesture of courage,[30] and as he contemplates the act in a rare soliloquy, Antony is drawn, uncharacteristically, to a Roman image of contract: "Seale then, and all is done" (4.14.50). Yet this confident assertion is belied by what the audience has seen—Antony first asking his servant to kill him, then witnessing that servant bravely kill himself rather than execute his master, then botching his own suicide, before vainly pleading with his guards to finish the job, and finally being hauled up to his deathbed by (foreign) women. And there is something very wrong with this sentence: who is Antony's "Countreyman" if not a Roman? If the countryman is not a Roman, then what is Antony?

The first official report of Antony's demise, given by Decretas to Octavius explains that he died,

> Not by a publike minister of Iustice,
> Nor by a hyred Knife, but that selfe-hand
> Which writ his Honor in the Acts it did,
> Hath with the Courage which the heart did lend it,
> Splitted the heart.

> (5.1.20–24)

The awkward reference to Antony's "selfe-hand" might alert us to a problem. Hands are prominently portrayed throughout the play, shaken, kissed, read by a soothsayer.[31] But the lovers show a surprising lack of control over their own hands. When Antony exclaims, "[Cleopatra] hath betraid me, And shall dye the death," Mardian replies, "Death of one person, can be paide but once, / And that she ha's discharg'd. What thou would'st do / Is done vnto thy hand" (4.14.26–29). The phrasing here is odd, but telling: Mardian means that the action Antony would do (raise his hand to kill Cleopatra) has already been done; but in so doing, the act has been done "vnto thy hand," almost as if an attack *on* his hand. When Cleopatra goes to stab herself, she exclaims, "Quicke, quicke, good hands" (5.2.38), but Caesar's man Proculeius is too fast, and disarms her. And, in this case too, the hand is not under Antony's control: although Decretas talks of "that selfe-hand / Which writ his Honor," the audience already knows that Antony's first impulse is to use someone else's hand to do the deed: the hand of Eros.

Antony's confident assertion that he is "A Roman, by a Roman / Valiantly vanquish'd," and Decretas's report that he was killed by "that selfe-hand / Which writ his Honor in the Acts it did," need to be tempered by the knowledge of his call on Eros: to what extent is Antony really vanquished by a Roman, or by his self-hand? Significantly, even before his suicide, Antony's sense of a discrete self is already shaken: indeed, the scene opens with him asking his servant Eros the bewildering question "*Eros*, thou yet behold'st me?" (4.14.1). Although Eros answers in the affirmative, Antony objects that, as when we see clouds that bear a certain shape, "now thy Captaine is / Euen such a body: Heere I am *Anthony,* / Yet cannot hold this visible shape (my Knaue)" (4.14.12–14) as a result of Cleopatra's betrayal. In his mind, Antony cannot be seen, yet Eros assures him that *he* can see Antony: Eros's sight is required in order for Antony to be visible. Antony has some comfort for his servant:

> Nay, weepe not gentle *Eros,* there is left vs
> Our selues to end our selues.
>
> (4.14.21–22)

Antony's meaning, as will soon become explicit, is that he will end his own life. But his phrasing, using the plural form "Our," suggests something else: that it will take both of them to kill themselves. Antony's death then is not at the hand of Antony, but at the combined hand of Antony and Eros; his "selfe-hand" is not his own, but theirs jointly.

If Antony's "selfe-hand" is not his own, to what extent is he killed by a Roman? There is another element to Eros that urges us to question this. The incident appears, at first sight, to be taken directly from Plutarch:

> Now he had a man of his called *Eros,* whom he loued and trusted much, and whom he had long before caused to sweare vnto him, that he should kill him when he did command him: and then he willed him to keepe his promise. His man drawing his sword, lift it vp as though he had meant to haue striken his master: but turning his head at one side, he thrust his sword into himself, and fell downe dead at his maisters foote. Then said *Antonius:* ô noble *Eros,* I thanke thee for this, and it is valiantly done of thee, to shew me what I should do to my selfe, which thou couldest not do for me. Therewithall he tooke his sword, and thrust it into his belly, and so fell downe vpon a litle bed.[32]

However, as Leeds Barroll has demonstrated so convincingly,[33] in creating the man whom Antony asks to kill him, Shakespeare goes beyond Plutarch's account. Rather than the vagueness of the "long before . . . promise," whereby Eros inexplicably agreed to kill Antony if required, Shakespeare has Antony recalling a specific moment—"When I did make thee free, swor'st *thou* not then / To do this when I bad thee?" (4.14.82–83)—that makes Eros a freedman, an enfranchised slave.

Where does this notion of Eros as a freedman come from? Thomas North's translation describes him merely as "a man of his," while Jacques Amyot's French makes him "vn sien seruiteur."[34] In other late Elizabethan adaptations of the moment, Mary, Countess of Pembroke seems to follow North in referring to "*Eros* his man" in her closet verse drama *Tragedie of Anthonie* (1592);[35] the original of her translation, Robert Garnier's *M. Antoine, Tragedie* (1578), follows Amyot in using "Eros son seruiteur."[36] These epithets—"his man" and "his servant" (serviteur)—certainly seem to be standard for Eros: we might add contemporary allusions by Sir Richard Barckley in his 1598 *A Discovrse of the Felicitie of Man* to "his man *Eros*";[37] and Robert Allott, in his 1599 *Wits Theater of the little World,* where Eros is described as "the seruant of Antonius."[38] (Another variant from the Herbert circle, Samuel Brandon's 1598 *The Tragicomoedi of the vertuous Octauia* omits Eros.)[39] Plutarch's Greek, however, has something very different: Eros as "οικετης αυτον πιστος"—a trusted household slave of his, and emphatically not an απελευτηερον, one of his "infranchised bondmen." Shakespeare's Eros is thus notably different from other contemporary versions of story—but why? Barroll's inquiry is undertaken in the cause of dating the play, largely in relation to the 1607 revision of Samuel Daniel's closet drama *Cleopatra*—Daniel also makes Eros "his late infranchis'd seruant," suggesting he may have seen or read Shakespeare's play.[40] But what does it mean that Eros should be an enfranchised slave? A freedman was never fully free, but bound to the conditions of the freedman's oath (*iusirandum liberti*), by which the freedman might perform certain *operae* or services, perhaps a weekly ration of domestic or skilled labor, or working as a generalized procurator, managing the master's affairs.[41] But beyond this, the *operae* might include certain specific tasks—and it is this arrangement to which Antony refers.

In rendering Eros a freedman, Shakespeare draws (as Barroll suggests) not only on Plutarch's Eros but also on other characters in Plutarch's *Lives.* The first is Rhamnus, another servant to whom Antony turned in a low moment during the Parthian campaign: "*Antonius* called for one *Rhamnus,* one of his slaues infranchised that was of his guard, and made him giue him his faith that he would thrust his sword through him when he would bid him, and cut off his head, because he might not be taken aliue of his enemies, nor knowne when he were dead."[42] This identification of Rhamnus with Eros is strengthened by the fact that Antony urges Eros to "Draw that thy honest Sword, which thou hast worne / Most vsefull for thy Country" (4.14.80–81), implying that Eros has been a soldier, and that Eros himself alludes to the Parthian campaign in this final scene: "Shall I do that which all the Parthian Darts, / (Though Enemy) lost ayme, and could not" (4.14.71–72).[43] In Barroll's argument, Shakespeare's Eros "has in effect taken on the characteristics of Plutarch's suicide helper *B*—Rhamnus from the Plutarchan Parthian expedition . . . And the manumission (from Plutarch's Rhamnus) has become so significant in Shakespeare that it is part of the structure of Antony's effort to persuade Eros—a persuasion, indeed, telling enough to force Eros either to honor Antony's plea or to kill himself to avoid the debt."[44]

Second, Eros recalls the man who slays Cassius "at his earnest request . . . a faithfull seruant of his owne called *Pindarus,* whom he had infranchised."[45] Elsewhere, Plutarch elaborates that Pindarus was "one of his freed bondmen, whom he reserued euer for such a pinch, since the cursed battell of the PARTHIANS"; Pindarus decapitates Cassius as ordered, "but after that time *Pindarus* was neuer seene more. Whereupon, some tooke occasion to say that he had slaine his maister without his commaundement."[46] In dramatizing this incident in *Julius Caesar,* as Barroll notes "Shakespeare altered this sequence,"[47] making the enfranchisement a delayed reward contingent on the killing:

> In Parthia did I take thee Prisoner,
> And then I swore thee, sauing of thy life,
> That whatsoeuer I did bid thee do,
> Thou should'st attempt it. Come now, keepe thine oath,
> Now be a Free-man, and with this good Sword
> That ran through *Cæsars* bowels, search this bosome.
>
> (5.3.37–42)

Having performed the act, Pindarus meditates on his fate: "So, I am free, / Yet would not so haue beene / Durst I haue done my will," and decides to go into exile "Where neuer Roman shall take note of him" (5.3.47–50). The Cassius-Pindarus narrative, with its coercive promises and its shameful outcome, makes clear the dangerous bargain that is involved in this claim on the freedman, a bargain repeated in the Antony-Eros encounter. As Antony notes,

> When I did make thee free, swor'st *thou* not then
> To do this when I bad thee? Do it at once,
> Or thy precedent Seruices are all
> But accidents vnpurpos'd.
>
> (4.14.82–85)

Antony claims that unless Eros obeys, his previous *operae* are rendered redundant, the terms of his freedom violated.

In both cases, the bargaining of Cassius and Antony belies the supposed freedom of their erstwhile slaves as, despite their enfranchisement, Pindarus and Rhamnus—and, it follows, therefore Eros—are shown to be still committed to certain formidable duties for their masters. Elsewhere, Antony has invoked another freedman over whom he exerts control. After beating him, he tells Caesar's messenger Thidias to

> Get thee backe to *Cæsar,*
> Tell him thy entertainment: looke thou say
> He makes me angry with him. For he seemes
> Proud and disdainfull, harping on what I am,
> Not what he knew I was. . . .
> .   .   .   .
>   If he mislike,
> My speech, and what is done, tell him he has
> *Hiparchus,* my enfranched Bondman, whom
> He may at pleasure whip, or hang, or torture,
> As he shall like to quit me.[48]

(3.13.144–48, 152–56)

This Hipparchus is introduced by Plutarch as "the first of all his infranchised bondmen that reuolted from him, and yeelded vnto *Cæsar,* and afterwards went and dwelt at CORINTH."[49] It is clear from Antony's speech, however, that he still recognizes Hipparchus as his own to punish, despite his doubly removed status— freed from bondage and then revolted from Antony's mastery. This notion, thus insistently made, that manumission does not fully free an ex-slave, is betrayed in Samuel Daniel's 1607 revision of his *Cleopatra,* which critics have seen as drawing on Shakespeare's play. Following Eros's suicide, Daniel's Antony exclaims

> O *Eros,* . . . and hath fortune quite
> Forsaken me? must I b'outgone in all?
> What? can I not by loosing get a right?
> Shall I not haue the vpper hand to fall
> In death? must both a woman, and a slaue
> The start before me of this glory haue?[50]

Antony objects to the fact that two lesser beings, two non-Roman citizens in the form of a foreign woman (Cleopatra) and a slave

(Eros), have beaten him to the virtuous Roman act of self-killing. As Eros has just been introduced by Daniel as "his late infranchis'd seruant,"[51] this seems inconsistent, but the implication here must be that Daniel's Antony is registering the notion that a slave is never fully manumitted—and equally that a freedman is never considered fully a Roman citizen.

But there is another aspect to Antony's relationship to Eros, and it takes us back directly to Antony's relationship to Roman letters. Whereas in Plutarch's "Life" we are introduced to Eros only at the moment of Antony's attempted suicide, in *Antony and Cleopatra* he has made a series of important entries.[52] Eros first appears on stage in 3.5 in a brief encounter with Enobarbus, where, although his social function is not clear, he is seen to be in possession of "strange Newes come" (3.5.2), knowledge of Antony's whereabouts and action, and the detail that Octavius has accused Lepidus "of Letters he had formerly wrote to *Pompey*" (3.5.9–10). His second appearance is in 3.11, immediately following Antony's ignominious defeat at sea. In Plutarch's account, it is "*Cleopatraes* women," sometime afterward, who "first brought *Antonius* and *Cleopatra* to speake together, and afterwards to sup and lie together."[53] In the play, the scene occurs immediately after Antony has dismissed his attendants, and it is not solely Cleopatra's women who bring about the reconciliation. Eros enters alongside Charmian and Iras, leading Cleopatra; it is here his role to bring the two together, encouraging first the queen ("Nay gentle Madam, to him, comfort him," [3.11.25]) then the despondent general ("See you heere, Sir? . . . Sir, sir . . . The Queene my Lord, the Queene . . . Most Noble Sir arise, the Queene approaches . . . Sir, the Queene" [3.11.30, 42, 46, 50]). It is still not specified who Eros is, but unlike Cleopatra's women, he seems to be able to talk to both parties. His next appearance is in 4.4, as Antony calls for his servant to prepare him for battle: "*Eros,* mine Armour *Eros* . . . *Eros,* come mine Armor *Eros* . . . Come good Fellow, put thine Iron on" (4.4.1, 2, 3). This scene places Eros in competition with Cleopatra: Antony's calls for Eros are at first interrupted by Cleopatra's pleas for him to "Sleepe a little" (4.4.1) and then by her offers to help him arm. Although at first her attempts seem misplaced, soon Antony is impressed: "Thou fumblest *Eros,* and my Queenes a Squire / More tight at this, then thou: Dispatch" (4.4.14–15). Eros is here portrayed as the devoted servant, intent on arming his master before thinking of himself: when Antony orders him to "Go, put on thy defences," Eros puts him off with a "Briefely Sir" (4.4.10).

The servant's name, of course, is serendipitous,[54] and it is not left unexploited throughout these scenes. Antony constantly *names* Eros, often calling for him urgently—five times as Eros arms him (4.4), no fewer than fifteen times in the suicide scene (4.14). If Eros equals Love, however, there is no single way of reading that love. In bringing together Antony and Cleopatra following the sea disaster, Eros may be seen as pandering their affair, assuring heterosexual love; but it could equally be argued that Eros is in competition with Cleopatra for Antony's love, as they squabble over who should arm him. Both readings are possible in Antony's distracted speech, as his thoughts of the dead Cleopatra are interrupted by his calls for Eros:

> *Eros?* I come my Queene. *Eros?* Stay for me,
> Where Soules do couch on Flowers, wee'l hand in hand,
> And with our sprightly Port make the Ghostes gaze:
> *Dido,* and her *Æneas* shall want Troopes,
> And all the haunt be ours. Come *Eros, Eros.*
>
> (4.14.51–55)

But perhaps the most telling scene of their relationship arrives when Antony realizes that Enobarbus has gone, and he orders Eros to "send his Treasure after" him (4.5.12):

> write to him,
> (I will subscribe) gentle adieu's, and greetings;
> Say, that I wish he neuer finde more cause
> To change a Master. Oh my Fortunes haue
> Corrupted honest men. Dispatch *Enobarbus* [or *Eros?*][55]
>
> (4.5.13–17)

Antony expects Eros to draft the letter, according to his general instructions ("Say, that I wish . . ."), and he will provide the subscription and salutation. Clearly Eros is here functioning as Antony's secretary, a position in which many freedmen continued to serve their erstwhile masters: the most famous is probably Cicero's Tiro, who dealt with his master's finances, appeased his creditors, revised his accounts, supervised his gardens and building operations, and acted as his confidant, secretary, and literary collaborator.[56] To early modern readers, the secretary suggested a role of unparalled intimacy based not only on physical proximity (although Eros's duties in arming and disarming Antony also testify to such a relationship) but on the sharing of intellectual knowledge and secrets. In his 1592 discourse "Of the Partes, Place and Office of a Secretorie," Angel Day insists that the secretary is not made merely by "the praisable endeuour or abilitie of well writing or ordering the pen," but rather by his relationship with his master: his position thus "containeth the chiefest title of credite, and place of greatest assurance, in respect of the neerenesse and affinitie they haue of *Trust, Regard,* & *Fidelitie,* each with the other, by great conceyte and discretion."[57] Beyond this, and worryingly, the secretary writes both for and—as in this case—*as* his master, as he composes his words. As Richard Rambuss has shown, "Secretaryship ... does not simply mean transcribing, copying down the words of the master; rather it entails becoming the simulacrum of the master himself."[58] We see this phenomenon at work in Timon of Athens' steward Flavius, who preempts an order by Timon to go to the Senate and drum up cash by asserting,

> I haue beene bold
> (For that I knew it the most generall way)
> To them, to vse your Signet, and your Name,
> But they do shake their heads, and I am heere
> No richer in returne.
>
> (2.2.204–8)

It is not clear from Flavius's statement whether he has written a letter from Timon, signing it as his master ("your Name") and sealing it with his master's seal ring ("your Signet"), or whether he has merely spoken to the senators in his master's name, producing the signet ring as proof that he was speaking with Timon's authority. But whatever the case, it is beyond doubt that Flavius is comfortable and probably accustomed to speaking, writing and sealing as his master.

The letter-writing scene is unique to Shakespeare's play, without parallel in any of the possible sources. So why does Shakespeare make Eros a letter-writing secretary? I suggest that the scene is a deliberate foreshadowing of the moment when Antony will demand Eros's hand to perform another task on his behalf—his suicide. The link between these two secretarial, manual functions, writing and self-killing, is made explicit in Decretas's report: Antony is killed, he claims, by "that selfe-hand / Which writ his Honor in the Acts it did." By turning to the trope of a handwritten honor, Decretas unconsciously draws attention to the fact that Antony does not do his own writing, and perhaps he did not write his own honor. Antony's hand is shown not to be his own. Here, the contrast with Caesar is vivid: Octavius's focus on writing is entirely personal—he reads, gathers "sentences" from the great authors, writes on tables to prepare his speeches, and writes his own letters. Antony's writing, his very hand, conversely, is the joint work of himself and Eros, and therefore his self-killing cannot be the work of his hand alone. He knows this, and so he calls on his secretary to kill him; but ultimately, the true secretary—the man whose hand is his master's—cannot be his master's hand in this task. Eros thus refuses to do the ultimate secretarial act: to use his (self-)hand against his master's body.

In building the servant Eros into both a freedman and a secretary, the play deliberately complicates Antony's actions to the point that they no longer mean what he claims they do. The impossible dual place of the secretary—the servant who is also "the simulacrum of the master"—is imposed on the impossible dual place of the freedman, slave and Roman. Antony's "selfe-hand" is no longer his, and his position as a Roman, so much a part of his self-vision, is ultimately not assured.

* * *

If Octavius's Roman historiography fails, and even Antony's very status within Roman historiography is compromised, then how does Cleopatra fare? At the climax of *Antony and Cleopatra,* there is a missing letter. Plutarch relates how after a countryman had delivered a basket and figs, and Cleopatra had dined,

> she sent a certaine table written and sealed vnto *Cæsar,* and commaunded them all to go out of the tombes where she was, but the two women, then she shut the doores to her. *Cæsar* when he receiued this table, and began to reade her lamentation and petition, requesting him that he would let her be buried with *Antonius,* found straight what she meant, and thought to haue gone thither himselfe: howbeit, he sent one before in all hast that might be, to see what it was.

However, by that time, it was too late: despite running "in all hast possible," Caesar's messengers "found *Cleopatra* starke dead."[59] The play dispenses with Cleopatra's sealed letter to Caesar. Instead, "*an Ægyptian*" (5.1.48, SD) is sent with a verbal message from Cleopatra asking for Caesar's "instruction, / That she preparedly may frame her selfe / To'th' way shee's forc'd too" (5.2.54–56). The omission of this letter runs true to form with the play's depiction of Cleopatra as preferring verbal to epistolary communication, and, in that way, it might be said to support the notion that oral Egypt is presented in opposition to literate Rome. But the omission of the letter—or more precisely, the introduction of the Egyptian messenger—can be seen to challenge the efficacy of Rome's documentary culture.

In Shakespeare's treatment, it is this Egyptian's oral message that serves to interrupt Octavius's invitation to his men to view his writings. As noted earlier, the message alerts Octavius that Cleopatra may harm herself, and he gives orders for his men to prevent her doing so, not out of humane compassion, but, once again, with an eye to posterity:

> giue her what comforts
> The quality of her passion shall require;
> Least in her greatnesse, by some mortall stroke
> She do defeate vs. For her life in Rome,
> Would be eternall in our Triumph.
>
> (5.1.62–66)

If a living, captured Cleopatra in Rome will be eternal in Caesar's triumph (as Cleopatra also imagines), then it follows that her death in Egypt will be eternal in Caesar's defeat. This defeat is enacted when Dolabella reaches Cleopatra's monument, and a guard enters, noisily "*rustling in*" (5.2.318, SD) to announce that "*Cæsar* hath sent—" The sentence is unfinished, and in the First Folio unpunctuated (modern editors tend to add a dash), and Charmian finishes the sentence with the sardonic "Too slow a Messenger" (5.2.320). Here, the limitations of Caesar's network of messengers are revealed. While Caesar hoped to clinch the narrative by showing his letter-book to his Council of War, instead the Romans march into the monument to examine the corpses, hoping to understand the cause of death, while Caesar pays tribute to the future longevity of this couple's memory:

> No Graue vpon the earth shall clip in it
> A payre so famous: high euents as these
> Strike those that make them: and their Story is
> No lesse in pitty, then his Glory which
> Brought them to be lamented.
>
> (5.2.358–62)

Linda Charnes reads this as the crowning glory of the Roman success in historiography: "Upon learning of Cleopatra's suicide, Octavius understands immediately the political uses to which he can put a mythologized 'Antony and Cleopatra' . . . He swiftly translates them from rebellious figures who escaped his control and punishment into legendary lovers. . . . Antony and Cleopatra can become epic lovers in the world's report only once Octavius has full control of the machinery of reproduction. Only then can they be put to historiographic use."[60] But to what extent is this myth of Antony and Cleopatra as eternally embracing "legendary lovers" truly Octavius's impulse? The notion that the queen "shall be buried by her *Anthony*" (5.2.357) is the request contained in her sealed letter; Antony explicitly determined to "bee / A Bride-groome in my death, and run intoo't / As to a Louers bed" (4.14.100–102). The historical Octavius ignored Antony and Cleopatra in his autobiography: the queen disappears altogether, and Antony is evoked only obliquely as "the tyranny of a faction" that Octavius suppressed in his youth.[61] But Shakespeare's Octavius, far from having "full control of the machinery of reproduction" as he hoped to have with the letters in his tent, is forced to take Cleopatra and Antony's version of events; his only power is to enshrine it in Roman historiography.

In the play's final two scenes, then, we see competing memorializing impulses played out, in ways that insist again on opposing values of Rome and Egypt, as Shakespeare depicts them. For Octavius Caesar, the history of Antony and Cleopatra will be written from the epistolary evidence of his correspondence with Mark Antony. For Cleopatra, the history will be inspired by the physical tableau of the almost perfect female corpses, and the oral testimonies of the man who last saw alive, her guard. And, as Rosalie Colie observes, Cleopatra gets the last laugh: while Rome may seem to dominate the play—a play that "begins and ends with expressions of the Roman point of view," nevertheless, "seen from another angle, Egypt commands the play, where the action begins and ends and where all the major episodes take place."[62] Colie's formulation implicitly contrasts Roman "expressions" versus Egyptian "action," Octavius's words versus Cleopatra's gestures. In this, Colie subscribes tacitly to the oft-asserted association between Cleopatra and the theater, in which commonplace antitheatrical prejudice is deployed against the exotic, foreign, stagy queen.[63] Here, however, that same Egyptian theatricality becomes an effective challenge to

Roman historiography and, within the terms of the play, may be said to defeat it.[64] For the showing of these "Writings" is superseded by the call to see the queen: the play ends not in Octavius's tent, with the viewing of his letters, but—through heeding the oral message of her Egyptian servant—inside Cleopatra's monument. In allowing that image to occupy the final moments of the play, Shakespeare—or perhaps theater itself—comes down on the side of Egyptian spectacle, and against Roman letters.

Notes

I am grateful to James Shapiro and Garrett Sullivan for their comments on an earlier version of this article.

1. Unless otherwise noted, quotations of Shakespeare's plays follow the text *The First Folio of Shakespeare,* prep. Charlton Hiinman (New York: W. W. Norton, 1968), a facsimile edition of *Mr. William Shakespeares Comedies, Histories & Tragedies* (London, 1623). They are cross-referenced to act, scene, line numbers keyed to *Antony and Cleopatra,* ed. John Wilders (New York: Routledge, Arden Shakespeare, 3rd series, 1998); *Julius Caesar* ed. David Daniell (New York: Thomson, Arden Shakespeare, 3rd series, 1998); and *Timon of Athens* ed. H. J. Oliver (New York: Methuen, Arden Shakespeare, 2nd series, 1969).

2. W. B. Worthen, "The Weight of Antony: Staging 'Character' in *Antony and Cleopatra,*" *Studies in English Literature, 1500–1900* 26 (1986): 297.

3. C. C. Barfoot, "News from the Roman Empire: Hearsay, Soothsay, Myth and History in *Antony and Cleopatra,*" in *Reclamations of Shakespeare,* ed. A. J. Hoenselaars (Atlanta GA: Rodopi, 1994), 113. I am grateful to Garrett Sullivan for bringing Professor Barfoot's useful essay to my attention.

4. Garrett A. Sullivan, "'My oblivion is a very Antony'," in *Memory and Forgetting in English Renaissance Drama* (Cambridge: Cambridge University Press, 2005), 89.

5. Linda Charnes, "Spies and Whispers: Exceeding Reputation in *Antony and Cleopatra,*" in *Notorious Identity: Materializing the Subject in Shakespeare* (Cambridge, MA: Harvard University Press, 1993), 106, 107.

6. P. A. Brunt and J. M. Moore, eds., introduction to *Res gestae divi Augusti: The Achievements of the Divine Augustus* (Oxford: Oxford University Press, 1967), 1–16.

7. Simon Goulart, "The Life of Octaius Cæsar Augustus," in *The Lives of Epaminondas, of Philip of Macedon, of Dionysivs the Elder, and of Octavivs Cæsar Avgvstvs: collected out of good Authors; Also the liues of nine excellent Chieftaines of warre, taken out of Latine from Emylivs Probvs,* trans. Thomas North (London: Richard Field, 1603), e4r–g4r (51–75) at e4v–e5r (52–53).

8. Here I share common ground with Ronald Macdonald, who argues that Shakespeare indulged in "an historical questioning of classicism in general, the peculiar prestige accorded it in learned Renaissance circles, and its centrality for European culture. He came to see that the centrality of classicism was not a 'natural' phenomenon at all, but a cultural and historical construct, and one, like all constructs, embodied assumptions of an ideological kind, about what we know

and how, about the nature of history, about stability and order, and perhaps most of all, assumptions about language and its role in shaping the very assumptions we so often take for fact." Ronald R. Macdonald, "Playing Till Doomsday: Interpreting *Antony and Cleopatra*," *English Literary Renaissance* 15 (1985): 79.

9. Worthen, one of the few critics to comment on these letters, argues similarly: "Throughout the play, Caesar relies on narrative—the 'news' of Alexandria, Antony's 'reported' (I.iv.67) exploits in the Alps, perhaps even in the 'writings' he offers in his defense after Antony's death (V.i.76)—to characterize his general, means which enable Caesar more easily to assimilate Antony's actions to an interpretive text: Antony becomes the 'abstract of all faults / That men follow' (I.iv.9–10). Caesar's characterization of Antony consistently privileges the absent 'character' of history over the present 'character' of performance." "The Weight of Antony," 299.

10. Plutarch, *The Lives of the Noble Grecians and Romaines, compared together . . . Hereunto are affixed the liues of Epaminados . . . etc* [by Simon Goulart], trans. Thomas North (London: Richard Field for Thomas Wight, 1603), Llll 5v (946).

11. He later remembers that he has already sent Dolabella, too late, to implore Antony to yield.

12. For a recent analysis of this notion, see James Hirsh, "Rome and Egypt in *Antony and Cleopatra* and in Criticism of the Play," in *Antony and Cleopatra: New Critical Essays,* ed. Sara Munson Deats, 175–91 (New York: Routledge, 2005).

13. John F. Danby, *Poets on Fortune's Hill: Studies in Sidney, Shakespeare, Beaumont and Fletcher* (London: Faber & Faber, 1952), 140.

14. Maurice Charney, *Shakespeare's Roman Plays: The Function of Imagery in the Drama* (Cambridge, MA: Harvard University Press, 1961), 93.

15. See, for example, Charney, *Shakespeare's Roman Plays,* 93–112; Rosalie L. Colie, "*Antony and Cleopatra:* The Significance of Style," in *Shakespeare's Living Art* (Princeton: Princeton University Press, 1974), 168, 177, 179. The most recent Arden edition attests to the tenacity of this reading: "For the Romans the ideal is measured in masculine, political, pragmatic, military terms, the subservience of the individual to the common good of the state, of personal pleasure to public duty, of private, domestic loyalties to the demands of empire. Alexandria, on the other hand, is a predominantly female society for which the ideal is measured in terms of the intensity of emotion, of physical sensation, the subservience of social responsibility to the demands of feeling." Wilders, *Antony and Cleopatra,* 28.

16. Danby, *Poets on Fortune's Hill,* 151.

17. Jonathan Gil Harris, " 'Narcissus in thy face': Roman Desire and the Difference it Fakes in *Antony and Cleopatra,*" *Shakespeare Quarterly* 45 (1994): 408–25; Carol Cook, "The Fatal Cleopatra," in *Shakespearean Tragedy and Gender,* ed. Shirley Nelson Garner and Madelon Sprengnether, 241–67 (Bloomington: Indiana University Press, 1996); Hirsh, "Rome and Egypt."

18. In 1958, Benjamin Spencer argued that the play "shows . . . an as yet undefined synthesis lying beyond both Rome and Egypt but partaking of the values of both." Spencer, "*Antony and Cleopatra* and the Paradoxical Metaphor," *Shakespeare Quarterly* 9 (1958): 373–78.

19. "No one gets far into *Antony and Cleopatra* without discovering that it is a play swarming with messengers": Macdonald, "Playing Till Doomsday," 85.

20. Janet Adelman, *The Common Liar: An Essay on Antony and Cleopatra*

(New Haven: Yale University Press, 1973), esp. 34–39; Charnes, "Spies and Whispers"; Barfoot, "News from the Roman Empire."

21. Barfoot has commented similarly that "Verbally, orally, the Roman Empire is observed articulating itself, giving conscious expression to itself through word of mouth, and through deliberate acts of writing; and defining itself spatially, geographically, through the need to conduct business by letter and messenger, and historically by the provision of documents and of witnesses (since presumably what we see in the play, on and across the stage, is a mere fraction of all the messages that are being dispatched about the Empire)." However, Barfoot does not make a distinction, as I shall attempt, between Roman and Egyptian modes of communication. Barfoot, "News from the Roman Empire," 108.

22. F1 reads "abstracts"; F2 and all subsequent editions read "abstract." Wilders glosses "there" as "i.e., in the letter"; *Antony and Cleopatra,* ed. Wilders, 114, note on 1.4.8.

23. Barfoot notes, "Significantly, the main charge levelled against Lepidus when he is deposed is that he wrote letters to Pompey (3.5.8–10): clearly letter writing can be a contentious and dangerous occupation in the Roman Empire, and may be used in evidence against you." "News from the Roman Empire," 108–9.

24. John Michael Archer, *Old Worlds: Egypt, Southwest Asia, India, and Russia in Early Modern English Writing* (Stanford CA: Stanford University Press, 2001), 23–62. Archer discusses book 2 of Herodotus' *Histories,* trans. B.R. as *The Famous Hystory of Herodotus* (London: Thomas Marshe, 1584); Diodorus Siculus's *Library of History; Ethiopica,* trans. Thomas Underdowne in 1587.

25. Philemon Holland "The Summarie" to his trans., Plutarch, "Of Isis and Osiris," in *The Philosophie, commonlie called the Morals* (London: Arnold Hatfield, 1603), Qqqqqv–Qqqqq2r (1286–87).

26. Wilders sees this as a symptom of Alexandria's female/Egyptian emotionalism: "Hence Cleopatra must send to Antony every day a several greeting or she'll unpeople Egypt"; *Antony and Cleopatra,* 28. Barfoot would counter: "At first we may suspect that Cleopatra's tally of 'twenty several messengers' is a characteristic piece of self-indulgent hyperbole; but we have no reason for believing that it is, and if what we as the audience see in the three hours' traffic on the stage is anything to go by, for all we know there are twenty thousand envoys currently employed at any single moment through the length and breadth of the Empire." "News from the Roman Empire," 108–9.

27. Plutarch, *Lives,* Lllllv (938).

28. Samuel Brandon, *The Tragicomoedi of the virtuous Octauia* (London: William Ponsonby, 1598), B3r; for the letters see F8r (argument), F8v–H2r (Octavia to Antony), and H2r–H7v (Antony to Octavia); Samuel Daniel, "A Letter sent from Octauia to her husband Marcus Antonius into Egypt," in *Certaine Small Workes heretofore Divulged . . . & now againe by him corrected and augmented* (London: I.W. for Simon Waterson, 1607), F2r–G2v.

29. "Sir, he fell vpon me, ere admitted, then: / Three Kings I had newly feasted, and did want / Of what I was i'th' morning: but next day / I told him of my selfe, which was as much / As to haue askt him pardon" (2.2.79–84).

30. See Anton J. L. van Hooff, *From Autothanasia to Suicide: Self-killing in Classical Antiquity* (New York: Routledge, 1990); Timothy D. Hill, *Ambitiosa Mors: Suicide and Self in Roman Thought and Literature* (New York: Routledge, 2004).

31. For important considerations of hands in the early modern period, see Jonathan Goldberg, "Hamlet's Hand," *Shakespeare Quarterly* 39 (1988): 307–27; Goldberg, *Writing Matter: From the Hands of the English Renaissance* (Stanford, CA: Stanford University Press, 1990); Katherine Rowe, *Dead Hands: Fictions of Agency, Renaissance to Modern* (Stanford, CA: Stanford University Press, 1999).

32. Plutarch, *Lives,* Llll 5r–v (945–6).

33. Leeds Barroll, *Politics, Plague, and Shakespeare's Theater: The Stuart Years* (Ithaca: Cornell University Press, 1991), 160–65.

34. Plutarch, *Les vies des hommes illvstres grecs et romains, compares l'vne avec l'avtre* trans. Jacques Amyot with additions by Charles de l'Écluse (Paris: Pierre Cheuillot, 1579), EEE. iijr.

35. Mary [Sidney Herbert], Countess of Pembroke, *The Tragedie of Antonie, Doone into English* (London: William Ponsonby, 1595), F5r.

36. Robert Garnier, *M. Antoine, Tragedie* (Paris: Mamert Patisson, 1578), I.jr.

37. Richard Barckley, *A Discovrse of the Felicitie of Man, or His Summum bonum* (London: William Ponsonby, 1598), D6v–D7r: "*Antonius* turning to his man *Eros* whom he had prouided before to kill him if neede were, required him to performe his promise. *Eros* taking his sword in his hand, & making as though he would strike his master, suddenly turned the point to his own bodie, and thrust him selfe through, and fell downe dead at his maisters feet. Which when *Antonius* saw; well done *Eros* (quoth he) thou hast aptly taught me by thine owne example, that thou couldest not finde in thy heart to do it, and therewith he thrust the sword into his owne belly, & cast him selfe vpon his bed."

38. Robert Allott, *Wits Theater of the little World* (London: I.R. for N.L., 1599), K6v–K7r: "Eros, the seruant of Antonius, hauing promised to kill his Maister when hee requested him, drew his sword, and holding it as if hee would haue killed him, turned his Maisters head aside, and thrust the sword into his own body. *Plutarch.*"

39. Brandon, *Tragicomoedi of the virtuous Octauia,* F4v.

40. Daniel, "The Tragedie of Cleopatra," in *Certaine Small Workes,* G3r–Lr, at G8r. The scene (Dircetus's account to Caesar of Antony's demise) is not in earlier editions of the play.

41. There is evidence that freedmen filled the posts of *procurator* (general manager, often involving several other functions), *lorarius* (overseer), *cocus* (cook), *structor* (headwaiter or meat-carver), *cubicularius* (keeper of the bedchamber), *nomenclator* (who reminded the master of his social duties), *pedisequi* (footmen), *pedagogi* and *grammatici,* doctors, clerical staff, including private secretary—(*a manu* or *amanuensis*), *anagostae* (readers), *librarii* (copyists), *librarioli* (bookmakers), *glutinatores* (roll-makers)—and, notably, letter carriers. A number of high-grade bureaucrats were also freedmen. See A. M. Duff, *Freedmen in the Early Roman Empire* (Oxford: Clarendon Press, 1928), 90–91; Susan Treggiari, *Roman Freedmen during the Late Republic* (1969; repr., Oxford: Clarendon Press, 2000), 68–81, 145–49; Aaron Kirschenbaum, *Sons, Slaves and Freedmen in Roman Commerce* (Jerusalem: Magnes Press/Washington, DC: Catholic University of America Press, 1987), 98, 127–40.

42. Plutarch, *Lives,* Kkkk 5r (933).

43. The Rhamnus moment had earlier been dramatized by Samuel Brandon:

> That *Antony,* with feare of treason mooued,
> Made *Ramnus* humbly sweare vpon his knee,

To strike that head, that head so much beloued,
From of his shoulders, when he once should see
Vneuitable danger, to lay holde,
Vpon himselfe . . .

Brandon does not, however, confer any status on Rhamnus. *Tragicomoedi of the virtuous Octauia,* B6r.

44. Barroll, *Politics, Plague, and Shakespeare's Theater,* 163.

45. Plutarch, *Lives,* Iiii 5r (921).

46. Ibid., Rrrrv (1010).

47. Barroll, *Politics, Plague, and Shakespeare's* Theater, 163n14.

48. Again, the passage is taken from North's Plutarch: "Whereupon *Antonius* caused him to be taken and well fauouredly whipped, and so sent him vnto *Cæsar:* and bad him tell him that he made him angrie with him, because he shewed himselfe proud and disdainefull towards him, and now specially, when he was easie to be angred, by reason of his present miserie. To be short, if this mislike thee (said he) thou hast *Hipparchus* one of my infranchised bondmen with thee: hang him if thou wilt, or whippe him at thy pleasure, that we may crie quittance." Plutarch, *Lives,* Llll 4v (944). The character is named Thyrsus in North's Plutarch.

49. Plutarch, *Lives,* Llll 3v (942).

50. Daniel, "Tragedie of Cleopatra," G8v.

51. Ibid., G8r.

52. Wilders makes the general point, but somehow misses the earliest introduction of the character: "This is Plutarch's first reference to Eros, but Shakespeare introduces him as early as 3.11.24 [*sic*—it's in 3.5] and gives his name repeatedly in 4.4." On 258, note on 4.14.63–68.

53. Plutarch, *Lives,* Llll 3v (942).

54. In Edward Phillips's *The New World of English Words, or, A General Dictionary* (London: E. Tyler for Nath. Brooke, 1658), Antony's Eros is the definition of the word: "*Eros,* the servant of *Mark Antony,* who killed himself, because he would not see his master fall" (O2v). Only in the third edition of 1671 is the usual definition also given: "*Eros,* according to the *Ethnic* Poets the God of love, who in Latin is commonly called *Cupido,* also the name of *Mark Anthony's* servant who killed himself, because he would not see his Master fall, the word in Greek signifying love." *The New World of Words, or a General English Dictionary . . . the third Edition* (London: Nath. Brook, 1671), R2r.

55. F1 reads *Enobarbus,* while F2 gives *Eros;* editors often now follow F1, but separate "*Enobarbus*" from the imperative "Dispatch," turning it into a reflective sigh.

56. Kirschenbaum, *Sons, Slaves and Freedmen,* 135–38.

57. Angel Day, *The English Secretorie* (London: Richard Jones, 1592), P4v. On the figure of the secretary, see Jonathan Goldberg, *Writing Matter: From the Hands of the English Renaissance* (Stanford, CA: Stanford University Press, 1990), 231–78; Richard Rambuss, *Spenser's Secret Career* (Cambridge: Cambridge University Press, 1993), 30–48; Alan Stewart, "The Early Modern Closet Discovered," *Representations* 50 (1995): 76–100.

58. Rambuss, *Spenser's Secret Career,* 43. Rambuss cites a passage from Day's *English Secretorie,* whose elusive and fraught syntax betrays the concerns about the master-secretary relationship:

> Much is the felicity that the Master or Lord receaueth euermore of such a seruant, in the charie affection and regard of whome affying himselfe assuredly, hee findeth he is not alone a commaunder of his outward actions, but the disposer of his very thoughtes, yea hee is the *Soueraigne* of all his desires, in whose bosome hee holdeth the respose of his safety to be far more precious, then either estate, liuing, or aduauncement, whereof men earthly minded are for the most part desirous.

As Rambuss comments of the line "yea hee is the *Soueraigne* of all his desires," "Is the antecedent of 'he' the master, making the antecedent of 'his' the secretary? Or is it just the opposite?" The effect is that "Day does not allow the possibility of grammatically distinguishing between the master and the secretary, thus undoing the familiar and socially grounding distinctions between commander and commanded, disposer and disposed, sovereign and servant." Day, *English Secretorie,* R4v; Rambuss, *Spenser's Secret Career,* 46.

59. Plutarch, *Lives,* Mmmmr (949).

60. Charnes, 144–45.

61. "Annos undeviginiti natus exercitum privato consilio et privata impensa comparavi, per quem rem publicam a dominatione factionis oppressam in libertatem vindicavi" ["At the age of nineteen on my own responsibility and at my own expense I raised an army, with which I successfully championed the liberty of the republic when it was oppressed by the tyranny of a faction"]. *Res gestae divi Augusti,* ed. Brunt and Moore, 18, 19.

62. Colie, "*Antony and Cleopatra:* The Significance of Style," 180.

63. See, for example, Phyllis Rackin, "Shakespeare's Boy Cleopatra, the Decorum of Nature, and the Golden World of Poetry," *PMLA* 87 (1972): 201–12; Jyotsna Singh, "Renaissance Antitheatricality, Antifeminism, and Shakespeare's *Antony and Cleopatra,*" *Renaissance Drama* n.s., 20 (1990): 99–121.

64. Phyllis Rackin makes a similar argument for Cleopatra's supremacy: "By admitting the reality of Rome, Shakespeare is able to celebrate the power of Egypt: by acknowledging the validity of the threat, he can demonstrate the special power that shows have to overcome the limitations of a reality that threatens to refute them." Rackin, "Shakespeare's Boy Cleopatra," 207.

"Try what repentance can": *Hamlet,* Confession, and the Extraction of Interiority

PAUL D. STEGNER

IN HIS FILM ADAPTATION of *Hamlet* (1996), Kenneth Branagh underscores the confessional themes present in the play by setting two scenes in a Roman Catholic confessional box. In the first scene, Polonius interrogates Ophelia about her relationship with Hamlet—an interaction that reinforces the common association of the confessional with an obsession over female sexuality. In the second scene, Hamlet listens to Claudius's penitential prayer and becomes, as Mark Thornton Burnett notes, "an unpunctual but unconsoling father confessor."[1] By depicting Hamlet and Claudius in the confessional box, Branagh introduces a conspicuous anachronism since the device was never used in early modern England and did not experience widespread use in Catholic countries on the Continent until the seventeenth century.[2]

Yet Branagh's inclusion of the confessional makes visually explicit a long-standing critical association of Hamlet with a father confessor that began as early as A. C. Bradley. Discussing Hamlet's exhortations to Gertrude to repent her sins, Bradley concludes, "No father-confessor could be more selflessly set upon his end of redeeming a fellow-creature from degradation, more stern or pitiless in denouncing the sin, or more eager to welcome the first token of repentance."[3] Subsequent literary critics have expanded Bradley's position by positing that Hamlet takes on the role of a "Black Priest," "priest/king," and "priest manqué."[4] When viewed in the context of Branagh's inclusion of the anachronistic confessional box, the critical interpretation of Hamlet as a father confessor calls attention to another more conspicuous and charged religious anachronism present in Shakespeare's play. More specifically, the rite of private or auricular confession to a priest permeates *Hamlet* even though the rite was no longer considered by the Church of England to be a sacrament after the promulgation of the Thirty-nine Articles and, while retained in an altered form in the *Book of Common Prayer,* it effectively ceased to be administered in early modern England. Like the connection of the Ghost with the Roman Catholic doctrine of purgatory, Shakespeare's concentration on private confession signals a type of doctrinal simultaneity in which vestiges of the traditional religion coexist, trouble, and even threaten to undermine the current belief system.

Recent critics have observed the importance of confessional rites in *Hamlet* and early modern drama, but they have generally followed Foucault's connection of the rite to the establishment of a power relationship between the individual and authority figure and the development of individual subjectivity.[5] Foucault's interpretation of confession is nevertheless historically tendentious because it neither attends to pre-Lateran confessional practices nor acknowledges the reality that most medieval and early modern Christians made poor confessants.[6] Given pastoral constraints, such as the annual Lenten rush for confession leading up to Easter, traditional confessional practices offered little opportunity for a sustained imposition of ecclesiastical control over private life or an extended exploration of interiority, except for a small minority of the faithful.[7] Furthermore, Foucault's argument regarding confession points to the practice's capacity for social discipline and control, but his grafting of the consolatory potential of confession onto a power relationship forecloses the capacity for the penitent's genuine belief in the assurance of forgiveness.[8]

Against the Foucauldian emphasis on the connection between confession and social control, in this essay I posit that confessional rituals and language point to the diffuse tension between traditional rituals and inwardness that persisted throughout the early modern period and continued to be enacted on the English stage. In what follows, I demonstrate that *Hamlet* engages the changes in confessional practices by presenting both Catholic and Protestant confessional rites as offering the promise of consolation and reconciliation and indicating that these promises cannot be realized in the theological world of the play. I first examine the shifts in penitential practices during the period and the ways in which Hamlet's adoption of the role of confessor engages the ongoing theological and theatrical problem of determining the authenticity of another's confession. I then turn to consider how Hamlet's role as confessor complements his role as avenger and guides his attempts to negotiate the inherent tensions between inward thoughts and outward actions. Hamlet adopts and maintains the role of father confessor as part of an effort to validate his obligation to avenge the crimes against his father and himself.

Ritual Confession and the Problem of Assurance in Early Modern England

The presence of private or auricular confession and confessional language in *Hamlet* in many ways reflects the general trend on the early modern stage. The traditional rite appeared with noticeable regularity in almost every dramatic genre, ranging from early modern history plays (Peele's *Edward I* and Shakespeare's *Henry VIII*) to comedies and tragedies set in Catholic countries (*Measure for Measure, Romeo and Juliet, Much Ado About Nothing,* and Ford's *'Tis Pity She's a Whore*) to anti-Catholic polemical dramas (Bale's *King Johan,* Marlowe's *Jew of Malta,* Webster's *The Duchess of Malfi,* and Middleton's *A Game at Chess*). Either in terms of England's religious past or contemporary examples on the Continent, the connection between ritual confession and Roman Catholicism constitutes the common theme in the majority of early modern dramatic representations of the rite. The presence of the sacrament of confession in these plays often signals religious, historical, and social differences between Protestant England and Catholic countries. In *Hamlet,* however, Shakespeare depicts remnants of traditional confessional rites in a Protestant context by evoking Lutheran Wittenberg.[9] The representation of confession in the play thus corresponds to developments in penitential practices that occurred during the English Reformation: on the one hand, a general shift away from sacramental auricular confession toward an unmediated, faith-centered confession to God, but, on the other, a retention of remnants of traditional confessional practices.

Early modern editions of the *Book of Common Prayer* retained a form of auricular, private confession and absolution in "The Order for the visitacion of the Sycke," which directed the priest to evoke the power to absolve sins granted to the Church by Christ and state: "I absolve the from al thy sinnes, in the name of the father, and of the sonne, and of the holy gost. Ame[n]."[10] Furthermore, in "The order for the administration of the Lordes Supper, or holy Communion" the Prayer Book instructs ministers to exhort those who cannot "quiet [their] own conscience, but requireth further comfort of counsel" to "come to me, or some other discrete and learned Minister of Gods woorde, and open his griefe, that he may receiue suche ghostly counsaile, aduice, and comfort, as his conscience may be relieued."[11] In contrast with the medieval church's requirement of annual auricular confession, the rite functioned as an exceptional means for achieving consolation and assurance in the early modern Church of England. Further, the Established Church rejected the medieval understanding of the priestly absolution as effecting forgiveness "from the actual performance of the sacrament itself."[12] It instructed instead, as Richard Hooker explains, that "private ministeriall absolution butt declare remission of sins."[13] Except for a few notable examples, after the institution of the Prayer Book, the practice consequently all but disappeared in the life of the Established Church and was commonly associated with post-Tridentine Roman Catholicism.[14]

The figure of the father confessor, too, became a vestigial reminder of the traditional religion. English Protestants frequently associated the office with historical and contemporary Roman Catholic intrusions into individual consciences and impingements on Christian liberty. Traditionally, the Church grounded its authority over penitents in the power of keys that Christ grants to Peter: "And I wil giue vnto thee the keyes of the kingdome of heauen, and whatsoeuer thou shalt binde vpon earth shall be bound in heauen: and whatsoeuer thou shalt lose on earth, shal be losed in heauen" (Matthew 16:19, Geneva Version). During the Reformation, however, the power of the keys came to symbolize the abuses of the medieval church. Calvin's description of Roman Catholic confession as a "ruinous procedure . . . [by which] the souls of those who were affected with some sense of God have been most cruelly racked" reflects many early modern English theological and theatrical treatments of the rite.[15] Yet after the Reformation the position of confessor to the royal household and several penitentiary offices were retained, such as one held by Lancelot Andrewes at St. Paul's.[16] The underlying shifts in the penitential system nevertheless separated such offices from their sacramental beginnings and, like the diminution of the rite of private confession in the Prayer Book, they functioned as confessional institutions only in an attenuated sense.

This transformation of penitential practices reoriented the ways in which Christians achieved assurance of the forgiveness of their sins and reconciliation with God. With the English Church's move away from private confession, self-examination became the usual method for discovering and confessing sins and achieving reconciliation. This transformation protected the liberty of the individual conscience against perceived priestly intrusions and excessive anxiety in the penitential process. Alan Sinfield argues that the change from ritual confession to interior self-examination increased, rather than diminished, the anxiety of the faithful: "Protestant self-examination is in a way confession, but it shifts the whole business inside the consciousness. . . . This made the whole process more manipulable, for since there was no external resistance there could also be no external reassurance."[17] This description creates the impression that Luther's famous, though atypical, anxieties surrounding the sacrament of penance extended into and increased in the practice of private introspection.[18] Yet Sinfield's observation regarding the transformation of confession rightfully advances the degree to which the practice became internalized and situated within individual consciences. William Perkins's development of a form of English Protestant casuistry, which emphasized the laity's self-application of cases of conscience rather than priestly administration, provides further evidence for this confessional shift.[19]

The Protestant internalization of confession reflects the Christian tradition's privileging of interiority rather than exteriority in matters of faith because of the potential for outward dissimulation that originates as early as Christ's warning against the "hypocrisie and iniquitie" of the Scribes and Pharisees whose virtues exist only in outward appearance (Matthew 23:28, Geneva Version). "An Homilie of Repentaunce and of true reconciliation vnto God," the last sermon contained in the *Second Book of Homilies* (1562), continues this tradition by connecting exterior devotion to the corruption of the Roman Catholic sacrament of confession:

> Therefore they that teache repentunce without a liuely faythe in our Sauiour Jesu Christ, doo teache none other, but Judas repentaunce, as all the scholemen do, whiche do onlye allowe these three partes of Repentaunce: the contrition of the hart, the confession of the mouth, and the satisfaction of the worke. But all of these things we fynde in Judas repentaunce, whiche in outeward appearaunce, did farre excede and passe the repentaunce of Peter.[20]

The homily instructs that the exteriors should be distrusted, that "liuely faythe" is the true measure for gauging repentance, and that anyone who teaches "repentaunce without Christ . . . doe onlye teache Cains or Judas repentaunce."[21] In so doing, the homily cautions against what St. Augustine calls the "deceptive resemblance" between a virtuous appearance and inward vice.[22] To overcome the limitations of exteriors, the homily instructs that, like Peter, true penitents "must be cleane altered and chaunged, they must become newe creatures, they must be no more the same that they were before."[23] True repentance or *metanoia* consists solely of an interior change that depends on faith rather than exteriors.

This conception of interiority, particularly in terms of conscience and repentance, follows the orthodox interpretation regarding the inscrutability of the divine will. To presume the salvation or damnation of another would impinge on God's special providence and mercy. Nathaniel Woodes's *Conflict of Conscience* (1581), a dramatic rendering of the spiritual struggle and mysterious death of the Italian lawyer Francis Spira (Francesco Spiera) in 1548, contains variant conclusions that advance the uncertainty surrounding Spira's famous renunciation of Protestantism: one in which the protagonist is damned, the other in which he is granted forgiveness. In the case of the controversial death of Spira, however, early modern writers argued for and against his damnation, despite the accepted theological teaching regarding the impossibility of knowing the mind of God.[24] These attempts to interpret Spira's death point to early modern assumptions regarding the connection between interiority and exteriority.[25] Indeed, although John Foxe admits in the case of Sir James Hale, a Protestant who committed suicide, that "certain divines" doubted "whether he were reprobate or saved," Foxe nevertheless readily attributes signs of grace to the martyrdoms of Thomas Cranmer and other Protestants and reprobation to the deaths of Roman Catholics in *Acts and Monuments*.[26] In the search for self-assurance and assurance of another's spiritual state, the orthodox reservation of determining inward faith became secondary to practical theological, social, and political concerns.

The emphasis during the early modern period on confessions and recantations during public executions further signals the functional importance of repentance and confession.[27] Ecclesiastical and magisterial recourse to torture in order to secure confessions offers one example of the putative authority granted to confession.[28] Cranmer's initial recantation to the Marian authorities and his subsequent disavowal of it on the day of his execution stand as a prominent example for demonstrating not only the imputed and expected veracity of confession, but also the contested nature of its reception.[29] The stakes for both Catholics and Protestants were high: the Marian authorities celebrated Cranmer's rejection of Protestantism and return to Catholicism as a blow against the Protestant cause in England; Protestants trumpeted his actions during his final day as evidence of his adherence to the true faith. However, when confronted by Fray Juan de Villagarcia, Regius Professor of Theology at Oxford and the official who succeeded in obtaining Cranmer's recantation, that he received the sacrament of penance before his execution, Cranmer asks, "What if the confession is no good?"[30] In so doing, Cranmer questions the ability of the authorities to access his interiority and depends instead on his actions during his death as the finis coronat opus.[31] Catholic and Protestant accounts of his death, *Bishop Cranmer's Recantacyons* (attributed to Nicholas Harpsfield, ca. 1556) and John Foxe's *Acts and Monuments* (1563, reprinted in 1570, 1576, 1583), are surprisingly similar in describing the events of his death, but they differ widely in their interpretations.[32] For Catholics, Cranmer relapsed into Protestant heresy; for Protestants, he died a martyr of the true faith. Undergirding each position is the conviction that Cranmer's true beliefs and, by extension, the true Christian faith can be adduced from his final confession.[33] The staging and representation of scaffold confessions in turn signals a more generalized confessional phenomenon in early modern England: the semiotic incompleteness of confession necessitates some form of a public account or, in Hamlet's terms, "story" to situate and interpret interior beliefs and motivations (5.2.354).[34]

Instead of remaining hidden in the conscience, confession in early modern England functioned as an inward spiritual change that invited a social component to evince its authenticity in order to satisfy both the individual and the community of his or her spiritual state. The assurance of an effective confession thus contains two performances: an inward spiritual performance accessible only to the individual and God, and an outward social performance intended to reassure both the individual and others in order to facilitate a reintegration of the penitent into the community.[35] The scriptural account of Christ's healing of the leper advances the social performance of confession by concluding with Christ's command: "Go, *sayeth he,* and shew thy selfe to the Priest, and offer for

thy clensing, as Moses hathe commanded, for a witnes vnto them"
(Luke 5:14, Geneva Version). In the medieval administration of confession, penitents could ideally find inward assurance of the effectiveness of their spiritual performance of confession in its ritual
form, especially through the priest's speaking of the rite of absolution and laying on of hands, and then demonstrate their repentance
through the social performance of penance or satisfaction.[36] The
English Reformation's reorientation of traditional penitential practice resulted in a shift from private to public ritual. As such, in the
early modern Church of England, assurance of sins came to be situated in the general absolution given during the liturgy, except in
special cases of scrupulosity or doubt.

Confession thus became an intensely personal spiritual performance because, under ordinary circumstances, only the individual
rather than a confessor needed to determine whether or not his or
her inward penitence was authentic.[37] Hence Perkins's claim that
"it is a grace peculiar to the man Elect, to trie himselfe whether he
be in the estate of grace or not" indicates that self-assurance begins
and concludes in the individual conscience.[38] However, confession
continued to have a socially performative dimension because it depended on an individual's participation in common worship and
reception of the Eucharist.[39] The required ritual and social performance of confession in the Church of England reveals continuity between traditional and reformed penitential practices. Private
confession and the office of father confessor were anachronisms
that became more diffused and "internalised fully" by the middle
of the seventeenth century.[40] At the turn of the seventeenth century,
however, the reemergence of debates surrounding their place in the
Established Church and their ongoing presence on the stage indicates that they remained in transition.[41] In the muddied theological
world of *Hamlet,* Shakespeare offers a sustained engagement of
these shifts in penitential practices.[42]

Hamlet as Avenger and Father Confessor

Shakespeare represents the transitional state of ritual confession
through the Ghost of King Hamlet's contradictory positions on the
rite. At the opening of the play, the Ghost avers that he would not
suffer supernatural torments in his "prison-house" if his last rites,

including final confession (i.e., "disappointed"), could have been completed satisfactorily:

> Cut off even in the blossoms of my sin,
> Unhousel'd, disappointed, unanel'd,
> No reck'ning made, but sent to my account
> With all my imperfections on my head.[43]

(1.5.76–79)

These remarks signal the Ghost's faith in the efficacy of the traditional sacramental system.[44] Yet in *Hamlet* only vestiges of it remain, and they are always relegated to the background, to a state of unrealized possibility. In act 5, the Doctor of Divinity similarly implies the efficacy of ritual through his prohibition of singing a "requiem" at Ophelia's funeral lest "[w]e should profane the service of the dead," but the results of the ritual are left to speculation (5.1.229–30). In addition, the Ghost intimates that a transformation of confession has occurred when he commands Hamlet to "[l]eave her [Gertrude] to heaven, / And to those thorns that in her bosom lodge / To prick and sting her" (1.5.86–88). Instead of emphasizing penitential rituals, the Ghost elevates unmediated, interior repentance and implicitly repudiates the rituals that he considered necessary for his salvation. The Ghost holds these contradictory positions in tension without ever reconciling them. This suspension indicates that Shakespeare's Denmark experiences a type of doctrinal simultaneity in which competing theological beliefs coexist.

Like his father, Hamlet reveals a striking degree of doctrinal heterogeneity. As a student at the University of Wittenberg, he is closely connected with the Lutheran rejection of the dominical status of the sacrament of penance.[45] For Roland Mushat Frye, "The Prince 'smites' his mother in the ways that might be expected of one who was educated at Wittenberg," that is, as part of the Protestant understanding of the "priesthood of all believers."[46] Yet Hamlet's emphasis on auricular confession contradicts the Reformation context of the play. Even though Hamlet reveals a general Christian desire to bring his mother to repentance, I would argue that he assumes the role of father confessor intent on extracting the consciences of others in order to assure himself not only of their guilt or innocence, but also to achieve support in his role as avenger. Hamlet's adoption of the role of father confessor becomes a subversive action that realizes all of the Protestant concerns about Roman Catholic intrusions of confessors into individual consciences and the *arcana imperii* of royal authority, demonstrated with striking effect in Hamlet's eavesdropping on Claudius's private confession to God. At the same time, this role establishes a means to negotiate the prison of Denmark. Father confessor and avenger merge into mutually constitutive roles that allow Hamlet to penetrate through the network of secrets, lies, and half-truths that circulate in Claudius's court. And cross-fertilization occurs between these roles, for the avenger's aim to fulfill the Ghost's "dread command" collapses into the confessor's exercise of binding and loosing of sins (3.4.109). For Hamlet, the scriptural validation of priestly authority over the spiritual states of others to which he lays claim throughout the play becomes radically literalized and, in the process, destabilized when yoked into the service of revenge.

Hamlet's fulfillment of his dual role as father confessor and avenger depends on the occlusion of his own interiority until he can successfully extract the conscience of others. When discussing his mournful appearance and behavior with Gertrude, he states:

> Seems, madam? Nay, it is. I know not "seems."
> 'Tis not alone my inky cloak, good mother,
> Nor customary suits of solemn black,
> Nor windy suspiration of forc'd breath,
> No, nor the fruitful river in the eye,
> Nor the dejected haviour of the visage,
> Together with all forms, moods, shapes of grief,
> That can denote me truly. These indeed seem,
> For they are actions that a man might play,
> But I have that within which passes show,
> These but the trappings and suits of woe.
>
> (1.2.76–86)

Hamlet's distinction between outward seeming ("trappings and suits of woe") and inward being ("within which passes show") signals the limitations of external appearances to convey interior thoughts and thereby injects suspicion into the direct correspondence between the visible signs and interior disposition. The "inky cloak" reflects Hamlet's internal state and suggests a form of inexpressible sadness over his father's death, but the limitations of these outward appearances to "denote me truly" evinces the existence of a disjunction between them. Put differently, Hamlet intimates that only he possesses access to the fullness of his interiority within, and suggests that it, though remaining "unspeakable" in its entirety, can be willfully revealed or concealed.[47] The language of the theater accordingly indicates the artificiality and limitations of that which can be shown and Hamlet's presumption of the capacity to manipulate those "actions that a man might play." His revelation to Horatio and Marcellus that he intends to "put an antic disposi- tion on" manifests his confidence in being able to manipulate exte- riors and mask his true motives (1.5.180). Hamlet's insistence that his companions do not reveal "aught of me" implies that he consid- ers the only possibility for revealing the inauthentic nature of his madness comes from without (1.5.187). For Hamlet, his "mind's eye" functions as an interior space over which he believes that he exercises dominion and controls access (1.2.185). Nevertheless, at the conclusion of his first soliloquy, "But break my heart, for I must hold my tongue," Hamlet reveals that inward and outward exist in a tension in which the heart desires to be revealed, but must be held in check by the tongue (1.2.159).[48] Significantly, Hamlet most fre- quently identifies this resistant, sometimes volatile interiority with conscience and employs the term not only to refer to a set of divine moral imperatives (as in the case with the prohibition against sui- cide), but also to function as a semiotic passkey to that within which passes show.

Through speech as well as voluntary and involuntary actions, Hamlet affirms that the consciences of others can be accessible if properly interpreted, extracted, or triggered. In his initial encoun- ter with Rosencrantz and Guildenstern, he declares his suspicions about friendship being the purpose of their visit: "Anything but to th' purpose. You were sent for, and there is a kind of confession in your looks, which your modesties have not craft enough to colour. I know the good King and Queen have sent for you" (2.2.278–81). Rosencrantz and Guildenstern's "guileless revelation of some oc- culted guilt" contrasts them with Hamlet's theatricality, but it also reveals Hamlet's assurance in his abilities to bridge the divide be- tween nonverbal confession and internal motivations.[49] He further displays this assurance by supplying the reason for which his childhood companions were summoned, once Guildenstern con- fesses, "My lord, we were sent for" (2.2.292). Hamlet's behavior during this encounter implies that he distinguishes his own in- wardness from nontheatrical individuals who cannot hide their consciences. Indeed, he confronts Guildenstern with attempting to "pluck out the heart of my mystery" and then stymies any efforts to gain access into his interiority: "Call me what instrument you will, though you fret me, you cannot play upon me" (3.2.356–63). Hamlet is aware of Claudius and others' capacity for dissimulation, explaining "one may smile, and smile, and be a villain—/ At least I am sure that it may be so in Denmark," but he identifies himself as the only one capable of preventing an unwanted revelation of his true state (1.5.108–9). Hamlet remains confident that even Claudius's interiority can be extracted once the appropriate external device triggers a verbal or nonverbal confession. He accordingly designs *The Mousetrap* to "catch the conscience of the King" (2.2.601) and declares that his uncle's conscience will be outwardly detectable: "I'll observe his looks; / I'll tent him to the quick. If a do blench, / I know my course" (2.2.592–94).

Hamlet does not act alone in this conviction, for Claudius, Rosencrantz, Polonius, and Guildenstern attempt to determine the motives for Hamlet's antic disposition. Claudius may initially gesture toward the direct correspondence between inward and outward by declaring that "Hamlet's transformation" indicates that "nor th' exterior nor the inward man / Resembles that it was" (2.2.5–7). But his employment of Rosencrantz and Guildenstern to discover "aught to us unknown" about Hamlet's antic behavior and belief that it may be "open'd" displays his suspicions regarding the potential for separating inward motives and outward appearance (2.2.17–18). In response to Claudius's frustration over their failure to determine the reason for Hamlet's aberrant behavior, moreover, Rosencrantz and Guildenstern similarly reply:

> *Ros.* He does confess he feels himself distracted,
> But from what cause a will by no means speak.
> *Guil.* Nor do we find him forward to be sounded,
> But with a crafty madness keeps aloof
> When we would bring him on to some confession
> Of his true state.   .
>
>   (3.1.5–10)

The description of Hamlet's disposition as "crafty madness" suggests Guildenstern's perception of what Hamlet later reveals to Gertrude in the closet scene, that is, "I essentially am not in madness, / But mad in craft" (3.4.189–90). By developing Rosencrantz's language of confession, Guildenstern indicates his awareness that present beneath Hamlet's initial confession of being distracted is a "true state" that could be uncovered if he could penetrate through external posturing. Even though Hamlet claims that his interiority cannot be expressed or accessed beneath its seeming exterior, his reference to its very existence in the opening act presupposes the potential for discovery and propels attempts to uncover the secrets that continually circulate throughout Claudius's Denmark.[50]

Hamlet, however, stands apart in the play because he alone desires to uncover and judge the conscience of others. Claudius may obsess over discovering the cause of Hamlet's antic disposition, but his concerns are grounded in self-interested, political pragmatism and contain no concern over the prince's spiritual state. Hamlet adopts the role of father confessor because his obligation to revenge his father's murder depends on verifying the truth of the Ghost's story. Moreover, Claudius provides Hamlet with a predetermined role for enacting revenge by assuming the part of a perverse father confessor.[51] Claudius's penetration of the orchard and poisoning of the king through "the porches of [his] ears" functions as an inverted image of auricular confession that evokes Reformation anti-Catholic polemic against the malign effects of "confession in the eare" (1.5.63).[52] While Claudius may have bound King Hamlet to a purgatorial existence "[t]ill the foul crimes done in [his] days of nature / Are burnt and purg'd away" (1.5.12–13), political and romantic motivations fueled the murder. For Hamlet, however, the confessional resonances of Claudius's poisoning of the king initiate a role to be emulated and imitated.[53] Consequently, Hamlet seeks to overgo Claudius by transposing the confessorial role from the secular to the spiritual, securing his uncle's damnation. Hence Hamlet spares Claudius's life in the prayer scene not because of the tension between Christian and vengeful impulses, but rather because of the spiritual imperative governing his conception of revenge. Unlike Laertes, who declares his willingness "[t]o cut his [Hamlet's] throat i'th' church" (4.7.125) and thereby implies that satisfaction can be accomplished in natural actions, Hamlet considers damnation necessary for satisfying the Ghost's dread command, for to slay his uncle in penitential prayer would be "hire and salary, not revenge" (3.3.79). Consequently, he aims to catch the conscience of the king in the sense not only of extracting his interior conscience, but also of trapping it in a state of sin.

In so doing, Hamlet rightly perceives Claudius's reaction to *The Mousetrap* as evidence of guilt, but wrongly interprets the sincerity of his uncle's repentance in the famous failed prayer scene. In

many ways, the private setting of the scene gestures toward the relationship between Claudius's interior and exterior state. Claudius
believes himself to be alone during his penitential prayer, and
Hamlet assumes that his uncle remains unaware of his presence.
For Hamlet, private penitential prayer would thus avoid the necessary cautions regarding the equivocations and dissimulations present in public speech. Yet Shakespeare manifests the limitations of
Hamlet's faith in the relationship between interior and exterior
through the dramatic timing of the scene: Hamlet does not overhear
Claudius's mental wrangling over his inability to repent, but only
him "a-praying"; and Claudius remains unaware of Hamlet's presence and unknowingly saves his own life by attempting to repent
sincerely (3.3.73). Given Claudius's remark that "[m]y words fly up,"
he presumably prays audibly rather than silently (3.3.97). Hamlet
therefore bases his judgment that his uncle is "in the purging of his
soul" (3.3.85) and "is fit and season'd for his passage" (3.3.86) on,
as Claudius reveals after Hamlet exits, "[w]ords without thoughts"
(3.3.98). Hamlet thus demonstrates a hermeneutic naïveté by accepting Claudius's penitential prayer as satisfactory because of his awareness of his uncle's characteristic adeptness at concealment and
manipulation. Hamlet may suspect Claudius's insincerity elsewhere,
but identifies private penitential prayer as a privileged discourse in
which words and intentions exist in direct correspondence. If the absence of the content of the prayer in printed editions of the play corresponds to its formulaic nature or its ambiguity (Claudius's prayer
was meant to be spoken aloud but unintelligible to the audience) onstage, it reinforces the rashness of Hamlet's willingness to overlook
the possibility of Claudius's inability to repent.

Claudius's prayer thus becomes a lacuna into which Hamlet
reads his uncle's successful repentance in terms of Protestant penitential practices.[54] In accepting Claudius's prayer as authentic, he
demonstrates his assumptions regarding the efficacy of unmediated
penitence, an attitude germane to his studies at Wittenberg. He believes that Claudius is able to and does receive forgiveness for the
murder of King Hamlet and Gertrude through *metanoia*. According
to Anthony Low, Hamlet's perspective on repentance differs from
that of Claudius, who identifies penitence with the traditional confessional rite: "Because he belongs to the older generation of King
Hamlet, Claudius understands that if only he were to consent to
give up his ill-gotten gains—his queen and his kingdom—he could
repent, confess his sins, and receive absolution. . . . In contrast,

Hamlet and Horatio, although their spiritual state is not depraved like Claudius's, have forgotten what Claudius knows but cannot put to use."[55] Yet Claudius never refers to ritual in the prayer scene; on the contrary, when Claudius debates, "Try what repentance can. What can it not? / Yet what can it, when one can not repent?" the language of ritual present in the Ghost of King Hamlet's speech is absent (3.3.65–66). Claudius may display a remnant of traditional beliefs in beseeching angels for help ("Help, angels!"), but he attempts to offer a satisfactory penitential prayer rather than seek a priestly mediator (3.3.69). By refraining from killing Claudius, Hamlet simultaneously reveals a Protestant belief in the sufficiency of private repentance and a traditional conception of the spiritual powers conferred on priests in the sacrament of confession through his evocation of the priestly role of binding sins.

Under the burden of the Ghost's dread command, however, Hamlet departs from the role of a conventional Christian father confessor because the revenge narrative leads him to base his determination of the moral state of others not on divine law, but on his conscience's judgment of their involvement in King Hamlet's murder.[56] Once he discovers Claudius's intent to kill him, he argues that his revenge against Claudius is supported by "perfect conscience" (5.2.67).[57] Furthermore, Hamlet condemns those whom he deems supporters of Claudius because they would prevent him from enacting vengeance. Hence, without compunction, Hamlet dispatches Rosencrantz and Guildenstern to their death "[n]ot shriving time allow'd" because he judges them as Claudius's agents and thus implicated in his uncle's crimes (5.2.47): "They are not near my conscience, their defeat / Does by their own insinuation grow" (5.2.58–59). Conscience functions for Hamlet as the central point of reference for determining the sinfulness or virtue of others through the position as father confessor that in turn justifies his actions as an avenger.

The most explicit association of Hamlet with a father confessor occurs in the closet scene with Gertrude. His determination to confront his mother with her sins in many ways corresponds to the traditional instilling of shame in an unrepentant sinner. Further, the Ghost commands Hamlet to "step between her and her fighting soul . . . Speak to her," and thereby take on the part of a spiritual mediator (3.4.113–15). The similarities between Hamlet's treatment of Gertrude and the sacrament of confession lead Harry Morris to conclude that Hamlet "uses directly the terms of the sacrament: 'Confess yourself to heaven [confession], / Repent what's past [contrition], avoid what is to come [satisfaction]'" (3.4.151–52).[58] Yet Hamlet's remark, "And when you are desirous to be blest, / I'll blessing beg of you," suggests not only a deferral of the rite of absolution, but also an indeterminacy regarding the agency of who will bless (that is, absolve) Gertrude (3.4.173–74). The question of whether he means himself, God, or even a minister remains unclear, and thus registers the theological uncertainties that govern the world of the play. In this sense, Hamlet's role as avenger supports his role as father confessor insofar as it confirms his ability to bind his victims to damnation. However, this same conviction does not transfer to securing the forgiveness of others. Like the Ghost, then, Hamlet holds competing doctrines regarding repentance in a suspension that renders them already deferred and lacking resolution. Yet despite the incompleteness of Gertrude's repentance, Hamlet accepts her exclamation of contrition, "thou has cleft my heart in twain" (3.4.158), and the fact that he never again mentions Gertrude's incestuous relationship with Claudius—even at her death—suggests his confidence that she has "[a]ssume[d] a virtue" and avoided further sexual relations (3.4.162).[59] Hamlet's faith in the success of Gertrude's repentance therefore reinforces his role as an avenger because it redresses Claudius's usurpation of the royal marriage by fulfilling the Ghost's command to "[l]et not the royal bed of Denmark be / A couch for luxury and damned incest" (1.5.82–83).

By framing the closet scene with the death of Polonius and the removal of his body offstage, though, Shakespeare points to the tensions caused by Hamlet's roles as father confessor and avenger. After mistakenly killing Polonius, Hamlet initially calls him a "wretched, rash, intruding fool, farewell. / I took thee for thy better" and treats his death as completely justifiable (3.4.31–32). But Hamlet then takes responsibility for the killing, "I do repent," only to abandon this position and again attempt to exculpate himself by imputing responsibility to his role as a revenger: "but heaven hath pleas'd it so / To punish me with this and this with me, / That I must be their scourge and minister" (3.4.175–77).[60] By further shifting from assuming of culpability (cf. 3.4.178–79) to mistreating Polonius's corpse (cf. 3.4.214) to jocularly referring to Polonius's spiritual fate (cf. 4.3.19–25), Hamlet manifests his ongoing conflict of conscience. These shifts reflect the tensions inherent in his theatrical roles as avenger and father confessor, for the impulse to revenge his father's murder overrides his Christian concern for repentance. The killing of Polonius in fact unwittingly condemns Hamlet to the spiritual irresolution that marked his father's death. In response, Hamlet capitulates to ignorance and the indecipherability of Polonius's spiritual status by declaring him "now most still, most secret, and most grave" (3.4.216)—language that parallels his description of his father: "And how his [King Hamlet's] audit stands who knows save heaven?" (3.3.82). For Hamlet, then, death forecloses access to interiority. This confrontation with the uncertainties surrounding Polonius's death pressures Hamlet to recognize that in the roles as both father confessor and avenger his conscience must couple oppositional impulses that cannot be reconciled, except through "answer[ing] well / The death I gave him" with a type of atonement through death (3.4.178–79).

Instead of withdrawing from his earlier confidence regarding his capacity to exact vengeance on those he considers damnable, however, Hamlet responds to Polonius's death in the final act of the play by reinforcing his role as an avenger and father confessor. In the final act, Hamlet may accept the orthodox Christian position on the inscrutability of the "special providence" of God; but, like his early modern contemporaries, he acts with assurance regarding the damnation and salvation of those around him based on external evidence (5.2.215–16). Indeed, once Laertes declares, "The King—the King's to blame" (5.2.326), Hamlet wounds Claudius and proclaims with certainty his uncle to be a "damned Dane" at the moment of death (5.2.330). Laertes' revelation of Claudius's involvement in poisoning Gertrude and Hamlet provides the prince with the opportunity for confirming his uncle's damnable state—the very opportunity frustrated by his misreading of Claudius's penitential prayer. Hamlet momentarily experiences self-assurance in his role as an avenger through the outward assurance of Laertes and, moreover, fulfills his role as father confessor by "exchang[ing] forgiveness" with Laertes through a type of mutual absolution:

> *Laer.* Mine and my father's death come not upon thee,
> Nor mine on me!
> *Ham.* Heaven make thee free of it! I follow thee.
>
> (5.2.334–37)

This interchange places Hamlet in the role of father confessor loosening Laertes' sins through a deathbed absolution. Yet Hamlet's statement, "I follow thee," indicates that he still does not consider himself free from the tension inherent in these roles and his crimes because he uses the imperative form of "follow" at the moment of Claudius's death, exclaiming, "Follow my mother!" (5.2.332). In this context, the term most likely refers to death rather than a spiritual state. In contrast with Laertes' apparent acceptance of Hamlet's absolution, moreover, Hamlet does not apply Laertes' absolution to himself, but only requests that "Heaven make thee free of it!" By denying the adequacy of his satisfaction for Polonius's death and maintaining the inexpressibility of his interiority, Hamlet reconciles himself to the incompleteness of his confession and the impossibility of resolution: "Had I but the time—as this fell sergeant Death, / Is strict in his arrest—O, I could tell you / But let it be" (5.2.341–43). In this transition from confessor to confessant, Hamlet gestures at the possibility of explaining his part in "this chance" and "this act," but this revelation remains deferred and unresolved (5.2.339–40). Hamlet's "true story," as Michael Neill observes, is "tantalizingly glimpsed only as Hamlet himself is about to enter the domain of the inexpressible."[61] The disjunction between Hamlet's presentation of the inscrutability of his interiority and his attempts to extract the interiority of others signals the underlying tension between Christian repentance and revenge tragedy.

By excluding others from his true inward state, Hamlet succeeds in exacting his revenge and satisfying the Ghost's command, but his retreat into silence leaves his own spiritual state uncertain. His final confessional speech offers the promise of complete revelation, but remains beyond reach, finding resolution only in the substitution of his "wounded name" (5.2.349) for his impenetrable identity and the circulation of Horatio's posthumous presentation of Hamlet's "story" (5.2.354). Hamlet's "dying voice" (5.2.361), which concentrates on Fortinbras's election to the throne, withdraws his interiority behind the veil of death, concluding his final speech with "the rest is silence" (5.2.363). This turn toward posthumous fame and the political future of Denmark evinces Hamlet's conviction regarding the impossibility of fully expressing his own story through a deathbed confession. Moreover, for Hamlet, the problem of his confession is identical to the problem of his inwardness: he professes the belief that neither can be expressed in its entirety. At the same time, this turn demonstrates Hamlet's deathbed attempt to overwrite the silence of interiority and death through the translation of his story into public narrative. Horatio's prayer that "flights of angels sing thee to thy rest," drawn from the Catholic prayer for the dead *In paradisum de deducant te angeli,* begins this process by joining Hamlet's spiritual state to the traditional ritual system espoused by his father's ghost (5.2.365). And Fortinbras's declaration of Hamlet's fortitude as a soldier and proclamation to let the "rite of war / Speak loudly for him" further indicates the transformation of Hamlet's inexpressible interiority to a comprehensible public figure (5.2.404–5).

Yet given the ineffective coexistence of conflicting theological rituals and doctrines in the world of the play, this announced presentation of Hamlet leaves the audience doubtful if not "unsatisfied" (5.2.345). Between Hamlet's inwardness and Horatio and Fortinbras's public narrative exists a breach that cannot be filled through a return to the traditional rites of, to use Catherine Belsey's terminology, "a much older cosmos."[62] Indeed, the different doctrines coexisting in the play effectually cancel each other out, for the only rituals presented in the action of the play are, in the words of Laertes, "maimed," either through insincerity (Claudius's penitential prayer), deferral (Gertrude's repentance), doubt (Ophelia's death), or parodic inversion (Eucharistic themes in the final act) (5.1.212).[63] The frequent recourse to these traditional rituals manifests the vestigial traces of their former function in society. Nevertheless, the ambiguity, failure, or deferral of resolution promised in both the traditional sacrament of confession and the Protestant confessional forms indicate that they have become ineffectual in the larger social, political, and theological upheavals affecting Hamlet's Denmark. As Steven Mullaney observes, "Whether sacred or secular, ritual relies upon and produces a certain consensus of belief; although highly dramaturgical, it functions effectively only in a relatively stable hierarchical society."[64] However, the only stability present in *Hamlet* exists in its ritual past, the world of sacraments and confessors, or its martial future, a world of the avenger-warrior Fortinbras—two worlds in which Hamlet can participate, but cannot inhabit fully.

By situating *Hamlet* in the context of Reformation Wittenberg, Shakespeare deploys the space of the theater to signal the spiritual and emotional repercussions resulting from the Church of England's reorientation of the traditional means for achieving assurance and consolation. Theatrical space intensifies rather than resolves the difficulties of determining inward and outward sincerity, for it accentuates the limited points of access into the conscience through a fundamental reliance on visual and auditory externals. Even the audience, who occupies a privileged perspective by witnessing the performance in its entirety, remains dependent upon what is revealed and concealed on- and offstage. Shakespeare's presentation in the play of the hazards of misinterpretation thus advance the inherent risks of determining another's conscience and suggest the possibility of misreading signs of one's own salvation or damnation. Consequently, Shakespeare withholds the anticipated resolution promised by traditional and Protestant confessional acts to illustrate that they could not guarantee assurance and consolation in Wittenberg, in England's Catholic past, or in the seventeenth-century Established Church.

Notes

I wish to thank Patrick Cheney, David Scott Kastan, Garrett Sullivan, and Jonathan Gil Harris for their generous suggestions on various revisions of this essay.

1. Mark Thornton Burnett, "'We are the makers of manners': The Branagh Phenomenon," in *Shakespeare after Mass Media,* ed. Richard Burt, 88 (New York: Palgrave, 2002).

2. Henry Charles Lea, *A History of Auricular Confession and Indulgences in the Latin Church,* 3 vols. (London, 1896), 1:395–96.

3. A. C. Bradley, *Shakespearean Tragedy: Lectures on Hamlet, Othello, King Lear, and Macbeth,* 2nd ed. (New York: St. Martin's Press, 1981), 138.

4. Roy Battenhouse, "Hamlet's Evasions and Inversions," in *Shakespeare's Christian Dimension: An Anthology of Commentary,* ed. Roy Battenhouse, 400 (Bloomington: Indiana University Press, 1994); Harry Morris, *Last Things in Shakespeare* (Tallahassee: Florida State University Press, 1985), 54; and John Freeman, "This Side of Purgatory: Ghostly Fathers and the Recusant Legacy in *Hamlet,*" in *Shakespeare and the Culture of Christianity in Early Modern England,* ed. Dennis Taylor and David Beauregard, 248 (New York: Fordham University Press, 2003).

5. See Michel Foucault, *The History of Sexuality, vol. 1, An Introduction,* trans. Robert Hurley (New York: Vintage, 1990), esp. 59–63. Foucault revisits the subject in *The Hermeneutics of the Subject: Lectures at the Collège de France, 1981–82,* ed. Frèdèric Gros (New York: Picador, 2005), 363–66. Important recent interpretations that concentrate on the relationship between confession and power include Stephen Greenblatt, *Renaissance Self-Fashioning: From More to Shakespeare* (Chicago: University of Chicago Press, 1980), esp. 85–86, 117–19, and 245–47; Steven Mullaney, *The Place of the Stage: License, Play, and Power in Renaissance England* (Chicago: University of Chicago Press, 1988), 88–115; Jeremy Tambling, *Confession: Sexuality, Sin, the Subject* (Manchester: Manchester University Press, 1990), 2–10 and 73–81; and Alan Sinfield, *Faultlines: Cultural Materialism and the Politics of Dissident Reading* (Berkeley: University of California Press, 1992), 163–64. For a response to Mullaney, see Huston Diehl, "'Infinite Space': Repre-

sentation and Reformation in *Measure for Measure,"* *Shakespeare Quarterly* 49 (1998), esp. 408–9. Of course, the association of confession to the use and abuse of power precedes Foucault, but his influential analysis of it continues to set the terms for many critics.

6. For a critique of Foucault's treatment of the history of confession, see Pierre Payer, "Foucault on Penance and the Shaping of Sexuality," *Studies in Religion/ Sciences Religieuses* 14 (1985): 313–20.

7. Even in the Catholic Counter-Reformation, regular confession was relegated to the elite; see R. Po-Chia Hsia, *The World of Catholic Renewal, 1540–1770,* New Approaches to European History 12 (Cambridge: Cambridge University Press, 1998), 199. On pre-Reformation confessional practices in England, see Ann Eljenholm Nichols, "The Etiquette of Pre-Reformation Confession in East Anglia," *Sixteenth Century Journal* 17 (1986): 145–63; and Eamon Duffy, *The Stripping of the Altars: Traditional Religion in England, 1400–1580* (New Haven: Yale University Press, 1992), 60.

8. I am here drawing on the interpretation advanced by Jodi Bilinkoff, *Related Lives: Confessors and Their Female Penitents, 1450–1750* (Ithaca: Cornell University Press, 2005), 24–27.

9. In many respects, Shakespeare's problematic representation of ritual confession in a Protestant context resembles Marlowe's depiction of the rite in *Doctor Faustus.* For discussions of Lutheranism in England, see Basil Hall, "The Early Rise and Gradual Decline of Lutheranism in England (1520–1600)," in *Reform and Reformation: England and the Continent, c. 1500–c.1750,* ed. Derek Baker, 103–47 (Oxford: Basil Blackwell, 1979). On late sixteenth- and early seventeenth-century English attitudes toward Lutheranism, see Anthony Milton, *Catholic and Reformed: The Roman and Protestant Churches in English Protestant Thought, 1600–1640* (Cambridge: Cambridge University Press, 1995), 384–95.

10. *The booke of common praier, and administration of the Sacramentes, and other rites and ceremonies in the Churche of Englande* (London, 1559), Pir.

11. *The booke of common praier* Mvir. For a similar instruction, see Richard Hooker, *Of the Laws of Ecclesiastical Polity: Books VI, VII, VIII,* ed. P. G. Stanwood, in *The Folger Library Edition of the Works of Richard Hooker,* gen. ed. W. Speed Hill, 7 vols. (Cambridge, MA: Belknap Press, 1977–98), 3:101–3.

12. Thomas Tentler, *Sin and Confession on the Eve of the Reformation* (Princeton: Princeton University Press, 1977), 25.

13. Hooker, 3:97.

14. Richard Greenham, for instance, used a Protestant form of private confession in his ministry; see Kenneth L. Parker, "Richard Greenham's 'spiritual physicke': The Comfort of Afflicted Consciences in Elizabethan Pastoral Care," in *Penitence in the Age of Reformations,* ed. Katharine Lualdi and Anne Thayer, 73 (Aldershot: Ashgate, 2000).

15. John Calvin, *Institutes of the Christian Religion,* trans. Henry Beveridge, 2 vols. (Grand Rapids, MI: Eerdmans, 1953), 1: 548.

16. The office of confessor to the royal household is discussed in an unsigned editorial reply in *Notes and Queries,* 1st ser. 10 (1854): 9–10; and J.K., "Confessor to the Royal Household," *Notes and Queries,* 2nd ser. 7 (1859): 252. Andrewes held the prebendary of Pancratius (St. Pancras) at St. Paul's, which had been used in the Middle Ages for administering the sacrament of confession, from 1589 until 1609 and, in this position, he attempted to revive the custom of Lenten confession

during this period. For a discussion of Andrewes's role as a confessor, see Peter McCullough, "Donne and Andrewes," *John Donne Journal* 22 (2003): 168, and Mc-Cullough's entry for Andrewes in the *New Dictionary of National Biography.*

17. Sinfield, 163.

18. On the exceptional nature of Luther's anxieties in confession, see Thomas Tentler, "The Summa for Confessors as an Instrument of Social Control," in *The Pursuit of Holiness in Late Medieval and Renaissance Religion,* ed. Charles Trinkaus with Heiko A. Oberman, 124 (Leiden: Brill, 1974).

19. Catherine Belsey notes the popular application of English Protestant casuistry in "The Case of Hamlet's Conscience," *Studies in Philology* 76 (1979): 132–33.

20. "An Homilie of Repentaunce and of true reconciliation vnto God," in *The seconde Tome of Homilies* (London, 1563), fols. 281v–82r. For a similar English Protestant interpretation, see Richard Stock, *The doctrine and vse of repentance* (London, 1610), 7–9; and John Coxe's translation of Bullinger's *Questions of religion cast abroad in Helvetia by the aduersaries same: and aunswered by M. H. Bullinger of Zvrick* (London, 1572), 53r–54v.

21. "An Homilie of Repentaunce," fol. 282v.

22. St. Augustine, "Letter 167," in *Letters: 165–203,* trans. Wilfred Parson, Fathers of the Church, vol. 30 (Washington, DC: Catholic University of America Press, 1955).

23. "An Homilie of Repentaunce," fol. 282v.

24. Many early modern writers, including Calvin, Foxe, Peter Martyr Vermigli, Edwin Sandys, and Arminius, nevertheless interpreted Spira's death as a sign of his damnation; see Lily B. Campbell, "Doctor Faustus: A Case of Conscience," *PMLA* 67 (1952): 19–39, and M. A. Overell, "Recantation and Retribution: 'Remembering Francis Spira,' 1548–1638," in *Retribution, Repentance, and Reconciliation: Papers Read at the 2002 Summer Meeting and 2003 Winter Meeting of the Ecclesiastical History Society,* ed. Kate Cooper and Jeremy Gregory, 159–68 (Woodbridge: Boydell Press, 2005).

25. For a discussion of this connection in the context of common worship and the theater, see Ramie Targoff, "The Performance of Prayer: Sincerity and Theatricality in Early Modern England," *Representations* 60 (1997): 49–69.

26. Cited in Richard Wunderli and Gerald Broce, "The Final Moment before Death in Early Modern England," *Sixteenth Century Journal* 20 (1989): 271–72.

27. For a discussion of the relationship between authority and scaffold confessions in relation to the trial, confession, and execution of Robert Devereux, second Earl of Oxford, see Karin S. Coddon, "'Such Strange Desygns': Madness, Subjectivity, and Treason in *Hamlet* and Elizabethan Culture," *Renaissance Drama,* n.s. 20 (1989): 56–57.

28. On the connection between confession and torture, see Foucault, *History of Sexuality,* 59. On the early modern awareness of the limitations of confession under torture, see Donne's Fourteenth Meditation in *Devotions Upon Emergent Occasions.*

29. The most detailed account of Cranmer's final days appears in Diarmaid MacCulloch, *Thomas Cranmer: A Life* (New Haven: Yale University Press, 1996), 554–605.

30. Cited in MacCullough, 603. On the problem of determining intentionality in public confession, see Janet E. Halley, "Heresy, Orthodoxy, and the Politics of

Religious Discourse: The Case of the English Family of Love," in *Representing the English Renaissance,* ed. Stephen Greenblatt, 316–19 (Berkeley: University of California Press, 1988).

31. On the disjunction between outward behavior and internal beliefs in scaffold confessions, see Katharine Eisaman Maus, *Inwardness and Theater in the English Renaissance* (Chicago: University of Chicago Press, 1995), 6–7. And for a discussion of the problematic relationship of external authority and individual faith, see also Claire McEachern, *The Poetics of English Nationhood, 1590–1612* (Cambridge: Cambridge University Press, 1997), esp. 67–72.

32. On confession in Foxe as a "privileged kind of discourse" that reveals the conscience, see Marsha S. Robinson, *Writing the Reformation: Actes and Monuments and the Jacobean History Play* (Aldershot: Ashgate, 2002), 62.

33. For a discussion of the difficulty of identifying true martyrs in theological polemic, see Brad Gregory, *Salvation at Stake: Christian Martyrdom in Early Modern Europe* (Cambridge, MA: Harvard University Press, 1999), 339–41.

34. Unless otherwise noted, citations of *Hamlet* are taken from Harold Jenkins, ed., *Hamlet,* Arden Shakespeare, 2nd ser. (London: Methuen, 1982). Citations from passages not included in the 2nd Arden are taken from Paul Bertram and Bernice W. Kliman, eds., *The Three-Text Hamlet: Parallel Texts of the First and Second Quartos and First Folio* (New York: AMS Press, 1991). For a discussion of interiority and exteriority and scaffold confessions, see Maus, 11; and Peter Lake and Michael Questier, "Agency, Appropriation and Rhetoric Under the Gallows: Puritans, Romanists and the State in Early Modern England," *Past and Present* 153 (1996): 64–107.

35. On amendment of life being a requirement of a good confession in the late medieval period, see Tentler, *Sin and Confession,* 120–23, and 132.

36. As part of the rite of confession, satisfaction underwent a dramatic reorientation during the English Reformation. For an analysis of the relationship between these changes and early modern revenge tragedy, see Heather Hirschfeld, "Compulsions of the Renaissance," in *Shakespeare Studies* 33 (2005): 112–13.

37. On Calvinist pressure to determine election or reprobation, see Baird Tipson, "A Dark Side of Seventeenth-Century English Protestantism: The Sin against the Holy Spirit," *Harvard Theological Review* 77 (1984): 301–30.

38. William Perkins, *A treatise tending vnto a declaration whether a man be in the estate of damnation or in the estate of grace* (London, 1590), A3v; the original is printed in italics.

39. The Prayer Book instructs ministers to exhort the congregation to receive communion and thereby reinforces the ecclesiastical expectation of receiving communion; see *The booke of common praier,* Mviir.

40. Tambling, 92.

41. At the turn of the seventeenth century, private confession became the subject of debate in Cambridge and London, primarily as a result of avant-garde conformists like Andrewes; see Nicholas Tyacke, *Anti-Calvinists: The Rise of English Arminianism, c. 1590–1640* (Oxford: Clarendon Press, 1990), esp. 110–11 and 221–22.

42. I explore the implications of this debate in the context of Shakespeare in "A Reconciled Maid: *A Lover's Complaint* and Confessional Practices in Early Modern England," in *Critical Essays on A Lover's Complaint: Suffering Ecstasy,* ed. Shirley Sharon-Zisser, 79–90 (Aldershot: Ashgate, 2006).

43. On the connection between "disappointed" and sacramental confession, see Jenkins, 220.

44. For a discussion of the Ghost's faith in the Catholic sacrament of Extreme Unction, a traditional rite that contains sacramental absolution, see Andrew Gurr, *Hamlet and the Distracted Globe* (Sussex: Sussex University Press, 1978), 71.

45. Shakespeare's knowledge of the retention of a reformed model of private confession and confessors in evangelical Protestantism remains unclear. On the subject of ritual confession in Lutheran theology, see Ronald K. Rittgers, *The Reformation of the Keys: Confession, Conscience, and Authority in Sixteenth-Century Germany* (Cambridge, MA: Harvard University Press, 2004), and his subsequent article, "Private Confession and the Lutheranization of Sixteenth-Century Nördlingen," *Sixteenth Century Journal* 36 (2005): 1063–86.

46. Roland Mushat Frye, "Prince Hamlet and the Protestant Confessional," *Theology Today* 39 (1982): 35 and 32. This argument is incorporated in "Gertrude's Mirror of Confession," in his *The Renaissance Hamlet: Issues and Responses in 1600* (Princeton: Princeton University Press, 1984), 151–66.

47. Maus, 1.

48. This tension between Hamlet's inward feelings and speech is not registered in the First Folio's version of Hamlet's first speech to his mother which Jenkins adopts in his conflated text. Instead of the Folio's reading of "good mother," the Second Quarto reads "coold mother," and thereby suggests that Hamlet struggles to contain his true feelings regarding her marriage to Claudius (1.2.76).

49. Paul A. Kottman, "The Limits of *Mimesis:* Risking Confession in Shakespeare's *Hamlet*," *Shakespeare Studies* (Japan) 42 (2004): 57.

50. The prominence of secrets in the theatrical space has been the subject of numerous critical studies; see Coddon, 51–71; Mark Thornton Burnett, "The 'Heart of My Mystery': *Hamlet* and Secrets," in *New Essays on Hamlet,* ed. Mark Thornton Burnett, 35 (New York: AMS Press, 1994); Patricia Parker, *Shakespeare from the Margins: Language, Culture, Context* (Chicago: University of Chicago Press, 1996), 229–72; and Richard Wilson, *Secret Shakespeare: Studies in Theatre, Religion, and Resistance* (Manchester: Manchester University Press, 2004), 26–28.

51. On the confessional aspects of King Hamlet's murder, see Tambling, 73–76, and Freeman, 253.

52. John Bale, *The seconde part of the image of both churches after the most wonderfull and heavenly revelacyon of Saynt Johan the Evangelyst* (Antwerp, 1545), 135v.

53. John Kerrigan observes that emulation and imitation represent common themes in early classical and early modern revenge tragedy; see John Kerrigan, *Revenge Tragedy: Aeschylus to Armageddon* (Oxford: Clarendon Press, 1996), 16–17.

54. On the connections between Claudius's penitential prayer and the Church of England's conception of private repentance, see Eleanor Prosser, *Hamlet and Revenge,* 2nd ed. (Stanford, CA: Stanford University Press, 1967), 185–86.

55. Anthony Low, *Aspects of Subjectivity: Society and Individuality from the Middle Ages to Shakespeare and Milton* (Pittsburgh: Duquesne University Press, 2003), 126. On another interpretation of the Catholic undertones of Claudius's prayer, see Arthur McGee, *The Elizabethan Hamlet* (New Haven: Yale University Press, 1987), 124–25.

56. On medieval and early modern understandings of conscience, see John S. Wilks, "The Discourse of Reason and the Erroneous Conscience in *Hamlet*," *Shakespeare Studies* 18 (1986): 117–44.

57. Hamlet's judgment of others is more forceful in the First Folio: he justifies his treatment of Rosencrantz and Guildenstern by remarking, "Why man, they did make loue to this imployment" (5.2.57); and he explicitly connects his "perfect conscience" to the killing of Claudius by rhetorically asking, "is't not perfect conscience / To quit him with this arme?" (5.2.67–68).

58. Morris, 56, brackets in original. For a precursor of this interpretation, see J. Dover Wilson, *What Happens in Hamlet* (New York: Macmillan, 1935), 256.

59. The meaning of "assume" in this line has been the subject of critical debate. Interestingly, the *Oxford English Dictionary* uses it to illustrate the meaning of "assume" as "To take to oneself in appearance only, to pretend to possess; to pretend, simulate, feign" (def. 8). For a reading of "assume" as a reference to the practice of virtue, see Jenkins, 329.

60. For a discussion of the significance of Hamlet's roles as scourge and God's minister, see Fredson Bowers, *Hamlet as Minister and Scourge and Other Studies in Shakespeare and Milton* (Charlottesville: University Press of Virginia, 1989), 98.

61. Michael Neill, *Issues of Death: Mortality and Identity in English Renaissance Tragedy* (Oxford: Clarendon Press, 1997), 242.

62. Catherine Belsey, *The Subject of Tragedy: Identity and Difference in Renaissance Drama* (London: Methuen, 1985), 42.

63. In his recent literary biography of Shakespeare, Stephen Greenblatt imagines a situation somewhat analogous to the doctrinal tension present in *Hamlet,* hypothesizing that John Shakespeare may have been simultaneously both a Catholic and Protestant; see *Will in the World: How Shakespeare Became Shakespeare* (New York: Norton, 2004), 102. If Greenblatt's theory is correct, the collapse of the effectiveness of ritual in *Hamlet* suggests that Shakespeare considered such a position to be ultimately untenable, a realization that John Shakespeare, if his so-called "spiritual testament" is to be held as authentic, had arrived at before his death.

64. Mullaney, 91. Social anthropologists have challenged this interpretation of ritual; see Catherine Bell, *Ritual Theory, Ritual Practice* (New York: Oxford University Press, 1992), 182–96. Yet in representations of ritual in early modern English drama, ritual and authority are frequently connected.

REVIEW ARTICLES

Dollimore's Challenge

Ewan Fernie

Radical Tragedy, which was first published by Prentice Hall / Harvester Wheatsheaf in 1984, was indisputably one of the most original and influential critical books of its time. But I want to argue here that the different and much more neglected position Jonathan Dollimore has developed in recent work is even more singular and challenging. It's also more radical in the sense of going to the root of something, its aim being no less than to uncover a constitutive dilemma of human history and self-experience as it is revealed in the arts in general and in literature in particular. This painful truth, Dollimore argues, has been especially complacently evaded by contemporary critics; but then, as he demonstrates, it has typically been avoided by criticism, as perhaps it must be by any human rationalization of art or life experience. Dollimore claims, therefore, to have identified, or returned to, the real challenge of art. Shakespeare plays a central if not unique role in his argument, which —even if he's only partly right—has extraordinary and comprehensive implications for contemporary critical practice.

Radical Tragedy was a fierce and (as it turned out) effective assault on an essentialism in English studies that Dollimore perceived as complacent and inherited (rather than freshly thought) and as lazily conservative—aesthetically, existentially, and politically. One reason still to value the book more than twenty years after its first publication is that it has *atmosphere:* a complex and affecting mood of grim, melancholy desire, come to think of it, not unrelated to the affect of Jacobean tragedy itself. The passion for the future that propels Dollimore's debut isn't simple; it's always born out of and dialectically intensified by a lucid apprehension of the deep structures of the world we inherit. Dollimore stresses, in his introduction to the third edition, that "the historical conditions of thought matter" and it was Thatcher's Britain that hurt intellectuals like him into hope as burning as it was beleaguered.[1] *Radical Tragedy* reads Jacobean tragedy for the complication, contradiction, and disorder where the promise of an alternative life lies lurking, but that promise is never overestimated: Dollimore recognizes the amazing contingency of the social order—that which isn't natural CAN be changed!—only to realize simultaneously that the social order, contingent though it is, may be harder to refashion than nature itself. And *Radical Tragedy* is a *historical* book, so its epiphanies have to be regarded as moments of possibility that opened like flowers in the night of what actually, historically prevailed. Dollimore resists the temptation to elaborate these into anything more, in implicit recognition perhaps of the almost unprecedented luck and labor needed to redeem such lost potentialities in the actual achievement of a better world.

But one of the most important reasons to value Dollimore is that he's continued to think. Almost uniquely in a context in which academics are expected to maintain a consistent position, *Dollimore changes his mind.* While he does claim a certain continuity for his project, he's not afraid to rearrange it all around a new and startling inspiration. Looking back at his introduction to the second edition of *Radical Tragedy* published (also by Prentice Hall / Harvester Wheatsheaf) in 1989, one notes a willingness to develop and consolidate his original case in relation to succeeding work and debates; but in the new introduction to the third edition, Dollimore stakes out a position that is shockingly disjunct, not just from the contemporary critical consensus he ignores but even from his own earlier position as *Radical Tragedy* records it.

While he is still, no doubt, opposed to the corruption of particular political regimes, Dollimore is now disposed to see order as such as fundamentally necessary, as a form of identity without which we are flooded by apprehensions of loss and chaos that are endemic to our culture.[2] Concomitantly, he entertains a darker, more generally libidinized view of subversion as the upwelling of suppressed disorder, and more inclined to violate and wreck civilization than reform it. Dollimore is now more interested in deformation than reform, in self and society imperiling desire, in what Nietzsche thought of as "death-welcoming moods" (*RT*, xxxii).[3]

And what he presents is nothing less than a vision of the full sweep of human history. It is a vision and a history of human beings on the rack of their own self-constituting repressions, of civilization barely, precariously, and inconsistently maintained.

Dollimore locates this startling new view in relation to the history of humanism, and his narrative makes for extremely interesting reading, not least because it fundamentally challenges contemporary criticism's conception of itself. Such criticism, including *Radical Tragedy,* defines itself squarely against humanism. But Dollimore now argues that, at least in its strongest forms, humanism is intellectually, ethically, and existentially admirable and interesting. This is because it confronts "what is refractory and intractable in human history and human desire," even if only to overturn it (*RT,* xii). One of the more sensational surprises of Dollimore's recent writing is its sudden sympathy for such woefully unfashionable figures as Herman Hesse and F. R. Leavis. Like them Dollimore acknowledges the destructive power of dissident desire, and like them he equally acknowledges the need to repress it in the name of civilization, sanity, ethics, identity, and love. He differs from them in arguing that "the aesthetic vision has been most captivating precisely when it exceeds and maybe violates the humanitarian one," and that "[t]o take art seriously must be to recognize that its dangerous insights and painful beauty often derive from tendencies both disreputable and deeply anti-social" (*RT,* xi). Dollimore deliberately takes up the suppressed intensities of an avowed inhumanity as his special critical and existential field, writing as follows, "Let us say at the very least that the ethical and the humane, in order not to atrophy, must be constantly exposed to their own vital exclusions—exposed, that is, to what allows them to be what they are. But without any guarantee they can survive that exposure. That is the promise and the danger of art" (*RT,* xxxiv). How does current criticism fit in here? Well, for all its self-defining animus against humanism, Dollimore argues it in fact is humanism by other means. Far from ditching humanism's ethical program, it has pursued it on the extended terrain of the political. To this extent it is humanism reinvigorated. But modern criticism is also a weak form of humanism inasmuch as it is complacently blind to the daemonic forces that undermine human history and personality from within.

Dollimore kicks off his introduction to the latest edition of *Radical Tragedy* with a surprising celebration of Hesse's "fierce spiritual flame" (*RT,* xix). The German author stood, in the midst of the First World War, for "an international world of thought, of inner freedom, of intellectual conscience" and a belief in "an artistic beauty cutting across national boundaries" (*RT,* xiv).[4] In addition, he insisted, "I shall always, incorrigibly, recognize in man, in the individual man and his soul, the existence of realms to which political impulses and forms do not extend" (ibid.).[5] Much later he explained in his Nobel Prize letter of thanks that "the hardships of the National Socialist period" had wrecked his health but testified, as Dollimore emphasizes, "*Still, my spirit is unbroken . . .*" (ibid.).[6]

Dollimore admits, "*Radical Tragedy* . . . attacked just these ideas: essentialism in relation to subjectivity, universalism in relation to the human, and the belief that there was an ethical/aesthetic realm transcending the political" (*RT,* xv). But what he now admires in Hesse is his ethical intensity, and the existential and rhetorical intensities it enables. Such passions show up the relative insipidity and meaninglessness of much right-minded current work, and they derive from their real opposition to something: all the daemonic political barbarism of the last century. Dollimore writes, "the full significance of an aesthetic humanism becomes apparent in relation to artists like Hesse in a way it doesn't in, say, the squabbles within the English literary critical tradition in the last quarter of the last century. More specifically, the critique of humanism never properly engaged with people like Hesse, preferring instead easier targets in academic literary criticism" (*RT,* xv). But if Dollimore admires the "high European humanism" of Hesse, he has less respect for the more muted version that is revealed in W. H. Auden's eloquent poem "1st September 1939." Auden's "affirming flame" is expressly weaker than Hesse's. Rather than being fired by spirituality, according to Auden, human beings are "composed . . . [o]f Eros and of dust," "[b]eleaguered by . . . negation and despair." The most "the Just" can muster up are "[i]ronic points of light" (*RT,* xix).[7] Dollimore observes:

> Together with its near cousin ambiguity, irony becomes the crutch of "late humanism," at once guarantee of its sophistication, and confession of its uncertainty; irony provided the intellectual with a rationale for non-commitment, and enabled the academic critic to contain anything which disturbed, by putting it in an imaginary, neutralising tension or balance with what didn't. Yeats saw through this kind of irony, which is why it's almost obligatory now to cite him: the best lack all conviction while the worst are full of a passionate intensity. (*RT,* xix–xx)

In other words, a sophisticated, ironic, or liberal response avoids or elides the lived antinomies of life. Dollimore prefers a humanism that lives out of such contraries, strenuously opposing the obscene energy of what it regards as evil. What he prefers to that is an existential and epistemological stance that counts the cost of desublimating repressed desire and chooses to pay it anyway.

The daemonic is domesticated by the sort of ironic humanism that half allows it but, for Adorno 'to write poetry after Auschwitz is barbaric" (*RT,* xxi):[8] the devil is dancing through the ruins of the humanism creed. And not just because, after such knowledge, art can only be a sick mystification of evil and suffering. As George Steiner observes, "We know now that a man can read Goethe or Rilke in the evening, that he can play Bach or Schubert, and go to his day's work at Auschwitz in the morning. To say that he has read them without understanding, or that his ear is gross, is cant" (*RT,* xxi).[9] This raises for Steiner what for Dollimore too is "a compelling question": "[w]hat are the links, as yet scarcely understood, between the mental, psychological habits of high literacy, and the temptations of the inhuman?" (*RT,* xxii).[10]

After the Second World War, the daemonic was pushing perceptibly through "the mental, psychological habits of high literacy" so that Steiner and others struggled to redeem and fortify the humanist faith. Perhaps foremost among them, in Dollimore's narrative, is Leavis. According to Dollimore, Leavis saw the need to "strengthen his ethical humanism by injecting it with a dose of diluted vitalism, thereby suggesting its origins in the life force with which, in reality, it was in permanent tension." "The truth is," Dollimore writes, "that the ethical order which we all live by and utterly depend upon, repeatedly turns away from life's energies." He contends that "humanism is most compelling when it honestly acknowledges the price, in terms of repression, renunciation and control, of adhering to humane values; when, in other words, it takes upon itself the responsibility for limiting human aspiration and acknowledging that humane values and human desire will always be in tormenting conflict" (*SLC,* 123). And yet Dollimore doesn't finally convict Leavis of dodging this sort of agonized honesty and responsibility; rather he finds it etched on his face in "a memorable picture" taken in June 1973: "Looking austerely fragile, still indomitable yet deeply exhausted, he recalls Mann's Aschenbach, burnt out by the unsustainable effort of speaking on behalf of civilisation. Wrecked by discrimination" (ibid.). It is a moment of particularly pressured intensity in Dollimore's recent work, and one that bespeaks a strange and telling identification. Thomas Mann's Gustav von

Aschenbach from *Death in Venice* ultimately and fatally succumbs to daemonic desire, and the reference to him here confounds Leavis, the heroic victor over such tendencies, with his own opposite. There is also a strange symbiosis between Dollimore's prose and its subject here, with the exceptionally careful writing—each word really counts in this passage—itself expressing Leavis's exhausting discrimination. Such self-wrecking restraint is curiously akin to self-imperiling indulgence, and it is impossible to resist the thought that Dollimore sees himself and his own struggle reflected back at him in Leavis's strained visage. It is partly a matter of having a worthy enemy, partly a genuine sense of sharing much common ground, if not common cause, with Leavis's existentially troubled and committed work. Dollimore wants criticism that really matters to the writer—and, indeed, how else could it matter to its readers? As a result he seems now to feel closer to Leavis than to many who would suppose themselves his followers and fellow travelers.

But if Dollimore finds a perverse refuge in the "high humanism" of Leavis and Hesse, he can find no such thing in its current manifestations. In some circumstances the humanist faith seems to have disappeared altogether from contemporary life. Dollimore comments, for instance, on the aftermath of 9/11: "Whereas in September 1914 Hesse passionately affirms the humanist aesthetic as an answer to war, in September 2001 it was as if such a vision had simply been forgotten: one listened in vain for significant voices promoting art as an articulation of civilised values transcending cultural, racial and religious conflicts" (*RT,* xviii). What we heard instead were appeals to "cultural and racial difference," epitomized by the fact that "Britain's Prime Minister, as he commuted the world in October 2001, shoring up support for the coalition against terrorism, allowed it to be known that, as he travelled, he read translations of the Koran" (*RT,* xvii). A vogue for the ethics of difference has equally swept through the academy in recent years, and to this extent the academics and the politicians are singing from the same hymn-sheet, which absolutely wasn't the case when *Radical Tragedy* challenged Thatcherism. It's notable that, although he acknowledges the need to correct the blindness and exclusivity of the old humanist universals, Dollimore does not celebrate the intensity of ethics of difference in the way that he celebrated the ethical humanism of Hesse. This is partly because such ethics seem implicated in a global capitalism that simultaneously spices up the market by selling "ethnic" or "gay" products at the same time as cultivating racial and social minorities as special-interest markets. It is also because where global capitalism has become "an aggressive economic and military imperialism which exacerbates cultural antagonisms . . . the multicultural can shift very quickly from being the imagined resolution of these antagonisms, to being the ground where they intensify" (ibid.): hence, for instance, the escalating tensions between the British government and British Muslims. If, beyond this, Dollimore seems to feel that ethics of difference can't sustain the sort of fierce spiritual flame shown forth by Hesse, that's perhaps because difference, as such, just isn't very lovable. Love is highly particular and correspondingly exclusionary. You love this and/or that singular thing or things; unless you're a post-structuralist philosopher or a mystic, it's difficult to love an open array of differences, which is largely why the ethics of difference, both beyond and within the academy, often degenerate in practice into the pieties and lip service of political correctness. By contrast, humanism knew what it loved: an elevated, theoretically universal human nature that was nonetheless concretely defined in experience by what it refused and excluded.

But if humanism has lost force in the political arena, Dollimore observes that in exhausted if not cynical form it nevertheless continues to underpin the humanities education system and the culture industries. Dollimore quotes Sir Claus Moser expressing its core belief—that art is a profoundly civilizing force—in October 2000 and comments:

> In short, I have deep respect for Hesse's advocacy of humanism in 1917; but I can't but regard Moser, writing in 2000, as deeply complacent. Far from being liberating, the humanist aesthetic has become a way of standing still amidst the obsolete, complacent and self-serving clichés of the heritage culture industry, the Arts establishment, and a market-driven humanities education system. The aesthetic has become an anaesthetic. (*RT*, xxii)

Whereas the humanism Dollimore now admires confronted, even while it refused, the most recalcitrant and troubling dimensions of human life and politics, in its current, degenerate and empty form, it merely props up a range of vested interests.

But, according to Dollimore, a healthier mutation of humanism survives within the academy: as the radical materialist criticism of the '80s and after, to which *Radical Tragedy* itself powerfully contributed. This movement represents not so much the final defeat of humanism it proclaimed as a late development of that creed. There is a fundamental moral continuity between humanism and contemporary materialist critics. For even while they have tended to despise humanism as benightedly ideological, such critics have fiercely competed with it for the high moral ground. To the extent that they have been able to raise humanist ethics onto the extended plane of politics, they've won an important victory, although often at the cost of the sort of ethical and existential intensity Dollimore admires in Hesse and Leavis. Moreover, even if they have fortified humanism by enlarging its political scope, they have weakened it in another important respect. Because whereas traditional or "high" humanism did real battle with the refractory forces of barbarism and evil, radical criticism has for the most part refused even to recognize the adverse impulses and conditions of human nature. As Dollimore puts it:

> With laudable political intent, and real insight into the ideological underpinning of supposedly natural and inevitable inequalities, political critics, like philosophers, rationalize reality. For instance, human violence is regarded not as the unavoidable manifestation of an innately violent human nature, but as the product of unjust social conditions: by altering the conditions we control the violence. This works. Yet if doing that leads us to believe it is only a question of social conditions, we deceive ourselves. (*SLC,* 126)

He's right, of course. The pitfall for political criticism is a naive optimism that humiliatingly fails to have much impact on a recalcitrant world.

The best of such works, like *Radical Tragedy* itself, don't underestimate the terrific difficulty of making a difference. But they do underestimate, where they do not entirely discount, what Dollimore now insists on: the dark and retrograde potential of desire itself. This is most flagrantly the case, as Dollimore shows, with queer theory.

> Every individual experiences the struggle to a greater or lesser degree: instinct, id and the unconscious are always there to wreck what precious equilibrium is achieved by the ego. But the sexual radicals argued that this force, instead of wrecking the individual through repression, might be liberated and turned against the society doing the repression. It's a momentous turn-about: now sexuality is not the reason we are rad-

ically unfree, but the impetus for a radical vision of freedom. Instead of being the source of torment, guilt and death, sex now involves liberation and happiness. It is hardly surprising that this reversal involved a taming of desire which amounted to a new kind of repression. Sexual radicalism wanted desire to subvert some things but definitely not others; it had to destroy the old order but serve the new. The hope is that liberated desire would, as it were, civilise itself. But it is unwise to rely upon desire to discriminate between good and bad social orders, and the very radicalism which made so much of the idea of the return of the repressed would repeatedly encounter the return of its own repressed. (*SLC*, 77–78)

To put it bluntly, desire isn't simply good. To see it as such is not only ethically complacent and inevitably very harmful (both to the un-self-censoring subject of desire and to anyone unfortunate enough to come in his or her way), it also denies the complex and often painful astringencies involved in the real experience of desire, and sex.

Dollimore writes:

In some elusive and incomplete way we are the embodiments of something called sex. "Desire" is the correct word, but let's for once use "sex" if only because it has a density, directness and yet a degree of indeterminacy which makes it occasionally right. We cannot step outside the force-field of sex any more than we can step outside the language we speak. Sex is profoundly cultural and not simply a natural given. And yet any attempt to explain exclusively in terms of culture will always fail. And when it does, we relive the experiential complexity of sex, and realize the futility of trying to evade it via the spurious complexities of theory. To be alive is to desire; to desire is to be deeply and maybe destructively confused, sooner or later. (*SLC*, 36)

"Theory": the word confesses the weakness. Dollimore now stresses that theoretical thought will tend to rationalize, and therefore censor, reality. Theory must therefore always, and urgently, be exposed to experience, and potentially transformed by it. That's why where once Dollimore attacked the complacent essentialism of English studies, he now has in his sights the complacencies that attend its more recent anti-essentialism. Thus, for instance,

[t]he historical approach to death insists that it is not some essential thing, but a socio-historical construct; it tells us that to look for the transhistorical continuities in the human experience of death is funda-

mentally misguided; on the contrary, we must understand death as something which changes across time within any one culture and which fundamentally differs between cultures (and religions). So, in the latter case there will be, e.g., a Buddhist conception of death, and a Christian one; in the former, there will be a medieval way of dying and a Victorian one, and so on. Difference is all.

This is true, as far as it goes. But as is often the case, the agreeable truth (diversity and difference) is used to evade the less agreeable (the anguish of mortality).[11]

Which is to say, Dollimore's case against the salient historicism of recent literary studies is that it collects historical differences as a way of ignoring the most terrible facts of history. He goes on:

Historicism performs this evasion not just with respect to specific topics like death, but in its very methodology, and especially in its assumption that anything in the past can be explained if its full history can be retrieved. Of course historicism knows that full history is rarely if ever retrievable, but the assumption that all would be revealed if it were, is the ideal to which the historian aspires. In other words, nothing of itself, and in relation to us, is inexplicable in principle, only in practice. Nothing more than inadequate historical data stands between us and a full understanding of the past. To the extent that this assumption pervades historicism of all kinds it entails a certain irony: this most empirical of procedures has at its methodological heart something of the *a priori*.[12]

As I have implied already, Dollimore is himself a rationalist inasmuch as he is a markedly lucid thinker and writer. But to think lucidly about reality is not the same as reproducing reality in the image of such thinking. The nub of Dollimore's critique of modern criticism is this: for all its savvy transcendence of a tweedier past, it's *frightened of life*. Of course, Dollimore's own work, as well as the best humanist scholarship, has shown there's good reason to be. The high humanists tried strenuously to wrest life's humane elements from its persistent inhumanity. Dollimore is different in that, although he admits life is indeed frightening, disturbing, even partly evil, he remains fully intellectually and even spiritually committed to it. To that extent he's a movingly affirmative thinker.

Dollimore respects humanism but insists nonetheless on "that underlying longing to reject prudential living . . . in favour of its opposite: risk, and an ecstasy inseparable from destruction including self-destruction" (*SLC*, 64). He doesn't romanticize this: humane values are essential to the health and well-being of any self or society. They've fallen into ideological disrepair, but, as we have seen, modern criticism has struggled to redeem them, even while defining itself against humanism. Within the ruins of that still necessary creed, Dollimore descries what is always there as humanism's opposite and occasion: "the aesthetic where dangerous knowledge crosses with dissident desire" (*RI*, xxiv). Art, according to Dollimore, unceasingly confesses and explores the dialectic between humanism and the inhumane; and whereas philosophy, and all more rational discourse, censors the latter, art recklessly tests and even privileges it. Of the thrilling agonies of the inhumane, Dollimore has made himself the lonely critical laureate, but we mustn't imagine any easy, self-congratulatory sneer. For he reckons the cost, envisions the blazing world, and then goes ahead and lights the match, writing grimly, "we are most ourselves when we are in this destructive, dangerous and suffering state of freedom," not only "violating the restraints of the very history which has produced us" but living to the full the intensifying contradiction of human nature (*RT*, xxxi).

Dollimore's great philosophical precursor is Nietzsche, but he in turn looks back to Shakespeare. Dollimore notes that whereas "[t]he rationalist might regard the accumulation of knowledge as a progressive and irreversible consolidation of civilisation," Nietzsche finds in Shakespeare "another kind of knowledge, one which does not consolidate civilisation, but threatens it." Its final revelation is "that civilisation is at heart illusory" (*RT*, xxxi).

That is the burden of Nietzsche's reading of Hamlet—"he has 'seen through' the illusions by which his culture maintains itself; inaction derives not from confusion and doubt, but too much certainty" (*RT*, xxxii). But whereas Hamlet stands at the wan end of the civilizing process, Macbeth is as much about "*affirming* what has been repressed, of desublimating the life force itself, of holding it up against civilised morality, and even celebrating its destructive power" (ibid., my italics). Dollimore goes on as follows:

So it's a mistake, says Nietzsche, to think that Shakespeare's theatre was aiming for moral effects. In this regard *Macbeth* does not warn against hubris and ambition; on the contrary it affirms their attraction. And the fact that Macbeth "perishes by his passions" is part of his "demonic attraction." By demonic [*dämonisch*] Nietzsche means "in defiance *against* life and advantage for the sake of a drive and idea"

[*Gedankens und Triebes*]. He adds "Do you suppose that Tristan and Isolde are preaching *against* adultery when they both perish by it? This would be to stand the poets on their head: they, and especially Shakespeare, are enamoured of the passions as such and not least of their *death-welcoming* moods." Shakespeare, like other tragic poets, "speaks . . . out of a restless, vigorous age which is half-drunk and stupefied by its excess of blood and energy—out of a wickeder age than ours is." But the guardians of high culture in our own day disavow this: they seek to "*adjust* and *justify* the goal of a Shakespearean drama" precisely in order that they (and we) "not understand it." (RT, xxxii)[13]

Dollimore explains how Shakespeare and his critics "fall on opposite sides of Nietzsche's great divide between those who affirm the life-force and those who turn away from it: between, in other words, the demonic and humanitarian" (*RT,* xxxii). And he observes that, in *The Gay Science,* "this distinction is expressed in terms of two distinct kinds of sufferer—those who suffer from a superabundance of life and those who suffer from an impoverishment of life" (ibid.). In Nietzsche's scheme, Shakespeare willingly confronts "the terrible and questionable . . . every luxury of destruction, decomposition, negation," while his critics prefer "mildness, peacefulness, goodness in thought and deed . . . a certain warm, fear-averting confinement and enclosure within optimistic horizons" (*RT,* xxxii–xxxiii and "Afterword").[14]

Dollimore now concurs exactly with this pitiless recognition of critical bloodlessness and bad faith, but his reading of Shakespeare and of life isn't exactly Nietzsche's. He points out, for instance, that the philosopher "wilfully misconstrues *Macbeth,*" agreeing that it "is indeed a profound exploration of the daemonic" but insisting "its *tragedy* is the deep and recalcitrant conflict between the daemonic and humane, between the Macbeths' 'black and deep desires' and the 'milk of human kindness'" (1.4.52, 1.5.15; *RT,* xxxiii).[15] Such conflict is what Dollimore proclaims the subjective truth we all inherit and the dialectic of civilization itself.

It is most completely embodied in Angelo, "A man of stricture and firm abstinence" who "scarce confesses / That his blood flows" (1.3.12, 51–52) and one who, as Dollimore says, "has hitherto been sublimating his own sexuality into strict government not just of himself but of his society, such that the opportunity to suppress illicit sexual desire in the community in his new capacity as deputy is a self-realization more than usually charged with libidinal energies." "But," Dollimore goes on, "this is also why the executing of power, initially a compensation for repression, becomes the occasion for its return" (*SLC,* 80). In Angelo we see how "desublimated desire has a virulence which is not the opposite of civilisation but its inversion"; we see "desire returning via the 'civilising' mechanisms of its repression, mechanisms it is still inseparable from even while it violates them" (*SLC,* 80–81). As Dollimore emphasizes, "only the highly civilised can be truly daemonic": lillies that fester. . . .[16] Here is Shakespeare's severe judge in the midst of his agonized arousal:

> Having waste ground enough,
> Shall we desire to raze the sanctuary
> And pitch our evils there? . . .
>
> . . . .
> Dost thou desire her foully for those things
> That make her good ?
>
> (2.3.174–76, 178–79)

Angelo exemplifies the coalescence of the political and the personal, the *formal* coincidence between social form and the individual identity that is vested in it. In violating the civilized world, he violates himself—and what is so starkly true of him would be fundamentally true for all of us. In Angelo, as Dollimore writes, desire "is hardly conscious." Moreover, "it is a pressure not so much for fulfilment, but to be free of something in itself which it cannot fully understand, something which, in effect, it does not desire" (*SLC,* 81). We approach a strange and compelling truth here: desire both is and is not mine, both is and is not *me.* As Dollimore writes, "'Angelo", devastated by the ferocity of his own vicious passion, is doubly mutilated: first by the repression, then by the return" (ibid.). Desire wrecks everything I am, not just my body, but also my spirit, and yet in so doing seems bitterly to introduce me to myself as if for the very first time.

The intense mysteriousness of this example evinces the phenomenological possibility of Dollimore's position as a way of allowing, accessing, and analyzing aesthetic and life experience. In this respect, Dollimore's recent work could be characterized as expanded humanism, one that entails a fuller accounting both of humanity and of the energy and authority that humanism derives from the challenge of the inhumane. This entails an important corrective to what might be described as the ethical kitsch of much modern scholarship. No ethical criticism deserves the name that doesn't in-

volve the rigorous examination of its own conscience, but an absolute (if not unthinking) righteousness comes easily to the
politically correct. Dollimore is more responsive to the ethical densities and provocations of life in general and of aesthetic experience in particular.

A case in point is his extraordinary analysis of the following
lines from *Othello:*

> *Othello.* And yet how nature, erring from itself—
> *Iago.* Ay, there's the point; as, to be bold with you,
>   Not to affect many proposèd matches
>   Of her own clime, complexion, and degree,
>   Whereto we see in all things nature tends.
>   Foh, one may smell, in such, a will most rank,
>   Foul disproportions, thoughts unnatural!
>
>   (3.3.232–38)

Dollimore first observes the amazing compression, suggesting that
if "poetry is, in essence, language at its most powerfully concentrated, this is pure poetry"; but he further observes that "it is also
pure evil of a most modern kind: here in just a few lines racism,
xenophobia and misogyny are imaginatively fused" (*SLC,* 131). He
goes on:

> Desire and revulsion: both are there, feeding the other. That is one of
> the things that could give this scene its intensity. The disgust is concen-
> trated in the multiple meanings of "will"—which could mean volition,
> sexual desire and sexual organs—and "rank"—which could mean lust,
> swollen, smelling, corrupt, foul: "one may smell, in such, a will most
> rank." Such words make for an imagery which is intensely voyeuristic
> even as it is so dense as to be beyond visualisation. Compressed in the
> next line is a pornographic fantasy of "foul disproportion": the mon-
> strously phallic black man violating the white woman. Again there is
> an allusion here to Iago's earlier taunt: "an old black ram / Is tupping
> your white ewe" (1.1.88–89). If Shakespeare dramatizes a pornographic
> imagination through Iago, it is also as a dramatist that he reveals how
> central is that imagination to a certain kind of ambivalent racism in
> which disgust and desire escalate dialectically (*SLC,* 132)

Fearlessly disclosed here is an intense and tangled imbrication of
the personal and political. It could not be more political: as Dollimore writes, "[t]he lynched, castrated black man is prefigured

here, in this scene from *Othello*" (*SLC,* 132). But nor could it be more personal, and not just for the dramatic characters but equally for any audience or reader: "One kind of political critic is inclined to say that Shakespeare is complicit with the racism of *Othello,* another that Shakespeare is clearly repudiating the racism he represents. Either view is too comfortable, and each ignores the element of fantasy in this scene" (ibid.). Dollimore's uncompromising point is that to read over the dialogue at this point in the play is, however fleetingly, to entertain a hateful pornographic fantasy. He goes on, "It seems bizarre to think of a play, performed on a stage, as a sexual fantasy: the one is overtly public, the other essentially private. But the language of the play is at this point steeped in fantasy. And anyway, fantasies, like plays, are typically visualized; they are enacted in a scene. Here the scene is what Iago/Shakespeare imagines" (ibid.). *Othello* is undeniably concerned with hateful fantasy; it is hateful fantasy that overruns and prevents Othello's life and love at their source, like foul toads who knot and gender there (cf. 4.2.63–64). In the very temple of true love Shakespeare forces a connection between desire and depravity. And yet, if Dollimore is right to stress that our best impulses are complexly entangled with their opposites, he is also right to say that there is no decadence without its ethical contrary and substrate: the most obscenely delicious depths are tasted in the same cocktail as the highest spiritual transports. This is because perverse desire depends on and solicits what it violates. It also stimulates the humanism it offends to respond with all the reinvigorated energy of outrage. The Good is inseparable from that which it seeks to defeat for good, and at once the fundamental dimension of human experience and a mere aphrodisiac. Art knows this, and keeps telling its knowledge in spite of the evasions and embarrassments of criticism.

Of course, Dollimore's view of art and life is a particular one. He wavers between recognizing that it's limited—truer at certain times than others, truer of certain literary forms or works than others—and asserting its validity for all. It seems true that mortality and its legacies of desire are freshly and inimitably troped in every authentic human life and action, though a full account of such tropes is beyond the scope even of Marcel Proust's *À la recherche du temps perdu.* Dollimore's view can account, as we have seen, for Angelo the severe judge as well as Angelo the would-be rapist, and to that extent it has plasticity and extensiveness sufficient to drama. But if Dollimore's freshly felt and perceived opposition between law and desire defines an "objective" position from which you could write a play, he equally stakes out a subjective position, making an open-eyed choice for desire at all costs. Dollimore is a thinker who insists on the existential consequence of viable theory and carries it in the direction of the lived truth. Reading him is an induction into a certain philosophy of life and a vicarious experience of it from a highly personal point of view. Such reading is perhaps above all an experience, and its fraught inconsistencies are indissociable from its meaning.

The energy of Dollimore's recoil from the merely academic derives from his tragic commitment to life. If he admires the existential consequence of Leavis's ideas, he also admires Nietzsche "for trying to live . . . a spirituality . . . at once austerely severe and romantically excessive" even though it cost him his sanity and he would otherwise have probably killed himself.[17] Such fierce subjectivity seems germane to drama inasmuch as theater gives human selfhood its own concentrated present in a body within a thoroughly embodied context—I take the animation of Hermione's statue in *The Winter's Tale* to enact this profoundly basic process of the art. Theater is a laboratory for testing and dramatizing subjective truth, by which I mean not so much what is merely true for me (such as that I like or dislike orange or oranges) but truth as it declares itself inwardly and to the world in its subjective experience and aspect. Hamlet, Macbeth, Othello, and Angelo are names of truths more complex and intensely felt than any that could be conveyed by a mere abstract noun or systematic analysis. Bradley knew this but modern theoretical criticism has, for the most part, forgotten. Shakespeare's characters have become anemic ciphers for dramas of ideas less vivid and compelling than those originally embodied in them. Recent criticism has been insufficiently based in the passions of the individual human being—and after Dollimore we're in a position to see that all the scholarship lavished on their alien embeddedness in the early modern period may in the end be a way of evading them. Such remoteness from experience explains why mainstream modern criticism has ceded its popular appeal so entirely and totally to the biographers and to Harold Bloom. In this connection, one massive gain in Dollimore's recent work is that it enables him to write directly about Shakespeare's major characters and with an existential inwardness that is one with the terrible appeal and force of the plays themselves.

Dollimore's recent work has freshly identified a structure of human experience that is so basic that it underpins both individual identity and civilization itself. He's no doubt right to say that art gives the daemonic more house room than more rational discourse, and perhaps even right to imply that art is ultimately the devil's house. I have indicated that he's always moving between an "objective" perception of an essential problematic of human nature and a fiercely subjective preference for desire over the law. As a result, during certain, more heated passages, it can seem that the devil not only has all the best tunes in Dollimore's work, but that there isn't any other music at all; but, as in a more philosophical mode he recognizes, there *are* Apollonian intensities in life and art. As his own portrayal of Leavis no less than his example of Angelo makes clear, the form-seeker isn't necessarily a dispassionate man. Nor is he always simply in flight from his real daemonic nature. Aeneas forsakes a self in forsaking Dido but gains a better one in founding Rome; and that is at least partly true of Hal's sacrifice of Falstaff to become the great King Henry V—although he, admittedly, is a daemonic figure of desire as much as an Apollonian bringer of new light and order.

In Dollimore, the underlying principle of life and literature is the violent dialectic between order and energy, law and transgressive desire, and we all are gored on its horns. But is there really no escaping this fate? Not in Dollimore, and yet one thing traditionally transcends his tearing contraries: love. St. Paul writes in terms that are surprisingly reminiscent of Dollimore's in the Epistle to the Romans:

> What shall we say then? Is the law sin? God forbid. Nay, I had not known sin, but by the law, for I had not known lust, except the law had said, "Thou shalt not covet." But sin, taking occasion by the commandment, wrought in me all manner of concupiscence. For without the law sin was dead. For I was alive without the law once: but when the commandment came, sin revived, and I died. And the commandment, which was ordained to life, I found to be unto death. For sin, taking occasion by the commandment, deceived me, and by it slew me. Wherefore the law is holy, and the commandment holy, and just, and good.
>
> Was then that which is good made death unto me? God forbid. But sin, that it might appear sin, working death in me by that which is good; that sin by the commandment might become exceeding sinful.
>
> For we know that the law is spiritual: but I am carnal, sold under sin. For that which I do I allow not; for what I would, that I do not; but what

I hate, that I do. If then I do that which I would not, I consent unto the law that it is good. Now then it is no more I that do it, but sin that dwelleth in me. For I know in me (that is, in my flesh) dwelleth no good thing, for to will is present with me; but how to perform that which is good I find not. For the good that I would I do not, but the evil which I would not, that I do. Now if I do that I would not, it is no more I that do it, but sin that dwelleth in me.

I find then a law, that, when I would do good, evil is present with me. For I delight in the law of God after the inward man, but I see another law in my members, warring against the law of my mind, and bringing me into captivity to the law of sin which is in my members. O wretched man that I am! Who shall deliver me from the body of this death?

(Romans 7.7–24)[18]

This, of course, is written from a position opposite to Dollimore's grim advocacy of desire: that is, from an agonized and failed commitment to the law. But such opposites resemble each other closely, and Paul portrays much the same structure of experience that Dollimore evokes. If we gloss "sin" and "evil" as transgression—and in doing so we lose, along with a more archaic sense of convinced and absolute values, a certain ontological density that Dollimore would probably want to retain—this becomes apparent. In Paul as in Dollimore, identity is impossible. The law simultaneously begets the desire to transgress it. That desire wrecks the law-abiding, civilized self yet simultaneously reveals or even *manufactures* an alternative, daemonic—or, according to Paul's Judeo-Christian view, a specifically demonic or satanic—self: "sin that dwelleth in me." This presents another way as well as another form of being, "another law in my members, warring against the law of my mind," a violently oppositional ethics. Entertaining movingly wistful fantasies of an anterior wholeness—"I was alive without the law once"—the subject, tragically, experiences itself as its own ruination: "the body of this death." No wonder Paul cries out, "O wretched man that I am!", expressing some of the morally honest and representative self-division that is equally and importantly a feature of Dollimore's work.

No text, to my mind, resonates more with Dollimore's recent output than this amazing passage from Romans. But of course Paul doesn't end there. The agonized, self-gnawing subject he pictures is suddenly lifted into overflowing bliss by the love revealed in Christ: and this private effect has salutary ethical and political consequences since the bliss overflows as loving thankfulness. After reading Dollimore, the question is whether this specifically credal solution to the violent dialectic of human being can work—can be translated in any way—in our secular present. The subject can't fulfill the law, Paul argues, but it is instead fulfilled by a divine gift of unconditional love. No longer under the law, its loving response to this gift now nonetheless fulfills the law easily and incidentally, because love (which always puts the other or the many before self) is the spirit of the law. It's a brilliant maneuver, whereby the subject is saved and made whole at the same time as the law is not just divorced from the ruinous impulse to transgress it but actually united with that impulsiveness which opposed it in its unregenerate state.

But does it really work? Does a gift of love really abolish the impulse to transgress? Doesn't it at least potentially produce, together with the loving thankfulness, the opposite impulse: a desire to strike out—to strike back at—the one to whom one is so profoundly indebted? Isn't something very like that what motivates Milton's Satan? Even so, the Pauline model of love does have considerable experiential plausibility outside its religious context. In happy, loving relationships (whether of an erotic or a filial character), we do feel somewhat "justified," more indifferent to social or professional judgments. "Being in love" is typically characterized by feelings of freedom, capacity, benignity, boundlessness. Of course, such feelings aren't permanent, but they can recur and breathe through a human life or relationship as its atmosphere or guiding light. Indeed, a certain continuity and interpenetration between divine and human love is expressed in the Song of Solomon, in Dante's love for Beatrice, and in the Persian poet Rumi's love for Shams; and it's worth remembering here that the love of Christ is always partly love for an embodied, wounded, mortal man. In the tenderness of love, desire isn't opposed to but largely coincides with the humane. In Shakespearean terms, much of this is visible in *Romeo and Juliet,* where the immature principals are completed in love and become tragic vessels of its boundlessness and beneficent influences. Paul's religious solution to the dilemma Dollimore poses seems worth taking seriously.

Love does powerfully surface in connection with sexual dissidence at the end of Dollimore's book on that subject.[19] But Dollimore otherwise has to exclude love, because to dwell on its humane gratifications would soften the terror of desire, which is his subject and inspiration, and perhaps fatally weaken the spe-

cifically aesthetic force of his grim vision. And if such love as
Romeo and Juliet's remains an experiential possibility for all, in
truth it is rarely achieved or sustained—hence its glitteringly poi-
gnant rarity and short lease of life in the play. Similarly, if Apollonian intensities are glimpsed in Hal's progress or in Prospero's
project, they're admittedly less vividly and importunately dramatized in Shakespeare than are daemonic temptations. Dollimore's
exclusion of such things keeps faith with the terrible regularity
with which a ruinous price for desire is exacted in art, life, and history.

Dollimore's conspectus of the history of criticism is also a form
of valediction. It is not just that he has left the academy, although
that in itself is powerful testimony to his alienation from current
criticism. Given the excessive professionalization of English, we
need people like Dollimore to write from outside the field. But Dollimore now lines up with art rather than with those who comment
on it. All criticism is humanism; indeed, all reflective or heuristic
discourse is, insofar as it simplifies and tidies up experience according to the dictates of a reasonable intelligence. Art has more
body than this, and is more written out of one. It lets in the mess
and intensity of experience and is exposed to the concomitant ethical and existential challenges. In the end then, it's not the nobly
beleaguered humanists with whom Dollimore most identifies, surprising though it was to see him lean in that direction. He stands
ultimately with those creative writers with the power to effect "a
shattering of the self into a vulnerable, receptive authenticity"
(*SLC,* 105). Among them are Shakespeare, Yeats, Gide, Lawrence,
Thomas Mann, and not the Hesse of the high humanist priesthood
so much as the one who wrote the daemonic *Steppenwolf.* Dollimore also makes less already canonical selections, like Oscar
Moore, who wrote *A Matter of Life and Sex* in the first aftermath of
the AIDS crisis.

We are a long way from the prescriptions and prejudices of current scholarship. Dollimore rejects the narrowness that confines
you to your specialism, whether medieval, early modern, antebel-
lum American, crime fiction, the long poem, or whatever. And
surely he's right to do so: rehearsing even so many prohibitively
restrictive classifications is almost infinitely wearying. And it's
equally refreshing to read Dollimore's analysis of Shakespeare and
then this extraordinary passage he excerpts from James Baldwin:

He stood there, wide-legged, humping the air, filling his barrel chest, shivering in the rags of his twenty-odd years, and screaming through the horn *Do you love me? Do you love me? Do you love me?* . . . This, anyway, was the question Rufus heard, the same phrase, unbearably, endlessly, and variously repeated, with all the force the boy had. The silence became strict with abruptly focused attention, cigarettes were unlit, and drinks stayed on the tables; and in all of the faces, even the most ruined and most dull, a curious, wary light appeared. . . . And yet the question was terrible and real; the boy was blowing with his lungs and guts out of his own short past; somewhere in that past, in the gutters or gang fights or gang shags; in the acrid room, on the sperm-stiffened blanket, behind marijuana or the needle, under the smell of piss in the precinct basement, he had received the blow from which he would never recover and this no one wanted to believe. (*SLC,* 166)[20]

The compelling message in this saxophone solo of desire's affinity to lack, obscenity, and suffering expresses a whole life and captivates and troubles everyone who hears it. It tells its own story but, like Shakespeare, is also a particular revelation of a much larger one. Utterly of its own historical and cultural context, it nonetheless draws all the ardent sadness of human history into its own supercharged density, the expressive density of each screaming note. It exemplifies the extraordinary expressive power of art and literature as Dollimore now sees it. Who really reads, for pleasure and edification, only early modern texts? Dollimore's transhistorical perspective combines with his respect for experience to allow for the intense copresence of works from different traditions and periods in the minds and lives of passionate and intellectually curious readers. In any case, there's a name for those who read essentially by period: historians.

As we have seen, Dollimore also rejects the historicist faith that everything changes historically as a frightened evasion of our mortal conditions. But, most devastatingly and profoundly, he fingers criticism's cornerstone claim to privileged and illuminating power over literature as self-serving fraud. In his view, literature speaks wild truth, which criticism will always evade. Nor is this any kind of mysticism, for the wild truth he points to bears intimately and ultimately on all kinds of human identity and conduct.

But where does this leave him? Or to put it another way: if that's the way he sees criticism, what's left for him to do? Well, Dollimore now is orientated toward that which can't be explained. He avowedly admires "a spiritual perspective," which "might (for example)

accept in principle that the object of its understanding may be ultimately incomprehensible, or comprehended fully only at the cost
of undermining what currently counts as understanding."[21] Such
epistemological openness is certainly pertinent to the literary,
whose own resistance to paraphrase bespeaks its utter incommen-
surability with even the most responsive formulation. Dollimore
propounds a self-deposing criticism always laboring at its own
frontier.

Temperamentally unlikely to go in for mysterious Heideggerian
gestures toward the ultimate mystery, he hunts after the intolerable
rather than the ineffable. Or, more precisely, his argument is that
some things are ineffable *because* they are intolerable; unamenable
to the ordered system of reason, they're quite literally unspeakable,
and to that extent they can't straightforwardly be thought at all. But
it is just such things, Dollimore maintains, that come to vivid and
unique life in art: "I disagree with Plato when he says that art does
not tell the truth about reality (the deep truth). The kind of art I am
describing might be said to undermine reason precisely because it
searches for the deeper truth. Put another way, Plato wanted to ban
art not because it told lies about reality, but because it refused his
own censorship of the real" (*SLC,* 150). The question—what to
do?—remains. Criticism laboring at its own frontiers must always
point beyond itself toward the dissolutely threatening truth of art.
This is the sort of criticism Dollimore has offered in recent work
alongside his theoretical argument. Much of it, as we have seen, has
been brilliantly illuminating, but it has also been somewhat short-
winded. Dollimore has not, for instance, offered a full-length reading of a Shakespeare play recently.

Dollimore is moving away from criticism as it has been traditionally practiced. The other thing he could do, of course, is write cre-
atively. Of the aesthetic where dangerous knowledge crosses with
dissident desire, he has written—"One might promote this as a
manifesto—as a demand for what art should be now"—and, unlike
academics as a tribe, he's always been a talented writer (*RT,* xxiv).
I've tried to indicate that his recent work has to be read partly aesthetically, because it is unusually concerned to adumbrate a vision,
but also because its expressive densities and intellectual rhythms
are basic to its meaning. Dollimore's style is also significant. His
characteristic idiom is reticent, distinguished by salient and sustained syntactic and lexical brevity: it has snap. It's marked by a
preference for natural language and, where necessary, a philosophi-

cal vocabulary distinguished by a tough concreteness as well as a skeptical and killing wit. But equally Dollimore is unbridled. Famously (or notoriously) sexually frank, he's been just as open about suicidal depression. And he flouts Anglo-American decorum in other ways as well: he's seriously interested in eros, religion, spirituality, and other such "deep" subjects, and his crisp and disciplined prose is permeable to passions of, for example, desire, solidarity, scorn, and hatred. The overall effect is of tension, a paradoxically passionate carefulness, struggled truth, exploding concentration.

Of course, the effect of all this taken together is of *character*. An irony of recent critical history is that it's been so preoccupied with subjectivity and yet so bare of the "subjectivity effect" itself. One of Dollimore's achievements is to have reflected and reflected on his own experience in a way that is a reminder of human self-experience as such, in all its quiddity, flux, and force, and of the sort of effects that reading—that is, *really reading*—can have upon identity. Although recent critics have been alert to the external conditioning of the self, they have been strangely indifferent to the subjective power of literature itself over the existentially susceptible and changing reading subject. I have commented already on Dollimore's powerful restraint, and it would be a mistake to see his self-revelation as in any way absolute or indulgent. The effect of passionate and even scandalous inwardness under such control as to be raised to representative, even symbolic power is reminiscent of Robert Lowell or Sylvia Plath. And perhaps we should also think of Rimbaud. Dollimore's life bears comparison with Rimbaud's in certain respects, but I'm more interested in the fact that Rimbaud's successive impulses to speak and be silent coexist in a fascinating and telling tension in Dollimore's work, which is reflective of the dialectic between freedom and restraint he writes about.

It may seem embarrassing to compare a critic to creative writers. But we've seen that Dollimore opposes art and criticism and gravitates to the former as a domain of secret and forbidden knowledge. After the attenuated abstractions of theory, criticism could learn much from art's embodied choreography of thought, its "musical" properties (of rhythm and of counterpoint) that are one with its subtle process of truth. Dollimore insists on the truth of art, but art's truth and credibility depends on form, and it is time for current criticism to pay more attention to its own formal processes. Dollimore's recent work persuades substantially because, as much in its style as in its content, it dramatizes its own struggle, but it is clear that Dollimore has the potential to go much further beyond conventional critical forms. I hope he will. Academic prose and production—from refereed journals, to career-making monographs, to textbooks—have become too exhaustively professionalized. If they lack experiential force and intensity, as Dollimore claims, that's partly owing to their standardized corporate forms. Dollimore calls for a more exposed encounter with literature. I believe the only way of fulfilling his demand is for criticism to come to resemble its subject more closely. There's a long way to go.

Notes

1. Jonathan Dollimore, *Radical Tragedy: Religion, Ideology and Power in the Drama of Shakespeare and his Contemporaries,* 3rd ed. (New York: Palgrave Macmillan, 2004), xv. Further references will be given parenthetically in the text as *RT* followed by the page number.

2. See Jonathan Dollimore, *Sex, Literature and Censorship* (Cambridge: Polity, 2001), 35. Further references will be given parenthetically in the text as *SLC* followed by the page number.

3. See also Friedrich Nietzsche, *Daybreak: Thoughts on the Prejudices of Morality* [1881], trans. R. J. Hollingdale, intro. Michael Tanner (Cambridge: Cambridge University Press), 140–41.

4. See also Herman Hesse, *If the War Goes On: Reflections on War and Politics* [1946], trans. Ralph Manheim (London: Pan Books, 1974), 16–17.

5. See also Hesse, *If the War Goes On,* 11.

6. Ibid., 141.

7. See also W. H. Auden, *Collected Poems,* rev. and reset ed. (London: Faber, 1994).

8. See also Theodor W. Adorno, *Prisms,* trans. Samuel and Shierry Weber (London: Neville Spearman, 1967), 34.

9. See also George Steiner, *Language and Silence: Essays on Language, Literature and the Inhuman* (New York: Athenaeum, 1977), ix.

10. See also Steiner, *Language and Silence,* ix.

11. Jonathan Dollimore, afterword to *Spiritual Shakespeares,* ed. Ewan Fernie (New York: Routledge, 2005), 213. Hereafter referred to as "Afterword."

12. Ibid., 213–14.

13. See also Nietzsche, *Daybreak,* 140–41.

14. See also Friedrich Nietzsche, *The Gay Science* [1882/1887], ed. B. Williams, trans. I. Nauckhoff (Cambridge: Cambridge University Press, 2001), 234.

15. All quotations are from *The Norton Shakespeare,* ed. Stephen Greenblatt, Walter Cohen, Jean E. Howard, and Katherine Eisaman Maus (New York: W. W. Norton and Company, 1997).

16. "Afterword," 217.

17. Ibid., 218.

18. I quote from the Authorized or King James Version.

19. Jonathan Dollimore, *Sexual Dissidence: Augustine to Wilde, Freud to Foucault* (Oxford: Clarendon Press, 1991), 356.

20. See also James Baldwin, *Another Country* (London: Michael Joseph, 1963), 16.

21. "Afterword," 214.

THWS, CWWS, WSAF, and WSCI in the Shakespeare Book Biz

BRUCE R. SMITH

The Age of Shakespeare, by Frank Kermode (New York: Modern Library, 2004), 204 pp., $21.95.

Shakespeare, by Michael Wood (New York: Basic Books, 2003), 344 pp., $29.95.

Shakespeare: The Biography, by Peter Ackroyd (New York: Doubleday, 2005), xvi + 548 pp., $32.50.

Shakespeare: The Seven Ages of Human Experience, 2nd ed., by David Bevington (Oxford: Blackwell, 2005), xi + 258 pp., $19.95 paperback.

Shakespeare After All, by Marjorie Garber (New York: Pantheon, 2004), xii + 906 pp., $40.00.

Shakespeare for All Time, by Stanley Wells (Oxford: Oxford University Press, 2003), xxi + 424 pp., $40.00.

Shakespeare's Face: Unraveling the Legend and History of Shakespeare's Mysterious Portrait, by Stephanie Nolen with Jonathan Bate, Tarnya Cooper, Marjorie Garber, Andrew Gurr, Alexander Leggatt, Robert Tittler, and Stanley Wells (New York: Free Press, 2002), xvii + 334 pp., $27.00.

Will in the World: How Shakespeare Became Shakespeare, by Stephen Greenblatt (New York: Norton, 2004), 390 pp., $26.95.

A Year in the Life of William Shakespeare, 1599, by James Shapiro (New York: HarperCollins, 2005), xix + 376 pp., $27.95.

Reviewed by Bruce R. Smith

SITTING JUST A FEW INCHES under yᵉ olde blacke beames in Hussain's Restaurant in Church Street, Stratford-upon-Avon, I once had the melancholy thought that the historical William Shakespeare (THWS), for all the omnivorous appreciation of human experience registered in his plays, and despite having gone to school (probably) just down the street, had most likely never tasted a good lamb vindaloo. Since then, however, I have come to associate "Shakespeare," if not THWS, with the smell of espresso. The books listed above have a lot to do with that association. Most of them have found a spot on the Drama or Literature shelves of Borders and Barnes & Noble, some of them cover-side out, a few of them cover-side out on a display table at the end of the aisle. Most readers of this journal will, I suspect, agree with the following responses to this phenomenon:

- Seeing the subject of one's professional expertise for sale in Borders and Barnes & Noble is like seeing a place you know well in a commercially successful movie. You feel validated.
- As a result of all those Foucault-inspired sessions at MLA and SAA in the 1970s and '80s you have to wonder what the commercial viability of these books (price: $19.90 to $40.00) means politically. What kind of "social work" are these books doing?
- At the same time, you can't help wondering why that person over there with the Prada shoulder bag—yes, *him*—is pausing at the Shakespeare table on his way to the Self-Help section.
- You're envious that no one has offered *you* a six-figure advance to write a book like one of these.

With these nine books it's probably fair to say that critical reception in academic journals has stood in inverse proportion to each book's commercial success. All nine principal authors have written for a "general" readership. It would be altogether hypocritical of me to follow the example of other academic reviewers, since, with respect to subjects other than early modern England ca. 1550–1700, I myself am just such a "general reader." As the sixty-year-old version of the child who would take to bed a volume of *The World Book Encyclopedia,* 1956 edition, I still maintain a general reader's interest in anthropology, art history, history, linguistics, musicology, philosophy, and psychology—this despite Prof. J. W. Johnson's warning in graduate school that I was a dilettante and would never get anywhere in this profession if I didn't settle down. The best way to keep up with these diverse fields, I've found, is not to wander aimlessly in the journals section of the university library but to read the reviews in the *TLS,* to which I've subscribed since 1972, the first year I could afford it, and use those reviews to choose books for sampling and, on rarer occasions than I'd like to admit, for cover-to-cover perusing. I am to anthropology what an anthropologist is to Shakespeare, and I've read these nine books with that fact in mind. Who or what is "Shakespeare" in each case? What kind of story does the author tell? To what ends? My angle here is, I suppose, narratology, but with awareness of political consequences (what kind of negotiation is this author making, or refusing to make, with the dire events of 2002–5) and psychological factors (why do readers want to encounter just this story?).

About What and in What These Nine Books Are

Why these nine books? Why now? The few documented facts about THWS are, after all, already well established. Almost all of these authors refer and defer to Sam Schoenbaum's *William Shakespeare: A Documentary Life* (1975). The "Shakespeare appropriation" business is likewise well covered already. In addition to Schoenbaum's *Shakespeare's Lives* (1991), we have Michael Bristol's *Shakespeare's America, America's Shakespeare* (1990), the essays collected in Jean I. Marsden's *Appropriating Shakespeare* (1992), Michael Dobson's *The Making of the National Poet* (1992), Tom Cartelli's *Repositioning Shakespeare* (1999), Ania Loomba's *Shakespeare, Race, and Colonialism* (2002), not to mention a new electronic journal, *Borrowers and Lenders: The Journal of Shakespeare and Appropriation.* As Alan Sinfield puts it in *Faultlines* (1992), "Shakespeare is a powerful cultural token, such that what you want to say has more authority if it seems to come through him."[1] Even readers outside the academy can't help being aware of the huge disparity between, on the one hand, the 218 documents reproduced in Schoenbaum's *A Documentary Life* and, on the other, your local rep theater's production of *Love's Labor's Lost* set on Mars in the year 2407, just before the planet is smashed by a meteor. "Shakespeare" is positioned somewhere in between Schoenbaum's historical documents and last night's stage production. It is to that vast space—"Shake-scene" in Robert Greene's coinage, "Shakespace" in Donald Hedrick and Bryan Reynolds's[2]— that these nine authors address themselves. What they find there and convey to their readers, their "general readers," gives a much better idea of the place of "Shakespeare" in public discourse than most academic books can manage. After all, the academic books are *about* "Shakespeare" in public discourse, not *in* it.

As apologists for the Earl of Oxford's authorship case are fond of pointing out, it is curious that early eyewitnesses to THWS's plays in performance do not mention the author by name. Thomas Platter, Simon Forman, Henry Jackson: in their brief jottings these witnesses to performances of *Julius Caesar, Macbeth, Cymbeline, The Winter's Tale,* and *Othello* during THWS's lifetime cut straight to the fictions they saw performed and the fictional persons who happened to strike them. Who wrote the scripts seems to have been unimportant to them. When THWS does figure in sixteenth- and seventeenth-century documents, he is only a name—a name that gradually emerges with more authority as time goes on. The name inscribed in ecclesiastical records in 1564 (birth), 1582 (marriage), 1583 (fatherhood), and 1585 (fatherhood) becomes: a factor in a lawsuit in 1589; the occasion for a punning sneer by Robert Greene in 1592; the signatory to dedicatory epistles (but not a title page author) with the publication of *Venus and Adonis* in 1593 and *Lucrece* in 1594; a payee in court financial accounts in 1595; the object of a peace-bond and the petitioner for a coat of arms on his father's behalf in 1596; the recorded purchaser of a prime piece of Stratford real estate in 1597; at last a title-page author with the publication of quartos of *Richard II, Richard III,* and *Love's Labor's Lost* in 1598; and finally, in 1623 (seven years post-obit), "Mr. WILLIAM SHAKESPEARE" in all caps on the title page to the First Folio.[3] The rest, as they say, is history. Who the subject of that history might be remains in doubt. What is Shakespeare? A word. What is in that word "Shakespeare"? What is that "Shakespeare"? Air. A trim reckoning![4]

In addition to the two syllables, we might locate "Shakespeare" in the engraved face that stares at the viewer with two left eyes in Martin Droeshout's portrait in the 1623 folio or perhaps in the stout trunk, two arms, two hands, one neck, one head, two lips indifferent red, one nose, and two eyes with lids to them that compose the monument on the north wall of Holy Trinity Church, Stratford-upon-Avon, or even in the bones that may or may not still lie under the stone inscribed "GOOD FREND FOR IESUS SAKE FOREBEAR TO DIG THE DUST ENCLOSED HERE." Beyond that, there is not much to go on. Greenblatt acknowledges as much. Near the beginning of his preface to *Will in the World,* Greenblatt announces that his aim is "to discover *the actual person* who wrote the most important body of imaginative literature of the last thousand years" (12, emphasis added); near the end, he confronts the impossibility of knowing for sure just which "Simon Hunt" in surviving written records was master of the Stratford grammar school when the "*Gu-*

lielmus filius Iohannes Shakspere" of the parish register may or may not have been a pupil there and confesses, "in these details, as in so much else from Shakespeare's life, there is no absolute certainty" (19). One has to face the fact that THWS is a function of the system of words within which "Shakespeare" happens to figure at a given moment, in given circumstances. Different forms of discourse need a different "Shakespeare," and the nine books under review here deliver several.

Rather than examine each of the nine books individually—other reviewers, after all, have done that—I will ask eight questions and see what Peter Ackroyd, David Bevington, Marjorie Garber, Stephen Greenblatt, Frank Kermode, Stephanie Nolen, James Shapiro, Stanley Wells, and Michael Wood have to say for themselves, or rather, what they have to say *for* themselves *to* general readers *about* "Shakespeare." Here are the eight questions:

- Who is the protagonist?
- Who are the antagonists?
- What is the shape of the story? What constitutes that story's beginning, middle, and end?
- What marks the turning point?
- What shapes up as the denouement?
- How is the story told? How much visual evidence is included and how important is it? Is the reader told about external events or invited to imagine interior experience? Does "evidence" come from texts of the plays and poems themselves, or from *con*-texts, from documents, artifacts, visual images, architectural remains? Is the story's narrator absent or intrusive?
- How does the story engage with political issues? How does it negotiate power differences between genders, sexual-identity groups, social classes, ethnicities?
- Where does the story's interest reside? What accounts for the story's hold on the reader?

My overall goal is to use the answers to these questions as reference points for distinguishing and naming the different ideas about "Shakespeare" that these nine writers have put on the shelves of Borders and Barnes & Noble—and hence into public discourse.

Who Is the Protagonist?

"Ask Shakespeare a question about anything and he is likely to come back with an amazing answer, or, more importantly, a still more puzzling question," Bevington observes near the beginning of *Shakespeare: The Seven Ages of Human Experience* (2). There is a "he" in this sentence, but the "Shakespeare" in Bevington's title is clearly not just THWS but the placeholder for a body of work. Wells in *Shakespeare for All Time* points out that the word "Shakespeare" can mean various things, including (1) THWS, (2) a subject studied in school, and (3) "the constantly evolving mind and imagination from which all the works emanated" (169). The prefatory epistles and poems printed with *Mr. William Shakespeare's Comedies, Histories, and Tragedies* encourage the last view: "Shakespeare" is everything that THWS wrote. That is to say, William Shakespeare is to be understood as the Collected Works of William Shakespeare (CWWS). Shapiro observes how Hemmings and Condell helped to mystify the life of THWS by printing the plays, not according to chronology, but according to genre. In Bevington's formulation, it is CWWS, and not THWS, that remains present in 2007 to answer our questions. "Shakespeare" in Bevington's preface also occupies what Foucault has called "the author function."[5] If there is a text, we tell ourselves, there must be an author of that text, and "Shakespeare" is it—not *him,* but *it.* Thus Bevington goes on to praise "the ways in which Shakespeare sought to balance ironic and satiric observation with charity and compassion. It is in this balance that we find what is so deeply humane about him" (6). The "he" here is William Shakespeare as Author Function (WSAF). In effect, Wells in *Shakespeare for All Time* delivers not only THWS, CWWS, and WSAF but a fourth "Shakespeare" whose fortunes in the seventeenth, eighteenth, nineteenth, and twentieth centuries provide the subject of most of Wells's book. These stories concern William Shakespeare as Cultural Icon (WSCI). Garber in *Shakespeare After All* remains skeptical of WSAF even as she embraces CWWS and acknowledges the inescapability of WSCI. Chapters on each of the plays individually are proceeded in Garber's book by an introduction in which "Biography and Authorship" figures as the shortest section. Positioning herself at Schoenbaum's end of the great divide, Garber offers only the barest facts about THWS. No speculation here about religion, "the lost years," the nature of Shakespeare's married life. THWS, Garber implies, remains elusive. He has disappeared into his characters, into CWWS. "Every age creates its own Shakespeare" (3), Garber declares. Most readers take that "Shakespeare" to be WSAF, but really "he" is a combination of THWS (less important), CWWS (more important), and WSCI (most important of all).

No more striking example of Garber's proposition could be found than the early seventeenth-century portrait of a young man that forms the subject of Nolen's *Shakespeare's Face.* A foreign affairs reporter for the Toronto *Globe and Mail,* Nolen wrote a story for the paper in 2001 about a portrait that had been passed down in the family of one of her parents' friends. Oral tradition in the Sanders family that the portrait represented William Shakespeare seemed to be corroborated by an inscription on the painting's surface dating the picture to 1603 and a linen label on the back that read—or once read—"Shakspere/Born April 23 = 1564/Died April 23– 1616/Aged 52/This Likeness taken 1603/Age at that time 39 ys." Although the costuming of the image, carbon-dating of the wood panel, and x-ray analysis of the layers of paint all point to the painting's origins in the early seventeenth century and confirm its largely original condition, what the Sanders portrait really has going for it is the pensive, personable face—so much more inviting to twenty-first-century eyes than the too-flat Droeshout engraving or the too-fat Stratford church monument. Nolen's book comprises not only her own account of the Sanders portrait's trajectory from hanging on a dining-room wall to storage under a bed to safekeeping in a bank vault to special exhibition at the Art Gallery of Ontario to notoriety to inconclusiveness to (one suspects) hanging on a dining-room wall—but interspersed chapters by art professionals and Shakespeare scholars, including Marjorie Garber. Taking a cue from Foucault's AF, Garber writes about "the portrait-function," which she defines as "a reflection-effect, holding, in the case of this author above all others, the mirror up to Shakespeare, showing the very age and body of the time his form and pressure" (177)—the time being *ours,* not *his.* Garber cites with glee the response of the culture correspondent of the *Los Angeles Times* to the Sanders portrait: the face in the picture, the reporter observed, strongly resembles Joseph Fiennes, the actor who impersonated the author-function in *Shakespeare in Love.* We come close here to Mars in 2407.

The protagonist in Kermode's *The Age of Shakespeare* falls somewhere in between THWS and WSAF. Kermode's short study (just over 200 pages) is part of a series called "Chronicles Books" that includes titles on literary genres (James Wood on the novel), ideas (Edward J. Larson on the theory of evolution), and institutions (Catharine R. Stimpson on the university) as well as times and places. "Shakespeare" functions for Kermode as a stand-in for an age, in just the way Napoleon does in another book in the series by Alistair Horne. The protagonist of Kermode's narrative is both a product of social and political history and an agent in his own right: "just as his was only the grandest of companies, Shakespeare was only the grandest of the poets writing for the many and various audiences who were in effect his patrons. He was, under one aspect, a very successful businessman, a type that was common at the time in other professions, but he was also a poet who had certain aristocratic contacts and, as a liveried servant of the Crown, a minor courtier, one who eventually had his own coat of arms—a man acquainted with much that went on in social ranks both above and below him" (7). As a stand-in for an age, *his* age, "Shakespeare" functions for Kermode as a kind of synecdoche.

All the other writers under review here—Wood in *Shakespeare,* Ackroyd in *Shakespeare: The Biography,* Greenblatt in *Will in the World,* Shapiro in *A Year in the Life of William Shakespeare, 1599*—purport to offer up THWS. Who in each case is that person? For all four of these writers, "Shakespeare" is a boy from the provinces who made good in London. Wood and Ackroyd stress his rural origins in Warwickshire. "Unlike the works of most of his urban or university-educated contemporaries," Wood begins, "Shakespeare's plays are full of images of flowers, trees and animals. His linguistic roots are here too—not in the more socially acceptable speech of London or the court. Shakespeare spoke with a Warwickshire accent" (17). After a brief introductory chapter on Shakespeare's birth date, Ackroyd, author of *Albion: The Origins of the English Imagination* (2002), is even more emphatic about the place of Shakespeare's birth and upbringing: "Warwickshire was often described as primeval, and contours of ancient times can indeed be glimpsed in the lie of this territory and its now denuded hills. It has also been depicted as the heart or the navel of England, with the clear implication that Shakespeare himself embodies some central national worth. He is central to the centre, the core or source of Englishness itself" (6). Wells likewise emphasizes THWS's provincial origins, although he devotes more attention to Shakespeare's local education than he does to Shakespeare's experiences in the Warwickshire countryside. Greenblatt's Shakespeare is also "a young man from a small provincial town—a man without independent wealth, without powerful family connections, and without a university education" who nonetheless becomes the world's most celebrated author (11). What distinguishes Greenblatt's Shakespeare from his peers, as we discover in chapter 1, paragraph 1, is his fascination with language, an obsession with "the magic of words" (23). Shapiro, because his interest is directed toward the single year 1599, is less concerned with Shakespeare's origins than with Shakespeare's professional achievements and habits of writing. "The Shakespeare who emerges in these pages," Shapiro warns in the preface, "is less a Shakespeare in Love than a Shakespeare at Work" (xviii). Shapiro's protagonist combines shrewd business acumen with imaginative genius. *As You Like It,* one of the plays produced during the 1599–1600 season, gives Shapiro the occasion for a freestanding chapter on "The Forest of Arden," but the subject this time is not THWS's wanderings among green fields and forests but his investments and business dealings.

The most "rounded" of the protagonists in these nine books (to use E. M. Forster's phrase from *Aspects of the Novel*) is Wood's. The Shakespeare who gives Wood his one-word title is a Catholic, a dutiful family man, and a bisexual who stops short of physically consummating his passion for the young man of the sonnets. The Catholic element looms large. John Shakespeare and Mary Arden, Wood is convinced, were devout Catholics who compromised outwardly to avoid persecution. He imagines the young Shakespeare overhearing adult conversations about the government's increasing severity: "When seen in the eyes and heard in the whispers of one's parents, such struggles of power and conscience are things a child never forgets" (46). Shame in the sonnets is interpreted as the result of Shakespeare's Catholic upbringing. If the plays do not trace "a religious trajectory" (270), it is because THWS kept his own counsel on matters of religion: "He listened to Protestant sermons, but he also knew about the 'touch of the holy bread' and the 'evening mass'" (271). Despite his absence from Stratford for months at a time, THWS remained a devoted husband and father. "It might seem as if he had in some sense abandoned his family, if not financially, then emotionally," Wood concedes. "But people have to adapt to their circumstances. London was where his employment lay—and therefore his income, which supported them. No doubt he wrote home, and both sides would have had to accommodate themselves to the situation as best they could" (165). Later, when he buys New Place: "Shakespeare clearly felt the need for some practical and emotional input in Stratford" (213). On THWS's sexuality Wood is less certain and more anxious. First he says that the passionate love for the young man expressed in certain sonnets "was *possibly* non-sexual" (177, emphasis added), then a few pages later the poet's feelings have become "*apparently not* physically consummated" (187). The slights of literary hand whereby these subjectivity effects—and displays of conventional middle-class morality—are created will occupy us shortly, but suffice it to say for now that Wood delivers up THWS in the guise of WSCI for postal code NW3 and zip code 20016, a man who exactly matches the sensibilities of the people who viewed the televisual version of this project over BBC2 in 2003 and later over PBS in the United States.

Who Are the Antagonists?

That a good story needs an antagonist is something that WSAF apparently knew well. Petruccio needs Kate, Richard III needs Henry Richmond, Achilles needs Hector, Othello needs Iago, Hamlet needs Laertes. And THWS, despite his successes, needs detractors and blocking figures. The historical record provides several candidates: Robert Greene, who in the first surviving reference to THWS as a theater professional derides him as "the only Shakescene in a country," and Ben Jonson, who manages to slide a sneer about THWS's "small Latin and less Greek" into his commendatory verses for the First Folio. Greene and Jonson make their adversarial appearances in the nine books under review here: Greene in Ackroyd's, Greenblatt's and Kermode's (along with Kyd and Marlowe) and Jonson in Wood's. Shapiro, given his focus on "Shakespeare at Work," positions THWS more generally vis-à-vis the playwrights competing for artistic and commercial success in London's busy theater scene. Alone among his peers, Shapiro's Shakespeare realizes that London audiences, able to see so many plays week in and week out, were capable of ever more sophisticated and discriminating responses: "He committed himself to writing great plays for the Globe but also to nurturing an audience comfortable with their increased complexity" (19).

For Garber, Wells, Bevington, and Nolen the antagonists hail, not from the sixteenth and seventeenth centuries, but the twentieth and twenty-first. Skeptical as she is of THWS, and committed to giving each play its fifteen- to twenty-page due, Garber casts as adversaries those critics who assume that masterpieces must be the products of one mind only. She loves to champion plays like *1*

Henry VI, often despised as being a collaborative play that lacks the workmanship of later plays more securely attributable to THWS alone. "The 'Shakespeare' that we have come to admire, revere, quote, and cite," she argues, "is often in part a composite author, since his works, even the most greatly honored ones, have been improved and altered over time by the conjectures of editors trying to make sense of what may appear to be gaps or errors in the printed text." As for *1H6,* it is "a lively, smart, sophisticated, and well-designed play, full of strong characters and fast-paced action. It plays exceedingly well onstage, and it does not deserve the literary condescension that has sometimes come its way" (90). Wells, whose book starts with "Shakespeare and Stratford" and ends with "Shakespeare Worldwide," finds his antagonists in the anti-Stratfordians, who make a three-paragraph appearance in the final chapter. Who knows what motivates them, Wells wonders. Snobbery? "Those who take this line tend to understate the value of a Stratford education, and to overvalue the talents of the aristocracy" (388). The desire for ten minutes of fame? The media love "new" news about WSCI. "Or is it mere eccentricity, bordering even on mental instability . . . , a perverse desire to challenge orthodoxy in the face of reason?" (388). Bevington's celebration of the complexity and resilience of CWWS is designed to preempt the partialities of "feminists, deconstructionists, Marxists, traditional close readers, Christian interpreters, students of cultural studies, you name it. Despite his chronological antiquity, he speaks today to the condition of each of these methodologies" (2). In the book's final chapter Bevington casts the entire academic enterprise as an agon. After a distinguished career of nearly fifty years, he ought to know. "Ideological rivalries," Bevington observes, "encourage young teachers to find out who the Enemy is, and to move ahead in the academic world by overthrowing older and presumably outmoded ways of thinking about Shakespeare (or any other subject). These are the hazards. . . . The hope lies in Shakespeare's malleability. He is eternally relevant because he responds acutely to virtually any question that is put to him, and does so often by disconcerting us with questions of his own" (238). Nolen's story of the Sanders family's attempt to authenticate their portrait of THWS at age thirty-nine finds its antagonists among the museum curators, auction-house experts, and Shakespeare scholars, all of whom doubt, albeit politely, the family legend about the portrait's origins.

What Is the Shape of the Story?

1564 April 26 Guilelmus filius Iohannes Shakespere

[15 March 1595] to Willi^am Kempe Will^am Shakespeare & Richarde Burbage ser-
   vaunts to the Lord Chamberleyne . . . xiij^l vj^s viij^d

1616 April 25 Will Shakspere gent.[6]

In rough outline the beginning, middle, and end of the story of
THWS are dictated by the surviving life-records. WSCI begins with
comedies, middles with histories (*OED* "middle" v. 6.c⊥), and
ends with tragedies. The story of WSAF is curiously symmetrical.
It stretches, in the Oxford second edition, from *Two Gentlemen of
Verona* (1589–91) to *The Two Noble Kinsmen* (1613), those two
plays about pairs of male friends set at odds by a woman. *The Life
of Henry the Fifth* (1598–99) and *The Tragedy of Julius Caesar*
(1599) come halfway through. For the most part it is the life-records
associated with THWS that govern the shape of Greenblatt's and
Wood's narratives. Each of them first situates THWS solidly in
Stratford-upon-Avon, then takes him to London, and finally returns
him to Stratford in unapologetically sentimental circumstances.
"He made a decision early in his life," Greenblatt avers in the closing pages of *Will in the World,* "or perhaps a decision was made for
him: he had something amazing in him, but it would not be the gift
of the Demiurge; rather, it would be something that would never
altogether lose its local roots" (389). Wood's protagonist is a loving
husband and father; Greenblatt's, only a loving father: "What
Shakespeare wanted was only what he could have in the most ordinary and natural way: the pleasure of living near his daughter and
her husband and their child" (390).

The three-part structure of Greenblatt's and Wood's stories become seven in Bevington's attempt to use Jaques' set piece on "the
seven ages of man" as a way of bringing together the known facts
about THWS, the evidence of life experience in CWWS, and the
continuing fascination of WSCI. The life-narrative is confined to
just a few pages in the first chapter, followed by a consideration of
the Oxford authorship case, but passing references to THWS's life
circumstances are made throughout Bevington's book. Thus THWS
wrote his comedies about love when he was twenty-six to thirty-
six. In the 1590s he wrote about "The Coming-of-Age of the Male"
in the history plays (80–101), turning about 1600 to "Love and
Friendship in Crisis" in the problem plays and *Hamlet* (102–28),

confronting "Political and Social Disillusionment, Humankind's Relationship to the Divine, and Philosophical Scepticism" in his midcareer tragedies (129–59) and "Misogyny, Jealousy, Pessimism, and Midlife Crisis" in the tragedies he wrote later (160–89), before turning to "Ageing Fathers and their Daughters" in the romances (190–211). "We do not know what Shakespeare's relationships with his immediate family were really like," Bevington is careful to say. "We can spectulate, however, that the story of Pericles' separation from and eventual reunion with wife and daughter was just the kind of tragicomic dream to give Shakespeare the chance to express, in a play, the sorts of feelings that a man might have in rejoining his wife and daughter after so long a separation" (193).

Genealogies of John Shakespeare's family and Mary Arden's figure in most of these books, but Ackroyd, Kermode, and Wells expand the time frame in significant ways, while Shapiro collapses it into a single year. Ackroyd and Kermode both reach into the past, Ackroyd to the primeval "Albion" into which THWS was born, Kermode to the political problems of the Tudor dynasty's claim to the throne and the controversies over religion. Wells's sights are turned in the opposite direction, toward what has happened to WSCI in the four centuries since THWS's death in 1616. The last of Wells's three biographical chapters is focused on "Shakespeare the Writer," a segue into the history of productions, adaptations, and cultural appropriations that occupy two thirds of Wells's book. Shapiro's story in *A Year in the Life of Shakespeare, 1599,* is in a way all middle, although he of course gestures toward the past and the future in the careers of THWS and WSAF. The year itself is organized into four seasons—winter, spring, summer, autumn— which makes sense in terms of the performing calendar (in addition to appearing at the royal court and the Inns of Court during Christmas festivities, playing companies like the Lord Chamberlain's Men seem to have enjoyed their best box offices in the stretch between Christmas and Lent) if not in the reckoning of the new year's beginning at the vernal equinox in March. The sequence of seasons from winter to autumn gives Shapiro's epilogue a certain elegiac quality, as the annus mirabilis of 1599 was succeeded by the political disillusionment of the Essex Rebellion and a relatively fallow period for Shakespeare as a scriptwriter.

In contrast to these various schemes for aligning THWS, WSAF, and WSCI, Garber by and large refuses narrative and the discriminations and distortions that beginnings, middles, and ends entail.

Her forty-one-page introduction, about twice the length of her longer chapters on plays like *Hamlet,* comprises sections on "The Stage and the Page," "Biography and Authorship," "the Theater in Renaissance England," "Shakespeare and Culture," and (best of all) "Planet Shakespeare." If there is a story here about CWWS, it is not linear. Near the beginning of the introduction, Garber insists that in her pages "Shakespeare" is nowhere to be found. After a survey of postcolonial readings of *The Tempest,* Garber poses the question that her reader must be thinking: "But where did 'Shakespeare' stand on these questions? As I will suggest through the chapters that follow, the brilliant formal capacities of drama are such that the playwright's voice is many voices. Shakespeare is Prospero, Caliban, Ariel, and the wondering Miranda" (6). The introduction concludes with a gesture toward those would-be authority figures who step forward at the end of WSAF's scripts—Fortinbras in *Hamlet,* Albany (or is it Edgar?) in *King Lear,* Leontes in *The Winter's Tale*—would-be authority figures whose stories are patently *not* the stories that other characters onstage (not to mention the audience in the house) would tell about the events that have just transpired.

What Marks the Turning Point?

Getting to London, of course. After that, writing *Hamlet.*

Ackroyd's account is the most grandiloquent. Leaving a not to-tally happy marriage might have been part of THWS's reasons for leaving Stratford. The opportunity to join a troupe of traveling players might have been another. But Ackroyd finds the ultimate reason in the stars: "In the lives of great men and women, however, there is a pattern of destiny. Time and place seem in some strange way to shape themselves around them as they move forward. There would be no Shakespeare without London. Some oblique or inward recognition of that fact spurred his determination" (108). This from the author of *London: The Biography* (2001). Greenblatt and Wood rehearse more circumstantial explanations for how THWS found himself on the road to London, but the journey thither occupies the same pivotal position in both stories. Greenblatt imagines THWS joining a group of actors who tour the southern counties before they get to London—a possibility that is appealing in part because it lets us imagine Shakespeare's first view of London as just what we see in those often-reproduced bird's-eye views from the south. Ackroyd's THWS approaches from the north, of course—from "the heart or the navel of England"—via Aldersgate or Bishopsgate. Among the writers under review here, only Kermode and Wells resist the London passage. Kermode imagines THWS leading "a double life," in two locales, London and the country—an arrangement that was not possible for professional writers who hailed from farther away. Wells calls attention to the regular communications that Stratford had with London (there was apparently twice-a-month goods carriage between the two places, and letters indicate frequent visits to London by Stratford town officials and merchants) as well as THWS's continuing investments and real estate transactions back in Stratford. In sum, "Shakespeare was, I suspect, our first great literary commuter" (37).

As for WSAF, CWWS, and WSCI, the turning point is just where we would expect it to be from the chronological printing of the plays and poems in the Oxford second edition: in 1599. Wood, who casts Jonson as THWS's main antagonist, momentarily entertains the possibility that *Julius Caesar* might be WSAF's breakthrough text, a response to Jonson's classicizing critique, but most of the writers here (excepting the antinarrativizing Garber, of course) locate the pivot of THWS's career just where it has been located since the early nineteenth century, in *Hamlet.* Kermode finds in the play a decisive shift from old to new styles of language as well as from old to new styles of acting. Wood calls attention to 1599 as the midpoint in THWS's career and sees *Hamlet* as the culmination of a burst of creative energy that includes *Richard II, 1* and *2 Henry IV,* and *A Midsummer Night's Dream.* "It is no surprise," Wood says, "that from this time Shakespeare spread his wings and his art widened and deepened" (160). The chapter subheading on *Hamlet* is entitled, without embarrassment, "The Invention of the Human" (238ff.)—a formulation that Greenblatt confirms. With this play, Greenblatt claims, WSAF "made a discovery by means of which he relaunched his entire career" (323). That discovery turns out to be not just the extended soliloquy as a dramatic device but "radical excision" (323) that implies a consciousness behind the words. What is more, if Wood can be believed, *Hamlet* shows THWS, a Catholic, coming to terms with his country's religious history at an epochal moment: "The pre-Reformation past is beginning to recede, and now Shakespeare can dramatize it, exorcizing the ghosts" (240).

It is Shapiro who gives this epochal moment its fullest treatment.

The year 1599 witnessed the crushing of the Irish rebellion, the launching of the East India Company, the weathering of another Armada threat, and the transfer of the Lord Chamberlain's Men from their hired quarters at the Curtain to the new Globe Theater they had erected on the Bankside, as well as the year in which WSAF wrote or saw produced *Henry V, Julius Caesar, As You Like It,* and *Hamlet.* "I've chosen to write about 1599," Shapiro says in the preface, "not only because it was an unusually fraught and exciting year but also because, as critics have long recognized, it was a decisive one, perhaps *the* decisive one, in Shakespeare's development as a writer" (xvi). The turning point within the turning point comes in the first chapter of the "Autumn" section: "In *Hamlet,* Shakespeare once again found himself drawn to the epochal, to moments of profound shifts, of endings that were also beginnings. . . . In *Hamlet* he perfectly captures such a moment, conveying what it means to live in the bewildering space between familiar past and murky future" (279). In particular, Shapiro contrasts the collapse of the age of chivalry and the beginnings of the age of mercantilism, empire, and globalization. That turning point was played out in 1599 between, on the one hand, Essex's attempt to act the chivalric hero in Ireland and, on the other, the founding of the East India Company. It is telling, Shapiro observes, that *Hamlet* is a remake of a play that was holding the stage when Shakespeare first arrived in London. It is "a play poised midway between a religious past and a secular future" (301).

What Shapes Up as the Denouement?

As far as THWS is concerned, the story ends as all human stories do, with death. What immediately precedes that event varies: the pleasure of living near his daughter Susannah and her husband and their child (Greenblatt), using his will to settle the score with his troublesome daughter Judith (Ackroyd), a final bout with alcoholism (Wood). On the subject of THWS's retirement to Stratford, Wood's range of reference is the broadest: "Had he perhaps lost the fierce creative energy that had driven him to such spectacular results in the late 1590s and early 1600s? . . . Was he burnt out? Was this a long-planned retirement? Had Anne finally put her foot down? Or did he simply not want to work so hard? Realistically, this is as good a guess as any" (300). For WSAF the denouement is less certain. Which among the several possible consummations is most devoutly to be wished? *The Tempest,* in Bevington's view, remains WSAF's "last play," even though he later collaborated on others. It was written as "a way of demonstrating the things he could do best" (219). For Garber, *The Two Noble Kinsmen,* as WSAF's *last* last play, represents "the melting of two (kinsmen, authors) into one" and thus the elimination of "friction and rivalry, but at the price of death" (906). More uncertain still is the denouement of WSCI's story. A short-range conclusion is provided by Kermode, who ends his book with the heightening of economic and social conflict in the years after THWS's death and the eruption of civil war in 1642. More optimistic, indeed triumphalist, endings are provided by Bevington and Wells, who celebrate the staying power of WSCI across the four centuries since THWS's death. Bevington's WSCI is, as we have seen, ready for any and all questions that might be thrown at him. Wells's is more subject to mutability. The international presence of WSCI may continue to increase, but in ways about which Wells registers ambivalence. Productions of all sorts continue to flourish on the world's stages, but WSCI seems not to have inspired many musical adaptations since Benjamin Britten. Is the growth of "the heritage industry" with its assorted T-shirts and tchotchkes to be celebrated or scorned? What about the "frenetic" workings (399) of the academic "Shakespeare industry" (including this review)?

How Is the Story Told?

There are four axes to be considered here:

- the ratio of visual images to written text
- the degree to which evidence is culled from WSAF's plays and poems, as opposed to other documents
- the balance between reportage of external events and appeals to interior experience
- the reticence or intrusiveness of the narrator.

One hundred twenty full-color illustrations in Wood, 31 in Wells, 23 in Nolen, 14 in Greenblatt, 14 in Shapiro, 11 in Ackroyd: perhaps the most striking difference between these cover-side-out books and the academic books lower on the shelf (or available only on special order) is production values. Wood's is by far the most visual in the way it conveys information, as one might expect from a book that was produced to accompany the television series *In Search of Shakespeare,* broadcast over BBC2 in 2003 and later over PBS in the United States. In fact, the dust jacket on the Basic Books edition carries an emblem saying "SEE IT ON PBS." See it, not read it. To the credit of Wood and his designers, the book is full of illustrations presenting places, faces, and objects beyond the usual suspects like Anne Hathaway's cottage, and to see already familiar images—the records of THWS's christening and burial, title pages to various quartos and the 1623 folio, the Earl of Southampton with his black cat, William Camden's limning of Queen Elizabeth's funeral procession—in full texture-rich color is to discover a startling, emotional, tactile immediacy. Most of these expensively reproduced images remain, however, mere illustrations—glanced at in the text but not subjected to detailed scrutiny. Notable exceptions are the illustrations Wood provides of black people in Shakespeare's London. Wells's images (in addition to the 31 in color there are 147 in black-and-white) likewise include unexpected items—a sixteenth-century hornbook with its handle, a page from William Lily's *A Short Introduction of Grammar* showing phrases repeated in the schoolroom scene in *The Merry Wives of Windsor,* the reconstructed Blackfriars Theater in Staunton, Virginia, assorted production stills from the nineteenth and twentieth centuries—and in general those images are coordinated with the written text more closely than they are in Wood. Nolen's account of the Sanders portrait includes a useful gallery of other portraits that have been taken to represent Shakespeare, as well as interesting reproductions of cross-section analysis of the painting's wooden support and layers of pigment. In general, however, images in all the other illustrated books provide little more than period atmosphere. They do not figure in any sustained way in the books' arguments. Other than the covers (all three in full color), Kermode, Garber, and Bevington are not illustrated at all.

One curious feature of Wood's *Shakespeare* deserves comment. Many of Wood's illustrations of places are Victorian photographs. Holy Trinity Church in 1870, London's Green Dragon inn in the 1880s, a lane near St. Helen's Bishopsgate in 1886, the Southwark docks in 1881, sixteenth-century houses in Bermondsey Street Southwark in 1893, the street called Cloth Fair in Smithfield in the late nineteenth century: with the exception of Holy Trinity Church,

none of these structures and street scenes is to be seen today
(though Cloth Fair comes close), but Wood's choice washes the
whole enterprise in a sepia-toned, fuzzy-focus nostalgia all too familiar from "the heritage industry." As Trevor Nunn observes in
the introduction to the film script of *Twelfth Night* (1996), a Victorian setting is comfortable for most contemporary viewers: distant
enough to seem "not now" but recent enough to appear imaginable
and inhabitable.[7] That is especially the case in Britain, where nineteenth-century buildings still dominate many cityscapes. To judge
from Merchant-Ivory films of classic novels and any number of BBC
and PBS dramatizations, not to mention Kenneth Branagh's films of
Much Ado About Nothing (1993) and *Hamlet* (1996), the nineteenth
century has become "the default past" for the sorts of people likely
to buy any of these nine books. And so it is in Wood's *Shakespeare:*
the reader is invited to see early modern England through a sentimental Victorian filter that lets in bisexuality but keeps out the possibility that personhood in 1599 might have been a very different
thing from personhood in 2003.

To what extent do these nine authors turn to contextual documents for their evidence about THWS and to what extent do they
depend on internal evidence from the plays and poems themselves? Kermode, with his insistent focus on political and social
history, is probably the most contextual of the nine authors; Bevington, the freest in extrapolating biography from WSAF's fictions.
Kermode's is primarily a historical narrative, in which the question
of Tudor succession, religious controversies, fluidity of class structures, the Essex Rebellion, James's accession, and so on. become
the main events that "explain" THWS's life. At the opposite extreme is Bevington's conviction that the THWS's life-experiences
are registered in WSAF's scripts, a situation that unlocks "the mystery of why he engages our imaginations so deeply. He writes of
desire, jealousy, ambition, ingratitude, misanthropy, and charitable
forgiveness because he has known what it is like to be there" (284).
The other writers (except for Garber, who does not concern herself
with biography after the introduction, and Nolen, who hardly concerns herself with the scripts at all) can be ranged between these
two poles:

Kermode | Wells | Shapiro | Ackroyd | Wood | Greenblatt | Bevington

Wells's account of THWS's life in Stratford is based on not only
the manuscripts and printed records that all these writers cite but,

to a much greater degree than anyone else, on the archaeological evidence of the surviving buildings associated with THWS. The built environment likewise figures in Shapiro's imaginative synthesis of a huge amount of printed evidence in reconstructing not only the events but the feel of THWS's life in 1599. "Winter," for example, opens with Shakespeare and company arriving at Whitehall Palace on Tuesday, December 26, 1598, for an evening performance. Shapiro uses Paul Hentzner, Thomas Platter, and other travelers' descriptions of the palace to set the scene in amazingly precise detail—and then introduces THWS amid those details and endows him with a consciousness. "A short detour up the staircase into the privy gallery overlooking the tiltyard led Shakespeare into a breathtaking gallery," Shapiro relates. "Its ceiling was covered in gold, and its walls were lined with extraordinary paintings" (25). Despite Shapiro's protestations in the preface that we can never know what THWS felt, he nonetheless is a master at making us feel that we do. It's plausible, of course, that THWS might have gone up the staircase to the privy gallery. But who would have given him permission? Who would have unlocked the doors? Hentzner, Platter, and the other foreign visitors who have left accounts of the space had access because of connections and letters of introduction. Hentzner was tutor to a young Silesian nobleman, Platter was a medical student with important London contacts. THWS and company figured, in the eyes of some members of the court at least, as the hired help, brought in for the evening's entertainment. In general, though, Shapiro is too smart for such slips. More typical of his magisterial arrangement of the evidence is his locating both THWS and Edmund Spenser at Westminster in December 1598. The possibility that Spenser might have seen the Lord Chamberlain's Men perform *2 Henry IV* at Whitehall Palace on December 26 gives Shapiro his prompt for considering impressment as a concern in both *2H4* and the English military occupation of Ireland. Spenser's death and funeral in Westminster a few weeks later provokes reflections on differences between Spenser and THWS with respect to circumstances, careers, and writings.

Like Wells, Ackroyd is interested in the evidence of timbers and plaster, in the arrangement of rooms in John Shakespeare's Henley Street house, the activities that took place in each one, the furnishings, the sounds, even the smells of leather-curing out back. "No other Elizabethan dramatist employs so many domestic allusions," Ackroyd observes. "Shakespeare maintained a unique connection

with his past" (33). In his determination to set down THWS amid
the quotidian realities of Elizabethan life, Ackroyd is willing to
take more risks than Wells and Shapiro. He begins with the documentary facts—the record of THWS's christening, known facts
about John Shakespeare and Mary Arden, the visits of the Queen's
Men and the Earl of Worcester's Men to Stratford in 1569, and so
on—and proceeds to fill in circumstantial detail from social and
political history—producing, in effect, historical "thick description." Usually the risks work. Ackroyd reports, for example, that
an inventory of Mary Arden's father's possessions includes several
painted cloths: "Mary Arden was bequeathed at least one of these
painted tapestries in her father's will, and it is most likely to have
ended up on a wall in Henley Street" (31). He proceeds to make
suggestive connections with painted cloths in WSAF's scripts:
Macbeth's reference to the "Eye of Child-hood that feares a painted
Deuill" and Falstaff's reference to "Lazarus in the painted cloth"—
which put me in mind of Lucrece's use of the Fall of Troy, painted
on a wall or on a cloth, to make sense of her misfortune. Painted
cloths, Ackroyd establishes, were something THWS likely knew
firsthand as a child, perhaps even had studied with the intensity of
a Lucrece. Likely. Perhaps.

Wood's way with evidence is more adventurous still. At first
blush his narrative reads as if it were absolutely factual. A great
deal of material, economic, and social history is put in place, then
THWS is introduced into the midst, with only the occasional foray
into what THWS "must have felt" (for example, the child listening
to his parents talk about religion). Wood's evidence is unapologetically *circumstantial* evidence. In several places he introduces what
he calls "shadow lives," excursions into biographies of people like
Robert Southwell and Emilia Lanier, whose lives may have inter-
sected with THWS's. There are also "shadow texts" like Samuel
Harsnett's *A Declaration of Egregious Popish Imposters,* invoked in
connection with *Lear,* and Virgil's *Aeneid,* in connection with *The
Tempest.* Often this circumstantial evidence leads Wood to strikingly original observations, such as the use he makes of two
"joyned beds" included in the inventory of the goods of Anne Hathaway's father, recently deceased when THWS came courting. At
the time, only Anne and her brother Bartholomew lived in the
house at Shottery, "so, although pre-marital sex among the young
usually took place in the open air in those days, the Hathaway
home must have been especially attractive to William and the mis-

tress of the house" (81). But how sure can we be that premarital sex usually took place outside? It does in "It was a lover and his lass . . . who through the green cornfields did hie." But did it always? Wood notes that, although the path from Stratford to Shottery now skirts allotment gardens and housing estates, THWS "would have passed through cornfields on either side" (81)—*green* cornfields, one imagines. Wood's circumstantial evidence works best when he is staying closest to his documentary sources. Wood is at his interpretative best when he describes his retracing of THWS's visit to the College of Heralds in London when he was renewing his father's application for a court of arms. The physical premises today are different, but the documents that Wood examines there—the interviewers' scribbled notes of his interview with THWS, the multiple drafts of the grant—create "one of the most intimate moments of the biography" (167).

Wood's incursions into the plays and poems are surprisingly rare. "It is often said that we can't find out from his works what Shakespeare believed," Wood admits, "and to a degree that assertion is true of his plays, which were crafted for their audience. But his poems are different because in most of them he was free to say what he wanted, and the indications are that he did so. A few scholars have dismissed the search for real people in the sonnets as fantasy. But there are strong reasons to think that Shakespeare used his poems as ways of getting things off his chest" (177). At this game Greenblatt is both more daring and more subtle. In his attempt to "discover" the actual person who wrote the most important imaginative literature of the past thousand years Greenblatt cultivates a double consciousness not unlike that possessed by WSAF. "Since the actual person is a matter of well-documented public record," Greenblatt says, *Will in the World* "aims to read the shadowy paths that lead from the life he lived into the literature he created" (12). Greenblatt finds this double life even in the sonnets, which seem so direct: "To be a very public man—an actor onstage, a successful playwright, a celebrated poet, and at the same time to be a very private man—a man who can be trusted with secrets, a writer who keeps his intimate affairs to himself and subtly encodes all references to others: this was the double life Shakespeare had chosen for himself" (249). External events—books read, people met, scenes observed, conversations overheard—become, along the shadowy path that Greenblatt treads, words in the theater. Internal experience figures as the way station between these events. The effect is to create an illusion of presence. "Shakespeare" becomes the placeholder between people and events in the historical record and the representation of those people and events in Shakespeare's plays and poems. As a result, "Shakespeare" seems both *there* and *not there.* Sometimes he is intimately present, as in Greenblatt's treatment of the sonnets as records of erotic imagination, but more often he is curiously absent: "Shakespeare was a master of double-consciousness. He was a man who spent his money on a coat of arms but who mocked the pretentiousness of such a claim; a man who invested in real estate but who ridiculed in *Hamlet* precisely such an entrepreneur as he himself was; a man who spent his life and his deepest energies in the theater but who laughed at the theater and regretted making himself a show" (155). Academic readers have tended to write off *Will in the World* as a work of fiction. Greenblatt's skill in cultivating a double consciousness—so like the skill of an actor pretending to be someone else—produces a story that, for me at least, is just as plausible as the stories that stay closer to external evidence.

These differences among the nine writers in (1) the kind of evidence they marshal and how they handle it are allied with (2) the different degrees to which the narrator in each case recedes or intrudes and (3) the very different balances these narrators set up between external third-person narrative and appeals to first-person subjectivity. The most insistently present narrators here are Bevington and Wells. Both authors offer their books as summations of lifetime experience with "Shakespeare." In the first sentence of the preface Wells declares that his book "is based on a half-century's engagement with Shakespeare" (xviii) and provides an account of that engagement, beginning with Wells's grammar-school teacher in Hull, memorable performances he saw as an undergraduate in London between 1948 and 1951, and later as director of the Shakespeare Institute in Stratford-upon-Avon and vice-chair of the governors of the Royal Shakespeare Company. Bevington is no less present in the pages of *Shakespeare: The Seven Ages of Human Experience.* The book is presented to readers as the record "of a continuing journey of discovery" (xi) that has involved colleagues and students across nearly fifty years. Amid the ideological bickering of the academic establishment, amid terrorism, rapid social change, environmental degradation, and name-calling that passes for political discourse, Bevington professes personal loyalty to the "Shakespeare" who can be depended on "to question our answers" (247).

At the opposite extreme, in splendid third-person detachment, stands Kermode. The others are ranged in between, with Ackroyd closer to the first-person side and Shapiro closer to the third-person side. With respect to the subject at hand, "Shakespeare," a sense of intimacy is not necessarily allied with the forwardness or diffidence of the storyteller. The most intimate "Shakespeare" among these nine accounts is Greenblatt's, even though Greenblatt as author function maintains a respectful distance. The trick in achieving this subjectivity effect is deftly to fuse THWS with CWWS without directly appealing to WSAF, all the while casting WSCI as more a magician with words than a recorder of historical events.

How Does the Story Engage with Political Issues?

Despite the political turn in academic criticism since the 1970s, the Literature and Drama shelves in Borders and Barnes & Noble are usually closer to the History and Philosophy shelves than they are to the Politics and Political Science shelves. One might have supposed that these nine books, commercial products designed for "general readers," would have little to say about the politics of THWS, WSAF, CWWS, or even WSCI. That is not the case. What varies among the books is the focus—politics *then* versus politics *now*—and the terms in which political interests are framed. The explicit concern in most of these books is turned toward the politics of THWS's own time and place. Political and social history is, indeed, the main subject of Kermode's book. However, Kermode's concerns with the big questions about succession and royal power, social mobility, and economic history turn out to be anything but typical. In most of the other books, the obsessive interest falls instead on one question: was or was not THWS a Catholic?

Wood answers that question with an emphatic yes. Other political happenings—the Essex Rebellion, for example—are very much "shadow events" in comparison with religious politics. Wood's most interesting gambit is to read *Henry VIII* as an attempt, late in WSAF's career, to bridge the Catholic-Protestant divide. Wells treats the Catholic hypothesis about "William Shakeshafte" cautiously, pronouncing it "an intriguing theory" (21) and ultimately deciding that "the absence of dogma" in WSAF's writings offsets the altogether circumstantial evidence about THWS's Catholic connections. Greenblatt gives the Catholic hypothesis more sympathetic play but concludes, "Out of a tissue of gossip, hints, and obscure clues a shadowy picture can be glimpsed, rather as one can glimpse a figure in the stains on an old wall" (103). For Greenblatt, as for Wells, WSAF fails to pass the ultimate test: how Catholics and Catholic dogma are portrayed in CWWS. In sum, "If his father was both Catholic and Protestant, William Shakespeare was on his way to being neither" (113). Shapiro's THWS and WSAF are likewise secular. The question of THWS's religious sensibilities is approached by Shapiro obliquely, via Flavius's use of religious terms in his iconoclastic instructions to Marcus in *Julius Caesar:* "Go you down that way towards the Capitol; / This way will I. Disrobe the images / If you do find them decked with ceremonies" (152). The translation of religious terminology to a theatrical space is symptomatic, Shapiro argues, of the transubstantiation whereby the secular stage in the later sixteenth century took on the functions of the religious rituals of pre-Reformation England. Ackroyd's range of political reference is broader, but he too gives the Catholic hypothesis full consideration and concludes that the presence of a large Catholic constituency in the Stratford of THWS's youth "does not necessarily imply that Shakespeare himself professed that faith— assuming that he professed any—only that he found the company of Catholics familiar" (39).

The desire to establish that THWS was secular, skeptical, tactical, or at least only conventionally Protestant makes sense for the latte-drinking buyers of these books, but concern about religion suggests more than a narrowly historical interest. It points, I believe, to an absolutely contemporary, early twenty-first-century anxiety about the place of individuals within cultural pluralism. The ideological standoffs that Bevington finds characteristic of late twentieth-century academic criticism—feminists, deconstructionists, Marxists, close readers, Christian interpreters, students of cultural studies all competing to deliver The Truth—have been supplanted, among academics at least, by a political culture of accommodation in which the supposed Catholic identity of THWS emerges as an exemplary test case.

What Accounts for the Story's Hold on the Reader?

That man with the Prada shoulder bag on his way to the Self-Help section—why would he want to buy one of these books? Probably for the same reason that he might decide to buy a copy of *People* magazine in a supermarket checkout line: to find out something behind or beyond or under or perhaps within an otherwise opaque, publicly available image. Is there an inside to this outside? WSCI is the reason these nine books have sold well. "How Shakespeare Became Shakespeare"—that is, how THWS became WSCI—is Greenblatt's subtitle. Shapiro, too, confesses, "At the heart of this book is the familiar desire to understand how Shakespeare became Shakespeare" (xiii). Bevington alludes to "the mystery" of why "Shakespeare" continues to engage "our imaginations" (284). Wood deploys the same mystery-motif when he chooses to begin *Shakespeare* with the whitewashing of the wall paintings in the Guild Chapel in Stratford three years before Shakespeare's birth. "So here's a parable at the start of our tale, but one full of ambiguity," Wood declares. "What lies under the whitewash? What lies behind actions and words in an age when covering up, concealment and dissimulation became the order of the day? Such questions are as relevant to the life of the greatest poet of all time as they are to untangling the tale of his father and his neighbors in his home town" (11). Wood's *Shakespeare* is all about a mystery that has been covered up, about getting at the truth that four centuries of Shakespeare scholarship and high-culture imperialism have whitewashed.

So what's behind the whitewash over "Shakespeare"? I personally can think of a few possible things: that THWS was a sodomite, that he was very ready to sue a tenant over unpaid rent, that he wrote the two plays per year that his agreement with his fellows demanded and no more than that. But, no, what lies behind Wood's whitewash is something much more mundane: Shakespeare's regional accent, the likelihood that he was a Catholic, perhaps his chronic depression as registered in Antonio in *The Merchant of Venice.* These are things that I, the guy in the checkout line at Borders, standing behind the guy with the Prada shoulder bag, can relate to. *Madame Bovary, c'est moi.* William Shakespeare, that's me. I disappear into "Shakespeare." In that respect, Nolen's quest for *Shakespeare's Face* may be the most basic and honest book here. It trades on the need to find a psychologically compelling likeness to put to WSAF. And the more that face "likes me," the better. As Alexander Leggatt in his contribution to *Shakespeare's Face* frankly admits, "Pictures can help us organize our ideas, and a picture of a writer can help us organize our ideas about the writer" (281). The versions of "Shakespeare" on display in these nine books are, with the exception of the Sanders portrait in Nolen's book, verbal representations, not visual. All the more reason, perhaps, that they should return our gaze so intently. But, of course, words printed on the page and pigments suspended in oil are not the same thing as a person. What captures our imagination is an illusion. It is the elusiveness of the face in the Sanders portrait that Leggatt likes most. "The Droeshout Shakespeare gives us a flat stare," Leggatt observes, "the Sanders Shakespeare looks away; the Sanders Shakespeare is more human. That face keeps its secrets—including the secret of its identity. The fact that it does so may be, paradoxically, one of the best arguments for seeing it as the face of Shakespeare" (297).

The last two sections in Garber's introduction, "Shakespeare and Culture" and "Planet Shakespeare," demonstrate how "Shakespeare literacy" has changed over time. Earlier assumptions, in the eighteenth, nineteenth, and twentieth centuries, that readers and listeners would know all about specific plays and the contexts from which quotations are taken, have been supplanted by a free-for-all in which lines are cited out of context as guarantors of cultural wisdom and the correctness of the writer or speaker's own position. "One touch of nature makes the whole world kin": you can buy a coffee mug inscribed with that line from *Troilus and Cressida,* but in its original context the line refers, not to the common humanity that people share across times and cultures, but to the sexual impulses that humans share with beasts. Garber cites from *The Congressional Record* a number of outrageous examples of such misappropriations. At the same time, I would observe, the plots of WSAF have been cut loose from the words in which they once were embodied, so that sisterly rivalry in *The Taming of the Shrew* can become a contemporary teen flick in *Ten Things I Hate About You.* And academics love the validation.

Is it Mercury, Clio, or Narcissus who serves as muse to these nine books?

Notes

1. Alan Sinfield, *Faultlines: Cultural Materialism and the Politics of Dissident Reading* (Berkeley: University of California Press, 1992), 11.

2. Robert Greene, *Greene's Groats-worth of Wit* (1592), excerpt repr. in *The Norton Shakespeare,* ed. Stephen Greenblatt, Walter Cohen, Jean E. Howard, and

Katharine Eisaman Maus (New York: Norton, 1997), 3321–22; Donald Hedrick and Bryan Reynolds, "Shakespace and Transversal Power," in *Shakespeare Without Class: Misappropriations of Cultural Capital,* ed. Hedrick and Reynolds (New York: Palgrave, 2000), 3–47.

3. These references to Shakespeare's name are collected in William Shakespeare, *The Complete Works,* ed. Stanley Wells, Gary Taylor, John Jowett, and William Montgomery, 2nd ed. (Oxford: Clarendon Press), lxv–lxvi.

4. My reference is to *2H4*, 5.1.133–35, in Shakespeare, *Works,* ed. Wells et al., 2nd ed., 506.

5. Michel Foucault, "What is an Author?" (1969), in *Language, Counter-Memory, Practice,* trans. Josue V. Hatari, repr., among other places, in *Criticism: The Major Statements,* ed. Charles Kaplan and William Davis Anderson, 4th ed. (Boston: Bedford/St. Martin's, 2000), 544–58.

6. S. Schoenbaum, *Shakespeare: A Documentary Life* (New York: Oxford University Press, 1975), 21, 136, 250.

7. Trevor Nunn, *William Shakespeare's Twelfth Night: A Screenplay* (London: Methuen, 1996), unpaginated.

Shakespearean Localities and the Localities of Shakespeare Studies

Alexander C. Y. Huang

Local Shakespeares: Proximations and Power
By Martin Orkin
London and New York: Routledge, 2005

World-wide Shakespeares:
Local Appropriations in Film and Performance
Edited by Sonia Massai
London and New York: Routledge, 2005

I

Do THE LOCALITIES of literary works and their critics matter in literary criticism? With the historical hindsight of such cases as Erich Auerbach and Paul de Man, the answer is a resounding yes.[1] But how do these localities relate to one another? The question of where we are now in what might be called studies of Shakespeare's textual and performative afterlife is ultimately connected to the question of where the critics and audiences are located, as the vicissitudes of Shakespearean localities are intimately connected to the localities of Shakespeare studies. Michael Neill, among other critics such as Edward Said, has argued for the importance of recognizing the fact that "reading is always done from somewhere."[2] These localities constitute the crux of criticism and Shakespeare's extensive posthumous encounters with the world.

At stake is not simply the temporality but also the locality of these encounters, for to study the presence of "Shakespeare" is to study the "arts of transmission" (Francis Bacon's term from a different context), the practices of appropriating and transmitting location-specific Shakespearean epistemologies. By locality criticism and local "Shakespeare" I mean interpretations that are inflected or marked by specificities of a given cultural location or knowledge derived from a specific geocultural region. Locality, in the full sense of the word, denotes the physical and allegorical coordinates of Shakespearean performance, appropriation, and criticism. While it has now been recognized that "Shakespeare has occupied an international space" from the beginning (in terms of the settings of the plays and their sources),[3] the theoretical implications of the international space of representation and criticism remain unclear.[4] Constituting these localities are physical performance venues, criticism, editorially mediated modern editions, and translations.

I would like to begin with the troubled relationship between performance studies and Shakespeare studies. The fact that Shakespeare has been "made the touchstone . . . of the surety and verification of issues of our—or any—time," as theorized by Marjorie Garber,[5] has prompted scholars to forsake classical character criticism as practiced by A. C. Bradley and G. Wilson Knight, and turn to a number of different modes of interpretation, lodging a Shakespearean play script in its social networks, thereby multiplying its interpretive possibilities. Early modern stage is one of the fields that are transformed by New Historicism, cultural materialism, and the renewed attention to the interplay between the different social forces present at the sites of performances. Elizabethan "local" knowledge has been perceived to constitute important social and ideological forces that define Shakespeare's theater.[6]

However, the same cannot be said of the contemporary counterparts of these performances. The local knowledge generated by an informed contemporary performance has remained marginal in the theoretical reflection on the meanings of "Shakespeare," for these contemporary localities—Anglophone or not—are often seen as obscure bits of Shakespeariana and therefore detached from what has been perceived as the core of Shakespearean knowledge. Robert Shaughnessy speculates, among other scholars, that as opposed to the early modern stage's perceived "amenability to critical appropriation," contemporary Shakespearean performance "may be less inviting on these terms," thereby remaining "peripheral to the concerns of theory" until relatively recently.[7]

Similar problems plague reception studies, despite its recognized status as an integral part of a vast field that encompasses postcolonial criticism and theater practice. Shaughnessy's observation anticipates Linda Hutcheon's more recent proposal to "interpret an adaptation *as an adaptation*," to treat adaptation as "what Roland Barthes called, not a 'work,' but a 'text,' a plural 'stereophony of echoes, citations, and references.'"[8] Performance criticism and reception studies are not exempt from the pitfalls in various versions of "morally loaded discourse[s] of fidelity" that lead to what Alan Dessen terms "the Blame Game, the academic process of fault finding wherein the director becomes a vandal sacking the sacred text."[9] Recent work has shown an acute awareness of these perils. For example, William Worthen's *Shakespeare and the Force of Modern Performance* (2003) and others in the same line of work problematize the relationship between script and theater, treating the specificities of performance—"stage *behaviors*"[10]—not as appendages that give way to the literariness of the Shakespearean script but as agents that participate in defining the play.

However, performance onstage and performance on-screen met different fates. Although a genre with a considerably shorter history than theater,[11] Shakespeare on film has quickly established itself as a viable and vital subfield in Shakespeare studies, with an abundance of theoretically informed filmographies, monographs, and collections, as well as "well attended sessions on [the topic]" at major conferences, as observed by Peter Donaldson.[12] Further, cinematic Shakespeare has had an intimate connection to pedagogy, because rather than theatrical production, filmed Shakespeare is how most nonspecialists, especially high school and college students, come to know Shakespeare's plays.

The opposite is true of studies of dramatic adaptations or translations deriving from and designed for decidedly local and even foreign contexts. Granted, due to the ephemeral nature of theater works and their contexts—even the most commercially successful and the most extensively toured—live theater can never be as accessible as film (and the cultural barrier may be prohibiting), but two of the main forces that propel this segregation are closely connected to politics of the field and problems in methodology: (1) the misconception of the referential stability of performances and appropriations from familiar centers, such as England, Canada, and the United States; and (2) the prevailing reportage mode deployed on panels and in articles dealing with Shakespearean appropriations, which reduces their subjects of study to temporary news items. These days both translation studies and reception studies panels abound, and many more scholars are engaged in related fields.[13] Publications in major venues now regularly feature articles and reviews on related topics. However, until recently many of these contributions amount to nothing more than factual reports without theoretical reflection.[14] The reportage mode—rather than a lack of relevant publications—has accounted for the disinterest by the Shakespeare studies community at large, furthering the ghetto-ization of reception studies. Paradoxically, as the cultural practice of appropriation and an increasing number of adaptations are "fa-miliarly known," they become ornamental, if not predictably ex-otic, objects for exhibition that invite only brief glances and are therefore not positioned to be properly known.[15]

Martin Orkin and Sonia Massai set out to change this critical im-passe. Massai's *World-wide Shakespeares: Local Appropriations in Film and Performance* addresses this first problem. The historically grounded and critically alert studies in Massai's collection demon-strate that "instability, dissonance and oppositional negotiations over Shakespeare's works are a common phenomenon throughout the field," and not only at the traditionally defined peripheral or postcolonial localities (9). Addressing the second problem and drawing upon African readings, Martin Orkin demonstrates in *Local Shakespeares* the relevance of "local knowledges in the con-text of Shakespeare production and its reception" (43) and analysis of power. He contends, "the historically contingent . . . impact of any critical practice, together with the knowledge-systems that in-form it, may in turn be taken as evidence for the relativity of any dominantly exclusionist policy towards particular local knowl-edges lying outside currently dominant critical terrain" (2).

II

To contextualize Orkin's and Massai's volumes and to under-stand the critical impasse they reacted against, it is necessary to survey developments in the field and the concept of "appropria-tion." Despite the significance of textual and performative appro-priations, critical ideologies and biases have, for a long time, relegated them to the periphery and limited the interpretive possi-bilities. As late as 1988, "localization" was still viewed as "intoler-able, imprisoning," according to Leah Marcus. She traced the attitude back to 1623:

Even though every interpreter of Shakespeare depends on the work of previous "localizers" for such basic things as determining the order of the plays' composition and establishing the texts in which we read them, we have tended to set such work apart from the mainstream, as though by assigning the localizers to a fenced-in preserve we can minimize their impact on something we are willing to perceive only as universal and without limits. The tendency is not new. Even though the word *localization* dates only from the nineteenth century, resistance to the activity it names goes back, in the case of Shakespeare, at least as far as 1623. More than any other English writer, Shakespeare has been made the bearer of high claims for the universality of art.[16]

If the textual and performative reconfigurations can be broadly categorized as acts of appropriation, being appropriated are certainly not only Shakespeare's texts as presented during his lifetime but also local (in temporal and spatial terms) politics. As evidenced by Heiner Müller, Ariane Mnouchkine, Yukio Ninagawa, and Ong Keng Sen's productions,[17] the act of staging a Shakespearean play is not simply a process of representing that play itself but rather the dynamics between the locality Shakespeare represents and the locality the performers and the audience represent. In other cases, these appropriations themselves become subjects to be appropriated; historically, the works that constitute Shakespeare's afterlife do not always remain secondary. Many works have had afterlives of their own.[18]

Even though worldwide appropriation of Shakespeare is hardly a new phenomenon, this cultural practice did not become a subject for serious scholarly analysis until the early 1990s with the emergence of a handful of works on related topics, such as Michael Bristol's *Shakespeare's America, America's Shakespeare* (1991). When Jean I. Marsden published the landmark study, *The Appropriation of Shakespeare* (1991), she lamented the lack of scholarly attention to "Shakespeare after the Renaissance" and pointed out that "it is this void that [her collection] address[ed]."[19] Recognizing that "what we think of 'Shakespeare' is . . . culturally determined," Marsden contends, Shakespearean appropriations "present a view of Shakespeare embedded not only in his own culture but in ours, forcing us to consider both the impact we have on the plays and the impact they have on us."[20] Dennis Kennedy's groundbreaking works, *Foreign Shakespeare* (1993) and *Looking at Shakespeare* (1993; 2nd ed., 2002)[21]—though with an Anglo-European focus similar to Marsden's volume—made "foreign" Shakespearean appropriations theoretically important subjects of further scholarly inquiry. The 1991 World Shakespeare Congress in Tokyo fueled the interest in the subject and led to the publication of *Shakespeare and Cultural Traditions* (1994), a collection of essays that examine the traffic between Shakespeare and world cultures.[22] A decade of theoretical reflection and historical studies culminated in the launch in 2005 of a new peer-reviewed journal, *Borrowers and Lenders,* edited by Christy Desmet, Sujata Iyengar, and Robert Sawyer, that is devoted exclusively to the study of Shakespeare and appropriation.

Studies in the field broadly conceived as reception studies (performance, film, popular culture) can be categorized into three related but different lines of work. The first mode of research brings critical theory to bear on various modes of representation (on and beyond the stage), as has been energetically pursued by Michael Bristol, James Bulman, John Joughin, Barbara Hodgdon, Christy Desmet, and W. B. Worthen, among other key critics.[23] The second mode of research draws upon case studies or specific stage histories. Some studies draw upon more personal experiences, such as John Russell Brown's *New Sites for Shakespeare: Theatre, the Audience and Asia* (1999), while other studies concentrate on practices in specific cultures and their theoretical implications.[24] Still others focus on less familiar appropriations in Europe, Africa, Asia, and other locations, and provide analyses of important materials from these sites that contrast those sites that have been privileged by Anglo-American criticism. This line of work has broadened the horizon of Shakespeare studies.[25] There are many more country- or region-specific stage histories of Shakespeare. A third mode of research engages the histories and reception of Shakespeare's images, biographies, and reputation. One of the best-known works in this category is Gary Taylor's *Reinventing Shakespeare* (1989; reprinted 1991).[26] A new contribution is *Shakespeares after Shakespeare*, edited by Richard Burt (2006), a two-volume encyclopedia chronicling bits of Shakespeariana in mass media and popular culture.[27]

While textual variations and editorial interventions raise similar issues and share general avenues of approach, the textual permutations have not been widely recognized in terms of their "appropriation" of Shakespeare. A few works, however, do begin to treat textual strategies as acts of appropriation.[28] It is also worth mentioning that as appropriation received more critical attention in Shakespeare studies, other relevant fields were also affected by a renewed interest in the theoretical implications of adaptation as a genre. Film studies, in particular, witnessed the emergence of new works that revisit the question of authorship and representation.[29]

The rise of reception studies has led to a reassessment of the concept of appropriation. Historical circumstances have shown that the concepts of afterlife and appropriation can be paradoxical. If, as the critical language of our time suggests, literary works could not contain meanings in and by themselves,[30] the notions of appropriation and the original would be redundant, for the "text" is constituted of nothing other than these permutations. On the other hand, if meanings were defined by nothing but the literary artifact, appropriation—in the sense of making something one's own—would not be possible.[31] These issues form the core of critical debates not only in Shakespeare studies but also in fiction, film adaptations, and performance studies, prompting recent works to revisit the very problem with naming. In her 2006 book, *A Theory of Adaptation,* cultural theorist Linda Hutcheon devotes the preface and entire sections in chapter 1 to discuss these problems.[32] Daniel Fischlin and Mark Fortier, coeditors of the latest critical anthology of Shakespearean adaptations, similarly devote a section in their introduction to the problem of naming (which considers the inadequacies of terms such as adaptation, appropriation, parody, offshoot, alteration, spinoff) and a section to the relationship between adaptation and contemporary cultural theory, emphasizing that adaptation is "not a simple rejection" of the notions of the author and the canon. Fischlin and Fortier argue that "to understand the cultural politics of adaptation, we must also examine how adaptation takes place within a certain structured relationship to . . . a broadly accepted group of works that is a consensual (though not uncontested) site of foregrounded study within the academy."[33]

III

Thus configured, studies of appropriation have returned to the question of locality. A recent wave of scholarship is seeking to redefine the localities of Shakespeare studies in relation to the localities of performance by taking into account their physical and geocultural dimensions and not simply their temporal dimension, which has traditionally received more attention. This new mode of criticism is articulated in a move to specify the universal (as opposed to Harold Bloom's tendency to universalize the specifics),[34] refiguring the relationship between politics and aesthetics.

While it is commonly acknowledged that theater works are best understood by careful examinations of their temporal and spatial configurations, and that the meanings of literary works are intimately connected—in similar ways—with their temporality as well as the local knowledge of their readers, much attention has been directed toward how "the past and the present might be put into meaningful dialogue with one another."[35] The concept of locality in performance studies and textual criticism has remained undertheorized. The recognition of the role of local knowledge and the locality of performance has remained a rhetorical rather than sustained reorientation. Since "local" Shakespeares have always been part of the global Shakespeare industry, it is important to consider, in dramaturgical terms, the dynamics between Shakespearean localities, the localities of the critics, and the localities where Shakespeare's works are (re)presented.

However, this is not how the local has been configured by practitioners and critics. From the perspectives of what Martin Orkin has called a Eurocentric "metropolitan bank of Shakespeare knowledge" (1), Shakespearean performances beyond the Anglo-European world often appear "remarkably localized," and "richer in sounds, music, and presentational support."[36] What do local and localization mean? Massai asks an important question: if certain performances are more localized, does it imply a normative standard from which these performances depart? (9) Orkin's and Massai's volumes usefully highlight a number of alternative modes of research that "provincialize" cultural locations, especially those that are traditionally perceived as central and normative.[37] Just like their "foreign" counterparts, English-language performances also articulate local anxieties brought forth by the diversified and internationalized contexts of globalization.

The deployment of locality as a critical category in recent works by Robert Shaughnessy, Martin Orkin, Susan Bassnett, and Sonia Massai, among others, has added locality and spatiality to the equation that has traditionally focused on the temporality of literary artifacts. The contested viability of Shakespeare's texts begs the question of the value of local reading positions, and whether there is any position that is not "local." The concept of locality foregrounds not the less productive dichotomy of local and global, but rather a recognition that representations signify *relationally* and contextually.

This move has shifted the terms of ongoing debates about Shakespearean representations from their historicity to their spatiality.

Its deferral of global judgments of truth also signals a form of intellectual self-restraint and a renewed sense of critical sensitivity to shifting contexts. Indeed, a survey of the history of Shakespeare editions, performance, and appropriation shows that at stake is the interplay between the locality where authenticity and intentionality is derived and the locality where differences emerge.

The term "local Shakespeare" has hence evolved from a binary opposition to "global Shakespeare" (which is believed to be founded on canonical metropolitan English-language representations) into a celebration of the possibility to articulate difference. Local readings of Shakespeare are no longer treated as mimicry of originals of a higher order, but as new epistemologies that actively participate in the formation of Shakespearean knowledges (Orkin 2005, 1–4). In an essay titled "On Location," Robert Shaughnessy argues that performance space and the cultural location of a production play a key role in configuring the meanings of the production. Performers and audiences negotiate these meanings on-site.[38] Locality is an integral part of any form of representation of literary artifact, especially Shakespeare's works, because Shakespeare's currency is developed through the tensions among various sites that include the allegorical, cultural, and physical locations of the representation.

IV

The volume edited by Sonia Massai, *World-wide Shakespeares,* addresses these complexities. Its use of the term "local Shakespeare" emphasizes the "increasingly syncretic combination of frames of reference which are available to local *and* to international audiences" in the disparate cases studied by the contributors (10). The volume demonstrates an awareness that "the field of Shakespeare Studies has been radically transformed by the emergence of significant world-wide localities, within which Shakespeare is made to signify anew" (8) by establishing how the global is "the product of specific, historically and culturally determined localities" (9). Arguing against the tendency to condemn the homogenizing function of the global institutional uses of Shakespeare, Massai points out in her introduction that the global and the local should not be understood solely in terms of an imaginary hierarchical dichotomy. Conversant in not only scholarship of Shakespearean appropriation but also global/local studies, Massai urges her readers to reconsider the function of Shakespeare in a wide range of "textual strategies" including those that originated in complex contexts that cannot be properly described as postcolonial.

Building on the connotation of "local" as pertaining to "a position in space" and " a particular place in a system," Massai reconsiders the categories of local and global in the history of the afterlife of Shakespeare's texts (1). Recognizing that "any signifying practice . . . is local," she cautions against both "under-theorized eulogies" and "skeptical responses" to interculturalism (5). Prompted by the diverse appropriations addressed by contributors to the volume—many of which originated in locations that cannot be "adequately described as post-colonial"—Massai turns to a model, inspired by Pierre Bourdieu, "Shakespeare as a global cultural field," to accommodate the range of textual strategies found in these appropriations. This theoretical framework treats post-mid-twentieth-century Shakespeare as "a field of forces as well as *genuine* struggles" (7).

Truly global in scale, the collected essays in *World-wide Shakespeares*—which grew out of a seminar at the World Shakespeare Congress in Valencia (2001)—work toward a variety of theoretical models that address the dialectic relationship between the global and the local, taking into account the variety of localities where Shakespeare is appropriated. One of the unique contributions of this volume is its theoretically informed comparative analyses of appropriations from worldwide localities. The majority of monographs and collections so far are either strongly Eurocentric in terms of the cases and histories chosen for analysis, or focused on single countries or homogeneous localities (postcolonial Shakespeare, Japan, Brazil, Romania, Germany, and others). The volume's comparative scope and investigations into a wide variety of localities complement other studies that focus on the role of Shakespeare in the formation of individual national cultures. Its juxtaposition of English-language appropriations, "performed in well-established theatrical venues, or widely distributed in cinemas around the world," and "foreign and unfamiliar ones" demonstrates how "local, partisan and unstable the center(s) of the field" actually are (8). While acknowledging the need for more contextualization of Shakespeare in nontraditional sites, Massai rightly points out that an exclusive focus on non-Anglo-European Shakespeares is not an effective approach to counter the current Anglo-Eurocentric tendency, for it only reinforces "lingering notions of

English Shakespeares as a normative standard" (9) and fails to recognize that all appropriations operate at local levels.

The local, regional, and transnational positions taken by the artists analyzed by the contributors, along with the nature of their target audiences, inform the three-part structure of the volume: "Local Shakespeares for Local Audiences" (essays by Tobias Döring, Suzanne Gossett, Elizabeth Klein and Michael Shapiro, Ruru Li, and Poonam Trivedi), "Local Shakespeares for National Audiences" (essays by Boika Sokolova, Sabine Schülting, Marcela Kostihová, Ton Hoenselaars, Lukas Erne, Sonia Massai, Alfredo Michel Modenessi, Robert Shaughnessy, and Maria Jones), and "Local Shakespeares for International Audiences" (essays by Margaret Jane Kidnie, Mark Houlahan, and Saviour Catania). Barbara Hodgdon's inquisitive afterword rounds up the volume with a reflection on critical categories and a series of thought-provoking questions about the nature of the act of appropriation—literary, performative, and critical. Noting that "the 'dramatic field' not only abuts the 'litcrit' field but also extends Shakespeare's reach beyond the borders of both: . . . occurring in various sites and citings, deploying a wide range of theatrical-textual strategies, encountering local cultural fields," Hodgdon argues that Shakespeare has been appropriated by the critical discourse (represented by the volume and elsewhere) as a "resource for mapping the poetics and politics of cultures" (157). Some of her questions derived from these complexities: "what relations . . . 'should' pertain between or among a specific performance, new historicist or cultural materialist readings and present-day events and histories?" She also probes the ways in which "audiences transform what they hear and see," a less theorized area as opposed to what "critical and theatrical practitioners bring to bear on what they read and witness" (159). The layerings of memory have important roles to play in the ephemeral performance culture, producing and reframing discourses at all levels.

Analyses of locations that range from Europe to the Asia Pacific in the seventeen engaging essays raise a wide range of theoretical issues. I would like to mention a few that engage the notions of locality from contrasting perspectives. The opening essay by Döring problematizes the act of naming ("local" Shakespeare) and the "act of siting which localizes experience" (15). Taking it one step further, Mark Houlahan, after examining the logic of cultural exchange in Don Selwyn's Maori *Merchant of Venice,* cautions that the global should not be simply taken as "the multinational and the corporate, blandly disseminating sameness throughout the world; and the local [as] the heroic, small-scale attempts to sustain specific difference" (141). Drawing on Derek Walcott's metadrama, *A Branch of the Blue Nile,* Döring's essay relocates Walcott to his position within Caribbean culture rather than cosmopolitanism, because "meaning is a localized product resulting from a specifically situated act of reading" (18). Gossett's analysis of how two political productions of *Pericles* in Washington, D.C., made the play meaningful to audiences that were decidedly local demonstrates the "inevitably local nature" of interpretations (30). Along similar lines, as Robert Shaughnessy's analysis of Peter Brook, a Royal Shakespeare Company, and a Shakespeare's Globe's productions of *A Midsummer Night's Dream* reveals, English-language "cultural centers" are prone to the "ambiguities and the nervousness of contemporary 'English' Shakespeare in the cultural and economic context of globalization" (113). Ton Hoenselaars examines Philip Purser's *Friedrich Harris: Shooting the Hero,* an overlooked offshoot inspired by Laurence Olivier's *Henry V,* a film epic based on a play with a "special place in the definition of British nationhood." He argues that Purser's novel actively participates in a post–Second World War discourse that uses Shakespeare to explore fascism, hero worship, and stardom (87). Like Shakespearean appropriations, critical discourses are not immune to locality-inflected specificities despite their claim to universal truth. This is the position Lukas Erne takes in his essay on Friedrich Dürrenmatt's adaptation of *Titus Andronicus,* which contains "fascinating misreadings of the Shakespearean original that are profoundly and inevitably local" (94), defending the interest of specific communities—scholarly and otherwise.

V

The shift from global Shakespeare to local Shakespeare corresponds to the increasingly complex negotiations between value systems that are far from unilaterally antithetical. A culmination of at least a decade of research, beginning with his essay "Whose Things of Darkness? Reading/Representing *The Tempest* in South Africa after April 1994," in *Shakespeare and National Culture,* edited by John J. Joughin (1997), Martin Orkin's *Local Shakespeares* situates the local within that which is "epistemologically current" in each reader's culture (2). While Massai's volume theorizes the

impact of locally conceived Shakespeare on localities at different
levels (local community, national, international), Orkin's book is
divided into two parts that examine, respectively, the reciprocal
impact of "the traveling but always local reader" and "the seventeenth-century and still iconic Shakespeare text" on each other, focusing on what he calls "unruly masculinity" in *Pericles,
Cymbeline, The Winter's Tale,* and *The Tempest.* He brings such
local knowledge systems as Tswana notions of conflict resolution
to bear on *Cymbeline* in order to complement and demonstrate the
inadequacy of "metropolitan knowledges" (4). Located outside of
Anglo-European metropoles himself, Orkin recognizes his critical
and geocultural positions and develops the notion of local knowledge that encompasses local communities in specific cultural locations, bodies of Shakespeare scholarship that practitioners and
audiences draw upon, archives and educational systems that influence the readers, as well as the broader social milieu that fashion
and are fashioned by these intertextual maneuvers. He locates this
"common bank of Shakespeare knowledge," or the "Shakespeare
metropolis," at the junctures where these communities encounter
the Shakespearean texts (1). However, the assumed commonality of
this bank of knowledge is not unproblematic, for "none of our present-day locations can be equated with what we know about seventeenth-century London" (1). It is important to examine this rupture
in order to fully recognize the discursive richness of Shakespearean
transmissions.

In the past decade, scholarship produced from within and beyond the "Shakespeare metropolis," to borrow Orkin's phrase, has
underlined the value and reciprocity of non-Anglophone Shakespearean appropriations and the act of reading. Stanley Wells,
among others, maintains that adapting Shakespeare is "a two-way
process, blessing those who give as well as those who receive."[39]
However, this gradual change of attitude notwithstanding, the tendency to privilege and neutralize select historical moments of the
text, especially its perceived point of origin, prevails. Orkin's mode
of reading (underlining the presence of present-day readers) challenges "existent epistemological certainties" that Orkin believes
will be "adjust[ed]" by local knowledges (4). He takes issue with
the historicist tendency represented by David Scott Kastan's work,
and contends that while this view may acknowledge the reader "as
part of the transaction in the encounter with literary text," it does
not grant enough agency to present-day readers with their temporarily common historical circumstances (4).

While the local knowledge systems (Tswana, Zulu, and others) Orkin draws on are African, *Local Shakespeares* has a different agenda than its predecessor, *Shakespeare in Africa* (1998), by Lemuel A. Johnson. Orkin usefully points out that one of the new directions for future research on cultural encounter is not a recursive insistence on difference or deconstruction of binary opposites, but rather the development and deployment of the notion of "proximation" that "unsettles the binaric mode of conceptualization inferred in the term 'the other' " (12–13). From a series of case studies on masculinity in Shakespeare's late plays as text and as adaptation, Orkin extrapolates the concept of proximates, which plays a crucial role in his model of approximation. Men and women, as well as different localities, are ultimately proximates rather than " 'opposites' of one another" (12).

In the three chapters in part 1, "Local Knowledges and Shakespeare's Global Texts," Orkin establishes how specific local knowledges can illuminate particular Shakespearean plays. Among cases he focuses on are the famous essay, "Shakespeare in the Bush," by Laura Bohannan, which chronicles a cultural anthropologist's mid-twentieth-century encounter with West Africans through *Hamlet,* established interpretations of the myth surrounding Othello's handkerchief, as well as *uMabatha* and *SeZaR,* two South African adaptations of *Macbeth* and *Julius Caesar,* respectively. Bohannan's case exemplifies how intersecting knowledges transform the active readers (26–27), while Othello's handkerchief, an object of continued fixation, is shown to contain multiple dimensions in light of non-Western evidence and knowledges.

Orkin's model of proximation in the power network is founded upon the problematic of the self and the other, or singular author and the ideal reader, as critical categories. These correlative terms are defined by the presence of each other. The self is often the true other, and the other the forgotten self. Orkin's model renders disparate meaning-making agents "proximates" that cross-fertilize rather than absolute opposites. In the case of Bohannan's encounter with the Tiv, what is most striking is the attention given, on the part of both the Tiv and Bohannan, to the "story." The interaction sharpens our awareness of the social basis of knowledge. Both the Tiv and Bohannan improvised to come to terms with each other's visions. Cultures do not clash with one another; local epistemologies do.

In the five chapters in part 2, "Encountering Men in Shake-

speare's Late Plays," a group of Shakespeare's late plays are selected for comparative analysis, and for good reasons. *Pericles,
Cymbeline, The Winter's Tale,* and *The Tempest* all feature travel
and encounters with unknown localities. Their thematic focus parallels Orkin's juxtaposition of "metropolitan knowledges" and
local knowledges that elicits the possibilities of gender and cultural
equivocation (7). Orkin's unique focus on unruly masculinity, in
travels within Shakespeare's text (e.g., *The Winter's Tale*) and in
Shakespeare's traveling text (e.g., Pedro Almodóvar's *All About My
Mother*), yields a reading that registers the complex proximations
and "heterogeneities in experience that the language of patriarchy
would expel" (169). Orkin maintains that such proximations
counter patriarchy's violence—symbolic or real. The afterword
cites the volatile situation between Isreal and Palestine in a hopeful
tone, suggesting that cultural encounter, as exemplified in the practice of active reading and articulated by Caliban, "need not be . . .
only threatening" (170).

What can we gain from such studies of the afterlife of a literary
work? It is important to study the critical and performative practices named by "localization" not because we can add to the already long list of variations and literary locations, nor because we
can show what is different (as in footnoting existing theoretical
models) or what the current models missed. It is important because
it creates new space between dichotomized poles of the text and
the reader, the ideas of the original and the intertextual, as well as
authorship and intentionality. It is important because such engagement destabilizes the assumptions of contemporary theory and the
established interpretations, which promotes a dynamic mode of research that reflects the changing circumstances of history and disparate localities.

Notes

1. Edward Said attributes Auerbach's fresh perspectives on European literature to his exile and new locality outside the Continent. Said argues that *Mimesis*
"owed its existence to the very fact of . . . exile and homelessness," considering
Auerbach's book as a work that is "built upon a critically important alienation"
and "an agonizing distance" from the Western cultural tradition it engages. Edward Said, *The World, the Text, and the Critic* (Cambridge, MA: Harvard University Press, 1983), 8.

2. Said, *The World, the Text, and the Critic,* 5; Michael Neill, "Post-Colonial

Shakespeare? Writing Away from the Centre," in *Post-Colonial Shakespeares*, ed. Ania Loomba and Martin Orkin, (London: Routledge, 1998), 168.

3. Anthony C. Dawson, "International Shakespeare," in *The Cambridge Companion to Shakespeare on Stage,* ed. Stanley Wells and Sarah Stanton, 176 (Cambridge: Cambridge University Press, 2002).

4. When Ben Jonson hailed Shakespeare as a poet "not of an age, but for all time" in 1623, he configured the popularization of Shakespeare's oeuvre and its author in temporal terms, highlighting the tension between past and present. Ben Jonson, "To The Memory Of My Beloved, The Author, Mr William Shakespeare, And What He Hath Left Us," in *Mr. VVilliam Shakespeares comedies, histories, and tragedies* (London: Printed by Isaac Iaggard, and Ed. Blount, 1623), n.p.

5. Marjorie Garber, "The Transvestite's Progress: Rosalind the Yeshiva Boy," in *The Appropriation of Shakespeare: Post-Renaissance Reconstructions of the Works and the Myth,* ed. Jean I. Marsden, 146 (New York: Harvester Wheatsheaf, 1991).

6. Arthur F. Kinney, *Shakespeare by Stages: An Historical Introduction* (Oxford: Blackwell, 2003).

7. Robert Shaughnessy, introduction to *Shakespeare in Performance,* ed. Robert Shaughnessy (New York: St. Martin's Press, 2000), 12.

8. Hutcheon, *A Theory of Adaptation,* 6, italics in original; Roland Barthes, *Image—Music—Text,* trans. Stephen Heath (New York: Hill & Wang, 1977), 160.

9. Hutcheon, *A Theory of Adaptation,* 7; 11. Alan C. Dessen, "Teaching What's Not There," in *Shakespeare in Performance: A Collection of Essays,* ed. Frank Occhiogrosso, 112 (Newark: University of Delaware Press, 2003).

10. Worthen, *Shakespeare and the Force of Modern Performance,* 3, italics in original.

11. Cinematic Shakespeare began with British Mutoscope's *King John,* directed by William Dickson, in 1899. Filmed Shakespeare as an established genre and an industry flourished in the 1990s. Popular feature English-language films from this period include Kenneth Branagh's *Hamlet* (1996), Oliver Parker's *Othello* (1995), Baz Luhrmann's *William Shakespeare's Romeo + Juliet* (1996), John Madden's *Shakespeare in Love* (1998), and Michael Almereyda's *Hamlet* (2000).

12. Peter S. Donaldson, "Review of *The Cambridge Companion to Shakespeare on Film* and *A History of Shakespeare on Screen,*" *Shakespeare Studies*, vol. 31, ed. Leeds Barroll, 241–42 (Madison, NJ: Fairleigh Dickinson University Press, 2003).

13. Commenting on the lack of reciprocity between Shakespeareans in non-Anglophone countries (including Europe) and their English and American counterparts, Inga-Stina Ewbank candidly observed that even though "seminars on translation are now an inalienable part of Shakespeare Conferences and World congresses," very few native English speakers attend them, which she interprets as implying that this field may be "an interesting and harmless occupation for researchers abroad." Ewbank's observation a decade ago may not always apply today, as the conditions have evolved. Inga-Stina Ewbank, "Shakespeare Translation as Cultural Exchange," *Shakespeare Survey* 48 (1995): 1.

14. E. H. Carr's critique of a problematic model of historiography may provide a useful angel of reflection: "scissors-and-paste history without meaning or significance." E. H. Carr, *What is History* (Harmondsworth: Penguin Books, 1964), 29.

15. Cf. Hegel's conception of a paradoxical relationship between the familiar and thought (or knowledge): "Das Bekannte überhaupt ist darum, weil es bekannt ist, nicht erkannt." G. W. F. Hegel, "Vorrede," in *Phänomenologie des Geistes*, in *Werke in zwanzig Bänden* (Frankfurt: Suhrkamp, 1980), 3:35.

16. Leah Marcus, *Puzzling Shakespeare: Local Reading and Its Discontents* (Berkeley: University of California Press, 1988), 1–2.

17. Examples include Heiner Müller's *Hamletmachine* (1978), Ariane Mnouchkine's *Kabuki-* and *Noh*-inflected *Richard II* in Paris in 1981, David McRuvie and Annette Leday's *Kathakali King Lear* at the Globe in London in 2000, Yukio Ninagawa's multiple Shakespeare productions for European festivals, as well as Ong Keng Sen's *Search: Hamlet* with a multinational cast that appropriated European and Asian performance idioms (2002).

18. The Restoration and eighteenth century produced some of most perplexing cases. Nahum Tate's *King Lear* dominated the English stage until 1836, and David Garrick's *Catherine and Petruchio* was regularly staged until 1887. Goethe's *Hamlet*-inspired *Bildungsroman, Wilhelm Meisters Lehrjahre* (1796), has an extended presence in Novalis's *Heinrich von Ofterdingen* (1802) and Penelope Fitzgerald's *The Blue Flower* (1995). Beyond Europe, Tsubouchi Shoyo's translations have had a lasting legacy in Japan, while Lin Shu's rendition of Charles and Mary Lamb's *Tales from Shakespeare* has defined the first generation of Shakespearean performances in China and inspired a new project in 2001 to retranslate Shakespeare's plays in prose narratives—following the footsteps of the Lambs and Lin. See Alexander C. Y. Huang, "Lin Shu, Invisible Translation, and Politics," *Perspectives: Studies in Translatology* 14.1 (2006): 55–65; and Daniel Gallimore, "Measuring Distance: Tsubouchi Shoyo and the Myth of Shakespeare Translation," in *Translating Others*, ed. Theo Hermans (Manchester: St. Jerome, 2006), 2:483–92.

19. Jean I. Marsden, ed., *The Appropriation of Shakespeare: Post-Renaissance Reconstruction of the Works and the Myth* (New York: Harvester Wheatsheaf, 1991), 5.

20. Ibid., 8.

21. Dennis Kennedy, ed., *Foreign Shakespeare: Contemporary Performance* (Cambridge: Cambridge University Press, 1993); Dennis Kennedy, *Looking at Shakespeare: A Visual History of Twentieth-Century Performance* (Cambridge: Cambridge University Press, 1993; 2nd ed., 2002).

22. Tetsuo Kishi, Roger Pringle, and Stanley Wells, eds., *Shakespeare and Cultural Traditions: The Selected Proceedings of the International Shakespeare Association World Congress, Tokyo 1991* (Newark: University of Delaware Press, 1994).

23. Examples include such thought-provoking volumes as Michael Bristol's *Big-Time Shakespeare* (1996); James Bulman, ed., *Shakespeare, Theory, and Performance* (1996); John J. Joughin, ed., *Shakespeare and National Culture* (1997); Barbara Hodgdon's *The Shakespeare Trade: Performance and Appropriation* (1998); Christy Desmet and Robert Sawyer, eds., *Shakespeare and Appropriation* (1999); Courtney Lehmann's *Shakespeare Remains: Theater to Film, Early Modern to Postmodern* (2002); W. B. Worthen's *Shakespeare and the Authority of Performance* (1997) and *Shakespeare and the Force of Modern Performance* (2003); and Barbara Hodgdon and W. B. Worthen, eds., *A Companion to Shakespeare and Performance* (2005).

24. John Russell Brown, *New Sites for Shakespeare: Theatre, the Audience and*

Asia (London: Routledge, 1999); Alan C. Dessen, *Rescripting Shakespeare: The Text, the Director, and Modern Productions* (Cambridge: Cambridge University Press, 2002); Robert Shaughnessy, *The Shakespeare Effect: A History of Twentieth-Century Performance* (New York: Palgrave, 2002); Ton Hoenselaars, ed., *Shakespeare and the Language of Translation* (London: Arden Shakespeare, 2004).

25. Some recent examples include Sukanta Chaudhuri and Chee Seng Lim, eds., *Shakespeare without English: The Reception of Shakespeare in Non-Anglophone Countries* (Delhi: Pearson Longman, 2006); Irena R. Makaryk, *Shakespeare in the Undiscovered Bourn: Les Kurbas, Ukrainian Modernism, and Early Soviet Cultural Politics* (Toronto: University of Toronto Press, 2004); Martin Orkin's *Local Shakespeares* (2005); Sonia Massai, ed., *World-wide Shakespeares* (2005); Ton Hoenselaars, ed., *Shakespeare's History Plays: Performance, Translation and Adaptation in Britain and Abroad* (2004); Edward J. Esche, ed., *Shakespeare and His Contemporaries in Performance* (2000).

26. Gary Taylor, *Reinventing Shakespeare: A Cultural History from the Restoration to the Present* (Oxford: Oxford University Press, 1989).

27. Richard Burt, ed., *Shakespeares after Shakespeare* (Westport, CT: Greenwood Press, 2006).

28. See Peter Erickson's *Rewriting Shakespeare, Rewriting Ourselves* (1991), which examines Shakespeare's representation of women along with contemporary women's rewriting of Shakespeare; and *Textual Performances: The Modern Reproduction of Shakespeare's Drama* (2004), ed. Lucas Erne and Margaret Jane Kidnie, both of whom also contributed to Sonia Massai's *World-wide Shakespeares.*

29. See James Griffith's *Adaptations as Imitations: Films from Novels* (1997); Deborah Cartmell and Imelda Whelehan, eds., *Adaptations: From Text to Screen, Screen to Text* (1999); and James Naremore, ed., *Film Adaptation* (2000).

30. This tendency is reflected in critical positions held by the reader-response theorists, by Julia Kristeva's notion of intertextuality, by Derrida's conception of the "iterability" as the nature of all texts, as well as by some Shakespeareans who subscribe to presentism, such as Terence Hawkes and Graham Holderness. For example, Hawkes argues that texts cannot provide self-contained meanings; rather, "we mean by the text we choose" (3). Terence Hawkes, *Meaning by Shakespeare* (London: Routledge, 1992); Graham Holderness, *The Shakespeare Myth* (Manchester: Manchester University Press, 1988); Jacques Derrida, *Limited Inc.* (Evanston, IL: Northwestern University Press, 1988).

31. According to the *OED,* appropriation refers to the act of "taking as one's own or to one's own use." In 2002, the *OED* added another definition: "The practice or technique of reworking the images or styles contained in earlier works of art, esp. (in later use) in order to provoke critical re-evaluation of well-known pieces by presenting them in new contexts, or to challenge notions of individual creativity or authenticity in art."

32. Linda Hutcheon, *A Theory of Adaptation* (New York: Routledge, 2006), xi–xvi and 1–9.

33. Daniel Fischlin and Mark Fortier, eds., *Adaptations of Shakespeare: A Critical Anthology of Plays from the Seventeenth Century to the Present* (London: Routledge, 2000), 6.

34. Harold Bloom, *Shakespeare: The Invention of the Human* (New York: Riverhead Books, 1998), 430.

35. Stevie Simkin, *Early Modern Tragedy and the Cinema of Violence* (New York: Palgrave, 2006), 3.

36. John Gillies, "Shakespeare Localized: An Australian Looks at Asian Practice," in *Shakespeare Global/Local: The Hong Kong Imaginary in Transcultural Production*, ed. Kwok-kan Tam, Andrew Parkin, and Terry Siu-han Yip, 101 (Frankfurt/Main: Peter Lang, 2002). John Russel Brown, "Foreign Shakespeare and English-speaking Audiences," in *Foreign Shakespeare: Contemporary Performance* ed. Dennis Kennedy, 32 (Cambridge: Cambridge University Press, 1993); John Russell Brown, *New Sites for Shakespeare: Theatre, the Audience and Asia* (London: Routledge, 1999), 130.

37. Ania Loomba and Martin Orkin, eds., *Post-Colonial Shakespeares* (London: Routledge, 1998), 19.

38. Robert Shaughnessy, "On Location," in Hodgdon and Worthen (2005), 79 and 99.

39. Stanley Wells, forward to *Four Hundred Years of Shakespeare in Europe,* ed. A. Luis Poujante and Ton Hoenselaars, 7 (Newark: University of Delaware Press, 2003).

REVIEWS

Translating Investments: Metaphor and the Dynamic of Cultural Change in Tudor-Stuart England
By Judith Anderson
New York: Fordham University Press, 2005

Reviewer: William A. Oram

In her latest book on the functioning of metaphor in early modern England, Judith Anderson sets herself two related tasks. She tests the accounts of metaphor in contemporary linguistics (citing Jacques Derrida, Paul Ricoeur, and neocognativists like George Laikoff and Mark Johnson) against the theory and practice of writers in the early modern period. (She comments that "history and text have as much to tell theory as the reverse" [2].) On the other hand, she uses the period's treatment of metaphor to expose the halting, uncertain movement of early modern cultural change. In so doing she reads with characteristically searching attention an extraordinary range of cultural texts—literary works by Shakespeare, Donne, and Spenser, but also dictionaries and treatises on rhetoric, politics, theology, and economics.

Its punning title, *Translating Investments,* suggests in several ways the book's focus. *Translatio* is the Latin term for metaphor and Anderson argues that metaphor involves translation, a "carrying across" from one context to another. It is further a kind of Hegelian sublation, a "translation to a higher level incident on partial cancellation of the physical" (Ricoeur, quoted on p. 1). Metaphor is creative, giving a surplus beyond the original, physical meaning of the word, but the departure from the physical also involves a loss. (A "dead" metaphor, which has entirely lost its original, material sense, lacks compensating creative force and becomes no more than code for an abstraction.) The second term in the title springs from the Latin *in/vestire* whose original, physical sense of "to clothe" spawns a series of more abstract, metaphorical offspring:

"the idea of investment as the bestowal, possession, or acquisition of rights and powers, for example, slides readily into the idea of investment as dressing for advantage and thence into that of financial investment" (23). Much of the book is a tour de force meditation on how Renaissance writers developed this investment-metaphor.

Anderson's earlier book, *Words that Matter,* argued that early modern writers see words as having a kind of physical presence, a "materiality" uncharacteristic of either earlier or later periods. Here she returns to the issue, highlighting Renaissance word-consciousness in relation to the debate between Derrida and Ricoeur over the meaningfulness of etymology. For Derrida the etymology is a part of the word, "a vestigial mark, a trace" of its origins (16), where for Ricoeur those origins are lost in the word's dictionary meaning, which is in turn redefined by its place in the sentence. Anderson argues persuasively that in a world where the "grammar" one learned in school was Latin grammar, the etymologies of words become essential components of their meaning. Renaissance writers were much more keenly aware of the degree to which the ordinary words they used were translations, hence metaphorical. This word-consciousness appears in Shakespeare's uses of "invest" and "investment," in *Othello, Macbeth,* and *1 Henry IV,* but most strikingly in *Hamlet* 1.3 where Polonius's use of the word makes "sex, religion and commerce intertwine" (31) and in the fourth act of *2 Henry IV* where the word becomes a leitmotif: the king tries to "invest" in his son but fears that his son has prematurely invested *himself* with the crown. The financial resonances of the term complicate the psychology of the relationships between fathers and children.

Three chapters treat theology because, Anderson argues, the most telling accounts of metaphor came not from Renaissance rhetoricians but from Reformation theologians, for whom being right about metaphor was literally a matter of life and death. A defining question of the Reformation was what "is" meant in the words of institution in communion, "this is my body." Catholics (and Lutherans) took "is" literally, but many Protestants took it metaphorically—to mean "represents." Pressed on these words, Archbishop Cranmer asserted desperately that his Catholic interrogators did not understand tropes. The debate over the Eucharist opens up ontological uncertainties that subsequent centuries would only deepen. Both Protestants and Catholics accused one another of being materialists: Protestants argued that Catholics tried to invest the material world with sanctity, while Catholics accused Protestants of seeing only with a "material," outward eye. Anderson points to the way these accusations "open up a (pre)Cartesian chasm" (47) between words and the realities they are supposed to represent in the spiritual or material realms. The Eucharistic debate also furnishes a surprising entry to Donne's "Aire and Angels" and the twelfth of his *Devotions Upon Emergent Occasions.*

One of the most arresting chapters concerns the Vestiarian Controversy of the mid-sixteenth century. For Catholics "vestments were instinct with a dignity of their own" (80), embodiments of spiritual power, while for a doctrinaire Protestant like John Hooper they were the signs of the old law, the pope, and the devil. A moderate Protestant like Cranmer, on the other hand, retained most church vestments in order not to give scandal, and to emphasize the church's authority. Anderson's account of the quarrel between Hooper and Cranmer about what Hooper should wear for his investment as a bishop leads into a fascinating reading of Foxe's account of the examination and martyrdom of both Hooper and Cranmer. Here all the parties, Catholic and Protestant—and Foxe himself—attribute different meanings to the contested clothing. The final discussion of the martyrdoms—which includes a symbolic investing and *de*vesting of the Protestant bishops before they are martyred—forms one of the most brilliant analyses in the book. As in *Biographical Truth,* her earlier book on Renaissance life-writing, Anderson shows superbly the literary and ideological patterning that shapes these narratives. The topic of clothing leads into Donne's Third Satire, with its portraits of overdressed and underdressed sects, and ends with a discussion of Herbert's "Aaron." In this poem Anderson points out that there is no *literal* vestment at all: the external image of holiness in the dress has disappeared. In this instance of a translation from an external vesting to something "radically inward" there is a cost, a "narrowing and a personalizing of the power of the vestiary symbol which no longer has even a separably or externally actualized form. . . ." (110)

Two connected chapters study the relation between metaphor and catachresis (extreme or wrenched metaphor). The first focuses on a literary text, the much-discussed passage in the third book of *The Faerie Queene,* in which the female hero Britomart needs to negotiate the house of the enchanter Busyrane. The standard term for catachresis was *abusio* (in English, "abuse"), and Anderson argues convincingly that Busyrane becomes the image of a man who "abuses figuration outrageously, fantasizing that metaphor is the same as reality: feigning and faining [delighting in] rape" (112). By contrast a paired chapter develops an unexpectedly positive account of how classical and Renaissance rhetoricians view catachresis. Working with patient, detailed retranslation of Cicero and Quintilian, she stresses that they saw catachresis as useful, an extreme metaphor created to supply a current lack in the language. Renaissance writers, while varied in their response to catachresis, were much less hostile to it than modern accounts suggest.

A final chapter on the merchant/economist Gerrard de Malynes (fl. 1586–1641 treats his economic theory and his view of metaphor as analogous, and stresses the degree to which both are conflicted. Malynes is a man caught between an old world and a new one. While developing an early version of the quantity theory of money (the effect of the money supply on price), he would nonetheless have "like[d] money to have an intrinsic, substantive and definitive value. . . ." (196) His attitude toward metaphor is similarly double. While he uses metaphor, he distrusts its creative potential, preferring "similitudes" that are merely illustrative. Such similitudes "evoke a shared world, and most often a familiarly coded one" (177). The need to hold fast to traditional beliefs remains at odds with his recognition that the categories he inherits don't square with his empirical experience.

This is a rich, densely written book, working in a bravura variety of fields and full of shrewd insight. It has two great strengths. One is the extraordinary range of Anderson's learning, which moves with authority between modern linguistics and Renaissance dictionaries, drama and biography, theology and economics. This learning and imaginative width opens up ways of seeing changes in early modern culture through the perspective of metaphor. The second is her x-ray vision in treating particular passages. Time and again her searching examinations of particular texts leave one seeing them differently—and to some degree *seeing* differently. It's this precise, imaginative awareness of language in action that gives the book its closeness to individual moments of vision. At times, however, I would have liked a few more explicit claims about the work's larger thesis. Anderson is so careful *not* to distort her evidence, to stay so close to the complexities of particular texts, that the sense of what the whole adds up to sometimes gets lost. Yet one comes away from reading the book with a deeper and more precise

sense of how the early modern period moves piecemeal and hesi-
tantly toward the ontological uncertainties of the late seventeenth
century.

Manuscripts and their Makers in the English Renaissance
By Peter Beal and Grace Ioppolo
London: The British Library, 2002
and
Dramatists and their Manuscripts in the Age of Shakespeare, Jonson, Middleton and Heywood: Authorship, Authority and the Playhouse
By Grace Ioppolo
London and New York: Routledge, 2006

Reviewer: Heather Wolfe

Surprisingly (to me, at least), the field of early modern manuscript
studies still has a limited number of players, and just about every
one of them makes an appearance in *Manuscripts and their Makers
in the English Renaissance* (half of the ten essays are written by
members of the annual journal's editorial board and two by the coeditors). As rich and wonderful as *Manuscripts and their Makers*
is, and as distinguished as the contributors are, it is also a cry for a
new generation of voices to step up and be heard: so many manuscripts, so few scholars equipped with the paleographical and bibliographical skills to make sense of them. Based on conferences at
the University of Reading in 2000 and 2001, this fascinating group
of essays introduces new discoveries, new attributions, and new
readings of well-known manuscripts. The essays devoted to individual manuscripts read like detective's reports, the authors pro-
viding the results of successful *and* dead-end investigations of

dates, scribes, and owners with equal panache. *Manuscripts and their Makers* is a model of scholarly generosity, with the contributors frequently thanking each other for being pointed in the direction of hitherto unfamiliar manuscripts and leads. The physical descriptions of manuscripts are uniformly thorough and expert, and the essays always sound the same underlying theme: manuscripts must not be overlooked when trying to unravel the often mysterious roles of author, scribe, and printer in the production of literary and historical texts of this period. Many of the appendixes contain edited texts, and the footnotes are helpfully voluminous. The only shortcoming of this volume, and of the journal in general, is not the fault of the contributors or editors: the reproductions of the manuscripts are poor and frustratingly small, making it nearly impossible to read the handwriting.

Peter Beal kicks off the volume with a long essay on his discovery of another contemporary copy of Philip Sidney's *Letter to Queen Elizabeth,* purportedly sent by the poet to the queen in 1579 in an attempt to prevent her from marrying the Duc d'Alençon. This essay provides a useful supplement to Beal's discussion of the *Letter*'s manuscript circulation in his *In Praise of Scribes.* None of the surviving manuscript copies are authorial, making the *Letter,* like most texts transmitted in manuscript, highly unstable by modern standards. What is extraordinary about this new copy (National Library of Scotland, Adv. MS 33.3.11, fols. 104v–110r) is that it can be dated to the earliest period of the *Letter*'s circulation, and one of its scribes, whom Beal identifies as the Scottish scholar and spy Alexander Dicsone (1558–1603/4), can be directly associated with Sidney in 1583–84. Beal suggests that since two of the most contentious sections are "re-ordered" here and in two copies from the 1620s–30s, it is possible that the *Letter* was perhaps "released to the world" in a multiplicity of forms, at different stages of composition, revision, and copying, and that, quite possibly, the pages of one copy got disordered at some point, leading to a variety of transcriptions (16). A transcription of a letter from Dicsone to Robert Bowes, dated August 9, 1595, appears as an appendix.

Henry Woudhuysen discusses a fragment of Sidney's *Old Arcadia* discovered by Steven May, which survives today because it served as binding reinforcement for a folio-sized terrier belonging to Sir Edmund Huddleston (it has since been removed; Cambridgeshire Record Office, Huddleston Papers 488/M [R92/88]). Containing forty-four lines of text, the fragment was apparently discarded by the scribe because he miscopied part of "The Eighte songe" at the bottom of the page, and decided it was easier to start over on a fresh sheet rather than try to correct the problem. It is not the variants that prove revelatory, but the fact that its provenance, scribe, and date of copying can be ascertained, and that the numbering of the two poems is unique, "raising questions of composition and ordering" (54). Through watermark, paper, and handwriting analysis, Woudhuysen attributes the ca. 1580 copy to one John Paxton, a skilled penman and estate steward to Huddleston, a papist with recusant children. Woudhuysen provides biographical information on Paxton and Huddleston, and offers a few theories as to how Huddleston and Paxton might have come across a version of *Old Arcadia* to copy, primarily having to do with Huddleston's Roman Catholic and East Anglian background. Woudhuysen also points out the importance of the process of provenance investigation and scribal recovery: "it may shed some light on the contexts in which works were originally read and perhaps written. Furthermore, identifying scribes may one day allow their habits to be studied in the same way that analytical bibliographers, in their efforts to produce better texts, have examined the work of individual compositors" (63).

Folger MS V.a.89 (the Cornwallis-Lysons MS) is a well-known Elizabethan poetical miscellany owned by Anne Cornwallis, later Duchess of Argyll. The manuscript has been mined by textual editors of Sidney, Dyer, Raleigh, Oxford, and Shakespeare (for the poem, "when that thine eye hath chose the dame" that shows up in the 1599 and 1612 editions of *The Passionate Pilgrim*). Arthur Marotti casts fresh eyes on the miscellany, treating it as an organic unit rather than a series of individual poems (for example, he notes that almost half of the poems in the second part also appear in two other miscellanies, British Library Harley MS 7392 and Bodleian MS Rawlinson poetical 85). The first part of the manuscript contains seven unique poems by one John Bentley in an inexperienced secretary hand, while the second part contains twenty-seven poems of an amorous nature, written in a professional scribal hand and attributed (and sometimes misattributed) to, in addition to the aforementioned poets, Anne Vavasour, Richard Edwards, Sir William Cordell, and others. Marotti provides a valuable semidiplomatic transcription of "When that thine eye" with a full collation against four other sources (two manuscript and two print), and close readings and transcriptions of nine unique, anonymous poems from the second part. He ends his essay with a critique of "the author-centered focus of most textual editing," which has allowed these nine poems, rare examples that "help define a mid-Elizabethan courtly poetic idiom and cultural style," to be neglected (86). These poems reinforce the point that court poetry of this period shared a common idiom, which was part of its appeal, and which would have been warmly received by those who could recognize the variations upon a well-trodden theme. Appended to the essay is a first-line index of poems in Folger MS V.a.89, which, most usefully, includes appearances in other manuscripts.

Katherine Duncan-Jones provides a short essay on her 1997 discovery of an incomplete autograph manuscript of Hugh Holland's *Owen Tudyr* (1601) dedicated to Elizabeth I (Berkeley Castle, "Select Book [unbound] 81"). Hilton Kelliher offers a brilliant attribution argument for *The Newe Metamorphosis* (1600) by "JM," deciphering autobiographical allusions scattered throughout its 15,000 couplets in order to pin the poem on one John Mott, "an apprentice goldsmith, mercenary soldier and law student turned East Anglian squire of no other known literary attainments" (128; British Library Add MS 14824–6). Grace Ioppolo analyzes correspondence and other records relating to a breach of promise between the dramatist Robert Daborne and Philip Henslowe in 1613 and 1614 to show that Henslowe and his competitors strongly preferred to receive "fair" copies of contracted plays rather than "foul," and then tests her theory on Thomas Heywood's autograph manuscript of *The Captives* (British Library, Egerton MS 1994), which she describes as a foul copy. Her arguments in this important essay are almost entirely encapsulated in her subsequent book, *Dramatists and their Manuscripts,* which I will address later. In a fascinating essay on the manuscript sources for Constantijn Huygens's translation of four Donne poems into Dutch in 1630 (Koninklijke Bibliotheek, The Hague, MS KA XL^a 1630), Richard Todd explores how Huygens may have encountered the poems (*The Sunne Rising, The Anagram, Recusancy, A Valediction, forbidding Mourning*) before they appeared in print. He argues that Huygen had access to early scribal copies of Donne's poems, perhaps from the early 1620s if not earlier, and is able to situate the sources for the translations, which are the earliest known to exist, in the overall stemma for each poem. Cedric Brown introduces us to "the Black Poet of Ashover," one Leonard Wheatcroft (1626–1706), a church clerk and enthusiastic village bard whose two surviving manuscript books, a miscellany and an autobiography (Derbyshire Record Office, D.253 A/PZ5/1 and D.2079), reveal his familiarity with popular mid-seventeenth-century printed miscellanies such as *Wits Interpreter,* a conduct/courtship manual with plenty of poetry for copying and imitating. Wheatcroft's miscellany includes poetry (original and copied), courtship letters and poems embedded in a prose narrative about the wooing of his wife, and "An Elegey vpon the death of all the Greatest Gentry In darley dale," for which Brown provides an edited text in an appendix. Brown wonders how such a miscellany might function in a provincial town: Did the individual poems, songs, and elegies travel as separates that were then collected? And how were they read and used once they were collected into a single volume and stored in a private library?

The last two essays concern the editing of manuscripts. Steve May discusses the difficulties of deciding which verse anthologies to publish as editions, when over 170 survive from the Tudor period alone. Given the instability of poems as they travel among manuscripts, May tests out Jerome McGann's print-based theory of the "socially created artifact" on Marotti's argument that the poetry transmitted in manuscript was often subject to "recontextualization," supplementation, revision, and answering. If this is the case, then poetry that may have no place in an edition of an individual poet's ouevre could still be of literary interest as an instance of contemporary "social editing," demonstrating the accumulation of "culturally significant and interesting accretions at every stage of transmission" (206). Just as it seems that May is about to suggest that *all* miscellanies deserve editing, he then turns the tables and argues that in fact, the overwhelming majority of scribes *did* try to make accurate copies, or at least capture "the essence of the original text" (207). May provides examples of three poetic miscellanies copied from print sources with substantive deviation rates of just .015, .007, and .005. "Print" is the operative word, here. Texts deteriorated rapidly once they entered into manuscript circulation, probably because most miscellanizers were amateur copyists who wrote in sloppy, everyday hands that were misread by later amateurs, and so on. This is a far cry from social editing, and leads May to conclude that "average, 'run-of-the-quill' social editing will yield few if any miscellanies that cry out for a modern edition" (212). May then offers two principles for selecting manuscript anthologies worthy of editing for the purposes of textual and literary criticism: an edited anthology should preserve texts of aesthetic and cultural value, and it should provide texts that are both significant in content and are also extremely rare or unique.

In the final essay, "Systemizing sigla," Harold Love ventures into the textual apparatus jungle, suggesting that early modern literary historians follow the example set by musicologists, and standardize the coded abbreviations we use to refer to scribally transmitted texts when listing variants. Musicologists regularly generate sigla for manuscripts by relying on the RISM (Repertoire internationale des sources musicale) system: national identifier followed by library identifier and shelfmark. Love argues that such a system, equally intuitive and perhaps even more streamlined than RISM, would aid considerably in the comparison of multiple copies of poems, making it easier to discover variants that occur in both "genetic" and "genetically non-indicative" groups of manuscripts by looking at each source as a whole, rather than only at the works of a particular author in that source.

*   *   *

In *Dramatists and their Manuscripts,* Grace Ioppolo's main argument is that playwrights exerted much more authority over their plays, both pre- and postproduction, and their payments, than has previously been thought. In most cases, plays took a decidedly non-linear path from first draft to audience, unsteadily bouncing between author, scribe, censor, bookkeeper, actors, and printers. Her groundbreaking study convincingly shows that many playwrights had bargaining power in negotiating advances, payments, and bonuses for contracted plays, and slightly less convincingly, that they took great pride in perfecting their work. Previous scholarship on theater history has been hindered, she concludes, by four main factors: 1) the assumption that scribal practice, a fairly predictable affair, extended to authorial manuscript practice as well, which in fact, was anything but predictable; (2) the tendency of scholars to focus exclusively on the business of theater from the perspective of the owners, and not the authors; (3) erroneous conclusions drawn by eminent bibliographers with little manuscript experience have been unquestionably adopted and enlarged by others; and (4) current scholars tend to move backward from print to manuscript. These errors have perpetuated the myth that most playwrights were underpaid hack writers who had little control over their texts once they handed them over to playhouses, and that therefore their authorial (and messy) manuscripts should be distrusted as authoritative texts. In her thorough examination of a wide range of Elizabethan and early Stuart theatrical manuscripts, Ioppolo ably demonstrates that "it is impossible to study, interpret or define the transmission of an early modern printed dramatic text, or its use in the theatre before publication, without studying, interpreting or defining the role of manuscripts in those processes" (4). To aid the reader in understanding this role, she provides a useful ten-page primer on the Elizabethan secretary hand, paper, ink, and quill (80–89).

Ioppolo's analysis of surviving play manuscripts (foul papers and authorial and scribal fair copies) and other theatrical records (including revelatory correspondence between Edward Daborne and Philip Henslowe) in the context of both manuscript culture and playhouse practice leads to one of her most radical conclusions: the current working definition of "foul papers" as the author's last complete draft before the fair copy, established by W. W. Greg over seventy-five years ago and extended by Fredson Bowers and succeeding critics, is too constrictive. Foul papers should be seen not as final drafts, but as working drafts with inconsistencies, cuts, and additions that are often revised and resolved in the process of making the fair copy, which could also contain corrections and contradictions. *Dramatists and their Manuscripts* takes us on a tour of the Henslowe-Alleyn archive at Dulwich College, introducing us to the informal and formal, nonexclusive and exclusive, contracts between Henslowe and his dramatists, which usually demanded the delivery of a "book" (a fair copy) by a specific date. In Daborne's letters to Henslowe, he mentions "some papers I haue sent you though not so fayr written all as I could wish," and attempts to prove that he has not broken a contract by sending him "the foule sheet & the fayr I was wrighting" and promising that he "will not fayle to write this fayr & perfit the book." That is, Daborne was in the process of making a fair copy when Henslowe's agent arrived to collect it, so he sends part of the play to Henslowe in "foul" form until he has time to finish copying it out. Thus, the dramatist, and not Henslowe, was responsible for having his drafts converted into a legible playbook suitable for licensing. Daborne's letters to Henslowe also corroborate evidence in the Henslowe agreements that "acting companies frequently sought the advice of authors when casting actors in their plays and continued to turn to authors for other support during readings and rehearsal" (29). For example, Daborne reassures Henslowe in May 1613 that a play is forthcoming, and that he would be prepared to "meet you & mr Allin & read some for I am vnwilling to read to *the* generall company till all be finisht" (37).

By broadening the definition of foul papers, Ioppolo is able to increase the number of surviving early modern foul papers of dramatic texts from zero to at least four: Heywood's *The Captives,* Mountfort's *The Launching of the Mary,* the manuscript of *The Wasp or Subjects President,* and, although not a play, Jonson's *Entertainment at Britain's Burse.* Other manuscripts fall into the category of partly foul, partly fair, such as *The Book of Sir Thomas More,* Heywood's *The Escapes of Jupiter,* and Massinger's *Believe as You List. The Book of Sir Thomas More* has undergone intense scrutiny over the years because of the notorious "Hand D," which is responsible for three pages of the collaborative manuscript. Ioppolo tentatively accepts the attribution of this hand to Shakespeare, but vehemently disagrees with W. W. Greg's designation of these three pages as "foul papers." Rather, she reclassifies them as authorial fair copies of foul papers, written in a "slow, measured and flourished manner" with "a relatively high number of unlinked letters," in stark contrast to the fluent form of a rapid cursive that would have been used in the process of composition. Five of the nineteen authorial corrections to this section are the result of eye-skip error, which occurs when a writer is copying from another version and loses his place on the page, not when he or she is composing. Shakespeare is fine-tuning his contribution, apparently after the bookkeeper has tweaked it, rather than making significant *currente calamo* revisions. She then extrapolates from Shakespeare's habits in *More* to draw conclusions about the source texts for his printed plays, arguing that contrary to popular belief and Condell's claims in his preface to the First Folio, Shakespeare wrote, revised, and reconsidered his texts as much as the next guy, revisiting his plays at various points in the "circular" production process to meet a range of competing demands.

This is a study that cannot be ignored, as it challenges and revises most of our notions about the ways in which Jonson, Middleton, Heywood, Shakespeare, and other dramatists worked. By subjecting both well-known and recently discovered manuscript evidence to rigorous paleographical and textual analysis, she provocatively disagrees with many current scholars, and it is to be expected that her work will elicit responses from many of them.

Redefining Elizabethan Literature
By Georgia Brown
Cambridge: Cambridge University Press, 2004

Reviewer: Bart van Es

It is not so very long ago that C. S. Lewis wrote of the 1590s as a golden age of English poetry. By "Golden poetry," he explained, "I do not mean simply good poetry (that is another question) but poetry in its innocent—as the theologians would say, its 'once-born'—condition." There are few scholars today who find "once-born" innocence in the 1590s. Even so, Georgia Brown goes further than most when she argues that "shame" is the decade's defining characteristic. She puts her argument in its starkest terms when she claims that "literary production at the end of Elizabeth's reign is, quite simply, dirty" (50).

Redefining Elizabethan Literature sets out to change our understanding of one of the most important decades of English literary history. Brown's title refers not simply to her own scholarly project: in her assessment "redefining Elizabethan literature" is what a specific body of early modern writers set out to do. What she terms "the generation of shame" (a set of authors including Marlowe, Shakespeare, Nashe, Drayton, and Daniel) reacted collectively against Tudor humanism. In the face of earlier stress on didactic purpose, they worked to change the function of poetry so that "literature started to be conceived as a valuable activity in its own right" (4). That effort itself brought an uncomfortable degree of shame.

After an introduction that examines the anthropology of shame and the reception of Ovid, Brown's book falls into three chapters. The first is a case study of Thomas Nashe. The second is a survey of the epyllion. The third looks at female complaint in historical verse. Brown's chapter on Nashe fixes especially on issues of superfluity. "Excess," she tells us, is to her more helpful than Richard Helgerson's category of "the prodigal," something well illustrated through Nashe's embarrassment over the physical overproduction of texts. Nashe, placed between the worlds of patronage and commercial print, at once celebrates and deplores his own productivity. Literary ornament is particularly important here because it defines the literary, but also marks "the ontological threat posed to anyone who bases their identity in language" (47). The paradox in his output, Brown argues, is that Nashe makes authorial stability (and commodity) out of his very changefulness.

Brown's treatment of Nashe is illuminating, but the following chapter on the epyllion (at nearly twice the length) is considerably more ambitious. This enormously rich section of the book covers eleven epyllia, running from Thomas Lodge's *Scillaes Metamorphosis* of 1589 to John Weever's *Faunus and Melliflora,* published in 1600. Brown examines the erotic minor epic (most famously typified by Marlowe's *Hero and Leander* and Shakespeare's *Venus and Adonis*) from many angles: its association with youth and innovation; its political status in relation to the Virgin Queen; its tendency to feminize the act of authorship; and its connection with the shame of print. Throughout, Brown illustrates the connections between literary and erotic pleasure—connections that humanism tended to suppress.

One of the achievements of Brown's chapter on the epyllion is the way it expands interest beyond the familiar examples of the genre. Alongside Shakespeare and Marlowe, Brown draws attention to work by Henry Petowe, Thomas Heywood, and John Marston. The final chapter (again on a smaller scale) also does something to extend the canon by offering sustained attention to Drayton's *Englands Heroicall Epistles.* Here, too, Brown argues, we have a countercultural form that challenges the assumptions of the morally orthodox.

Redefining Elizabethan Poetry is a significant achievement; it should change the way the 1590s are perceived. The chapter on the epyllion is outstanding, but the book as a whole also makes important wider claims. Of course, Richard Helgerson's *Elizabethan Prodigals* (1976) already looms large in this area, but Brown's study complements and extends it in several ways. Her account of the connections between the minor epics is more extensive. Her insistence on the sexual content of this work is also instructive, and her analysis (which tends toward the psychoanalytic) is also different from what has come before.

Of course, a work that challenges orthodoxies will also invite opposition. At the most fundamental level, this is likely to come in response to Brown's key concept of "the generation of shame." By this oft-used phrase Brown denotes a very large body of writers unified by very particular concerns. Repeatedly, they are assessed as a collective. Thus "by setting narrative chronicles in dialogue with complaint," we are told, "the generation of shame re-examines the nature of the Tudor subject" (222). Similarly, "it is the mixture of gendered elements, or, to put it in different terms, the paradox of gender, that writers in the generation of shame find so productive" (223). Again, "the generation of shame is preoccupied with the fragmentable nature of culture" (224) and "the generation of shame defined itself in opposition to certain aspects of humanist ideology" (224). Such unity of purpose is open to doubt.

Even with Nashe (in whose works the importance of shame is clearly shown) Brown sometimes gives a programmatic impression. Describing *The Unfortunate Traveller,* for example, she writes that "Nashe acknowledges that the pursuit of the poetics of displacement, in this history of the reign of Henry VIII, not only undermines teleological structures, it also constitutes a highly unconventional kind of national chronicle" (178). This is plausible analysis, but it does imply a coherence of argument that is not easily found in Nashe's text.

Moving beyond the usual "prodigal" suspects (such as Nashe, Greene, and Marlowe) the case for a coherent "generation of shame" is still more difficult to sustain. Drayton is a case in point. Brown notes that he has generally been thought of as a conservative and moralistic writer. For her, however, his use of the female voice in *Englands Heroicall Epistles* becomes, of itself, an antiauthoritarian gesture. Thus "while the Tudor chronicles extoll an Early Modern version of the stiff upper lip, the historical complaints adapt the chronicle material to form a shameful counter-history which redefines the nature of Englishness and resists the values promoted by the chronicles" (222). Brown cites Holinshed in support of her argument. Yet these multiauthored volumes (including stories such as that of Cordelia's suicide) are hardly uniform in their intent. The *Epistles,* in contrast, condemn "the blamefulness of the persons passion" at their outset and conclude on chaste marriage and usurpation's just deserts.

Drayton, Brown contends, is profoundly concerned with the sexualized shame of authorship. In a dedicatory sonnet to Lucy, Countess of Bedford, she tells us, Drayton "describes an authorial fantasy of rape by the patron, in which the male author will be raped by his patroness" (108). Such a vision would certainly warrant a major reassessment. The sonnet in question, however, hardly fits the bill. Published when Lucy was twelve, it is begins "Great ladie, essense of my cheefest good, / Of the most pure and finest tempred spirit, / Adorn'd with gifts, enobled by thy blood, / Which by discent true vertue do'st inhert." From start to finish it is concerned with praise for Lucy's honor and good family. While the lines "Unto thy fame my Muse her selfe shall taske, / Which rain'st upon mee thy sweet golden showers" may glance at the story of Danae's impregnation by Jove, it is surely excessive to call this a "rape fantasy."

Brown's book contains other interpretations that will fail to convince all of its readers. Walter Ralegh's tale of exploratory derring-do, *The Discoverie of the Large, Rich, and Bewtiful Empyre of Guiana,* for instance, is summarized as "a defense of the imagination, a defense of the reader's ability to suspend judgement and entertain the fantastic." The land itself "is a substitute for Elizabeth and for Ralegh" (20). From Brown's description one would expect a narrative of the wildest Nashean fantasy, not a travelogue promoting a realistic colonial scheme. To write that "the factual status of Guiana is always at issue" (20) is either vague or nonsensical. Such readings will irritate the more historically minded reader, especially because they are not announced as speculative in any way.

Even at its wilder moments, however, Brown's interpretation remains insightful. Indeed, as she illustrates, interpretations like hers could fall within the range of early modern readers themselves. William Reynolds, admittedly, "appears to have been unstable," but his commentary on Shakespeare's *Venus and Adonis* "wherin the queene represents the person of Venus" (131) is fascinating nevertheless. It shows how deeply the connection between sexuality and power had penetrated what Louis Montrose has termed "the Elizabethan political imaginary." As Brown observes, "Epyllia, such as *Venus and Adonis, Endimion and Phoebe* and *Faunus and Melliflora,* are products of the generation of shame not only because of their shameless eroticism, but also because they express frustration with the politico-cultural stasis generated by the old Queen's prodigious ability to persist" (133).

Redefining Renaissance Literature shows us that such eroticism is, in fact, very rarely "shameless." Brown's book illustrates shame's pervasive presence: within systems of publication, patronage, politics, and nation-building, and within the very idea of "the literary" itself. The author presents an excellent case for reassessing the

1590s; still more valuably, she casts light on many hitherto ne-glected works. Her case for a generational project invites some skepticism, but we cannot doubt that this was part of the genera-tional experience. Without question, important further work in this area will follow. The 1590s has lost its "once-born" innocence; some natural tears we drop, but the world is all before us.

Prologues to Shakespeare's Theatre:
Performance and Liminality
in Early Modern Drama
By Douglas Bruster and Robert Weimann
London and New York: Routledge, 2004

Reviewer: Kiernan Ryan

Given the high proportion of early modern plays that feature pro-logues, it's surprising how little attention they have received from theater historians and critics. Prologues pave the way for almost half the plays that survive from the period between 1558 and 1642. The popularity of the device peaked in the 1580s and dipped sharply from the 1590s onward, as Benvolio's refusal to counte-nance a "without-book prologue, faintly spoke / After the prompter" in *Romeo and Juliet* (1596) attests. Within a decade of that dis-missal the *"Prologus Laureatus"* to *The Birth of Hercules* (1604) felt constrained to announce: "I am a Prologue, should I not tell you so / You would scarce know me; 'tis so long ago / Since Prologues were in use." In its heyday, however, this arresting theatrical ploy could boast of having spawned the dazzling manifesto that trum-pets the advent of *Tamburlaine* (1587): "From jigging veins of rhyming mother wits, / And such conceits as clownage keeps in pay, / We'll lead you to the stately tent of war." During its decline, paradoxically, Shakespeare produced the consummate instance of the art in *Henry V* (1599): "Admit me Chorus to this history, / Who Prologue-like your humble patience pray / Gently to hear, kindly to judge, our play." And he was still eager to enlist its aid in *Henry VIII* (1613) at the close of his career: "Such as give / Their money out of hope they may believe, / May here find truth."

The reasons why the early modern dramatic prologue—with the exception of Shakespeare's most famous choruses—has suffered such critical neglect are not hard to discern. Prominent among them is what Douglas Bruster and Robert Weimann perceive as a "reluctance to study conjunctures of dramatic form and social function" (2), a reluctance that anyone more interested in the plays themselves will readily understand. But the chief reason lies with the ostensibly extraneous, disposable nature of the device, whose archaic air of obsequious artifice only compounds the impression of redundancy. The prologue dwells in a paratextual twilight zone, at once beyond and yet within the boundaries of the play it precedes. Viewed from one angle, it's an integral part of the ensuing drama, the point at which the whole theatrical event begins; viewed from another, it's an optional extra that can be unplugged from the play proper in performance, and deleted from published versions of the script, without the least compunction.

For Bruster and Weimann, however, it is precisely in this curious liminal quality that the key to the prologue's dramatic and cultural significance is to be found. Far from being of merely peripheral import, they contend, the prologues of this period allow us to trace through their mutations the emergence and evolution of new forms of theatrical communication in the drama of Shakespeare and his contemporaries. In a culture that could no longer count on stable structures of authority and signification, the commercial theater was obliged to forge its own warrant to depict the world on its own unpredictable terms, and the prologue provided the perfect means of inducting the audience into this dynamic theatrical dispensation. From Marlowe to Peele to Lyly to Shakespeare, the story the prologues tell is one of increasing complexity and contingency, as the power to determine a play's meaning came to reside in neither author nor actor nor spectator, but in the interaction of all three in the course of the performance.

Bruster and Weimann set the scene for that story with a prologue of their own, which takes the form of three chapters designed to define the manifold nature and diverse functions of the Elizabethan prologue as it morphed from fledgling appeal into full-blown monologue. The first chapter considers the prologue in its three closely entwined manifestations: as scripted speech, as the costumed actor who delivers it, and as the actual performance of the speech onstage. Although many prologues, including the remarkable discourse on theatrical mimesis that prefaces Lyly's *Midas,* were written in prose, most of them were composed in verse and displayed a marked bent for rhyme, especially in the capping couplet. The majority of prologues from dramas of the commercial playhouses were between fifteen and thirty-five lines long (Shakespeare's normally leaning toward the upper limit), and were traditionally delivered by an actor wearing a black velvet cloak and a wreath of bay leaves around his brow. At the most basic level they were, as Bruster and Weimann put it, "forms for mustering attention, part of a constellation of heraldic devices surrounding the performance of plays in the early modern era" (28). But they also served, more complexly, to demarcate and occupy "a zone of multiple transitions" (23).

What's at stake in the creation of this zone becomes clearer in chapter 2, "Prologue as Threshold and Usher." Rejecting Gérard Genette's *Paratexts* as "too wedded to a novelistic model of literary production to account for the complexities of collaboration involved in the early modern theatre" (38), the authors turn to the anthropological concept of liminality pioneered by Arnold van Gennep and developed by Victor Turner to explain the more profound objectives of the prologue. Although they perhaps discount Genette too hastily as unhelpful, they make a persuasive case for viewing prologues as initiating a rite of passage within a privileged space set apart from "the centres of London's commercial and political power": "By facilitating the transition from everyday world to playworld, from ordinary perception to imaginary reception, they reconstituted their own liminality in terms of textual and performative strategies. They thus helped conduct theatre-goers over the threshold of a fictional world that allowed new perspectives on a host of issues relating to these centres of power and their affect [*sic*] on playgoers' lives" (44). Quince's mangled, mispunctuated prologue to "Pyramus and Thisbe" in *A Midsummer Night's Dream* ("All for your delight / We are not here") and Rumour's bold arraignment of the audience in *2 Henry IV* ("which of you will stop / The vent of hearing when loud Rumour speaks?") are perfect illustrations of the prologue's capacity to transport the spectator into uncharted territory, where the responsibilities of reception are no less apparent than the vulnerability of the powerful to critique.

The third chapter tightens the focus on the prologue's penchant for serving as "a site of inquiry concerning authority" (57), taking its cue from one of Nathan Field's prologue figures, who likens "A man in Authority" to "a candle in the wind." Drawing on ideas developed in Weimann's *Authority and Representation in Early Modern Discourse* (1996) and *Author's Pen and Actor's Voice* (2000) as well as Bruster's *Shakespeare and the Question of Culture* (2003), the authors examine a range of pre-Shakespearean prologues, from Plautus and Terence to *Mankind* and *Everyman,* which "project diverse sources of theatrical authority" (61), in order to establish by contrast what makes Elizabethan prologues different. The sense of a radical departure can already be inferred from the exuberant prologue to Robert Wilson's *The Three Ladies of London* (ca.1581). "You marvel, then," declares Wilson's prologue, "what stuff we have to furnish out our show. / Your patience yet we crave a while, till we have trimm'd our stall; / Then, young and old, come and behold our wares, and buy them all." In this speech we can hear, as Weimann and Bruster show, "the language of a prologue authorized, it appears, almost exclusively by material performance requirements" (74): the language of a drama, in short, that has begun to locate its authority, its right to represent reality, within itself. Emancipated by the market, by the principle of exchange value, from the dictates of extrinsic authorities, whether religious or secular, the theater is empowered to please itself, provided that by doing so it pleases the audience. "Authority in this theatre, then," conclude Weimann and Bruster, "is shared with, even ostentatiously surrendered to, those who 'come and behold our wares'" (75).

The remaining four chapters of this brief but dense study are devoted to close readings of key prologues penned by Marlowe, Peele, Lyly, and Shakespeare respectively. Their aim is to trace the shifting balance of power in early modern theatrical productions as dramatist and spectator, actor and character, text and performance contend with each other for control of the play's significance. The general trend of these developments is clear enough—toward a more fluid, collaborative, open-ended exchange between all the parties involved, culminating in the startling usurpation of political power by theatrical power in the prologue to *Henry V.* But comprehending the detailed discriminations the authors strive to make within and between the works of each dramatist is another matter altogether. In Marlowe's prologues to both parts of *Tamburlaine* and *The Jew of Malta* can be found, we are told, a "new concept of writing" that "was prepared to advance accomplishment in authorship as itself a source and site of authority" (78). So far so good. "Here, then, in rudimentary, emergent form was a new economy of intellectual ownership in alliance with a new epistemology empowering a poetic language of writing as the dominant agency of knowledge, inspiration, and meaning" (81): no problem whatsoever. But by the end of the chapter on Marlowe the reader is struggling to make sense of sentences like this: "Investing into the duplicity of liminal space, the playwright comes close to assimilating a presentational *gestus* of delivery that deliberately addresses an otherwise unspeakable contrariety" (94).

The chapter on Peele, which revolves round the prologues to *David and Bethsabe* (1593/94) and *The Old Wives Tale* (1590), is clouded by a similar confusion about what distinctions and conclusions are being drawn, and to what end. On the face of it, the prologue to *David and Bethsabe* confirms Peele's kinship with Marlowe, inasmuch as "The dramatist's refusal to concede to the public stage any authority in excess of his own poetic medium of authorization appears to dominate the stage at large" (99). But in the earlier play, *The Old Wives Tale,* the authority of the author, it transpires, had already been displaced by "the dramatic assimilation of a preliterate story-telling culture to the author's written representations" (104). Our confidence in this claim is immediately scuppered, however, by another hapless resort to turgid abstraction: "Insofar as this perception is deceptive, the relation between the two cultures can be summed up best by saying that it is marked by affirmative uses of difference in a floating nexus of mutual engagements" (104). The gist of the chapter's argument is actually straightforward in retrospect: from Peele's two prologues it may be inferred that "there was in the early 1590s no unalterable or, for that matter, representative position in the authorization of stage plays" (107). But the reader would be hard put to grasp this as the punch line of the chapter while plowing through its congested analyses.

The penultimate chapter, "From Hodge-podge to Scene Individable: John Lyly," threatens to sink into a quagmire of tortuous pretension in the opening paragraph, which concludes: "Lyly must have felt free to use the opening of *Midas* (1589) for launching a remarkable précis on [*sic*] the new art of Renaissance representation—the more so because it anticipated and combined the Hobbesian politico-juridical notion of a contractual type of representative action and what Heidegger defined in modern epistemology as the setting forth of a masterful world-picture 'in relation to oneself' or one's emerging national culture" (117). Fortunately, however, things perk up from this point on. Even the opaque invocation of Gayatri Spivak's terms "portrait" and "proxy" can't prevent the authors making it plain as the chapter proceeds that "Lyly's prologue marked the advent of cultural practices on the Elizabethan stage that led to far-reaching complications within the circulation of authority in theatrical representations" (127). And they wrap the chapter up by spelling out what these complications boil down to: "Authority in the Elizabethan playhouse, then, was not unified, conclusive, or given prior to a performance; it needed to be validated by the audience and was implicated in the effect of and response to the theatrical production itself" (133).

Prologues to Shakespeare's Theatre almost secures its redemption with the final chapter, *"Henry V* and the Signs of Power,"* whose analysis of "what remains the most admired instance of the genre" (154) starts to unpack at last the critical implications of the prologue's cultural significance. Bruster and Weimann argue convincingly that through the Chorus of *Henry V* Shakespeare claims for his theater the capacity to cut the powerful down to size and call the legitimacy of their sway into question. The ordinary, largely illiterate members of the audience are empowered by the play to subject monarchy to their imagination and judgment: "In *Henry V,* the authorization of 'imaginary forces', the summons even to 'deck' royalty is deliberately tied to 'mean and gentle all'" and, as a result, "here was in action a new medium, usurping the 'authority of public instruction', abducting what was supposed to rest in the hands of 'Ecclesiastical Ministers, and temporal Magistrates'" (150). The Chorus's gestures of self-deprecation absolve neither author nor audience of "In little room confining mighty men, / Mangling by starts the full course of their glory," and reducing Agincourt to a "brawl ridiculous" fought with "four or five most vile and ragged foils." On the contrary, as Weimann and Bruster observe: "Suddenly, an unsuspected source of strength emerges out of 'this unworthy scaffold,' on which the representation of political power can literally be confined, if not mangled, by the imperfect, but for all that forceful, power of theatrical performances" (151).

The last chapter is so suggestive that it throws the book's shortcomings into sharp relief. Chief among these is the way it flinches from confronting the consequences of viewing the prologue "as both a seismograph of cultural change and itself a changeful vessel of theatrical convention" (115). For those consequences could be considerable as far as the interpretation and evaluation of early modern drama, and of Shakespeare in particular, are concerned. Most obviously, the kind of cultural historicism that assumes the theater's complicity with the throne and orthodox attitudes might have to think again. The achievement of the likes of Peele and Lyly, moreover, may warrant a radical reappraisal, involving detailed attention to the language and form of their plays that treats them as singular works of art rather than signposts on the road to Shakespeare. Above all, if we do find in the prologue to *Henry V* a "strange symbiosis of historiography and theatricality" that seeks "to legitimate the common stage as a public medium of historical understanding" and "sanction an entirely different type of history" (135, 136, 137), it may be that the relationship between Shakespeare's texts and their time will have to be rethought. After all, why labor to explain those texts by ensconcing them in their historical contexts, as most critics feel compelled to, if the whole point of Shakespearean drama is to create an alternative, imaginative version of its world that confounds the accounts of conventional historiography?

It's a shame that the authors are disinclined to do more than drop hints about the potential ramifications of their book, because by pulling their punches and forcing the reader to do so much work, they run the risk that its true importance will remain latent and its deepest insights overlooked. Nevertheless, even though reading *Prologues to Shakespeare's Theatre* is like being led to the place where the gold is buried and left to dig it up with a spoon, that should not deter anyone keen to break new ground in the field of early modern drama from delving into it.

Marvelous Protestantism: Monstrous Births
in Post-Reformation England
By Julie Crawford
Baltimore and London: Johns Hopkins
University Press, 2005

Reviewer: Mark Thornton Burnett

In this exciting study, Julie Crawford discusses representations of monstrous births in England from the 1560s to the 1660s, linking them to developments in Protestantism and the so-called "reformation of manners." She deploys monstrous births as a "rich source of information about, and creative re-imaginings of, particular social and religious controversies" (2), thus establishing, beyond any reasonable doubt, the status of "monsters . . . as texts" (3) and the multiple ways in which "marvelous Protestant" forms of literary and cultural registration "initiated an interpretive process" (3). In her endeavor, Crawford is often subtle and persuasive, energetic and absorbing, particularly at those points where she considers the centrality of monsters to the "polemically casuistical . . . battles of English Protestantism" (7): stories of monstrous births, she compellingly contends, "served as objects for Protestant education, reflection, and repentance, but they also made claims for the truth of specific, often controversial, Protestant doctrines and beliefs" (9). Not surprisingly, many of the authors involved were "Protestant ministers or proselytisers" (4) themselves and, hence, the concerns with which they wrestled spanned the spectrum of contemporary controversy, from "the form of marriage ceremonies to the nature of the indwelling of the Holy Ghost" (12). Three further dimensions to this study testify to its depth, importance, and appeal. The book is distinguished by its fine adjudication between events in London, the "publishing centre" (10), and practices and convictions in more regional peripheries; it recognizes and illustrates a "crisis" in the "reproduction of religious and social norms and institutions" (13), which necessitated a concomitant sixteenth- and seventeenth-century emphasis on "religious and behavioural conformity" (20), and it privileges in order to integrate a gendered perspective, understanding monsters as "figures for women" (49) and pursuing the beliefs of Protestantism via constructions of female imaginations. In these respects alone, *Marvelous Protestantism: Monstrous Births in Post-Reformation England* represents a significant contribution to the scholarship in its field.

Chapter 1 addresses "the complicated genealogy of the monk calf in the English popular press and imagination" (28). "While the monk calf originally appears as an indictment of Catholicism," Crawford states, "its most prevalent legacy lies in the history of the reformation of individual, often female, believers" (28); to support this thesis, the author traces a fascinating genealogy that begins in the 1520s, moves through to the 1560s, and ends with the early seventeenth century. En route, Crawford offers delightful and entirely plausible connections—between "fashion monsters," as they are termed, and "controversies over acceptable church vestments and appropriate secular fashions" (33), between the "monk calf" and the "cat," and between "beliefs about clothes . . . as sanctifying and efficacious holy objects" (35) and reconfigurations of "Catholic ritual" (37). Particular strengths of this chapter emerge in its elaboration of the anti-Catholic world in which printers circulated, in its suggestion that monsters legitimated if not prompted preaching and sermonizing, and in its hypothesis that the very same monsters, at a critical historical juncture, "clarified the basic tenets of Protestant faith . . . [and] provided a kind of supernaturally vetted form of socio-religious discipline" (45). On occasions, however, the discussion might have been finessed: errant apprentices, for instance, did not only have their "monstrous" clothes displayed (36) since they were simultaneously held up for public scorn in their own right.[1] I wondered, too, if the otherwise excellent discussion of the points of contact binding the monk calf and the cat might have been developed: there is no reference to a well-known 1573 anti-Catholic pamphlet about the birth of a monstrous cat, nor is there engagement with the transformation of the monk calf into related forms of papal monstrosity later in the century.[2] My point is that the phenomenon of the "fashion monster" did not peter out at the start of the seventeenth century, as the organization of the chapter might suggest; rather, conjunctions of clothes, fashion, women, and physical anomalousness continued well into the seventeenth century and beyond, reflecting more nuanced anxieties about sexual indeterminacy and constituting a further enmeshing and sophisticating of the relations between gender, religion, and the monstrous body.[3]

Chapter 2 continues the first chapter's example in its discussion of "birth monsters" and the extent to which the figuration of an extraordinary delivery articulated Protestant doctrine and practice. Once again, there is much to admire here, not least in the well-versed and shrewdly applied argument's recovery of printer-publisher networks, in its attention to a variety of contexts (including vagrancy and poor relief) and in its excavation of collaborative modes of literary production and dissemination. Protestant beliefs—the "use of the ring" (70), resolutions of "a case of conscience" (71) and the "divinely binding nature of marital contracts" (71)—are knowledgeably handled, especially at those moments when Crawford ties their inculcation and circulation to readings of the monster and women's contemporary predicaments. What the chapter does not address is the afterlife of the monstrous forms that precipitated religious inquiry, and it is in this connection, I think, that more speculation and pursuit might have been warranted. How was the monstrous birth configured in its extratextual manifestations? What geographical/cultural circuits of exchange did the monster move inside and to what ideological effect? What was the chronological trajectory traced by the anomalous birth, and in what ways did that trajectory enable or transform the expression of Protestant thought? One location answering to at least some of these questions was the fairground or marketplace, sites of monstrous exhibition and interpretation that *Marvelous Protestantism* eschews, possibly to its detriment. In 1583, John Taylor, a London fishmonger, visited Shrewsbury in order to display "a deade childe . . . which had ij heades . . . myraculously"; in 1660, John Evelyn took a trip to St. Margaret's fair in Southwark to view "a monstrous birth of Twinns, both femals and most perfectly shaped . . . having their arms throwne about each other thus"; and, in 1664, conjoined twin girls born in Salisbury were "Imbalmed . . . to be seen."[4] These alternative but also complementary fields of negotiation and understanding for "birth monsters" are, arguably, as central as the popular pamphlet or the cash-strapped parish, enshrining, as they do, a capitalist logic, an economic nexus, and a mode of inscription rife with peculiarly Protestant meanings and associations. At the same time, the more secular environment of these species of representation affords a window onto the conflicted discourses, and competing models of explanation, that marked the period at a critical stage of religious and political uncertainty.

The case study occupying the center of chapter 3—rector William Leigh's accounts of the 1612 birth of conjoined twins in the parish of Standish, Lancashire—is intriguingly mounted. Leigh published two quite different assessments of the birth: the first interpretation framed the event within a rubric of "punishment for local sinners" (88) while the second deemed the occasion a "Protestant portent" (88) with "national [and] . . . political implications" (88–89). With this later interpretive method, the monster becomes de facto both "a sign of England's imperfect union with God" (91) and "a symbol of a mixed Catholic and Protestant state" (102). Contextually, the chapter is typically informed and careful, elaborating Leigh's own resistant positions, the Protestant-Catholic tensions at work in the parish, and the status of "equivocation" in the emerging Protestant mind-set. Consideration of equivocation allows Crawford to make one of her most impressive moves, which involves a semantic and ideological mapping onto each other of the Standish monster, and its doubled-bodied significance, the gunpowder plot, the English body politic ("disordered less by two heads . . . than by two *faces*" [109, emphasis in original]) and the Janus-like situation of James I/VI himself. As elsewhere in the book, the claims are stimulating and engaging, although it would have been worthwhile, I think, to have incorporated more on the monarch's own imbrication in, and use of, monstrous discourses in his writings. I was uncomfortable with one assertion, however. Citing the line from *Macbeth* in which Macduff plans to have his nemesis "as our rarer monsters are, / Painted upon a pole, and underwrit / 'Here may you see the tyrant,'" the author states: this "refers to the displaying of broadsheet pictures and pamphlet frontispieces of monstrous births; of broadsheet portraits of traitors, often physiognomically inflected; and of pictorial libels of local malefactors, who were often represented as monstrously deformed" (104).[5] It is one of those moments in *Marvelous Protestantism* where neglect of a fairground/market incarnation of monstrosity in fact allows for the possibility of error, for the Shakespearean line is less informed by the broadsheet, the pamphlet frontispiece, and the pictorial libel as it is by the contemporary practice, in contexts of commercial demonstration, of displaying banners to draw attention to the "monster-booth" and the spectacle to be encountered inside.[6] Visual messages at the fairground were, as the *Macbeth* example suggests, accompanied by a textual announcement: both worked together as a specific modality of monstrous representation, one that operated in discrete and particular ways as a guide to interpretation and a prompt to consumerism.

"Heedless Women, Headless Monsters, and the Wars of Religion," chapter 4, is elegantly pitched toward analysis of mid-seventeenth-century views, as they were communicated through monsters, of the religious and social order. Greater account might have been taken here of the range of types of monstrous representation. For instance, for every registration of a "headless body," which is explained as "the monstrous product of popish resistance to Parliamentarian ascendancy" (139), there was in the period an equally emphatic emphasis placed upon parliamentarian types of monsters with multiple heads, perennial figures for discord, rebellion and the multitude.[7] By the same token, the same trope—of a many-headed beast whose significance resided in its flouting of authority—was enlisted by parliamentarians as an index of contemporary political crisis.[8] Monstrous figures flowed into each other and were distinguished at this juncture, serving across communities and constituencies as politically charged ciphers of obedience and resistance.[9] Too, echoing a concern voiced earlier, the commercial dimensions of the display of the horned woman, Margaret Owen (actually Margaret Vergh Griffith), who is discussed on pp. 118–19, might have complicated the public/private and truth/deception dichotomies the book at this point elaborates.[10] Nevertheless, the chapter is still absorbing, seeing as integrally related to each other headless monsters, material "beheadings" and contemporary efforts to assert control over "controversial religious rites" (130). Equally forceful, it recognizes the new prominence of women as speakers and petitioners, and finds in the phenomenon of the headless monster "a range of female desires, beliefs, public avowals, and activism specific to the religious and political turmoil of 1640s England" (116). Above all, as the chapter concludes, spectacles of headlessness in the period functioned to express even as they attempted to contain the material circumstances of those "women [who] *were* in fact committing 'treason' against their husbands" (126, emphasis in original) and constituted authority.

Chapter 5, "*The ranters monster* and the 'Children of God,'" is one of the best. Concentrating on New England in the 1630s, it assesses reports of monstrous births in the context of controversies "over religious toleration during the Cromwellian Protectorate" (155). The error of monsters is inseparable, Crawford argues, from "loosely organized forms of worship [that] inevitably fostered or led to sectarian error like that of the antinomians" (155). In these sections, the book is sensitive and expert, moving nimbly and authoritatively between more than one opposed sectarian position and winding up by positing the inscrutability of the monstrous body as indicative of "those 'invisible' sectarian Christians who resisted or ignored outward and public forms of religion" (160). The chapter's final move, which acknowledges the increasingly secular status of the monster, is judicious and well placed: it acknowledges the growing attention given to scientific inquiry without presupposing the dominance of this new interpretive paradigm. Precisely managed as well is the book's conclusion in which the emergence of the Royal Society is balanced against the religious modalities of analysis explored in the book as a whole. Correctly, I think, Crawford identifies later seventeenth-century monster texts as removing the "divine or maternal role" (181), yet, as she simultaneously suggests, no smooth development can be inferred, with the cult of the monster in its subsequent histories pointing to "no comprehensive erasure of pious or political interpretations" (233). The book is to be applauded here in going against a well-rooted critical tradition and in offering a salutary corrective to long-held assumptions.

Marvelous Protestantism is an insightful study and a significant critical statement. Yet, for me, some reservations still persist. Curiosity, as a secular response to the monster, occupies little space and might have been considered as a complement to, if not a necessary part of, religiously inspired readings. Inevitably, some monster texts appeared in the early modern period which do not fit into Crawford's scheme: what of them, and did every monstrous representation enter a specifically Protestant nexus of explanation?[11] Crawford's approach is, as I have intimated, broadly historical and contextual, but it is also one that is theoretical only at a fairly subdued level, with Antonio Gramsci (13), Stuart Hall (24), and Michel Foucault (25, 84, 169) making no more than occasional appearances. Given the book's pedigree and genealogy, this is somewhat surprising, although it may, of course, be indicative of no more than a recent turn in Renaissance studies back toward the everyday and the material. But the theoretical modesty of the scholarship does mean that key voices in monster studies, such as Jeffrey Jerome Cohen, and notable contributors to disability and gender studies, such as Margrit Shidrick and Rosemarie Garland Thomson, are overlooked, with the effect that some current questions are not allowed appropriate scrutiny.[12] It is in monster/disability studies,

indeed, that considerations about the peculiar cultural and ideological work performed by nonnormative anatomies are aired, and reflections upon the proximity of monsters and periods of crisis are
formulated—all are directly germane to Crawford's interests. Other
publication in the broad area of monster studies, much of it theoretically inflected, is not engaged with in this book.[13] The decision
represents something of a missed opportunity, I think, since the
plethora of recent work, among other lines of investigation, bears
witness to a fine-tuning of the relations between the monstrous and
the marvelous and a qualifying of, and probing at, many of the categories and classifications with which Crawford is preoccupied.

Earlier parts of this review identified moments in *Marvelous
Protestantism* where issues of display might have been further ex-
trapolated. To be sure, Crawford is interested in the idea of the
monster as an instructive example, referring to displays of criminals and conspirators (22, 104), the exhumation of monsters (98,
163), public exposure opportunities (182, 208), and the appearance
of monsters at court (201). Yet what did it mean, either in terms of
Protestant polemic or at the level of audience reception, when a
monster was demonstrated, to invoke the etymology, as spectacle?
What were the commercial and/or institutional considerations involved when, for instance, a "chylde . . . being deformed [with] . . .
no eyes but a printe wheare the eyes should stand" lived for fifteen
hours yet was "vewed and seene by dyvers people of the p[a]rishe'
in London in 1590, or when "Ye kinge" in 1633 "had a syght" of a
"monster" born in the same city "w[hi]ich had 2. hedds . . . [and]
ioyntes like unto that of a horse"?[14] Print, of course, was only one
of the media through which monsters were made visible in order to
be properly understood; I am interested here in the related, although not exclusive, idioms of performance through which the
meanings of what have been termed "extraordinary bodies" were
disseminated and distributed through the fabric of contemporary
life. Part of the performability of the monster resided in the mobility visited upon it. What species of regional/urban dialectic was
held in play when monsters were transported from the periphery
to the center, as in, for example, the conjoined twins and child with
ruffs born in Monmouth in 1585 and thereafter transported to London, or the conjoined female twins hailing from Salisbury who,
after death in 1664, were "*speedily . . . brought*" (emphasis in original) to the metropolis?[15] These are questions touching upon the
monster's transferability and the fluidity of its messages in different

contexts; they are also questions relating to the ideological topography of early modern England and, as such, bear directly upon this book's hypotheses. In performances there was profit and, whether it was parents being given money on compassionate grounds on the occasion of a monstrous delivery or a mummified political leader such as Cromwell being exhibited for lucre, the nonnormative body was at the center of an economic system that shaped and informed the range of its meanings and implications.[16] It was in the ballad, indeed, one of the literary forms concentrated upon in detail in this book, that the monster's ideological and economic valences were most fully revealed. Ballads, accessible via being performed—a kind of aural or visual literacy, if you will—could be made to measure, set in metre on demand as a particular monstrous event or happening saw fit.[17] Par excellence instruments of play and drama, ballads crystallized in their market or fairground unfolding many of the premises upon which constructions of the monster depended: they were narratives shaped by popular Protestant ideas, yet they were simultaneously demotic registrations of social and folkloric tensions at some remove from established thought. Contemplating the ballad and the monster enables us to recall, in turn, the monster and the fairground and, in particular, the spiel of the so-called "monster-mongers" as they touted for custom and advertised their wares, placing an interpretive frame upon the contents of the "booth." By not pursuing the monster to such commercial manifestations, *Marvelous Protestantism* passes over what is possibly the nonnormative form's ultimate destination—the language of the impresario, which combined miracles with monsters and politics with prodigies in a highly stylized, but still intensely communicative, fashion.[18] In so doing, this performed, rhetorical construction of monstrosity sublimated, at the same time as it conversed with, the religious and/or official strains of representation, which this book elsewhere so expressively discovers.

In addition, at times, *Marvelous Protestantism* is confusedly inconsistent, and erroneous, in its mechanisms of notation and reference. Hence, the broadside reproduced on p. 8 is incorrectly given as *Conjoined twins born in Middleton Stoney* (London, 1552) and is not accompanied by a *Short-Title Catalogue* (*STC*) number: it is, in fact, Mrs. John Kenner, *Thou shalt vnderstande* (London, 1553?; *STC* 14932.5). There are very few monster items not listed in *STC* or Wing; in the pre-1640 period, only two are known to me. One is the unique Bodleian Library copy of *The true description of a monsterous chylde borne in the cytie of Anwarpe* (London, 1564). (Incidentally, this is credited to John Barker, a well-known prodigy writer, and offers an arresting slant on the 1560s in terms of its anatomization and itemization of the monster's parts, instructions to read the "image" and conjunction of themes of death and repentance.) The other is a 1637 English ballad about Lazarus and John Baptist Colloredo now in a private collection. Many other items are disallowed *STC* or Wing numbers that the printed catalogs clearly provide. For example, the Jeffey entry (actually Jessey) in the bibliography can be found at Wing J694, while the Laurence Humphrey entry in the bibliography is at *STC* 13966. The list could easily be continued. There is a particularly difficult-to-follow entry for the pamphlet, *The strange monster . . . from Nottingham-shire* (1668): described as "STC 20863.5 10/23/47.8"; it is, in fact, Wing S5884A (*STC* 20863.5 appears neither in the printed catalog nor on EEBO). Further difficulties cluster around authorship, titles, and identification. *The true discription of a childe with ruffes* (London, 1566; *STC* 1033) should have H.B. as the author (i.e., it is not anonymous); the use of complete, long titles in the bibliography is not explained; and the genesis of a further work is misunderstood. Quoting from a mid-seventeenth-century publication, Crawford explains "Although the pamphlet is identified in both ESTC and EEBO as *Fire in the Bush,* the title on the pamphlet itself is *A Vindication of those Whose Endeavour is only to make the Earth a Common Treasure, called Diggers*" (227). Yet a quick check in the printed catalog of Wing reveals that these works are not separate or incompatible: *Vindication* (Wing W3056) is a canceled part of *Fire* (Wing W3043), and both are credited to Gerrard Winstanley.

This is unfortunate as it slightly detracts from the range of investigations conducted in the book as a whole. Crawford has worried and teased, sought and found, discovering salient instances of monstrosity in parish registers, quarter sessions records, and the transactions of local record societies and antiquarian organizations. The book showcases writing of rare virtue, and one of the author's great strengths is that her stories are also analyses, with the chapters combining keen exemplifications of particular moments of representation and charged encounters with monsters that are consistently illuminating and powerful. *Marvelous Protestantism* has identified a crucial topic of inquiry and does indeed establish a new model for a deeper understanding of post-Reformation English culture.

Notes

1. See, for example, Clothworkers' Company, Minute Book, 1558–81, fol. 90r; Corporation of London Records Office, Repertory 15, fol. 414v; Corporation of London Records Office, Repertory 17, fol. 78v. The particular mid-sixteenth-century controversy of apprentices, servants and their "monstrous hose" is rehearsed in Richard Edwards, *Damon and Pithias* (1564), ed. D. Jerry White (New York: Garland, 1980), ll. 1135–47.

2. William Bullein, *A dialogue bothe pleasaunte and pietifull against the feuer pestilence* (London, 1573; *STC* 4037), 106–10; I. L., *A true and perfecte description of a straunge monstar borne in Rome in 1585* (London, 1590?; *STC* 15107).

3. Andrew Clark, ed., *The Shirburn Ballads, 1585–1616* (Oxford: Clarendon, 1907), 133–39; John Holloway, ed., *The Euing Collection of English Broadside Ballads in the Library of the University of Glasgow* (Glasgow: University of Glasgow Publications, 1971), 439–40; William Parkes, *The curtaine-drawer of the world* (London, 1612; *STC* 19298), 30; Francis Rous, *Oile of scorpions* (London, 1623; *STC* 21344), 166, 173, 178. The seventeenth-century ballad, "Pride's Fall," about a gentlewoman who is so addicted to fashion that she gives birth to conjoined twins bearing a ruff and a mirror, was reprinted in the eighteenth century (a unique copy is at the Huntington Library, HN 289745).

4. J. Alan B. Somerset, ed., *Shropshire,* Records of Early English Drama, 2 vols (Toronto: University of Toronto Press, 1994) 1:237; John Evelyn, *The Diary,* ed. E. S. de Beer, 6 vols. (Oxford: Clarendon, 1955), 3:255; Holloway, ed., *Euing,* 387.

5. *Macbeth,* ed. Nicholas Brooke (New York: Oxford University Press, 1994), V.vii.55–7.

6. See George Chapman, *Bussy d'Ambois* (ca. 1604), ed. N. S. Brooke (Manchester: Manchester University Press, 1979), 3.1.25, 27–28; David Galloway, ed., *Norwich, 1540–1642,* Records of Early English Drama (Toronto: University of Toronto Press, 1984), 146; John Spalding, *Memorialls of the Trubles in Scotland and in England, 1624–1625* (Aberdeen: Spalding Club, 1850–51), 2:125.

7. G.A., *No post from heaven* (London, 1643; Wing A8), sig. A2r.

8. *The kingdoms monster vncloaked from Heaven* (London, 1643; Wing K587).

9. See *Mistris Parliament brought to bed* (London, 1648; Wing M2281), 1, 8; *Mistris Parliament presented in her bed* (London, 1648; Wing M2284), sigs. A1r, A4v; *Mris. Rump brought to bed of a monster* (London, 1660; Wing M2285), fol. 1r; *The Sovndheads description of the Rovndhead* (London, 1642; Wing S4722), sigs. A1r, A1v, A2v, A3r.

10. In addition to the sources referred to by Crawford, the horned woman is described in Thomas Dekker, *Old Fortunatus* (1599) in *The Dramatic Works,* ed. Fredson Bowers (Cambridge: Cambridge University Press, 1953–61), vol. 1, 5.2.16–18; John Marston, *The Malcontent* (1603), ed. George K. Hunter (Manchester: Manchester University Press, 1975), 1.8.18–20; Thomas Nashe, *Have with you to Saffron-Walden* (1596); in *The Works,* ed. Ronald B. McKerrow (Oxford: Blackwell, 1966), 3:77.

11. See, for instance, P.G., *A most strange and true report of a monsterous fish* (London, 1604; *STC* 11501.5); Oteringham, *A most certaine report of a monster borne at Oteringham in Holdernesse* (London, 1595; *STC* 18895.5).

12. Jeffrey Jerome Cohen, ed., *Monster Theory: Reading Culture* (Minneapolis: University of Minnesota Press, 1996); Margrit Shildrick, *Embodying the Monster: Encounters with the Vulnerable Self* (London: Sage, 2002); Rosemarie Garland Thomson, *Extraordinary Bodies: Figuring Physical Disability in American Culture and Literature* (New York: Columbia University Press, 1997).

13. See, for instance, Douglas Biow, *"Mirabile Dictu": Representations of the Marvellous in Medieval and Renaissance Epic* (Ann Arbor: University of Michigan Press, 1996); Kathryn Brammall, "Monstrous Metamorphosis: Nature, Morality, and the Rhetoric of Monstrosity in Tudor England," *Sixteenth-Century Journal* 27.1 (1996): 3–21; Mark Thornton Burnett, *Constructing "Monsters" in Shakespearean Drama and Early Modern Culture* (Basingstoke: Palgrave, 2002); Mark Thornton Burnett, "La fabrication des monstres sur la scène au temps de Shakespeare," in *Esthétiques de la Nouveauté à la Renaissance,* ed. François Laroque and Franck Lessay, 77–97 (Paris: Presses de la Sorbonne Nouvelle, 2001); William E. Burns, *An Age of Wonders: Prodigies, Politics and Providence in England, 1657–1727* (Manchester: Manchester University Press, 2002); Jerome Friedman, *Miracles and the Pulp Press during the English Revolution* (London: UCL Press, 1993); Laura Lunger Knoppers and Joan B. Landes, eds., *Monstrous Bodies/Political Monstrosities* (Ithaca: Cornell University Press, 2004); Stephen Pender, "In the Bodyshop: Human Exhibition in Early Modern England," in *"Defects": Engendering the Modern Body,* ed. Helen Deutsch and Felicity Nussbaum, 95–126 (Ann Arbor: University of Michigan Press, 2000); E. Sauer, " 'Monstrous altercations and barking questions': The Prodigious Births of Scylla, Mris. Rump, and Milton's Sin," *Ben Jonson Journal* 2 (1995): 171–90.

14. Guildhall Library, MS 9234/3, fols. 52r–53r; British Library, Additional MS 35331, fol. 54r.

15. Portskewett, *A right strange and wonderful example of the handie work of God* (London, 1585; *STC* 20127), title page; *The true picture of a female monster born near Salisbury* (London, 1664; Wing T2854).

16. Holloway, ed., *Euing*, 387; John Frederick Varley, *Oliver Cromwell's Latter End* (London: Chapman and Hall, [1939]), 50–51.

17. Nicholas Bownde, *The doctrine of the sabbath* (London, 1595; *STC* 3436), 241–42; Richard Brathwait, *Whimzies, or A new cast of characters* (London, 1631; *STC* 3591), 9; John Earle, *Micro-cosmographie* (London, 1628; *STC* 7439), fol. F2v; Henry Fitzgeffrey, *Satyres: and satyricall epigrams* (London, 1617; *STC* 10945), fol. A7v; Joseph Hall, *Virgidemiarum* (London, 1599; *STC* 12719), 47.

18. See Ben Jonson, *Every Man in His Humour* (1598), ed. Martin Seymour-Smith (London: Benn, 1966), 1.2.111–13; Jasper Mayne, *The City-Match* (1637–38?), in W. C. Hazlitt, ed., *A Select Collection of Old English Plays,* 4th ed. (London: Reeves & Turner, 1874–76), XIII, III.i.pp. 248–59; Thomas Randolph, *Hey for Honesty* (1626–28?; rev. 1648–49?), in *The Poetical and Dramatic Works,* ed. W. Carew Hazlitt, (London: Reeves & Turner, 1875), II, I.i.pp. 392–93; *The terrible, horrible, monster of the West* (London, 1649; Wing T765), passim.

Rogues and Early Modern English Culture
Edited by Craig Dionne and Steve Mentz
Ann Arbor: University of Michigan Press, 2004

Reviewer: Charles R. Forker

The literature of the Elizabethan underclass with its fascinating accounts of vagrants, peddlers, doxies, confidence tricksters, pickpockets, dissemblers, unemployed street entertainers, disabled veterans, masterless outcasts, beggars, and "upright men" (swindlers masquerading as respectable citizens) has attracted a formidable amount of scholarly attention in recent decades. Arthur Kinney's invaluable anthology of the major cony-catching texts by Walker, Awdeley, Harman, Greene, Dekker, and Rid (a second edition of Kinney's 1973 volume appeared in 1990) has contributed importantly to the trend; and a veritable battalion of literary critics, cultural historians, and sociolinguistic postmodernists have approached the subject with vigor and a bewildering complexity of attitudes and methods. The present volume, introduced by the editors with fierce awareness of their ideological valences, brings together some fourteen essays by contributors who fairly represent the discipline of vagabond-study as practiced in the academy today. Kinney contributes a learnedly insightful afterword, especially helpful in its acute discussion of the historiographical challenges that confront modern analysts of the material.

As is common with such collections, the value of the essays varies considerably, but what emerges from the book as a whole is the relentlessly reiterated conviction that writers such as Greene and Dekker, although seeming both to entertain and to moralize about the sorry state of social disorder in the realm, can no longer be read naively or taken at face value. Subjected as they are to strenuous historicizing, contextualizing, post-structuralist theorizing, ambiguating, and "problematizing," these somewhat slender writings, at once didactic and pleasurable to the common-sense reader, exemplify and embody contradictory "discourses," portray a world suspended uncertainly between fiction and fact or between affirmation and subversion of the established power structures, and reveal their authors as ventriloquists or equivocators, and sometimes as being more of the devil's party than they know or can acknowledge. The rogues they portray inhabit a world of "linguistic prowess and social dexterity" (1), defining a culture of gamesmanship and clever self-fashioning that evokes both "sympathy and disgust, admiration and fear" (8). Craig Dionne, for instance, views the Elizabethan con man as the prototype of the modern urban capitalist whose manipulative schemes of bartering, false advertising, and financial investment, skirting or co-opting the law when possible within a fraternity of like-minded entrepreneurs, was already implicit in the sixteenth-century rogue-enterpriser—a dark mirror, so to say, of the emerging self-made merchant. As with Tony Soprano, the popular Mafioso of American TV culture, we experience such figures with fascinated ambivalence, mingling shocked disapproval of their criminality with a certain delight in their daring, cleverness, and selective capacity for fellow feeling.

Four headings serve as category markers. The first group deals with theoretical overviews of the rogue and rogue studies. A second group discusses the economic and marketplace realities of vagabond culture in England. A third treats rogues in relation to urban environments (especially London), while a final group, entitled "Typologies of the Rogue," discusses particular figures such as the "low-life" characters of Shakespeare's *Henry V* (Bardolph, Pistol, Nym, Mistress Quickly), the French veteran-counterfeit Martin Guerre, and the reformed criminal Moll Flanders (the title figure of Defoe's eighteenth-century novel). In addition, this final catchall includes an essay on Dekker's "commercial deceit," an analysis by Laurie Ellinghausen of *Lantern and Candlelight* that convicts the author and, by implication, other cony-catching writers, of pretending to expose fraud while being themselves participants in what they would be seen to condemn. Still another essay examining Spenser's *View of the Present State of Ireland* (by Brooke Stafford) discusses English demonizing of the Irish—the habit of regarding their language and culture as barbaric, "other," and potentially criminal on analogy with that of the sleazy underclass in their own country. In the "fantasy" of writers such as Spenser, Ireland was a "nation of rogues" practicing their own particular cant, who served their would-be civilizers as a synecdoche "for the vagrants who posed a real and pressing problem for the English nation" (313).

Bryan Reynolds and Janna Segal coauthor a piece on Moll Cutpurse, Middleton and Dekker's transvestite heroine in *The Roaring Girl* based on the notorious "cultural icon" (68), Mary Frith. Probably the most unreadable essay in the book, this effort, more than usually obsessed with gender, class, and oppression, seeks "to simultaneously historicize, de-essentialize, and relativize" Moll, not as a dramatic character but as a "cultural product" to whom the language of "transversal theory" can be applied (62–63). Larded with pretentious inkhorn terms ("processually," "identitarian," "equivalential," "counterhegemonic," "celebrityness," "hierachicalizing," "heteronormative," "historicalities," "multidimentional positionality," "reparameterizes," "subfluxation," "biunivocal," "subjunctified," "non-state-promoting entities," "Marlowespace") and marred by lapses in grammar and euphony, this analysis invites us to "tango with [alternative] perspectives" as reflected in "materialist and constructivist accounts" of "Mary/Moll" "as a means by which to chassé into our own alternative theoretical understanding of deviant identity formations" (66–67). In his *Fraternity of Vagabonds* (1561), Awdeley provided a useful dictionary of canting terms. Would that Reynolds and Segal had followed suit with a glossary of their own obscurantist vocabulary.

With welcome (and contrasting) clarity A. L. Beier (in a reprint from *ELR*) reexamines Harman's *Caveat for Common Cursitors,* often considered the most reliable and complete of the vagabond books. Reassessing Harman from the perspective of New Historicism (as influenced by Marx, Freud, and Foucault), and unearthing new information about the author from archival research, Beier shows how important it is to test skeptical theories about the "truth" of rogue literature against what can be established from nonliterary sources. He concludes that although the *Caveat* "is a rich and complex text . . . open to a variety of readings," it "can still be productively studied with traditional historical methods." While giving respectful consideration to the politicizing and ideological approaches of much recent criticism, Beier recognizes that Harman's views on the sexual, economic, and social aspects of his subject are based upon more than personal interviews with "vagrants at his front gate" and must "be considered part of the mainstream of social and religious discourse in the 1560s" (112–13). In a related essay, Martine Van Elk explores parallels between popular literary accounts of rogue culture and the court records of Bridewell Hospital, a London penal institution that not only punished vagrants but that also purposed their reform. At Bridewell the examination of offenders, far from uncovering mere facts, usually took the form of moral categorizing or imposing generic identities, so that rogue tales in the pamphlets closely resemble those extracted from the prison confessions. As impersonation and counterfeited identity become prominent issues in both the vagabond literature and the Bridewell records, Van Elk suggests that the language of these narratives involves elements of negotiation and "social exchange," of stereotypical expectation and preconstruction, thus disclosing a culture that exploited "the easy assumptions and desires of others" (135).

One of the finest essays in the collection is Linda Woodbridge's wide-ranging, beautifully articulated discussion of Elizabethan merchandizing and shopping with its treatment of Thomas Gresham, builder of the Royal Exchange ("a veritable Tamburlaine of commerce") at the high end of the social spectrum, and the itinerate peddler at the lower end. Peddlers became the hated middlemen between local artisans or farmers and the rich livery companies who practiced international wholesaling and large-scale importing and exporting. With no fixed times or places of business and low overhead, here today, gone tomorrow, peddlers undercut merchants with permanent establishments and were commonly regarded as charlatans living by the sweat of other men's brows. Woodbridge describes the culture of fairs and shops, commenting perceptively on architectural change as a result of burgeoning capitalism and focusing on Heywood's two-part drama, *If You Know Not Me, You Know Nobody.* The play celebrates the opening of Gresham's Royal Exchange as a symbol of England's commercial eminence while characterizing Gresham ambiguously as a giant of national philanthropy who is nevertheless arrogant, stubborn, quarrelsome, and a poor judge of character. Interestingly, in the character of Tawnycoat, Heywood overturns the stereotype of the peddler as a cheat, making him the "one wholly admirable figure" (161) of the drama.

Taking up the later cony-catching writings of Greene and Dekker, Karen Bix perceives a shift from the moralistic condemnation of vagabonds to an attitude of greater toleration. Whereas earlier pamphlets had stressed the unbridgeable gulf between their predatory individualism and an ideal of social cohesion based on Christian brotherhood and charity, the newer writings tended to express greater admiration for commercial innovation, cunning, and ingenuity, and to see in certain elements of the underclass a commendable geniality and fellowship that helped to glamorize and even democratize urban success. The new model of confederacy by which rogues organized themselves rejected the "regimentation and status-based assignments" of the older fraternities to favor resourcefulness, improvisation, inclusion, "spontaneous social intercourse," and "the appreciation of individual talents" (185).

Nicholas Blount (alias Nicholas Jennings), the notorious vagrant whose multiple roles (epileptic, mariner, hatmaker, serving man, artificer) Harman describes so colorfully in his *Caveat,* becomes the focus of a thoughtful essay by Patricia Fumerton on the "economics of disguise" in the vagabond pamphlets. Countering the tendency of Greenblatt and others to treat Jennings as a prototype of the inherent "theatricality" of Elizabethan rogue culture, Fumerton takes the figure as a symbol of occupational displacement and the necessity of job-shifting in Tudor England at the end of the sixteenth century. As she sees it, Harman criminalizes what looked to him like sinister dissembling among a population of itinerant laborers and apprentices who had failed for various reasons to complete their terms of indenture, when in fact they were often simply victims of bad luck thrown by desperate need upon their own inventive resources.

Adam Hansen and Steve Mentz write provocatively on English rogue literature in relation to London, a locus of "hybrid sociogeography" (216) with its licit and illicit spaces cheek by jowl, thus constituting a Jerusalem-Babylon in which churches and brothels encroached upon each other symbolically as well as physically. Hansen argues that the authors of rogue literature, although adopting a tone of overt didacticism, recognized the considerable degree to which the underworld they were describing actually mirrored their own values. Dekker, for instance, did much of his writing in prison and could see the culture of cony-catchers through the eyes of the punished. Mentz is interested in urban experience as a cultural pressure on the evolving genre of the rogue pamphlet. As a case in point, he thinks, Greene's works of this type assimilate the exposure of London cheats and predators to prose romance, containing their stories "within a forgiving plot structure": they "serve as 'magic books' for London's citizen-readers, initiating them into the new languages of urban culture and making the city seem manageable if viewed through the lens of" a genre that "rehabilitates deceptive tactics and purges them of malice" (240–41). Much debate about Elizabethan rogue literature has centered on the question of whether it was genuinely subversive, giving voice to elements that dangerously threatened social stability, or was rather a means of containing such a threat, as argued by Greenblatt and his school. Mentz endeavors to step outside the subversion-containment controversy by reading the cony-catching pamphlets as "tactical instruction manuals for urban life" (244). To some his formulations may seem more ingenious than convincing, but his essay is among the most original and stimulating of the lot.

Linda Salamon's study of ex-soldiers, "abandoned to poverty, hunger, and disability" and generally "construed as a transgressive presence on the margins of public life" (262), considers a somewhat neglected aspect of rogue scholarship. She notes the increasing tendency of the unemployed, or unemployable, to impersonate war veterans, or, if genuine and armed, to become highwaymen, ravishers, and petty criminals preying on the gullible. Salamon takes Martin Guerre, the French soldier-thief-impersonator-husband whose sensational deception and subsequent execution intrigued Montaigne, as an icon of the ex-military vagabond occupying a liminal space between war victim and predator. If "ruffler" was the cant term for a phony survivor of battle, "falconer" was the label applied to the fraudulent author who cozened "patrons" out of their cash by cobbling up a book at his own expense with a flatteringly generalized dedication in which the names of multiple dedicatees could be secretly inserted. Ellinghausen regards Dekker, the professional writer who sees himself in outraged opposition to falconers and their ilk, as allying himself, if only half-consciously, with the scam artists he reprobates—as participating in a print culture that blurred "distinctions between criminal and scholar" (298). Her interesting analysis of *Lantern and Candlelight,* which describes an imagined hell in which members of the inherently deceitful book trade ply their craft, shows how three different voices of the work tend to merge or blend so that boundaries dissolve between the punished, the punishers, and the supposedly objective observer.

Stafford's essay on the English view of Ireland, which analogizes the language of a foreign culture to rogue's cant, makes suggestive observations and connections. She writes informatively of "the Old English," a group of settlers in Ireland who had gone native, assimilating linguistically and culturally to the "barbarism" that had once been alien—a group with which "the Roaring Boys" in England (313) shared certain traits. But her assertion that "the reader and the rogue become one" in the conclusion of Harman's *Caveat* strains too far. That readers engage to some extent with the vagabonds they are instructed to abhor is surely true, but this hardly means, as Stafford also asserts, that "the English reader becomes incorporated into a criminal community" (319) as a consequence of meeting it on the printed page. Taking vicarious pleasure in criminals and their world, whether in the study, the theater, or the cinema, does not *make* us criminals even if the experience may disturb us with fresh awareness of how the licit and illicit sometimes rub shoulders. The *Godfather* films of the 1970s allowed us to participate aesthetically in horrifying violence, glamorous criminality, lyrical nostalgia, and sympathetic domesticity, all intricately intermingled, without converting us to the values of la Cosa Nostra. Stafford's implication that English readers were inevitably a part of the corruption they enjoyed reading about seems unjustifiably puritanical. She seems to forget that a literary interest in crime is partly based on the invitation to moral holiday.

The excellent concluding piece on Defoe's *Moll Flanders* by Tina Kuhlisch pursues the tradition of rogue literature into the eighteenth-century picaresque, illustrating the English transformation of the Spanish *pícara* from a figure rooted in a culture of blood, class, and honor to one based upon the values of self-improvement and middle-class capitalism. As a repentant criminal who ultimately achieves status and respectability, Moll is the heroine and antiheroine of "a thoroughly double-voiced and double-structured work" (337). Overtly moralizing her own transgressions (theft, impersonation, prostitution), she nevertheless excuses her misdeeds as showing initiative and presenting opportunities for wealth and advancement. As opposed to signaling changes of fundamental identity, Moll's disguises represent merely the means of asserting her true self as a person bent on improving her lot. Kuhlisch interprets the novel finally as an essay in the instability of meaning, a fiction interweaving "contradictory discourses" (353) in which business success and traditional morality jostle each other uncomfortably.

The diversity of subjects and perspectives in this volume is welcome, nor can students of Elizabethan culture safely ignore it. Alas, the book is something of a chore to read. The high degree of abstraction and theoretical speculation makes for denseness, if not opacity, in the prose, as do the recurring ambiguities of focus and meaning on which so many of the authors insist. Nor is it reassuring that whoever copyedited the manuscript at the University of Michigan Press has permitted a surprising number of solecisms and stylistic infelicities. *Rogues and Early Modern English Culture* nevertheless contains important new thinking on a traditional subject.

Unsettled: The Culture of Mobility and the Working Poor in Early Modern England
By Patricia Fumerton
Chicago and London: University of Chicago Press, 2006

Reviewer: William C. Carroll

A seventeenth-century mariner named Edward Barlow figures largely in Patricia Fumerton's fascinating new book, *Unsettled: The Culture of Mobility and the Working Poor in Early Modern England*. Fumerton's book is ambitious, wide-ranging, and compelling, in part because she builds up to a detailed consideration of Barlow's life through a meticulous analysis of the conditions of the working poor in early modern England. The scope of her argument takes in many topics in early modern studies, as we will see.

Fumerton's book is divided into two related parts. The first half—"Unsettled Subjects"—stakes out a clear place among the recent studies of poverty and vagrancy in early modern England. Much of this resurgent interest in literary studies can be traced back to A. L. Beier's 1985 study, *Masterless Men: The Vagrancy Problem in England 1560–1640* (London: Methuen), a scrupulously careful historical work that crossed over numerous disciplinary boundaries.[1] In the wake of, and dependent on, Beier, a number of literary-oriented studies followed in the past two decades.[2] Fumerton's first three chapters intelligently and usefully engage with these studies, marking her own positions and carefully framing the strengths and limitations of her predecessors. Among Fumerton's most trenchant points is the predisposition of these earlier studies to fall back on, or end up in, the trope of "theatricality," inevitably heading toward analyses of the early modern theater itself, or plays staged in it: "The problem is that the term 'theatrical' implies a level of disguise or fakery not necessarily a part of everyday role-playing," hence in trying "to focus on the shifting 'I' of actual vagabonds and their laboring fellow itinerants, the notion of theatricality proves dangerously misleading" (52).

The first half of the book, instead, traces the slowly developing official consciousness of "a new category of poor—neither the deserving impotent nor the undeserving sturdy rogue, but the deserving, sturdy indigent who sought but could not find enough work" (26)—hence Fumerton's key term, used throughout the book, the "unsettled." Early modern theories of poverty could not account for some categories of labor—thus a peddler (a perfect instance of one who was "unsettled") was still said to be a vagrant, one without "work" or profession—or cycles of unemployment without falling back on the binary of impotent/deceitful (and many of the earlier literary studies have turned on this binary). One of the real strengths of Fumerton's book, then, is its examination of this other category of the laboring poor, and its reexamination of some familiar texts from earlier studies, such as Thomas Harman's *A Caveat for Common Cursitors Vulgarly Called Vagabonds* (1566). In her chapter on Harman, Fumerton covers well-trodden ground,[3] but as usual, sees it slightly differently. Where others have rightly emphasized Harman's fascination with beggars' disguises and role-playing, Fumerton notes that Harman's pamphlet "is an early response to the threat of an economy of unsettledness . . . His response was to translate displaced and makeshift labor into disguisings. Rather than shifting from job to job and place to place, Harman's vagabonds and rogues shift from disguise to disguise. He thus makes invisible (or barely visible) the unsettling economics that were to dominate the seventeenth century" (31). This kind of insight, building on the work of earlier studies, allows Fumerton to move to a different kind of analysis—not just of bodies, but of subjectivities.

What does Fumerton mean by "unsettled"? On one level, it refers to the physical wanderings of beggars and the working poor; their very mobility figured their lack of economic and social identity. Contemporary officials attempted to "fix" them in place, forcing them back to the towns from which they had come (though many did not know where they came from), whipping and punishing them if they returned. Such measures could be locally effective but were globally doomed. But Fumerton also wants to understand the term "unsettled" as a category of subjectivity, and here her book stakes out an ambitious (if somewhat less convincing) argument: that a type of early modern subjectivity can be identified: "as the felt experience of being unfixed, multiple, and displaced on the one hand; and as the inconsistent and intermittent awareness of such an unsettled experience on the other" (58). She is well aware of the difficulties posed by the available evidence, and she intelligently places her argument in relation to other models of early modern subjectivity.[4] What makes Fumerton's argument here slightly less convincing than the rest of her book is that her use of the central term, "unsettled," is, well, unsettled itself—too often applied in too many instances. But, as if anticipating such a criticism, Fumerton then anchors the second half of her book in a special, concrete category—the seaman—and one in particular, Edward Barlow.

The seaman is the perfect example for Fumerton's argument: classified as a vagrant (and much featured as a "disguise" in rogue pamphlets from Harman forward), the seaman is by definition unsettled, "a kind of 'nowhere'man,'" Fumerton notes, "detached not only from physical places or occupational jobs, but also from communal, personal, and familial connections" (74); "Laboring without tools, without a product from their 'craft,' and without a fixed 'home,' seamen are the *ne plus ultra* of the displaced laborer, quite literally landless or 'at sea'" (65). Such seamen, unless they ascended to the highest ranks, were the unlanded equivalent of the laboring landed poor, "one of the first and largest groups of free subjects within a new landless proletariat" (83). And even better, many of them kept journals of one kind or another. Among the most prolific was Edward Barlow. But before taking us to Barlow, Fumerton usefully describes the growing nature of the English seafaring profession, with some surprising observations about its size and importance (by the 1670s, "In London, probably more than a quarter of the population depended on the sea for its living" [89], in one form or another). There is even a fascinating chapter on the development of cartography in response to the growing needs of a mercantile fleet, with an analysis of the conception and mechanics of nautical chart books of all kinds, and an appendix on "the variation of the compass." Another of the strengths of Fumerton's study, which appears early on, is that she does not observe the dead-end wall of 1642 as her stopping point, a date that is not exactly arbitrary for many earlier studies, but one tied to the closing of the theaters. Instead, Fumerton ranges up toward the late seventeenth and early eighteenth century, rightly taking a long view of complex historical processes.

Having established a detailed historical context, Fumerton turns in detail to Edward Barlow (1641/42–1705–8). His journal/autobiography is "the only surviving such [secular] self-accounting made from the perspective of a poor seaman" (49), some 279 pages in manuscript, including 147 self-drawn sketches (sixteen of them are reproduced in the volume, one of which—Barlow's "leaving home, with his mother beckoning in the wheatfield, 1657"—is analyzed in great depth). This treasure trove of material is mined frequently and deeply. Fumerton quite rightly cautions that "we should resist upholding Barlow as entirely typical" (69), and the fact of his having written the journal in the first place proves just how untypical he is. Still, his unsettled condition as a seaman—his abrupt departure from his parents, his eventual marriage but physical and emotional distance from his wife and children,[5] his lifelong wandering—does make him one of the few secular sources of early modern subjectivity. Through the second half of her book, Fumerton goes at Barlow and his journal from several different directions, from analyzing his rhetoric (his use of the "I" pronoun) and reading his sketches (so many seacoasts, so few people) to offering in yet another appendix a thirteen-page record of Barlow's "mobility" on land and sea, year by year, from 1656 (about age fourteen) to 1706, when Barlow's ship *Liampo* (he has at last been made captain) is lost off the coast of Mozambique;[6] this record in itself is well worth reading simply for its extraordinary picture of the travels that were possible in the seventeenth century. Fumerton doesn't overly romanticize or sentimentalize Barlow, who could be callous indeed; he was often bitterly envious of those above him—whether justified or not is difficult to determine—and frequently disclaimed his own failings. What we get instead of the brave sea captains of contemporary pirate dramas is a full, rich portrait of a *very* complex human being—and, finally, his unsettled subjectivity.

In a final chapter, Fumerton analyzes a number of seaman ballads. Earlier she had argued that in addition to the usual sources about the unsettled poor and the culture of mobility, scholars should be looking at a different medium in addition to, or instead of, plays, namely, the broadside ballads, "which embraced the diverse labors of itinerant workers" (45). The book's final chapter on seamen's ballads argues their importance not only as they are *about* seamen, but that they were to some degree *for* them—a public aesthetic of unsettled subjectivity that complements the private one of Barlow's journal. Such ballads "deliberately market multiple perspectives" (141), projecting "a myriad of different roles or identities that may be promiscuously picked up and discarded by its audience upon hearing or viewing them" (146). One could say this about many art forms, but the "presenter," who at one moment sang the songs, inhabiting the personae of the characters, and in the next moment was hawking them as consumable objects, marks ballads as distinct forms of performance. There is much material of interest in this chapter, but to this reader it felt somewhat anticlimactic after the multiple fascinations of Barlow.

In the end, then, Patricia Fumerton's book is essential reading for anyone interested in the early modern period. She advances our understanding of the conditions and representations of poverty, crosses all kinds of disciplinary and chronological boundaries in fruitful ways, and presents a compelling case study of Edward Barlow.

Notes

1. Beier's influence was no doubt enhanced by his willingness to attend literary conferences such as the Shakespeare Association of America and Renaissance Society of America. Among other recent and influential historical studies are those by Ian Archer, *The Pursuit of Stability: Social Relations in Elizabethan London* (Cambridge: Cambridge University Press, 1991); Paul Griffiths, *Youth and Authority: Formative Experiences in England, 1560–1640* (Oxford: Clarendon Press, 1996); Valerie Pearl, "Change and Stability in Seventeenth-Century London," *London Journal* 5 (1979): 3–34; Paul Slack, *Poverty and Policy in Tudor and Stuart England* (London: Longman, 1988) and *The English Poor Law, 1531–1782* (Houndmills, England: Macmillan, 1990); and Keith Wrightson and David Levine, *Poverty and Piety in an English Village: Terling, 1525–1700* (New York: Academic Press, 1979).

2. Among them: Mark Thornton Burnett, *Masters and Servants in English Renaissance Drama and Culture: Authority and Obedience* (New York: St. Martin's, 1997); William C. Carroll, *Fat King, Lean Beggar: Representations of Poverty in the Age of Shakespeare* (Ithaca: Cornell University Press, 1996); Craig Dionne and Steve Mentz, eds., *Rogues and Early Modern English Culture* (Ann Arbor: University of Michigan Press, 2004); Heather Dubrow, *Shakespeare and Domestic Loss: Forms of Deprivation, Mourning, and Recuperation* (Cambridge: Cambridge University Press, 1999); Elizabeth Hanson, *Discovering the Subject in Renaissance England* (Cambridge: Cambridge University Press, 1998); Paola Pugliatti, *Beggary and Theatre in Early Modern England* (Aldershot, England: Ashgate, 2003); and

Linda Woodbridge, *Vagrancy, Homelessness, and English Renaissance Literature* (Urbana: University of Illinois Press, 2001).

3. Indeed, analyzing Harman's text has become a standard feature of earlier studies: Carroll, Hanson, Pugliatti, and Woodbridge all devote a full chapter of their studies to Harman, a practice justified, as Fumerton notes, because Harman's work "shaped representations of the unsettled poor for some forty years" (31).

4. Fumerton groups such efforts as those by "Marxist critics" who critiqued older humanistic notions (Francis Barker, Jonathan Dollimore, Catherine Belsey), "currently dominant reaffirmations of subjectivity, but only as dependent on social or political constructs" (Stephen Greenblatt, Jonathan Goldberg, herself), and religiously construed theories of subjectivity (Deborah Shuger, Katharine Eisamen Maus).

5. Fumerton points out that nowhere in his journal is his wife Mary actually named; only in his will of 1705—transcribed in an appendix here—do we learn her name and those of his living children.

6. As Fumerton notes, it's not clear whether Barlow went down with his ship in 1706; his will was proved in 1708, but there might well have been a lengthy delay in news of his death reaching home.

Before Intimacy: Asocial Sexuality in Early Modern England
By Daniel Juan Gil
Minneapolis: University of Minnesota Press, 2005

Reviewer: Stephen Guy-Bray

Daniel Juan Gil's book is a fascinating and novel study of sexuality in Renaissance literature. It begins with a short introduction, and since this introduction is in so many ways so different from the rest of the book, it seems appropriate to discuss it separately (and first). *Before Intimacy* begins, as so many books on sexuality in Renaissance literature now do, with the author's somewhat defensive situation of his project in relation to larger discussions about the use of the past and the role of sexuality in society. Gil argues strongly against seeing "the modern identitarian regime" of sexuality as inevitable, and he insists that early modern concepts of sexuality are very different from ours, rather than being merely nascent versions of them. This is a useful point to make, although it is compromised by Gil's use of the term "early modern," which is inescapably teleological: the early modern is what leads to us. When he says, for instance, that "much of the modern world that we still inhabit was consolidated" in the early modern period, he signals, perhaps without even knowing it, what he sees as one of the important things about the area we study. The book also begins with much citing of names: Norbert Elias, Luhmann, and Leo Bersani make an appearance in the first few pages. Gil appears to mention these names in order to give information about his theoretical background rather than to prepare the reader for the sort of analysis that follows.

These are not crucial objections, as the analysis that follows is very fine indeed. While a little more Bersani might have been useful—given Gil's interest in sexuality as something experienced by the self as disruptive or, in Bersani's terms, shattering—Gil's discussions are always original and perceptive. Basic to his view is the idea that in the Renaissance sexuality was something that was experienced as distinct from social life. He points out that we now tend to see male homoeroticism as either homosociality (male/male sex that can be accommodated within existing social relations) or sodomy (male/male sex that cannot be accommodated within existing social relations). Without arguing that these categories should be ignored, Gil asserts that in the Renaissance the emotions frequently served "as the basis of a powerful, asocial connection."

One of the main points that *Beyond Intimacy* makes is that emotions do not give us access to a character's interior life but rather work as a way for bodies to connect "when a functionally social connection between socially legible persons is impossible." Central to Gil's argument is what he sees as a conflict between the traditional view that identity and relationships depend on family and inherited position and the view, slowly becoming dominant throughout the sixteenth century, that humanity is a universal quality shared by all. Sexuality, then, becomes a way to forge new relationships, new ways of being social in the world.

The attempt to forge these new sorts of relationships is Gil's focus for the greater part of the book. In a series of illuminating discussions, he looks at lyric poems by Wyatt, the sonnet sequences of Sidney, Spenser, and Shakespeare, *Troilus and Cressida,* and the *Faerie Queene.* Because his theme is asociality, Gil is able to avoid what seems to me to be the main problem with much recent scholarship on the Renaissance: the tendency to see texts either as a way to see the author's life in its historical and/or political contexts or as a way to find out how people really lived back then. Instead, Gil produces a series of closely argued and convincing analyses of some of the most interesting texts of the English Renaissance.

His discussion of Spenser is particularly rich, and also particularly novel. When he speaks of "a privileged experience of asocial sexuality that is the real subject of the *Faerie Queene*," the sound you hear is Spenser rolling in his grave, but by the end of the chapter it is hard not to feel convinced by Gil's approach. Concentrating on the idea of civility, Gil provides a valuable new look at book 3, finding in it an exploration of "sociosexual alternatives that lie beneath or alongside the historical social world." A further benefit of Gil's analysis is that he complicates our typically unproblematic sense of Spenser as a middle-class poet on the make—not by rejecting it altogether, but by showing more clearly than most who have written on this topic just what that might have meant.

Most readers will probably find the last two chapters the most useful. In his discussion of *Troilus and Cressida,* Gil argues that Shakespeare, in essence, uses the Trojan War—and, in particular, the battle between the sexes, which is the play's main theme—as a kind of allegory for the conflict between opposing visions of society and sociality. In Troilus's doomed love for Cressida, a woman of no real status, for example, Gil sees a way out of homosocial competition and the traffic in women. Of course, like the love, this attempt to rethink what we now call heterosexuality is also doomed. In his discussion of Shakespeare's sonnets, Gil suggests that the poem's focus on asocial sexuality enables Shakespeare to present literature as a semiautonomous discourse—another doomed hope.

In the turn to personal reflection, which characterizes the end of the final chapter as well as the brief epilogue, Gil admits that later literature does not engage with the vision of sexuality that he sees in these Renaissance texts. Gil points out that what becomes typical instead is "the ideal of romantic, intimate sexuality that affirms rich individual personalities built on fully psychological emotions"—or, as it is technically called, tedium. As he says at the end of the last chapter, "if . . . these sonnets and the sexuality they depict represent a dead end, then it is all the more true that they are today a resource for rethinking, reimagining, and reconfiguring the most basic forms of sociability on which the modernity we now inhabit stands." One of the many virtues of Gil's valuable and consistently interesting book is that it insists upon and adumbrates the possibilities of this resource.

Science, Reading, and Renaissance Literature:
The Art of Making Knowledge 1580–1670
By Elizabeth Spiller
Cambridge: Cambridge University Press, 2004
and
Arts of Calculation: Numerical Thought
in Early Modern Europe
Edited by David Glimp and Michelle K. Warren
New York: Palgrave Macmillan, 2004

Reviewer: Denise Albanese

In the last ten years or so, there has been a growing interest among scholars and critics of early modern literature in problematizing the origins of the current conceptual and institutional gap separating the sciences from the humanities. Although attention to the "New Science" is at least as old as the influential studies of Marjorie Hope Nicholson, more recent inquiry has moved away from the way in which early modern texts thematized or contextualized astronomy or other physical sciences, and towards broader-ranging questions of epistemology and representation. Fueled in part by Foucault-inflected researches into the "sciences of man" and by feminist interest in embodiment, scholars first turned to historical body and its fluxes as such, thereby redressing a long-standing inattention to less emblematic, or perhaps less stereotypically empirical and remote, objects of scientific concern. Increasingly, however, nascent modern discourses of mathematics and the physical sciences have been read as generative, indeed as textual, by scholars less interested in the history of ideas (as Hope was) and more interested in enriching our understanding of a cultural moment when the authority of the scientific was far from secure, and its privileged form far from stable. The two studies under review are further contributions to this burgeoning area of specialization.

Elizabeth Spiller's *Science, Reading, and Renaissance Literature* encompasses such well-recognized figures of literature as Edmund Spenser, Sir Philip Sidney, and Margaret Cavendish, whose texts it juxtaposes with those by others, like William Harvey and William Gilbert, not usually read alongside them. Her aim in bringing texts that subsequent disciplinary taxonomies have dispersed is to argue against casting those taxonomies back in time, and to unite what has come to be known as science and literature under the aegis of "making." What both textual practices share at this moment of origin, she argues, is a dependence on fabricating, although when it comes to the "New Science" the constructed character of knowledge is covered over by a discourse of discovery, and undergirded by the presumption that to see is to know. Juxtaposing texts currently relegated to different historiographic traditions becomes a way to recapture similar strategies of construction or similar ways of making an argument or object.

Hence a good part of her title. As for the third term, "reading," however, it is not always clear how that functions alongside the other two; at any rate, it does not seem to have the same analytical continuity of Spiller's other terms. While the last two chapters present compelling arguments that the writer of one text was reading and responding to the other text to which it is conjoined, the first two chapters offer only conjectural connections, none of which is referred back to an early modern author as a point of origin. This difference in the source of reading—sometimes it is Spiller, attempting to recapture broad field of historical possibility; at others, it is one of her subjects, a trace of whose historical practice she has discerned—need not be disabling in itself. But it would have been good for Spiller to explain the distinction in practice, and to consider whether it was consequential for her argument. When, as the title suggests, "reading" is a central category of analysis, that it is unevenly grounded as a historical act in her study needs to be accounted for.

It must be said that *Science, Reading, and Renaissance Literature* does not entirely succeed in making a distinctive claim for the historical or analytical consequence of acts of reading as making—

although the study itself is strongest when Spiller is herself pursuing close reading as a strategy. When, for instance, she follows Cavendish's reasoning in the *Philosophical Letters* and charts in it the possibility of direct (if unmarked) responses to writing by Hobbes or Hooke, Spiller is convincing. And when in the strongest chapter of her study, devoted to Kepler's reading of Galileo, Spiller argues that Galileo's illustrated sunspots in *The Starry Messenger* collapse the distinction between viewer and reader, the claim vividly and elegantly supports her argument about the points of contact between early modern science and early modern texts. In contradistinction, Spiller's argument in her first chapter, concerning Sidney's *Defence of Poetry* and Gilbert's *De Magnete* as essays in worldmaking, is her least successful. Although her analysis of Gilbert's work in constructing magnetic *terrellae* offers a novel and welcome analogue to contemporary poetic production, the reading of Sidney to which it is linked seems largely familiar. Moreover, the overarching epistemological connection she draws between "small worlds" and hypotheses in experimental science on the one hand, and the production of literary worlds on the other, is in itself not particularly new, nor is her connecting both to colonialism. That is a shame, because the chapter would gain force from a rigorous engagement with prior, more theoretical articulations on the role of form in discursive homology and disciplinary differentiation.

To say as much is already to note one, conceptual, difficulty with the book. Another is rhetorical: at times Spiller's arguments seem centrifugal, whether in exploring the text at hand or in pursuing a seemingly digressive excursus on a critic or a debate. The second chapter on Spenser and Harvey, for instance, no sooner begins than Spiller turns to Thomas Laqueur, Stephen Greenblatt, the transvestite theater, and, finally, a critique of Laqueur's overemphasis on Galenism at the expense of Aristoteleanism. It is not, of course, illegitimate to bring any or all of these things to bear on how Spenser and Harvey think knowledge is propagated; far from it. (Indeed, later in the chapter Spiller goes on to draw a resonant if abbreviated connection between Aristotelian biology and Aristotelian models of poetry: for Harvey, both have beginnings, middles, and ends.) The problem lies in the abeyance of Spiller's overarching argument, which along with the ostensible subjects of the chapter seems to disappear without warning for pages at a time. In a related problem, what is useful in the study defies easy summary: Spiller offers many passing insights of great value, but because her control of her argument is not always sure, it is not clear how those insights mesh with each other, or reinforce an overarching claim. And although it is difficult to avoid using anachronistic terms in talking about embryonic discourses, Spiller's tendency to such imprecise words like "biology," "literature" and "art" without qualification undercuts the very clarity of her main point. When she writes in the second chapter of William Harvey and Edmund Spenser that "what they share is not so much a sense of how man is made but how knowledge is" (63), a more specific and marked sense of argumentative payoff is needed. That knowledge is constructed is, as I have said, an unexceptionable claim; even so, such an understanding is the starting-point of an argument rather than its destination. Similarly, when in her final chapter Spiller argues that unlike the members of the Royal Society, Margaret Cavendish is interested in making a different type of reader, the ends to which difference in reading as a historical project is put—whether to science, to literature, to an episteme, or the process of institutionalizing—are never specified. Moreover, that Spiller adduces her own close readings as proof of a claim about Cavendish's intent with respect to reading risks circularity by confounding argumentative means with analytical ends. As a result of logical and rhetorical flaws like these, the book unfortunately fails to register any cumulative force, although it offers many fine local arguments along the way.

Fortunately, the same cannot be said of David Glimp and Michelle K. Warren's well-edited collection, *Arts of Calculation: Numerical Thought in Early Modern Europe.* Even though as an edited collection the volume does not, indeed cannot, have an argumentative through-line, taken together the essays provide a provocative brief for the value of relating numerical formations in the early modern period to a broader literary and cultural context. Setting out such a brief is the work of the editors' excellent introduction (neither has contributed a separate essay): as they suggest, the volumes concern is less with "plastic or literal acts of calculation" than with the "abstractions" that accompanied these new material forms, and that could not but affect the "production, organization, and application of knowledge" (xviii). For all the systematicity of these terms, however, the way that "calculation" registers in these essays is plural, evidence both of dispersed and embryonic practices and of a dispensation on the part of the contributors to read instances of the mathematical against the grain. In the main, such thought here is considered concretely, and as an instance of local production, rather than as the immediately pervasive epitome of a universalizing modernity, although Timothy Reiss's summary essay is an exception in considering measurement, quantification, and Descartes' philosophical legacy as they might be associated with early modern military and colonial formations. More typical is the closing essay by Robert Batchelor, which also focuses on *mathesis universalis:* here, however, it is not introduced so much as a wide-ranging epistemological dominant for the age, but as the motive for Leibniz's very concrete and specific interest in a binary (base two) code. Indeed, the mathematician's desire to develop a universal character—a language that would, among other things, by apprehensible across otherwise vast geographical and cultural divides—led him to seek for unexpected connections between his privileged (and putatively "transparent") system of zeroes and ones and the Chinese *Yijing,* news concerning which was being disseminated in Europe by Catholic missionaries. As one might expect, Leibniz wholly lacked the linguistic and cultural requirements that would enable him to understand how the classical Chinese divination text ought to have been read. Still, as Batchelor argues, this misapprehension is less to the point than the historical fact of Leibniz's interest in looking to Asia to construct a broadly international system of knowledge. At times Batchelor's main line of argument gets submerged by the wealth of historical information he provides. Even so, this very amplitude is a further (if not entirely intentional?) confirmation of his claim: the systems of information by means of which Bruno Latour characterizes the "Modern Constitution" of science are themselves hybrid, methodologically inexact, and not without material friction. The same is true of that early modern network in which Leibniz was imbricated, the Republic of Letters.

Three other essays also consider exemplary figures in numerical thought, albeit in more local, European terms. J. B. Shank's "Fontenelle's Calculus" nicely argues that the French writer and academician, more often associated with popularizations of knowledge than with historically significant developments in it, demands to be taken seriously as a contributor to what he calls the "Calculus Wars" in France. As Shank suggests, few scholars of the early eighteenth century have studied Bernard le Bovier de Fontenelle's mathematical contributions in themselves rather than as regrettable exceptions to his more accessible writings; thus they have missed the connections that could be drawn between his work on infinitesimals and French rococo aesthetics, as well as the relation between this more "modern" form of mathematical analysis and courtly and administrative struggles over the extent to which such analysis should be purely an instrument of rule. In another engaging essay, Christopher Johnson pursues "Clavius's number"—the sixteenth-century Jesuit mathematician and astronomer's calculation of how many grains of sand it would take to fill the universe—across a series of seventeenth-century texts, where, like the rhetorical figure of hyperbole to which Johnson links it, the number becomes both a sign of intellectual accomplishment (or presumption) and a register of ineffability, a discursive hybrid of theology and mathematics. And in one of the strongest essays of the collection, Gordon Hull makes an effective case for taking Hobbes's "infelicitous forays into mathematics" (116) seriously, arguing that they are of a piece with his political philosophy. As Hull suggests, Hobbes's rejection of the more successful position associated with John Wallis (that number is an abstraction potentially immanent in nature rather than a convention of representation) led the former to prefer geometry, a referential and axiomatic science, as a mode of knowing the world. What was a residual position in mathematical thought paradoxically became a modern position in political discourse: just as, in Hobbes's view, mathematics needed to establish its constitutive autonomy from the natural realm in order to be considered a science, so too did civil philosophy. If number is a convention, then differences in quantity are not reducible to differences in quality: hence the equality of all men in a Hobbesian "state of nature."

One advantage of the decision to gather essays together under the rubric of calculation is that it enables the contributors to construe their analytical relationship to numerical thought rather broadly. A few essays, for instance, offer varied readings of the role of money. Joel Kaye's subtle and provocative essay on the role of monetization (that is, the system of exchange based on monetary equivalents) in the administrative life of scholastic philosophers is a good example. As he demonstrates, the bureaucratic role played by medieval masters at such universities as Oxford and Paris demanded that they quantify quality—assign ascending monetary equivalents, for instance, to ascending academic degrees. Kaye goes on to suggest that such work might well have had a subterranean effect on scholastic logic, since the pragmatic need to work with money demanded it be understood both as a "continuum of value and a measuring line" (8), a medium of exchange whose discrete technological form (in that money comes in countable units) covers over the fact that it operates in conceptual terms rather like a straight line, a system of potentially infinite points.

Other essays that devolve on money are less interested in the conceptual infrastructure of monetization than in the way monetary wealth signifies—as locus of conventional yet arbitrary value, as in Alina Sokol's fine close reading of Francisco de Quevedo's sonnet "To Gold"; or as a register of social relations, as in Benjamin Liu's nuanced study of the fifteenth-century poet Anton de Montoro, a tailor whose invoices in poetic form neatly underscore, even ironize, the socially enabling illusion that economic interest must be denied in courtly patronage interactions. And still other essays pick up on the figuration of mathematical thinking in literary texts characteristic of these last two essays, although they move away from money and into mathematics as sign, symptom, or cultural logic in early modern England. Patricia Cahill's contribution, "Killing by Computation," offers a Foucaultian-inflected meditation on how military formations, with their ways of aggregating manpower or, conversely, making a given force of men seem deceptively small, participate in a logic of interchangeable masculinity, of the male fighting body reduced to its strategic, place-holding essence. She then connects these "disembodied markers of collective military might" (173) with Marlowe's *Tamburlaine,* and offers a new, convincing reading of how early modern subjectivity—a marked if nascent form of individualism associated with Marlovian "over-reachers"—might look different when the unitary figure is oppressed by the weight of number.

Finally, two of the collected essays consider mathematics semiotically, either as affective sign or as a system where significance depends on a syntax, a system of meaning by position that tropes the cultural logic of succession. The seventeenth-century English Jesuit revenge play *Blame Not Our Author,* in which all actions occurs among geometrical figures made animate, is the focus of Carla Mazzio's essay "The Three-Dimensional Self," which links mathematics to melancholy. Via a wonderfully inventive and far-reaching argument, Mazzio indicates that the regularity of geometrical figures in the early modern world covers over a realm that is anything but regular and normalized, one that is riven instead by anxiety about authority, measurement, and "depth." As her essay suggests, the geometric characters of this drama, who are unsettled by the very rationalized space they inhabit, might serve as augurs of "Renaissance self-fractioning." And Eugene Ostashevsky's essay turns *Henry V's* introductory concern with ciphers, with the way a "crooked figure may/ Attest in little place a million," into a witty, revelatory exploration of the idea of place and value, of the way in which questions of numerical value map onto questions of political legitimacy. At a time when numbers could still be written "back-ward"—that is, from left to right as well as from right to left—the rhetoric of the preposterous, of ends that precede their beginnings, seems to pervade Shakespeare's play no less than the world of nu-merical calculation: Henry's right to succeed to the throne of France is, paradoxically (and preposterously) enough, guaranteed by the fact that as the latest—the last in place—to make the claim, he is in a position to give or deny value to competing political calculations.

Taken as a whole, this excellent collection ought to spur schol-arly interest in the way that early modern cultural logics can be im-bricated with the mathematical discourse that has for too long been kept in abeyance; as the essays suggest, numerical thought need not be read solely in terms of an orthodox historiography that has stressed order, transparency, and rationality, but might rather be set in less "proper" discursive spaces than those of Euclid and Des-cartes. Moreover, since many of the contributors are at compara-tively early stages of their careers, the volume also serves as the harbinger of longer, yet more stimulating projects to come.

Common Bodies: Women, Touch and Power in Seventeenth-Century England
By Laura Gowing
New Haven: Yale University Press, 2003

Reviewed by: Diane Purkiss

This is one of the best books of the decade in gender history, bring-ing together critical intelligence and outstanding reading skills. It also represents an attempt to produce genuinely interdisciplinary work. Gowing has read the work of Gail Kern Paster and Valerie Traub with as much attention and respect as she has the work of her fellow historians. And she is one of the few historians who has given serious thought to theory.

She also has a repertoire of wonderful and surprising stories to tell. Some make unsettling reading. We meet some assertive and strong-minded Kentish women who Gowing catches in the act of driving Joan Jacquett out of their parish at the very moment when she is about to give birth. We encounter Bess Bourne, subject of a scurrilous and reputation-ruining libel, which has her crying out with sexual pleasure during forced sex. We meet Martha Bevers, subject of her master's unrelenting sexual harassment. We see pregnant Marie Ryley, whose mother is chided for her failure to notice changes in her daughter's breasts that illustrate her pregnancy. Gowing's range of sources is astonishing. Broaching court records from consistory courts, quarter sessions, assizes, archdeaconry courts, and Bridewell records, she is also unafraid of printed works, using medical texts and household manuals as comparators. The attempt at comprehensiveness is refreshing in a universe of increasingly fragmented historical endeavors. It also allows her to make firm connections between materials.

Her first chapter illuminates the idea of the leaky body, already adumbrated by Paster's work in *The Body Embarrassed.* Through an attentive study of court records, Gowing is able to show that popular belief chimed surprisingly well with medical anxiety about the body and its humors. Using Mary Douglas's notion of the body and its boundaries, Gowing is able to demonstrate that the leaky idea of the body—there is a telling self-referentiality in the ideology—both reinforced and continued to trouble the patriarchy from which it was supposed to emanate. This notion of the body underpins separate studies of illicit sexuality, and of the bodily difficulties of maternity: pregnancy, birth, illegitimacy, infanticide.

Throughout, Gowing is excellent on the constructedness of states and ideas which ideology insists are natural. Pregnancy and maternity, she stresses, are not moments from which early modern women are free from ideology, but moments when they experience everything through it. Of course, this is no surprise; what is perhaps surprising and important about Gowing's work is that the discovery does not drain such states of meaning for those experiencing them, or for the reader.

Gowing decisively eschews both male myths about women in the period, and also more recent sentimentalities forged by an earlier generation of feminists. Her vivid study of early modern childbirth does away with any idea that all-women births were cozy and comforting affairs. Throughout, she is conscious of the way women regulate and control each other's behavior, acting as agents of men. Older women manage younger women, particularly through their role as the instructors of young servant-girls; married and widowed women police the acts and activities of single women. Any Shakespearean will think of Hermia and Helena, but perhaps also of Cleopatra and her maids, or Portia and Nerissa, Desdemona and Emilia; the last are especially illuminated, for perhaps it adds to the staining of Desdemona's reputation that she is manifestly unable to manage and control the tongue and sexuality of her servingwoman. Feminist history is now itself mature enough to begin to be answerable to uncomfortable truth, and Gowing's brave book is proof of this maturity. At the same time, she sees clearly that in thus controlling each other, women are acting as agents for patriarchs, not empowering themselves. She rightly criticizes Bernard Capp's idea that gossip is a way for women to acquire secret knowledge with which to blackmail men with threats of dishonor. For Gowing, men's honor is out of women's reach, but they can do plenty of harm to each other.

On witchcraft, Gowing follows the line laid down by Roper, Chaytor, and this reviewer, but perhaps does not quite see the oddity of the witch's body in the context of her own ideas. The strangeness of that body is that it is at once old, wizened, and hence hard like wood—as she shows—and also oddly flexible and aleatory, capable of clambering into churns and entering the bodies of others with eel-like agility. It therefore combines the menace of a woman whose telos has passed, who has lost maternal ability, with the overtly and overly maternal body that is far too capable of climbing into and controlling children of her body. Here, perhaps, we might sense that Gowing is supping with psychoanalysis but using rather too long a spoon. Luce Irigaray's marvelous essay "And the One Doesn't Stir without the Other" might have illuminated what is at stake for women in the perpetuation of such figurations, though Gowing is certainly right to claim that they ultimately serve patriarchy. Similarly, she is right to portray infanticide as a product of inexorable and insurmountable social pressures exacerbated by changes in the law concerning poor relief and bastardy, but she might also acknowledge more amply the difficulty for women in dealing with the simple mixed emotions of motherhood in a context where it was supposed to be a cause for divinely appointed joy.

A provocative conclusion questions the extent to which gender ideas shift in the tumultuous seventeenth century. Gowing's superb anthology of diverse texts concerning women's lives in the same century, *Women's Worlds in England, 1580–1720: A Sourcebook* (with Patricia Crawford) illustrates the way the apparent continuity of gender discourses—though themselves stirred by instability and anxiety—underlay and consoled in local or national turmoils. *Aristotle's Masterpiece,* that incarnation of bosh and bolshy ancient medical lore, and its persistence, is a bellwether of this unexpected continuity. But Gowing rightly sees that this forces us to ask how and when things did finally change. It is, she writes, assumed that the late eighteenth century sees a kind of passivication of women's desires and bodies, understood not as sexual but as teleologically maternal. But, says Gowing, the more nuanced history she has produced shows that the protest reformation's determination to elevate the household as the crucible of a just and godly society ensured that there were violent and punitive moral policies that impacted cruelly on single mothers and their babies, illegitimate mothers, and prostitutes. Implicit in these invasions of the space of women's bodies by church and state were the ideologies that would shape a later idea of woman as the guarantor of civility and culture within a household.

The only real reservation one might express about this wonderful and already germinal book might be a kind of unfair post hoc reflection. Is there a limit to what we can get from the court archives into which we have been happily burrowing? How typical are these women? Would we feel well represented by a similar survey of court cases and diaries, household manuals and medical texts? Would our states of mind be reliably inferred from a mix of the trials of Aileen Wurnos, Martha Stewart, Martha's baking book, and *Our Bodies Ourselves?* If not, where might we look for enlightenment? Many might say that our historians will look to blogs and e-mails. But these may give a false sense of immediacy; all readers of seventeenth-century diaries, Gowing included, know that nothing is more dominated by generic expectations than personal writings. In the end, this book reminds us that we cannot locate an absolutely authentic female voice anywhere—nor could the women of the past. Precisely because women are oppressed, what will sur-

vive of us is mediated, twisted, awry. But it is still of immense
value, because and not despite the fact that it emanates from lives
lived under the unbearable weight of ideology.

Reading Material in Early Modern England: Print, Gender and Literacy
By Heidi Brayman Hackel
Cambridge: Cambridge University Press, 2005

Reviewer: Alexandra Halasz

The history of reading practices is notably difficult to trace, for
reading leaves no necessary marks, and the mere existence of a
given material text provides no proof of its having been read, let
alone how it might have been read. Much of the direct evidence
for a history of reading practices is thus exceptional: it survives by
chance, an exception to the ephemerality of most reading experiences; and/or, it survives by virtue of intensely bookish contexts
and exceptional readers. Scholarly work on the "history of the
book" over the last two decades has afforded much indirect evidence about reading and brought the question of reading practices
to the forefront of inquiry. Heidi Brayman Hackel's book, *Reading
Material in Early Modern England,* offers a well-organized, well-
written, and comprehensive engagement with the current scholarship on reading practices and a pair of archival studies that makes
an original contribution to that scholarship.

   The brief Brayman Hackel sets for herself is to shift attention
from "extraordinary readers" to more ordinary ones and "to historicize, rather than idealize or merely theorize, the various experiences of early modern readers" (8). The task is a daunting one, not
least because the commitment to uncovering the experiences of individual readers risks foundering in anecdote and microhistory,
thus losing sight of the larger, indeed theoretical, issues. Because
so few ordinary readers can be identified, *Reading Material in Early*

Modern England builds its case by carefully laying out the scenes and habits of early modern reading. A chapter on "gestures and habits of reading" discusses the representation of reading on the stage, the spaces in which reading might happen, the variety of scriptive practices and surfaces (scripts, scribes, wall-writing), the sociality of reading (communal and aural), and the training to literacy (pedagogic practices, manuals, self-teaching). Another chapter provides an extensive survey of efforts to shape the reader, by policy (limiting the distribution of books or the spread of literacy), dedications, preliminary matter addressing the reader, and printed marginalia provided for the reader. These scene-setting chapters draw on and generously acknowledge an immense number of articles and books, thus affording an excellent introduction to research in the field.

The second half of *Reading Material in Early Modern England* presents two archival studies, one focused on readers' responses to Philip Sidney's *Arcadia* and Robert Greene's *Menaphon* (also known as *Arcadia* in seventeenth-century printings) and the other on the (reconstructed) libraries of two early modern gentlewomen. Each of these chapters opens with an extensive context-setting discussion that again includes an exemplary synthetic and critical discussion of existing research. The case studies themselves are the product of many hours spent in rare book libraries in Britain and the United States, "wandering through the archives" (13), as Brayman Hackel describes her initial methodological approach. The wandering evidently soon settled into a focus on well-known texts and artefacts chosen, in part, because they foregrounded women as readers and collectors of books.

For her discussion of the material traces left by readers, Brayman Hackel examined in detail some 150 surviving copies of Sidney's *Arcadia,* about fifty copies of quarto editions of prose fictions by Greene (only six were copies of Greene's *Arcadia*), and four intact commonplace books featuring extracts from the *Arcadia*s. Not all of them bore markings; the most common marks were signs of ownership and penmanship exercises that might be parsed to speculate about patterns of ownership and circulation, but reveal little, if anything, about practices of reading. The heavily marked volumes feature finding notes, plot summaries, source identifications, imitative poetry. One remarkable copy features what can only be described as a scholarly apparatus (commentary in four languages and extensive citation of authorities), an extensive index to the prose and a first line index to the poetry. Someone connected to the owning family clearly read the volume in a professional or quasi-professional manner, but the annotations afford no evidence as to whether or how less-learned readers followed the cues of the annotator. The cumulative evidence of the heavily marked volumes suggests that keeping track of character(s) and plot(s) motivated the more ordinary readers in their annotation. The commonplace books, in contrast, bear witness to a process whereby Sidney's plots and characters disappear; thematic passages are extracted and redeployed by the reader, to fashion, one might argue, their own "characters" and lives/plots. The same original material might appear under a rubric of "amorous speeches" or be used as a template and, heavily amended, stand as a statement about divine judgment. The radical de- and recontextualizing evident in the commonplace books not only blurs the distinction between reader and writer, as Brayman Hackel argues, but also suggests how one might begin to theorize reading in a historically sensitive fashion by considering such appropriative practices as shaped by and in turn shaping the habitus of readers.

Most of the annotations in books (aside from signs of ownership) and most surviving commonplace books are putatively male; tracing female readers is a more difficult proposition. The final archival study in *Reading Material in Early Modern England* was actually the first focused work in Brayman Hackel's research, a reconstruction of Frances (Stanley) Egerton's library from a manuscript short-title catalog prepared between 1627 and 1633. (An appendix transcribes the catalog and provides bibliographic identifications.) Brayman Hackel literally reconstructed the library, assembling copies of the volumes listed and arranging them on a shelf according to the cues afforded by the catalog's arrangement. What's at stake in the effort is our capacity to imagine the agency of early modern women readers, the evidence of a personal library serving as a proxy for reading. Egerton did not heavily annotate her books, though they bore marks of her, as opposed to family, ownership. Anne Clifford Pembroke, who commissioned a triptych portrait of herself featuring identifiable books in each of its panels and who left manuscript remains in the margins of books and in diaries (or summaries of diaries), affords a complementary case for imagining not only a gentlewoman's library, but her relation to books and reading. Brayman Hackel argues that Egerton constitutes a "normal exception," that is, an exception that is taken as representative in the absence of significant quantity of evidence; she considers Anne Clifford Pembroke, in contrast, to be exceptional. This distinction makes sense in the immediate context of Brayman's argument with the prevailing scholarly emphasis on limitations of women's access to (higher forms of) literacy. But both Egerton and Pembroke were highly privileged women, exceptional by virtue of their class position. More interesting evidence of "normal exception" arises from Pembroke's recorded practices of regularly supplying her domestic servants with books and adorning her rooms and walls with transcribed extracts from her reading.

Reading Material in Early Modern England is rich and informative in its accumulation of evidence about early modern reading practices. In the breadth of its survey and the depth of its close studies, it brings its readers into the archives and allows them to wander a bit. Brayman Hackel's reluctance to theorize the evidence she presents is at once a sign of the times (in which the archive and the empiricism it supports seems to afford a firm footing for humanities research otherwise in danger of not being credited) and a considered response to the methodological problem of constructing large arguments from microhistories. On the one hand, as William St. Clair remarks in his John Coffin Memorial Lecture in the History of the Book (http://ies.sas.ac.uk/Publications/johncoffin/st-clair.pdf), "we should beware of putting too much weight on anecdotal evidence whose representative quality is uncertain" (9); on the other, the accumulation of sufficient evidence and kinds of evidence to understand early modern reading practices and theorize their import requires an interdisciplinary and collaborative effort we have only begun to glimpse. Our own habits as readers and writers and the institutional pressures on our research practices make the desiderata of such an effort seem quixotic: a common repository for gathering and sorting the material traces we encounter in the archives (see, for example, the Reading Experience Database1450–1945 at http://www.open.ac.uk/Arts/RED/); an understanding of the demand curves of the book trade and how they shaped the material available for readers; investigation of the educational, social, and institutional practices that shaped multiple literacies; open discussion of theoretical models and disciplinary approaches. We need to follow the example of Anne Clifford Pembroke and post the material of our "storehouse" in digital rooms and on digital walls so that we may "descant on them" (231).

Joint Enterprises: Collaborative Drama and the Institutionalization of the English Renaissance Theater
By Heather Anne Hirschfeld
Amherst and Boston: University of Massachusetts Press, 2004

Reviewer: Richard Preiss

It does not go without saying that all scholarship is collaborative, and among the many virtues of Heather Hirschfeld's *Joint Enterprises* is its own exemplary collegiality: with inexhaustible diligence and expository skill, in its slim bulk it consolidates a vast range of previous theater-historical research together with the author's own original insights to advance, at least methodologically, a fertile new approach to its field. That field has in recent years become synonymous with the work of Jeffrey Masten—an ironic accolade, given his deconstruction of individual "hands"—and Hirschfeld devotes space in the first of two introductory chapters to asserting both the value and the recuperability of the cultural information that gets lost in his model. Rather than abstract collaboration from its institutional setting in order to generalize and extend it as a uniform poetics, that is, *Joint Enterprises* argues that dramatic collaboration was fundamentally premised on the professional autonomy and individualism of its members—just one of the competitive frictions on which its alchemy could operate—and accordingly that the subjects of our greatest interest are not the Beaumonts and Fletchers, those artificially and retroactively idealized patron saints of the practice, but instead the more numerous and minor writing teams whose very occasionality reveals the material pressures that brought them together and to which their efforts responded. The social metaphor of this bold rethinking is thus not the pair-bond but, by turns, the syndicate, the temporary alliance, the intermittent partnership, the one-night stand: or, more accurately, no normative metaphor at all, since she is primarily eager to analyze "the particular shape or mode of a writing group" within the nonrepeating parameters of its specific historical moment, and, where possible, to locate "a predominant interpersonal affect" for each project (8).

This yields for her a "rationale of the case-study," whose theoretical strengths also prove interpretive handicaps the book as a whole cannot always (nor, in its defense, does not attempt to) overcome. Heterogeneity makes for an unstable, shifting, opportunistic set of investigative procedures, and one senses immediately that the other collaboration on which her thesis rests—the very terms "collaborative drama" and "institutionalization" juxtaposed in her subtitle, seeming to offer a direct, parallel relation between the two—represents something of a paradox, the second term inevitably gesturing toward a more synthetic, developmental narrative, which the genre of the case study by definition resists. This strain is especially felt in the introduction, where Hirschfeld must establish historical and theoretical frameworks for readings that, in their ingenuity and nuance, usually end up exceeding the discursive taxonomies she initially assigns them. (The fault, that is, lies not in the quality of the ideas but in an overly formal deference to academic convention, a mannered tendency toward meta-argumentation that likewise disrupts the logical flow of her otherwise lucid prose elsewhere.) A crucial early appeal not to take "gentlemanly interaction" (10) as the sole measure of collaborative work, for instance, which might have lent more organized vision to the consistently antagonistic role played by the court in later chapters, instead leads to a digression on guild structures as a basis for company relations—a rubric that may push too far in the other direction, obscuring in collectivism the idiosyncratic agenda of dramatists on which her readings often depend. A defense of her "disynchronic" analytical process, furthermore, using both "the collaborative context to inform . . . the text" and "the text to inform . . . the collaborative context" (8), needlessly codifies her method into a circularity the reader was probably prepared to ignore. Most troubled, perhaps, is the attempt to posit (via Bourdieu) for each case study a "psychic dimension of collaborative work" as the linchpin bridging the theatrical, institutional, and political conditions of its composition with "how these strains and rewards registered in the plays themselves" (15), thereby giving the impression of a single, "psychomaterialist" hermeneutic. Not only do Hirschfeld's case studies rarely illustrate so neat and orderly a catalysis from public to private determinants (nor can they)—professional and personal motives instead variously jockey for superiority—but this formulation actually weakens the thrust of her larger claims, entailing a good deal of self-distancing from intentionality and psychologization, and more important, compromising the terms of her underlying bid to redefine collaboration criticism as, on some level, always a psychothematic exercise, a self-reflexive attention to the way every jointly authored play text preserves and reduces to the purely interpersonal complexities of its own genesis. Those complexities cannot be negated, but they can also be put into perspective: it seems to me that the merits of her intervention lie precisely in *not* trying to theorize dramatic collaboration as a necessarily "special case," viewing it instead as a continuous instance, multiplied and intensified by internal refraction, of the manifold shaping forces inherent in early modern theatrical production. Hirschfeld prompts us to ask, that is, just what it is about two or more poets working in tandem that seems to trigger psychic chemistries and investments beyond the tolerance of either the cultural poetics of New Historicism or the commercial imperatives of theater history. Her own repertoire draws generously from both schools, after all, and under the weight of the sociomaterial stakes she excavates beneath each project, the personalities of collaborating writers can sometimes register thinly indeed; then again, the fact that such readings do not always thematize collaboration is exactly what makes them refreshing. One suspects that, caught between competing critical vocabularies, none fully capable of containing or predicting her analytical moves, her efforts to harmonize their lines of communication with umbrella terms simply lets her keep her options open for the chapters that follow. A more aggressive engagement with the book's programmatic unclassifiability, however, might have better mapped out (and delved into) the theoretical fault lines its subject straddles, as well as underscored the innovation it thus represents.

Nevertheless, Hirschfeld's first chapter might profitably have been merged with her introduction, since as a sort of interchapter laying out the "baseline" conventions of collaboration in and across theatrical milieus in the late Elizabethan and early Jacobean years, it does much to historicize the grounds for privileging an authorial territorialism throughout the period that would have been especially volatile to joint work, and in the process firmly rooting its study within the Greenblattian dyad of "rhetorical performance and selfhood" (17). Beginning with the familiar dichotomy between institutional norms for collaborative writing at the adult, "public" amphitheaters and the boys' "private" halls ca. 1600–1607, she first demonstrates the incipient versions of intellectual property even the former was still capable of recognizing—in the "conservation of collaborators" across serialized plays among Henslowe's syndicates, for example (20)—before moving on to the more agonistic culture of solo gamesmanship, both enabled and made requisite by the higher degree of Latinity, learning, and coterie practices prevalent among the audiences of Paul's and the Blackfriars, evidenced variously by the *poetomachia,* the *Parnassus* plays, and manuscript circulation. Hirschfeld thus trains her sights on the emerging "ideology of rhetorical style" (28) that engendered in Jacobean playwrights an acute sense—despite the lack of an authorial copyright to concretize it—of literary identity and self-ownership, thus implicitly embedding the collaborative act in anxieties of rhetorical, socioeconomic, and institutional forms of contamination. Apart from fixing her initially vague "psychic" object of study within a set of real historical discourses, this survey provides an excellent segue into her next chapter, where she considers the remarkably rich layerings of text and subtext collectively posed by the *Hoe* "trilogy." The first of these, Dekker and Webster's *Westward Hoe* (1604), was also the first cowritten production at the reopened Paul's, and for her it is this specifically aesthetic incursion, crossing not so much professional borders as social and disciplinary practices, that incited Jonson, Marston, and Chapman to reply with *Eastward Ho,* a "parody . . . not only of representation but of production" (29). Staged at the Blackfriars, however, *Eastward* cannot but perpetuate and multiply the very transgression it mocks, and Hirschfeld ingeniously develops how the play's "scenarios of linguistic theft" (37)—what it does both to *Westward*'s mercantile plot *and* to Dekker and Webster—naturally "recoil" as a threat against and by the writers themselves, eliciting a collective verbal style of obsessive banality and pastiche whose ultimate goal, she argues, is to protect them from *mutual* appropriation in turn. Even if steeped in too much paradox—it is difficult to see the practicalities of three playwrights *collaborating* on a "rejection of the collaborative process" (46), or, conversely, how such a result did not still achieve the trio's original end—one is unlikely to find a more rigorous and unified genealogy of these plays' disunities, and while her claim that *Eastward*'s paranoia constitutes a fully realized "strategy of *anti*-self-fashioning" sounds overblown, her concluding appraisal of *Northward Hoe* compellingly illustrates how Dekker and Webster took it as just that.

For the same reason they build so well off each other, chapters 1 and 2 stand apart from the rest of the book, having more to say about how institutions *in* the theater interrogated the structure and meaning of collaborative drama than the reverse. As later chapters begin to address the institutionality *of* theater as a whole within a wider cultural and discursive field, meanwhile, the other half of Hirschfeld's equation correspondingly fades into the background; her emphasis, that is, becomes those particular *collaborations* that focalize such issues rather than "collaboration" itself. Chapter 3, for example, takes up a fascinating question from the previous two—how by the end of the first decade of the 1600s did collaborative writing at the private theaters go from anomaly to norm?—which it never quite answers in terms consistent with the scope of her governing inquiry. Hirschfeld proposes that the sudden swing toward collaboration registered among theater professionals a "critique of the court masque," foregrounding "key differences" between the two institutions' production methods and "hermeneutic situation[s]" (68). This thesis is as unique and inspired as it is tenuous, and while Hirschfeld lays extensive foundation for it in a well-researched (if slightly obvious) exposition of the masque's "hermeneutics of identification" (55)—its allegorical use of community as a performative pretext for hierarchies of social difference, including its own authorship as a singular mode—the claim's value as an interpretive springboard remains confusing and perhaps mishandled. For one thing, it does not translate into the hermeneutics of collaborative authorship one is led to expect: if masque promotes the very "principle of distinguishing participants" (59) we had earlier associated with the individualizing drives of private theater, why instinctively take the discriminatory challenge of collaboration as rejecting rather than merely amplifying those drives? More pertinently, if we accept that indoor halls writers now began aligning themselves against rather than with the court, what commercial or disciplinary factors *account* for this seemingly atavistic regression in institutional self-image, and thus for the "suspicion" of the genre she sees articulated in the inset masques of *The Maid's Tragedy* and *Two Noble Kinsmen?* The crux of this moment's relevance to a study of "institutionalization," such problems are withheld for the end, and although her hypothesis that the King's Men's new royal proximities demanded (ironically) their own statements of institutional self-difference—characterized in these plays by the failure of masque to arbitrate identities or reality (87)—seems on the mark, its belatedness hinders the chapter's coherence: we cannot properly understand the case study if we are not first given the case. Front-loading this explanation would have also buttressed readings that, while cogent within larger materialist critiques of court culture, never quite attain a truly *epistemological* divergence from the routine operations of drama itself. (These tragedies, on some level, convey the impossibility of making distinctions not just because they have masque elements in them but because they are tragedies.) Finally, since Hirschfeld admits that work specifically *by* collaborators bears only a secondary relation to her thesis, which is not "made visible in their plays alone" (68), she somewhat obviates her principle of selection, and one feels even a sidelong glance at texts like *The Tempest* (or, for that matter, the fully eligible *All Is True*) would have supported her arguments.

Chapter 4 attempts to correct course by returning to that staple of collaboration criticism, Renaissance friendship rhetoric—only here considered not in the well-worn context of Beaumont and Fletcher but in the unlikely, chronic partnership of Middleton and Rowley, where Hirschfeld can revise the discourse's habitual link with aristocratic aspiration. Again, however, despite a powerful central reading of *The Changeling*, the overarching trajectory from joint work to institutional politics remains loose: immensely absorbing analytical parts never entirely coalesce into a whole. An opening section on the shiftier term "fellow" and its exclusively theatrical usages, for example, provides a much-needed check to critics who take friendship as the epitome of professional relations, and "gentleness" as its ideological telos. This lets Hirschfeld argue Middleton and Rowley's own friendship as predicated on a "resistance . . . [to] aristocratic relations" (99), but since friendship now becomes the engine of her exegesis, the initial distinction with fellowship gradually disappears, and one is left uncertain what it contributes. Similarly, her notion that *The Changeling* perverts the topoi of friendship into exposing the extremes of lust, violence, and abjection they themselves already contain—doubly counterpointed not only by puns but by puns *about* marriage, friendship, and "fellows," linguistic intimacies that betray instead characters' total misapprehension of one another, their "sharing the same word for entirely opposite meanings" (110)—is brilliantly conceived and very persuasive. Yet apart from the clever observation that such drama depicts "precisely the opposite of mutually reinforcing joint work" (111), Hirschfeld is less assured about whence it comes and where it points. Middleton and Rowley's frequent couplings may have been elective, but we know too little about their bond to hypostasize it as the play's ideal, photonegative original, an "anti-allegory" of "its conditions of production," "the perverted result of the experience of its writers" (117)—not, at least, without longer discussions of other efforts (like *A Fair Quarrel*) that seem also to thematize friendship. If their probable friendship alone seems insufficient motive for such an otherwise narcissistic exercise, the mere fact of *The Changeling*'s court setting is likewise too generic from which to extract a critique of anything particularly "aristocratic," other than friendship discourse itself. What precise personal or material factors, in other words, framed 1622 as an "institutional" moment for this play and its putative anticourt cynicism? Meanwhile, avenues both more basic and more germane to Hirschfeld's twin concerns—like her utterly prescient choice of writers who *chose* to collaborate across company lines, and what that trend itself might indicate about institutional dynamics—are regretfully left unexplored.

Only in chapter 5 do the book's alternating poles finally converge, to produce a superb case of institutional tensions simultaneously inscribed in the work of a writing team they themselves directly selected. It helps, no doubt, that that team here consists of Thomas Heywood and Richard Brome, writers whose biographical and aesthetic disparity afford Hirschfeld a ready foil for deducing a rationale behind their lone collaboration, the 1634 "journalistic drama" *The Late Lancashire Witches* (the question of whether this was a revision of a 1612 play is set aside). In Hirschfeld's artfully managed exposition, the very differences that made them an improbable pair in any other circumstance turn out to underwrite the commonalities that joined them for this one: both writers shared strong commitments to a generational hierarchy of craft that, while sequestering old master from young (unrelated) apprentice, also defined "the stage as a business and a brotherhood, a profession" (123), and that galvanized both against the Caroline sponsorship of amateur, courtier aficionados like Davenant and Carew. Surprisingly resituating the play within the "second poets' war" usually confined to Massinger and Shirley, Hirschfeld connects the historical context of *Witches* to the escalating contest between "royal government and sociocultural activity" (129), in which both the Privy Council's intervention in the trial and Charles's reissue of James's *Book of Sports* forged a "synecdochal relationship" between the provinces and the public stage, forcing the latter into a cavalier paternalism of which it was increasingly leery. The King's Men's commission to propagandize for the prosecution, then, becomes instead a record of Heywood and Brome's attempt to "expose the self-interest that motivates" not only prosecution *and* defense but the persecution of the occult and the promotion of "sports" as interrelated policies. Accordingly, the play "renders judgment on the witches impossible" by depicting their mischief as "a form of festive inversion" indistinguishable from playmaking itself (134ff.). As throughout, there are shades here of Paul Yachnin's "powerless theater" idea, and one wishes Hirschfeld had more to say about how such periodic retreats to the rhetoric of less "legitimate" social forms alter our narratives of "institutionalization." But all the same, here her persistently court-reactionary argument finds real purchase, and this is ingenious historicist work balanced with finely tuned close reading. Moving from strength to strength, she adds a speculative conclusion on the case of inter*company* collaboration posed by the King's and Queen's Men's joint performance of Heywood's *Iron Age* (ca. 1610–13) that, in a mere eight pages, elevates her thinking on the subject to an exponentially higher order of sophistication. In terms of sheer critical psi, it is the most muscular section of the book.

Besides the floating definition of "institutionalization" and the reluctance to draw heavier narrative lines between its evidentiary constellations, *Joint Enterprises*'s other global flaws are more forgivable: the tacit conflation of dramatists' interests with those of actors similarly begs the question of a monolithic sense of "profession," while the fact that Hirschfeld bypasses the period of greatest collaboration and professional uniformity, the 1590s, perhaps avoids giving playwrights too little agency rather than too much. Yet this is all to say that the worst thing about the book is simply that it does not do more of what it already does; nor can these synopses appreciate the amount of local erudition and command concentrated in each page, disclosing institutional lives behind neglected texts that Hirschfeld persuades us should, if we reevaluate what collaborative authorship really represents, be more canonical than they are. The success of the book, fittingly, does not ultimately depend on that of its parts. While *Joint Enterprises* improves as it progresses, the inconsistent results of its individual case studies do little to diminish the generative power of Hirschfeld's approach—in fact, its very plasticity predicts them. To argue as she does, rather, that dramatic collaborations form suture points in which the negotiation of competing values not only is made visible but is constitutively *imbricated,* involved in yet not limited to the identities (however broadly or narrowly construed) of their authors, is conceptually to transform the field—and to bring it into alignment with how we have tended to read the "rest" of Renaissance drama all along. In a disciplinary climate already attuned to the vertically collaborative nature of theatrical production and its ideological freight, to anyone interested in the more formidable challenge of *horizontal* collaboration, *Joint Enterprises* establishes a blueprint for future studies.

Renaissance Drama and the Politics of Publication: Readings in the English Book Trade
By Zachary Lesser
Cambridge: Cambridge University Press, 2004

Reviewer: Marcy L. North

Zachary Lesser's *Renaissance Drama and the Politics of Publication* is a provocative and illuminating study of the Stuart book industry and the way it marketed printed play texts for its reading audience, sometimes several years after the plays were composed and performed. The study integrates in a fresh way the findings of book history, reception studies, and historicist and materialist approaches, but its most significant break with tradition is in its choice of an agent through which to read the plays. Instead of invoking the author as a source of meaning, Lesser turns to those booksellers and Stationers' Company members who *published* books, arguing that they are readers with an astute understanding of how printed playbooks fit into particular literary and political contexts. Using these publishers and their marketing niches as an interpretive lens, Lesser rereads with historical precision Stuart editions of several plays, among them, Beaumont's *Knight of the*

Burning Pestle (1613), Marlowe's *Jew of Malta* (1633), Webster's *White Divel* (1612), Shakespeare's *Othello* (1622), and Beaumont and Fletcher's *King and No King* (1619).

Lesser's premise is deceptively simple; he asks "why *that* play was published *then*" (16, his emphasis). This question conspicuously echoes the inquiries of New Historicists who envisioned literary texts as players in the political field, but Lesser answers his question by circumscribing the field very precisely. The "politics of publication," as he terms it, refers to the political, literary, and economic context created by a stationer's career specialization as it resonates for readers at particular historical moments (22–23). When stationers published a play, they necessarily and intentionally placed the play in the context of their book list, anticipating that readers would recognize their generic categorization of the text and perhaps even share their reading of it. Evidence of early reader response is notoriously scarce for this period of literary history, but Lesser argues convincingly that there is an untapped cache of evidence in the marketing strategies of these early publishers, whose livelihoods depended on their ability to predict audience interpretation.

An introductory chapter offers a tribute to and critique of the scholarship that has made Lesser's study possible, from the New Bibliographers who documented the work of the Stationers' Company, to the New Historicists, to more recent scholars looking for evidence of reading and reception in the margins of early books. Lesser observes that New Bibliography's quiet devotion to the author has obscured the importance of the publisher as a reader and producer of meaning (15). New Historicism has similarly overlooked the publisher by assuming that the author is the source of a work's political topicality. As such, historicists have failed to identify the readers *for whom* a literary work is political (22). Scholars investigating book ownership and marginal notation share Lesser's desire to recover readings, but their conclusions have been compromised by scarce evidence. Although he only briefly acknowledges their influence, Lesser seems quite closely aligned with scholars such as Roger Chartier and Adrian Johns, who value local studies and who make the market exchange and reception of particular editions critical interpretive tools.

Chapter 1 provides a concise history of print and traces the development of niche publishing in the English book industry. Lesser also makes some broad distinctions here between printers and publisher/booksellers. By focusing on the publisher, the agent who acquired a text, speculated on the financial success of the published book, and provided the capital for the printing project, Lesser steers us away from traditional print history with its focus on the products of particular presses. The wording of many title page imprints, he notes, announce that a book has been "printed by" a trade printer "for" a publisher/bookseller. Because publishers had the most at stake, Lesser argues, they tended to look at potential publications through readers' eyes, using "critical skills to judge the book's potential appeal and possible consumers, a judgment that depended on making meaning of the text of the book" (35). Over the course of the Elizabethan period, government regulation and market patterns slowly encouraged publishers to develop recognizable specialties and to evaluate prospective publications in light of their specialties. Trade printers, on the other hand, eventually became less specialized contractors who were paid by the project and who did not need to speculate on the success of a book. The divisions in the print industry between trade printers and publishers grew wider during the Stuart period, and the split, Lesser asserts, was well defined by the 1620s and '30s.

The distinctions that Lesser draws in this chapter are informative, but they are also a bit too uncomplicated. Lesser's persistent use of the term "publisher," for instance, can be confusing. The term succeeds in foregrounding the critical and interpretive activities of those stationers responsible for financing print projects, but it obscures the fact that these same individuals often referred to themselves as printers. They wrote prefatory letters to readers as "printers" and signed many errata statements as "printers." Many likewise took an active role in all stages of book production, including the printing. They may not have worked the press physically, but neither did they distance themselves from the physical production of the book. To his credit, Lesser acknowledges that "publisher" is anachronistic, but some scholars will still find the term too modern.

The first chapter nevertheless leaves a reader well equipped to enjoy the in-depth case studies that follow. In these four chapters, Lesser traces the long careers of four important stationers. The ways in which these stationers develop their specialties is intriguing, and Lesser manages to make excellent sense of some complicated book lists. Chapter 2's subject is Walter Burre, who specialized in publishing play texts, especially those that had failed as stage productions. Taking Beaumont's *The Knight of the*

Burning Pestle, Burre framed the play text in 1613 just as he had several Ben Jonson plays, as a work likely to appeal to discriminating wits rather than to the broad public. Rather than advertising the prominence of the author, whose name may not have been known to Burre, Burre used typographical conventions to establish the play's generic affiliation with other playbooks aimed at an educated audience. In many of Burre's dramatic publications, the contents complement the publisher's appeal to gentleman wits; the plays mock the newly wealthy who do not have the breeding to carry their privileges gracefully, and they position the audience as the "normative" wit or authority who judges the foibles of the characters (76). What Lesser also sees in Burre's well-developed publication oeuvre is a surprisingly early designation of play texts as literary. Previous critics have credited the book industry with elevating the status of literary authors in the seventeenth century, designating Jonson's 1616 *Workes* as pivotal in this evolution. Lesser refines this argument to suggest that the process was well under way before 1616. "Perhaps," Lesser writes, "it is not in theatrical repertories, nor solely in authors' self-constructions, but rather in the corpuses of people like Burre, in the commercial motives of publishers, that we should look for the schism that produced a 'high' dramatic culture" (79). This insight is one of several in *Renaissance Drama* that promises to change the way scholars of early modern literature think about the designation "literary."

In the third chapter, Lesser turns to the curiously late publication of Marlowe's *Jew of Malta.* Nicholas Vavasour published the play more than forty years after it was written, and Lesser argues that modern critical interpretations, which see the play as Marlowe's subversive and skeptical depiction of Christianity, overlook the play's topicality in 1633. Printed in the same year that William Laud became archbishop of Canterbury, *The Jew of Malta* contributed to Stuart debates about the cohesiveness and uniformity of the Church of England. In their arguments for uniformity, Laudian polemicists commonly drew analogies between Jews and sectarians, especially Dutch resident aliens. Lesser argues that in the 1630s, Marlowe's character Barabas would have been viewed against this backdrop as a schismatic, creating internal divisions among Christians, and his downfall would have represented a call for Christian unity. Lesser's Laudian reading of the play is supported by the fact that Vavasour subsequently developed a specialization in Laudian publications.

Webster's *White Divel* (1612), Dekker and Middleton's *Roaring Girl* (1611), and Marston's *Insatiate Countess* (1613, 1616) are nominally the focus of chapter 4, though by placing them in the context of the Stuart pamphlet war over the worth of women, Lesser questions conventional modern interpretations of a whole generation of misogynist publications. Lesser proposes that the dialogic publishing niche cultivated by Thomas Archer, who was unusual in publishing pamphlets on both sides of a debate, reveals the anti-feminist debate to be less adversarial than previously thought. Read together, the two sides give readers not a war between the sexes but a safe way to "negotiate marital tensions between patriarchal authority and mutual love" (136). The three plays mirror internally the dialogic arguments of the pamphlet war, and thus offer readers the vicarious pleasure of testing social and sexual extremes from the safety of conventional marriage. This reading of the plays is not entirely convincing, but the chapter succeeds because Lesser's reorganization of the *querelle des femmes* along the lines of Archer's publication list offers scholars an intriguing new perspective on the debate.

In chapter 5, Thomas Walkley's long career as a publisher of books and pamphlets on state affairs is the context for Lesser's re-readings of Shakespeare's *Othello* (1622), and Beaumont and Fletcher's *King and No King* (1619) and *Phylaster* (1620). Lesser argues that at the time of its publication, *A King and No King* was read as a commentary on the cooperation, or "marriage," of the king and parliament. Lesser sees echoes in the play of the "familial discourse" used to promote the model of mixed government espoused by Sir Henry Neville (169). Only later was the play viewed as concerned exclusively with kingship. Political marriage is also the backdrop for Walkley's other publications. In the context of Stuart negotiations over a Spanish match for Prince Charles, *Phylaster* and *Othello* depict foreign marriages as tragic decisions and suggest that James ought to support Continental Protestants instead by going to war against Spain. Later in his career, as the Civil War raged, Walkley's specialty came to be perceived as royalist even though his publishing politics had not changed. This case serves to illustrate one of Lesser's central points, that publishing specialties and the publications they frame resonate in different ways in different periods. Here, more than in other chapters, however, Lesser reads the three plays looking for analogies to particular events. This strategy threatens to oversimplify the plays, as Lesser acknowledges, but it also demonstrates just how politically publishers expected their products to be interpreted. As with the previous chapter, the critical lens through which Lesser reads the plays is somewhat more innovative and daring than the readings themselves.

In *Renaissance Drama*, Lesser's unique recontextualization of Stuart plays is so well formulated that it will strike some readers as simply common sense. It is much more than that. By making the publisher his agent and the publisher's specialty his backdrop, Lesser creates a new canon of literature for investigation and a new method for recovering early reader response. He also destabilizes many foundational principles of print history and literary criticism—that the author is the source of a text's meaning, that the print industry is a passive if unreliable conduit of meaning, and that the political culture that informs a text is the one in place when the text was composed. There are always dangers to introducing a new critical method, and I mention one here to encourage further research, not to detract from Lesser's considerable accomplishments. Lesser has chosen four publishers who were more successful than most and whose niches are relatively well defined. The specialties of other publishers may prove much harder to parse. Throughout the book generally, Lesser avoids messy exceptions to the histories and patterns he is tracing. Given how new his approach is, however, it is perfectly understandable that he chose clarity over subtlety. If scholars come to embrace Lesser's ingenious approach, as seems very likely, they (and perhaps Lesser himself) will no doubt complicate the notion of "political publication." Even in this introductory study, the critical approach that Lesser outlines is compelling and extremely promising, not only for the readings it makes possible, but also for the way it revitalizes historicism and bridges the divide between bibliography and literary criticism.

Citizen-Saints: Shakespeare and Political Theology
By Julia Reinhard Lupton
Chicago and London: University
of Chicago Press, 2005

Reviewer: David Hillman

There are all sorts of ways to become a citizen, and several ways to become a saint; and these, as Julia Reinhard Lupton shows in her elegant new book, need not be mutually exclusive. "Citizen-saints," in Lupton's epithet, are "figures who dwell in the frontier between the sacred and the profane; figures who, by virtue of embracing or embodying superceded historical and religious positions, become unlikely portents of social formations to come" (13). These include Saint Paul and Antigone, Marlowe's Barabas and Milton's Samson, Shakespeare's Shylock, Othello, Isabella and Caliban, and, ultimately, Shakespeare himself. The citizen-saint, in Lupton's definition, is one "who invests the regular intervals of citizenship with the ongoing potential for radical singularity" (140). All these exemplary figures embody radical exceptions to norms of universalization and naturalization—the norms of citizenship, which are marked by what Lupton terms a "salutary insufficiency" (208): "Citizenship as a category is both rooted in local practice, in the life of a polis or city with its own institutions, and embodies a standard that breaks away from its particular instantiations precisely because its formal definition does not gather into its reach all aspects of social life" (213). While "citizenship can offer a provisional ground of equivalence and a forum for deliberation and compromise for persons from diverse groups without equating politics with particular religious, cultural, or sexual identities" (210), it comes at a cost—that of shedding a vital part of one's previous affiliations, familial, tribal, religious, ethnic, and so on. And it is in this shedding—a kind of mortification or sacrifice, as Lupton describes it—that one nears the status of sainthood, at precisely the moment that one is moving into citizenship.

In approaching the ambiguous embrace of the polity—through ceremonies of conversion, manumission, marriage, or naturalization—the characters Lupton analyzes lose a substantial portion of their allegiances to the local habits and habitations of their origins. One of Lupton's main interests here is the relation between the universalized and the localized, the dominant polis and the various locales within or beside it in which these figures have lived out their prior identities: the ghetto, the wilderness, the convent, the desert, the island. Hence, for example, the importance of Venice in Shakespeare's "multicultural" plays *The Merchant of Venice* and *Othello:* a thriving polis struggling to incorporate in its commercial and republican pluralism outsiders of various kinds. According to Lupton's thesis, the city provided Shakespeare with a perfect test case for the dramatization of the tension between *ethnos* and *demos,* defined by Étienne Balibar as, respectively, "the 'people' as an imagined community of membership and filiation" and "the 'people' as the collective subject of representation, decision making and rights."[1] The eventual incorporation of these characters into the collective, sometimes civic, realm is always "structurally incomplete, maintaining memories of suspended modes of affiliation that never dissolve completely into a new identity" (101). The conversion of Shylock, like Othello's suicide (and like other key moments at the endings of the Shakespearean plays discussed— Isabella's prospective marriage to Duke Vincentio in *Measure for Measure,* and Caliban's final lines in *The Tempest,* his promise to be wise and seek for grace), are shown to be partial, unsatisfying; they thus figure the imperfect relation between the particular and the universal, the exceptional and the normative. It is in the shape of the Jew, the Muslim, the Pagan, the (Catholic) nun, and the not entirely human creature that Lupton discerns her complex figurations of "the uncivil core of civil society" (55), types of moral and aesthetic extremity—the indigestible exceptions within Hegel's *bürgerliche Gesellschaft.*

Citizen-Saints explores the vexed and ever-evolving relations between the political and the theological; it is interested in uncovering some of the roots of modern notions of citizenship: in Greek philosophy, the Bible, and early modernity. Lupton lists some of the questions the book takes on: "Who is my neighbor? Who is a citizen? What is a creature? What is a person?" (10); this brief list hints at the scope and ambition of the book. More specifically, the rubric of the citizen-saint implicates, for Lupton, the following kinds of questions:

How does circumcision operate as both a marker of ethnic membership and a means of conversion and civic naturalization across group lines? What vision of social equality is embedded in the injunction to Sabbath rest? How do antinomian suspensions, states of emergency, criminal acts of sovereign exception, and Messianic anticipations lead to reconfigured forms of and relations to law in its written and unwritten, political and religious forms? What styles of universality—ecological, trans-ethnic, or cross-gendered—are implied by the abject state of the pure creature, at sea in a creation abandoned by its Creator? (4)

It is at times hard to follow Lupton's subtle weaving of connections between these very diverse questions; the organizing categories and antinomies (norm and exception; *ethnos* and *demos; politeia* and *philôtes;* the civic and the civil; creature and Creator; and so on) overlap and don't line up neatly, but they are traced in highly intelligent, subtle, and resonant ways. Indeed, part of the resonance comes precisely from the "messiness" of the different types of messianic impulses interrogated. What Lupton calls "the literature of citizenship" encompasses "not only a group of texts that take their themes and modes of production from civic life, but also a way of approaching texts, of reading them for the styles of deliberation and debate, of address and redress, of bargaining and compromise, that they depict or instantiate" (214). The field available to this debate is thus very open, and Lupton moves deftly among an impressive array of texts and thinkers: biblical scholars, theologians, political theorists, philosophers, psychoanalysts, and literary critics. One of Lupton's greatest strengths is in her ability to unearth genuine dialogues between apparently quite diverse texts; these interconnections are often surprising, usually convincing, and never less than fascinating.

The first half of Lupton's book is under the aegis of Saint Paul, who provides her with an influential model for the notion of dying into citizenship. Both in his life and in his New Testament writings, she argues, Paul gives us the formative outlines of the idea of civic naturalization, negotiating between Jewish, Hellenistic, and Roman identities and circles of citizenship. In his writings, "the universality of Christian fellowship is both produced and limited by the dialectic between the open embrace of the Christian message on the one hand and the internal national coherence represented by the Jews on the other, a tension that provides a foundational mapping of Western ethno-political consciousness" (105). Paul's attempts to square the particularist impetus of Judaism and the universalizing ideals of Christianity converge in the issue of circumcision, a marker of unique ethnic identity as well as a means of conversion and civic naturalization, and hence potential universality, as Lupton explains: "Circumcision is both denaturing and naturalizing, an initiatory act of separation (from biology) and socialization (in a legally constituted membership set)" (34). The cut (or de-cision) of circumcision renders the body a member of the (absolutely exclusive) Chosen People but is simultaneously a purely covenantal or legal identity (thus making the group identity potentially permeable). Paul's supercessionary hermeneutics reinterprets circumcision as a question of pure faith, dissolving the central sign of Israel's covenantal bond into the metaphorized "circumcision of the heart," which, ideally, "joins both sexes, all peoples, and all classes into common fellowship with Christ" (42).

Lupton takes the Pauline discourse of citizenship as "one of the crucial mythemes of Western thought, a charged article that constellates biblical exegesis, Renaissance texts, and modern methods in relation to each other" (45). Her readings of the middle term of this triad are powerfully animated by the first and last. (Oddly, given the central role of Saint Paul here, the two Shakespearean plays most often associated with his writings—*The Comedy of Errors* and *The Winter's Tale*—go completely unmentioned in this book.) *Citizen-Saints* extends and deepens the investigation begun in Lupton's fine previous work on hagiographic echoes in Renaissance literature.[2] An essential methodology throughout is the typological reading, which provides Lupton with some of her most surprising and illuminating findings. She finds, for example, suggestive links between Samson's "O first created Beam" (quoted on 187), Caliban's "teach me how / To name the bigger light, and how the less" (quoted on 165), and Genesis's "God then made two great lights: the greater light to rule the day, and the less light to rule the night" (quoted on 166; cited from the Geneva Bible). Through typology, Lupton shows how each of these later characters is placed in a hierarchical relation to the first act of creation and hence to what Giorgio Agamben calls the "mere life" of creatureliness. Less surprising but equally revealing are the Abrahamic and Pauline echoes in both Shylock's evocation of circumcision and Othello's dying words, "I took by th'throat the circumcised dog, / And smote him, thus" (quoted on 118). The Old and New Testament meanings of circumcision shadow both Shylock's stab at "re-Judaizing" the Pauline notion of circumcision of the heart and Othello's equivocal effort to identify himself as both part of the Venetian polity (in slaying the circumcised other) and radically apart from it (in the ensuing reflexive act of self-circumcision). In each case, Lupton perceives an attempted renegotiation of the relations between citizen and alien other. This train of thought leads, for example, to an eye-opening reading of the character of Othello as a symbol of the potential of Christian universalism rather than of racial otherness: "In *Othello*," writes Lupton trenchantly, "religious difference is more powerfully felt, or at least more deeply theorized, than racial difference" (106).

While God, according to Nietzsche's all-too-catchy dictum, may be dead, theology—as Lupton amply shows—is very much alive and kicking. Building on Walter Benjamin's insistence on "both the *necessity* and the *evacuation* of theological frameworks" in the seventeenth century (163), *Citizen-Saints* provides an important corrective to some recent New Historicist and multiculturalist readings of the various early modern works discussed. Lupton's book pushes us back toward universalist readings of early modern texts—but with a crucial difference, since the very idea of universalism and its relation to particularism is one of the central issues being theorized here:

> It is precisely the particularism of "culture," set against a universalism presumed bankrupt, that neo-historicist readers of Shakespeare have attempted to salvage, whether in the guise of Othello's blackness, Shylock's Judaism, or Caliban's indigenous claims. In the process, however, the universal potentialities of these positions are necessarily ignored, reduced, or secularized. (176–77)

Lupton keeps history very much in the frame in this book, but it is history as seen through a longer—a two-thousand-year—lens than most recent accounts of the works she discusses. But—just as with the universalising ideals of citizenship—there are costs as well as benefits to this approach. One of these (and the parallels to Lupton's own account of the costs of entry into citizenship are inescapable) is the loss of some of the local context that recent criticism has brought to the foreground of our attention. Especially unexpected is the near-total disregard of the significance of the Reformation in the typological trajectories portrayed here. Some discussion of the difference the Reformation made to, for example, understandings of circumcision, or to the relation between familial and political allegiances would have been welcome here—as would, more generally, some assessment of the role of Protestantism in the emergence of modern ideas of citizenship.

A second kind of sacrifice made to the methodology deployed by Lupton—and in this I feel sure that not all readers will agree with me—might be said to be some part of the individuality of the characters or of the singularity of the plays discussed. *Citizen-Saints* may be characterized as a book not so much of literary criticism as of politico-theological philosophy. The critical energy flows in this direction: from the literary works to the politico-theological discussion more than vice versa. For a book ostensibly about Shakespeare, there is a relative paucity of quotation from the plays; at times there is a sense that Shakespeare's (and Marlowe's, and Milton's) works are used primarily as hooks for Lupton's deep musings about issues that lie not quite at the periphery but also not quite at the heart of these plays. Though powerfully engaged with the literary texts, Lupton's real passion seems to lie in rethinking their genealogies and politico-theological implications. One could say that she is more interested in the ways in which a character's extravagant particularity injects difference into the civic realm than in the precise quality of that uniqueness. To insist, as Lupton does, that "however ambivalent we may feel about Shylock's conversion, there is *nothing tragic* in his destiny" (101, Lupton's emphasis) is to view Shylock's fate from a perspective that appears to involve a certain distance, an insertion, say, of the politico-theological dimension between character and reader or viewer. Lupton's subtle readings undoubtedly illuminate neglected facets of these plays, but for me, they cannot be characterized as fully satisfying overall interpretations.

In the end, *Citizen-Saints* is a book about the roots of "modern citizenship and its discontents" (9). It is evangelical about the necessity and indeed desirability of exceptionality, the interpellation of something other—immeasurable, nonnegotiable, extravagant, messianic—into the fungibility, normativity, and regularity of civic life. It questions the ostensible impartiality of the civic ideal, its partial embrace of otherness:

> Can civic life survive as a valid and authentic form of existence if it operates at the expense of the alien, no longer conceived as the member of a recognized corporate community with its own distinct internal and external rights and charters, its own circles of citizenship, but now

stripped of property and dignity, criminalized and dispossessed, and fundamentally alone? (In contemporary politics, we would contrast here the permanent resident with the illegal alien, the immigrant with the refugee, the tourist with the terrorist.) Civic life is not only *at stake* in the case [of Shylock], but also *on trial.* (97)

The relevance and importance of these questions in a world of multiculturalism, multiple group memberships, and the much-heralded "clash of civilizations" is clear. Lupton concludes her book with a "Humanifesto" (205), an epilogue, the main thrust of which is to urge literary scholars in academia toward an engagement with the problematics of citizenship, in part as a way of infusing into the debates surrounding these matters a different perspective, but also in part as a way of healing the growing breach between scholarly pursuits and the public domain. Lupton offers the literature of citizenship "as a field of scholarly inquiry but also of artistic capacity that might draw humanists toward matters of public interest and consequence without diluting the integrity of what we do" (206). Lupton wishes "to reopen the civic envelope of liberal education in order to separate its critical and creative potential from its ideological functionalizations" (216)—a worthy ideal, and one that this book embodies superbly.

Notes

1. Étienne Balibar, *We the People of Europe,* trans. James Swenson (Princeton: Princeton University Press, 2004), 8.
2. Julia Reinhard Lupton, *Afterlives of the Saints: Hagiography, Typology and Renaissance Literature* (Stanford, CA: Stanford University Press, 1996).

The Children of the Queen's Revels
By Lucy Munro
Cambridge: Cambridge University Press, 2005

Reviewer: Darryll Grantley

In justifying her decision to undertake a study of the work of this boys' company, Lucy Munro argues that studying a company's repertory allows recuperation of neglected works and study of a wider range of the individuals who took part in the production of plays. This book richly achieves these objectives and a great deal besides, as it provides a perspective on English theatrical culture in the early modern period in general, but also makes a strong case for the ways in which dramatic texts need to be viewed in terms of a range of their determining contexts if they are to be read most productively.

Munro starts with what she calls a "biography" of the company, recognizing that her focus on the Jacobean period renders a clear divide between the Children of the Chapel and the Children of the Queen's Revels problematic, but pointing to new directions taken by the company in this period. She successfully presents a fresh view of the nature of a children's company, and this one in particular, interpreting Rosencrantz's "little eyasses" speech in *Hamlet* in different ways, including the idea that it might actually have been advertising the Queen's Revels. An overview is provided of the activities of the Children of the Chapel/Queen's Revels from 1600 to 1613, its move to the Blackfriars, and the appointment of Samuel Daniel as a licenser independent of the Master of the Revels, but her discussion ranges further over a number of particular qualities of this company as a children's troupe. These include practical matters such as the problems of recruiting and retaining actors, especially as the usual connection of Elizabethan boy actors with grammar schools became more complicated in the Jacobean period, and she discusses the lawsuit over the abduction of Thomas Clifton. She notes the difficulties the company experienced several times over the contentious nature of its plays, such as the loss of the queen's patronage in 1606 until its return to favor with a performance at court in 1608/9. The company's political positioning also has an effect on the work it produces, and Munro suggests that its patronage by and association with the queen's court, its connections with certain other royal or aristocratic figures and with the Inns of Court while having an uneasy relationship with the king's court made the Queen's Revels writers a sort of poetic "opposition."

Munro chooses to examine the Queen's Revels repertoire by genre, arguing that recognition of genre had considerable importance in the early modern period and also that the playing companies exercised considerable control over the dramatic product they produced. This is not presented as operating in any simplistic way, since her view is that it is unnecessary to look for a prime intelligence behind the plays performed by the Children of the Queen's Revels—rather that there was a network of allegiances among playwrights and shareholders that sometimes conflicted, and what emerges is a form of "collaborative authority." She contends that contrasts between the adult and boy companies have been exaggerated, and that the latter had a considerably wider range than the "railing" plays usually deemed to dominate their repertoires, something she goes on amply to demonstrate with reference to the repertory. On the other hand, she does then go on to make a case for the particular qualities brought by the Queen's Revels company to the early modern theater in London precisely by virtue of its performers being children. She discusses the problematic social status of young actors and the indeterminacy of their status as young performers, though the notion that these issues are of moment in what the plays have to say is perhaps slightly less convincing. However, an interesting point is made about the changing status of actors as they got older in James's reign, and their move from being objects to subjects and having a more active role in the company. She also interestingly comments that our understanding of acting style can be enhanced by knowing the ages of actors. A particularly worthwhile area to which she draws attention, and one that has relevance to later parts of her analysis, is the sexual interest in the young players on the part of both men and women, which has implications not only for performances but for the sorts of plays that would be written for this company. She examines the blurring of the boundaries between the genders in Chapman's play *May Day,* commenting that the young performers would have been able to create both disturbing and comic effects.

In line with Munro's focus on the genres of the Queen's Revels repertory, each of the next three chapters is devoted respectively to comedy, tragicomedy and tragedy. In chapter 2 she points out that laughter was not always regarded favorably in the early modern period and was associated with the young and the lower classes; thus the comedic material of the company is in one sense appropriate to it, while the elite status of its audiences, who are intensely aware of social hierarchy, paradoxically excludes those who are most associated with laughter. Munro suggests that the contradictory attitudes to comedy that this situation brings about can help unpack the problematic relationship between performers and audience—especially when it comes to jokes about social status. She argues that the fact that the company's audiences were more select was not the result of policy, but a by-product of the conditions in which they performed—small theatres with high entry prices—and she finds no indication of a "coterie" audience. Munro identifies a reflection in some Queen's Revels plays of tensions about social status, and though she possibly overstates this a little as a characteristic attributable specifically to plays of this company, she usefully challenges Steven Mullaney's view that children's comedies were less oppositional in their attitudes to the establishment than those of the amphitheater houses. The argument is supported by a discussion of the exploration of social tensions about status in a number of plays produced by the company, including *Eastward Ho,* by Chapman, Jonson, and Marston; Middleton's *Your Five Gallants;* Beaumont's *The Knight of the Burning Pestle;* and Beaumont and Fletcher's *The Coxcomb.* She highlights the importance of jokes in the Queen's Revels comedies especially as a means of regulating behavior but unpredictable in their effect and contends that the equilibrium of standard comic narratives is often upset by specific jokes, something indicating an awareness of the problematic aspects of comic closure.

The following chapter, on tragicomedy, is probably the most interesting of the three chapters on genre, particularly in that the company is credited with a considerable contribution to this mode of drama, since Munro presents tragicomedy as emerging from the collaborative practice of the playing companies, especially the Queen's Revels. She views the company's experiments with comedy as having a background of English pastoral tradition, its playwrights drawing on the work of John Lyly who also wrote for children. She counters charges that Fletcher's *The Faithful Shep-*

herdess was out of keeping with the "railing" plays of the Queen's Revels and points out that pastoral could also be used for social commentary, citing traditions of political pastoral and pointing out that the company's tragicomedies tended toward the comic and satiric. Marston's *The Malcontent* is suggested as a paradigm for later Queen's Revels tragicomedies, containing elements such as the disguised ruler motif and substantial intertextual quotation, especially in respect of its revenge tragedy tropes, and she also highlights the dark and corrupt sexuality present in several of the Queen's Revels plays.

In chapter 4, Munro makes the important point that, despite tending to be overlooked among the output of the children's companies, tragedy is a very significant part of the Queen's Revels repertoire and in fact constitutes the preponderant genre within it. As this was unusual for a children's company, she suggests that this possibly indicates their attempt to compete with and outdo the adult companies. The discussion in this chapter is focused on the malleability and mutability of the tragedies performed by the Queen's Revels, something that is ascribed partly to the idea that tragedy was influenced by the popularity of tragicomedy. She takes a detailed look at a play that has undergone revision, Chapman's *Bussy D'Ambois,* first performed by the Queen's Revels children around 1604 and subsequently revised for performance at the Whitefriars around 1611–12 to illustrate the flexibility of tragedy as performed by the company, in the hands of which it was a genre open to various forms of experimentation. She goes on to account for the unpopularity of Chapman's *The Revenge of Bussy D'Ambois* and Daborne's *The Christian Turn'd Turk* as conversely equally being due to the impact of tragicomedy, since these tragedies are insufficiently sexualized by comparison with more popular contemporary plays that both offered sexual titillation and were more generically fluid. It is also noted in this chapter that the tendency of the Queen's Revels company to permit their authors to print their plays usefully allows us to see how the authors reconstitute their works in print.

In her concluding chapter Munro stresses the influence of audience taste and the early modern theater's intermingling of aesthetics and commerce on the nature of the various products on offer in the theater, and also argues for the importance of the impact of the repertory on the writing of genres. Her contention is that the plays of the Queen's Revels provide illustrations of the various forces that operate in the period to determine the generic forms of the commercial theater, since they are tailored among a range of other determinants both to the capabilities and potentialities of the juvenile actors and the demands of their paying audiences.

As is the tendency in recent works of this nature, Munro provides a range of valuable appendixes that set out relevant data in a clear and accessible form, enhancing the general usefulness of this volume and allowing a ready reference to the material on which its arguments are based. These are: a chronological summary of the Children of the Chapel/Queen's Revels repertory, including authors, dates, first publication dates, and whether the plays had revivals; a setting out of repertory alphabetically by play with more data, a biographical summary of the people connected to the company including players, writers, patentees, and patrons; actors lists of the Queen's Revels productions; and a list of court and touring productions between 1600 and 1613, including patrons, payees, and sources of the data.

This is an important book that helps to illuminate the meaning of several early modern plays by placing them in one of their contexts of production. It provides valuable new perspectives on the theater company that is its topic, but also the particular qualities connected with children as performers and the troupes in which they worked. It additionally affords an insight into a significant part of the theatrical culture of the period, negotiating carefully through the data and being equally attentive to what can be gleaned from material historical data and from the plays themselves.

Shakespeare and Women
By Phyllis Rackin
Oxford: Oxford University Press, 2005

Reviewer: Valerie Wayne

In her concise, accessible, and important book, Phyllis Rackin shows us where feminist criticism of Shakespeare needs to go: not to laments about women's oppression but to discoveries of historical empowerment; not to texts and interpretations that reinforce patriarchy and misogyny but to those that resist it; not to timeless women but to women understood in relation to time, place, and circumstance. Rackin's concern is more with where feminist criticism is taking us than with where it has been, and her book moves us forward to a better place. Carefully organized and lucidly argued, it offers a fresh, energizing account of its subject and reminds us we have a choice about how we view history, texts, and ourselves. Since Shakespeare's writing "still has an authority unequalled by any other secular texts," many want to claim that authority for their own beliefs and opinions. However, "for women . . . what matters is not what Shakespeare thought and felt about us, but what the words he wrote enable us to think and feel about ourselves" (111). The book sees texts and authors in relation to their effects upon living persons, rejecting critical approaches that teach women to read from the subject position of misogynist men and affirming our ability to find the historical evidence we are looking for to create a history in which women have a meaningful and major part to play.

The first two chapters work as a pair, with the first explaining the kind of history we need but don't have because of an overemphasis on women's oppression, and the second serving as an example of the new history we can develop. Attending to Mary Arden and her family, to what we do and don't know about Anne Hathaway, to early modern women's importance as laborers and housekeepers and their participation in off-stage theatrical activities as well as their presence in the audience, this second chapter paints a different picture of Shakespeare's Stratford and London. On the topic of the exclusion of women from the English stage, which was anomalous in the larger context of Europe, Rackin posits that the professional companies "seemed to have exploited that anomaly in an effort to establish their business on a respectable footing" (43) in a culture that viewed theatrical impersonation with suspicion and traveling players as having low social status. Although this chapter could say a good deal more about the women who were writing at the same time as Shakespeare, it does propose that some of those anonymous plays may have been written by women, and it affirms the importance of female patrons for the London companies. As for members of the audience, "the collective economic power [women] possessed as paying customers in the playhouse meant that none of Shakespeare's plays could have been successful in his own time if it failed to please them" (47). When was the last time you read such an affirmation of women's cultural influence? Could one make the same statement about cultural phenomena today?

Chapter 3 argues that the plays we choose to read, study, and perform "tell us more about our own assumptions regarding women than about the beliefs that informed the responses of Shakespeare's first audiences" (49). These choices contribute to the greater estimation of *Richard II*, the two parts of *Henry IV*, and *Henry V* as compared to all three parts of *Henry VI*, *King John*, and *Henry VIII*, where female characters are more prominent; to the emphasis on *The Tempest* in contrast to the other late romances; and to *Hamlet* as compared to *Antony and Cleopatra*. Our preoccupation with the "crudely misogynist story" (53) of *The Taming of the Shrew* may also explain that play's exceptional popularity, which "seems to prefigure the most oppressive modern assumptions about women and to validate those assumptions as timeless truths" (54), especially when the induction is cut in performance. In place of *Shrew*, Rackin proposes we reconsider *The Merry Wives of Windsor*, the only Shakespearean comedy set in contemporary England, which demystifies male sexual insecurity by presenting Falstaff as "a beached whale, helplessly gasping on a shore he cannot navigate" (67), and offers female characters exercising power in their own persons as women.

In her next chapter, "Boys will be Girls," Rackin discusses crossdressing, not by focusing on the women in the comedies, but by taking a long look at Cleopatra as epitomizing the paradox of theatrical representation. In "The Lady's Reeking Breath" she takes up the sonnets, showing that Shakespeare critiqued the essential narcissism of Petrarchan conventions in remarks by the Dauphin and the Bastard in *King John* (2.1.497–510), that *Romeo and Juliet* stages a "complicated negotiation with the Petrarchan tradition" (99), and that the tradition was entirely consistent with misogyny, women's silence, and the devaluation of women's bodies. Then she provides a wonderful reading of sonnet 130, where the lady's reeking breath becomes her speaking voice, and her solid corporeality as she "treads on the ground" transforms her to an "active human presence" (109). The force of this reading almost overtakes the chapter, but Rackin repositions its sentiments as so "strikingly atypical . . . that they do not, therefore, provide any basis for claiming Shakespeare as a feminist *avant la lettre*" (110).

The last chapter critiques the ways in which Shakespeare's female characters have served as models of an unchanging female nature. The case is made largely by comparing Lady Macbeth with the Scotswomen in Holinshed's *Chronicles,* which leads to a discussion of the early modern controversy over women breast-feeding their own children. Shakespeare's anachronistic rendering of an old story is seen to restrict women "to a private, domestic sphere, defined by their 'natural' vocation as wives and mothers, which was to become a leading feature of modernity" although it was new at the time (134). There is some dissonance between this chapter, given its comments on the paucity of devoted mothers or good marriages in the plays, and the book's claim in its last sentence that "the women we see in his plays are inevitably limited by the range of possibilities we can imagine for ourselves" (137). Much of the book confirms that observation, but the chapter also points out the limitations present in the texts themselves, which could become an argument for reading beyond Shakespeare to his contemporaries, including women writers, and beyond all of them to other times and places. Nonetheless, Rackin consistently takes the difficult route of focusing on Shakespeare's texts that feminist criticism has undervalued or ignored, slighting the comedies and youthful heroines for the female characters of greater complexity and experience, confronting directly the problems posed by characters and passages most troubling to women readers. She writes with the urgency of someone who knows firsthand, as many of us do, how intensely these texts can affect our sense of ourselves as women, and she is committed to improving our critical practice as a way of improving the directions we chart for ourselves. This teachable book—for undergraduates as well as graduate students, with helpful suggestions for further reading at the end—deserves a wide and diverse audience. It challenges us to develop a criticism that is less concerned with making Shakespeare's texts look better, more complex, or more historical, than with making the world a better place in which to read—anything.

The Italian Encounter with Tudor England: A Cultural Poetics of Translation
By Michael Wyatt
New York: Cambridge University Press, 2005

Reviewer: Ian Frederick Moulton

Michael Wyatt's *Italian Encounter with Tudor England* opens with the description of England in John Florio's *Firste Fruites* (London, 1578), a book of Italian-English dialogues. Wyatt asks his reader to imagine what it would have been like for an Italian merchant to arrive in London in the late 1570s, speaking no English. According to Florio, he would have found himself in a country where the air is clear and the women are beautiful, where food is plentiful and good (though everyone prefers beer to wine), but also where *la gente vanno vestiti con gran pompa* ("the people go well appareled with great pomp") and *il denaro regge ogni cosa* ("money ruleth all things"). Other Italian accounts note the extraordinary social freedom enjoyed by Englishwomen, and our imaginary visitor might well have been surprised by the early modern English custom of kissing hello. He would also have found a small, but thriving Italian community, including merchants and court musicians. Best of all, Florio claims, the queen looks fondly on Italians and their culture: *si diletta di parlar con loro elegantissime* ("delightes she to speak with them eloquently").

Much has been written on the influence of Italian culture in sixteenth-century England. But Wyatt's book is something new: an engaging, if at times diffuse, examination of the contact between actual Italian people and England in the sixteenth century. Although the English fascination with Italian culture goes back at least as far as Chaucer, most early modern Italians did not reciprocate the interest. (Boccaccio, for one, held to the traditional Roman view that England was *remotissimus orbis angulus,* the farthest corner of the world). Nonetheless, individual Italians engaged with England in various ways throughout the sixteenth century, and Wyatt makes an eloquent argument for the importance of the cultural connection they embodied.

Wyatt's study is divided into two sections. The first surveys the Italian encounter with England from the earliest extant Venetian ambassador's report in 1498 to the death of Queen Elizabeth and beyond. The second focuses on the work of John Florio, the English-born Italian language teacher, translator, and lexicographer. The relation between the two sections is somewhat uneasy. The first is primarily historicist in tone and chronological in organization. The second is more theoretical, and its periodic focus on gender and sexuality—while fascinating—can seem a bit incongruous. One senses that Wyatt's book would rather be two books: one a reference work, listing and describing the prominent Italians who lived in, visited, or wrote on England in the sixteenth century; the other a historically specific theoretical exploration of translation and cultural difference. The dual focus of *The Italian Encounter* may trouble some readers, but the first section is so informative and the second so thought-provoking that it seems ungrateful to complain. Serious students of early modern English and Italian culture will learn much from both.

The first section, "'A parlar d'Inghilterra': Italians in and on Early Modern England," neatly divides Italian-English relations into three periods: before Henry VIII's break with Rome; the mid-century struggle between Reformation and Catholicism; and the long reign of la Regina Helisabetta.

Before the Reformation, contact between Italians and English tended to be at the highest social levels. In the fifteenth century, Italian humanists like Poggio Bracciolini and Tito Livio dei Frulovisi lived in English noble households. Pietro Carmeliano, a native of Brescia, served as Latin secretary to both Henry VII and Henry VIII. Even Baldassare Castiglione visited England briefly in 1507 to accept the Order of the Garter on behalf of the Duke of Urbino, his patron. But although Henry VII's tomb in Westminster Abbey was built by Pietro Torrignano, Italian artists did little work in England.

Prior to the Reformation, the Catholic Church provided the strongest institutional link between the two cultures. Not surprisingly, several English bishoprics were held by Italians in absentia. But Polidoro Virgilio, the author of the *Anglica historia,* lived in England for many years, first as deputy papal collector, then as archdeacon of Wells. And many of the negotiators between Henry VIII and the pope over the matter of Henry's divorce were prominent Italian clerics. When Henry broke with Rome, this complex institutional relation between England and Italy was abruptly severed.

According to Wyatt, initial Italian reaction to Henry's divorce was mixed; Bandello wrote a novella bad-mouthing him; Aretino wrote him a flattering letter (nothing out of the ordinary there). One of the best contemporary accounts of Edward VI's minority, the *Relazione d'Inghileterra* (Venice, 1552), was written by Petruccio Ubaldini, an Italian soldier and courtier who fought in English wars in the 1540s and '50s and settled permanently in England in 1563. Ubaldini warns of the dangers that attend a child king, and describes in disapproving detail the changes that the Reformation has brought to English religion. Under the Protestant Edward, England served as a haven for Italian Protestant refugees, many of whom were to flee again when Mary came to the throne. The two most prominent Italian refugees in London were Pietro Martire Vermigli and Bernardino Occhino. Occhino wrote a didactic antipapal tragedy in nine tableaux, published in John Ponet's translation as *A Tragedie or Dialogue of the uniuste usurped primacie of the Bishop of Rome* (London, 1549). Vermigli, more seriously, was involved in the articulation of Anglican theology and contributed to the writing of the *Book of Common Prayer.*

Edward's reign also saw the establishment of a small congregation of Italian Protestants in London. Like other foreign congregations, they worshipped at the Church of Austin Friars. Michelangelo Florio, a refugee from the Inquisition and John Florio's father, was their first pastor. A temperamentally difficult man, he had connections to both Archbishop Cranmer and William Cecil. His *Regola de la lingua thoscana* (London, 1553) was dedicated to Lady Jane Grey, and he also wrote an Italian account of her brief reign, published long after his death, in Middleburg in 1607.

When Mary ascended the throne, like her father she received a flattering letter from Aretino (he had skipped Protestant Edward). Mary's Catholicism meant she was well regarded in Italy, and Wyatt discusses the *Sponsalito,* an "oddball poem" written by Giovanni Alberto Albicante in 1555 to celebrate Mary's marriage to Philip II of Spain, as well as the description of Mary's reign in Girolamo Pollini's *Historia ecclesiastica della rivoluzion d'Inghilterra* (Rome, 1594). Pollini spoke for much Italian opinion when he described Elizabeth's ascension as the triumph of Satan over the English people.

During Elizabeth's reign, Italian culture was valued at court, if not in the country as a whole. Elizabeth herself spoke Italian; her court followed Italian fashions and was entertained by Italian actors and musicians. Wyatt attributes the queen's fondness for the culture to her Italian tutor, companion, and bodyguard Giovanni Battista Castiglione, who was her only link to the outside world during her confinement in the Tower in 1554. But paradoxically, this most Italianate of English monarchs had little contact with her Italian counterparts. Because of her Protestantism and the papal censure, the only Italian nobleman to visit Elizabeth was Virginio Orsini, a cousin of the queen of France and a nephew of the Grand Duke of Tuscany. He was lavishly entertained on a casual visit in 1601, and shocked to discover on his return to Italy that he was in the process of being excommunicated (his family connections ensured that he was ultimately absolved).

Under Elizabeth the tiny community of Italian Protestant refugees returned to London. Their numbers are hard to ascertain, but they were probably less than 500. (The French and Dutch refugee communities were much larger.) Despite Elizabeth's reputed fondness for their culture, most of the London Italian community had little contact with the court, and their influence on the larger culture was minimal. Their skills were sometimes valued by their employers, but the general public reaction to them was hostile.

Despite political and religious upheavals, Italians traded in England throughout the century, although their wares were valued more by the elite than by the general public. The Bardi-Cavalcanti company of Florence had an Italianate nineteen-room house on Throgmorton Street, near Austin Friars, the church of the Italian Protestant community. A 1599 map of London shows an open space called the "Giardin di Piero" in the same neighborhood, near Moorfields and Bishopsgate. Wyatt concludes his survey of Italian contacts with Tudor England with Giacomo Aconcio, an inventor and theologian who made the first request in England for the granting of a patent and also wrote *Stratagemata Satanae* (Basel, 1564; English translation, London, 1647), the first systematic defense of religious toleration written in England.

As is obvious from this brief summary, the Italian presence in sixteenth-century England was multivalent and resists generalization. The most striking thing is how small it was. English poets were obsessed with Petrarch; Spenser rewrote Ariosto and Tasso; English drama was set in Italy; Shakespeare adapted Italian novelle; Castiglione's *Cortegiano* was the bible of courtly conduct; Machiavelli and Aretino were icons of evil; Venetian courtesans epitomized sexual license, and the Venetian constitution fascinated English statesmen. But there were relatively few actual encounters between people from Italy and people from England. England was peripheral to the worldview of most educated Italians. And the number of Italians actually living and working in London was miniscule. Clearly, in this case, cultural transmission was more imaginative and textual than personal and practical.

This textual transmission of culture is the subject of the second half of Wyatt's book, "John Florio and the Cultural Poetics of Translation." Although he may be unfamiliar to modern readers, Florio was at the center of early modern English cultural exchange with continental Europe. An English-born child of Italian refugees who never set foot in Italy, he published two Italian-language instruction books as well as the first English-Italian dictionaries. He was also the first English translator of Montaigne. Wyatt deals with Florio's work both as language instructor and lexicographer, reading Florio's texts not only as pedagogical tools, but as evidence of cultural contact and conflict.

Florio's two books of instructional dialogues, *Firste Fruites* (1578) and *Second Fruites* (1591), make constant reference to the social and physical environment of early modern London, including the theaters, the court, and sumptuary laws. He also makes great use of proverbs and folk sayings. Wyatt argues for a connection between language learning and disguise in Florio's works, which he relates to the fundamental theatricality of early modern society. Florio, after all, was an Italian by language and culture, not birth or residence, and his uncertain national position makes him an ideal case study of cultural mutability and border crossing.

While focusing on Florio, Wyatt touches on the major influences on English views of Italy in the Elizabethan period: Roger Ascham's famous attack in *The Scholemaster* (1570) on "Italianate" Englishmen and corrupting Italian books; Philip Sidney's positive view in *The Defence of Poesy;* and the activities of John Wolfe's press, which published Italian books in London—including scandalous works by Machiavelli and Aretino. Wyatt's discussion of Wolfe is informative, but does not break much new ground. He does not raise the possibility that Wolfe's books may have been primarily intended for export (his Machiavelli and Aretino were common in contemporary Italian collections), and in general underestimates commercial motives in accounting for Wolfe's tendency to publish polemics on both sides of a given issue. Wyatt also strays a bit from his focus on Florio and Italians in a brief discussion of the French princess Katherine's language lesson in Shakespeare's *Henry V,* an iconic scene that has been much discussed in recent years.

The volume concludes with a chapter analyzing Florio's Italian-English dictionaries. Wyatt situates Florio in regard to the fierce sixteenth-century debates over the Italian language, demonstrating once again that Florio preferred living, spoken language to literary tradition. Wyatt also details the ways in which Florio's dictionaries can be used to read sexually explicit passages of Aretino's *Ragionamenti,* a text that Wolfe had published in London a few years earlier. This fascinating and entertaining passage seems a bit incongruous: issues of gender and sexuality that Wyatt has seldom addressed in previous sections of the text suddenly become central to the issues around cultural transmission, and there is little context provided for the discussion. The chapter ends with a brief analysis of Florio's treatment of gender in his dictionaries. Here too the arguments are intriguing, but could have been developed further.

The Italian Encounter with Tudor England is a much-needed book on a very large, complex subject, so it is not surprising that Wyatt touches on more issues and ideas than can be explored in the space of one volume. The Tudor period is crucial for the development of English culture and national identity, and too often it is studied only from English-language texts. Given the enormous influence England and the English language have had on the subsequent development of global culture, it is useful to be reminded that for many sixteenth-century Europeans, England was peripheral and curious rather than central and normative.

Index